THE GERMAN LEFT SINCE 1945

*Socialism and Social Democracy
in the German Federal Republic*

WILLIAM DAVID GRAF

*with an epilogue by Ossip K. Flechtheim
Professor of Political Science of the
Free University of Berlin*

The Oleander Press

The Oleander Press
17 Stansgate Avenue
Cambridge CB2 2QZ
England

The Oleander Press
210 Fifth Avenue
New York, N.Y. 10010
U.S.A.

Hardcover ISBN 0 902675 54 0
Softcover   ISBN 0 902675 68 0

Printed in Scotland by
JOHN G ECCLES PRINTERS LTD, INVERNESS

CONTENTS

PART C
OPPOSITION FROM BELOW 1960-1967

Abbreviations used in Text

BDA   Bund deutscher Arbeitsgeber (German Employers' Federation)
BdD   Bund der Deutschen (League of Germans)
BDI   Bund der deutschen Industrie (Federation of German Industry)
CDU   Christlich-Demokratische-Union (Christian Democratic Union)
COMINTERN   Communist Internaional
CP   Communist Party
CPF   Communist Party of France
CPI   Communist Party of Italy
CPSU   Communist Party of the Soviet Union
CPY   Communist Party of Yugoslavia
DAG   Deutsche Angestelltengewerkschaft (German Clerical Workers' Union)
DDR   Deutsche Demokratische Republik (German Democratic Republic)
DFG   Deutsche Friedensgesellschaft (German Peace Society)
DGB   Deutscher Gewerkschaftsbund (German Trade Union Federation)
DIHT   Deutscher Industrie — und Handelstag (German Chamber of Trade and Commerce)
DNVP   Deutsch-Nationale Volkspartei (German National People's Party)
DP   Deutsche Partei (German Party)
DPA   Deutsche Presse-Agentur (German Press Agency)
EDC   European Defence Community
EKD   Evangelische Kirche in Deutschland (Lutheran Church of Germany)
FDGB   Freier Deutscher Gewerkschaftsbund (Free German Trade Union Federation)
FDJ   Freie Deutsche Jugend (Free German Youth)
FDP   Freie Demokratische Partei (Free Democratic Party)
GDVP   Gesamtdeutsche Volkspartei (All-German People's Party)
IdK   Internationale der Kriegsdienstverweigerer (War Resisters' International)
IG   Industrie-Gewerkschaft (Industrial Trade Union)
Juso   Young Socialist
KdA   Kampf dem Atomtod (Fight Atomic Death)
KPD   Kommunistische Partei Deutschlands (Communist Party of Germany)
KPÖ   Kommunistische Partei Österreichs (Communist Party of Austria)
LDP   Liberal-Demokratische Partei (Liberal Democratic Party)
NPD   Nationaldemokratische Partei Deutschlands (National Democratic Party of Germany)

5

OECD	Organization for Economic Cooperation and Development
OEEC	Organization for European Economic Cooperation
OMGUS	Office of the Military Government of the United States
ÖVP	Österreichische Volkspartei (Austrian People's Party)
PPP	Parlamentarisch-politischer Pressedienst (Parliamentary-political Press Service)
SAP	Sozialistische Arbeiterpartei (Socialist Workers' Party)
SB	Sozialistischer Bund (Socialist League)
SBZ	Sowjetische Besatzungszone (Soviet Zone of Occupation)
SDS	Sozialistischer Deutscher Studentenbund (Socialist German Student League)
SED	Sozialistische Einheitspartei Deutschlands (German Socialist Unity Party)
SFG	Sozialistische Förderer-Gesellschaft (Society for the Promotion of Socialism)
SHB	Sozialdemokratische Hochschulbund (Social Democratic University League)
SMAD	Soviet Military Administration
SOPADE	Sozialdemokratische Partei Deutschlands im Exil (SPD Exile Party)
SoPo	Sozialistische Politik
SPD	Sozialdemokratische Partei Deutschlands (Social Democratic Party of Germany)
SPD (PV)	SPD Parteivorstand (SPD Executive Committee)
SPO	Sozialdemokratische Partei Österreichs (Social Democratic Party of Austria)
SRP	Soziale Reichspartei (Socialist Reich Party)
UAPD	Unabhängige Arbeiterpartei Deutschlands (Independent Workers' Party of Germany)
UPI	United Press International
USPD	Unabhängige Sozialdemokratische Partei Deutschlands (Independent Social Democratic Party of Germany)
USSR	Union of Soviet Socialist Republics
VUS	Vereinigung Unabhängiger Sozialisten (Union of Independent Socialists)
VVN/ VVNR	Vereinigung der Verfolgten des Naziregimes (Union of Persons persecuted by the Nazi Regime)
WWI	Wirtschaftswissenschaftliches Institut (Institute of Economic Sciences)
ZK	Zentralkomitee (Central Committee)

PREFACE

The subject of the socialist Left in the German Federal Republic, and its relationship to the Social Democratic Party, is one which surprisingly has not been examined intensively, either in the Anglo-Saxon countries or in Germany. The two works which encompass to some extent the material covered here neither account for the — arguably crucial — relationship between the Left and the SPD nor do they incorporate the larger social, economic and political context within which the postwar Left has developed.[1] (Nor were they intended to do so; both books were written, at a time of increased interest in the German Left, as general guides or background information, and both fulfil this purpose well.)

This dearth of information on and analysis of the system-opposed Left has given rise to a number of problems in the preparation of this study. It has been necessary to do a considerable amount of primary research on individual movements and topics but, given the relatively broad scope of the work, it has been impossible to present all the relevant material in detail. Hence the interested reader should note the references to individual subjects cited in the footnotes. Since, moreover, a great deal of information, upon which many of the conclusions here drawn are predicated, is relatively unknown, particularly to English-speaking readers, a certain amount of pure exposition has been necessary in order to support certain — and to some extent controversial — conclusions essential to the main line of argument. Finding an appropriate balance between exposition and analysis has been one of the major difficulties in preparing this investigation.

This problem has been complicated by the controversial nature of the topic itself and the difficulty of locating reliable sources. In Germany, many contemporary press accounts, general scholarly works and official sources diverge considerably from the writings and statements of the Left; then within the Left itself there is the proverbial plethora of individual views. And the Anglo-American literature on contemporary Germany is suspiciously uniform in its treatment of political life in the Federal Republic as (expressed simply) the gradual triumph of "pluralist liberalism" over the omnipresent "totalitarian fascist" past and the invidious "totalitarian communist" threat.

In the sense that this book implicitly or explicitly rejects much of what has been written about political and sociological developments in the Federal Republic, its claim to "scholarly objectivity" will necessarily be subject to challenges on many points. But where possible it does attempt to present alternative views or interpretations, though for reasons of space this has not always been achieved to a degree which would have been satisfactory to the author, whose views alone are herein represented.

7

In preparing and writing this study, I have accumulated a large number of obligations, some of which I should like to acknowledge here. The present book is essentially a doctoral thesis presented to the London School of Economics and Political Science in early 1975. To Professor Ralph Miliband, who supervised the original research from conception to completion, frequently over long distances, I am most indebted — in many ways. Without exception, all the persons with whom I conducted personal interviews also gave freely of their time, their experiences and their private archives. These were: Herr Arno Behrisch, Herr Peter Blachstein, the late Dr. Gerhard Gleissberg, Frau Lisa Huhn, Herr Fritz Lamm, Prof. Peter von Oertzen, Herr Nikolaus Ryschkowsky, Prof. Wolfgang Abendroth and Prof. Ossip K. Flechtheim. To the latter two, in particular, my intellectual and scholarly debt is considerable. Dr Gordon Smith, Professor Hans-Manfred Bock, Prof. David Childs and Professor Flechtheim read and made useful comments on various chapters.

For valuable assistance in locating and providing source materials, I am also grateful to the following: Herr Wolfgang Fischer and Herr Armin Sellheim of the archives of *Der Spiegel*, Hamburg; Dr. Dieter Schuster and his assistants of the DGB archives, Düsseldorf; Herr Horst Ziska and his colleagues at the SPD archives (Friedrich-Ebert-Stiftung) in Bonn; Frau Ruth Gleissberg, Hamburg, who made a number of items available from Gerhard Gleissberg's estate; and the librarians of the Wiener Library and Deutsches Kulturinstitut (London), the Düsseldorf Staatsbibliothek, and the Universities of Marburg, Bonn, West Berlin (Otto Suhr Institute) and Hamburg. I would also like to acknowledge a special debt to Dr Anne Bohm of the L.S.E. Graduate School. The indispensable financial assistance was kindly provided by the London School of Economics in the form of a studentship, the Canada Council with a doctoral fellowship and the University of London as an exchange scholarship with the Free University of Berlin.

And finally, to my wife, Martine, who did not spend many hours laboriously correcting drafts or typing and re-typing manuscripts, but instead, by pursuing her own studies and living her own life, enabled me to escape from the German Left when I wished to, this book is dedicated.

University of Maryland,
European Division,
Heidelberg,
Germany.   September 1976

REFERENCES
Preface
1 Nicholas J. Ryschkowsky, *Die linke Linke*, Munich 1969; and Ernst Richert, *Die radikale Linke*, Berlin 1968

I. PROLOGUE:

The Left and the Social Democratic Party in the Modern Capitalist State

One of the most central, most fundamental ways in which political parties, ideologies or regimes have been classified in modern times has been by locating them at some point between an hypothetical left-right continuum. This method of classification, which originates in the seating arrangements in the post-revolutionary French Assembly, applied originally to the new political constellations arising out of the transition from feudalism to capitalism:

> The king is put to death, the aristocracy made to abandon its privileges; to express the remaining unavoidable difference one resorts then to the least hierarchical of the spatial dimensions — left and right; but the cunning of this symbolic form is that at the same time as it denies hierarchy . . . , left and right also expresses hierarchies . . . Left and right then while stating an ideal, the absence of hierarchies, can also be used to describe the unavoidable hierarchies . . .[1]

The terms "Left" and "Right" only entered the vocabulary of politics during the eighteenth century, in connection with the rising middle classes' movement toward emancipation from the old feudal order. The concept of Left was thus from the outset connected with *opposition*, since it aspired to destroy the existing system of Throne and Altar. And it was *dynamic* because it arose and developed only in reaction against the "Right" or the established traditional order. More important, the Left, at this historical juncture, as the agent of the revolutionary bourgeoisie, was the champion of the *universal* principles: liberty, equality, fraternity. Marx has written that the revolutions of 1648 in Britain and 1789 in France

> . . . were not the victory of a *certain* class in society over the *old political* order; they were *the proclamation of the political order for the new European society*. The bourgeoisie was victorious within them; but the *victory of the bourgeoisie* was at that time the victory of the *new social order*, the victory of bourgeois over feudal ownership, of the nation over the province, of competition over the guild, of distribution over primogeniture, of the rule of the owner by the land, of enlightenment over superstition, of the family over family names, of industry over heroic laziness, of civil rights over medieval privileges. The revolution of 1648 was the victory of the 17th century over the 16th; the revolution of 1789 was the victory of the 18th over the 17th.[2]

If the Left in this period was embodied by liberalism, the subsequent alliance of the emancipated bourgeoisie with the ruling feudal classes created a new status quo. This alliance, which still exists in somewhat modified form today, was based on a mutuality of interests of the two classes: a common desire to preserve the system which guaranteed their social and economic pre-eminence. The fact that the industrial revolution and the bourgeois revolution in most western European countries occurred more or less simultaneously, indeed were interdependent, forged a lasting link between capitalism and liberalism:

> Despite structural variations in liberalism and its bearers from one country or period to another, a uniform foundation remains: the individual economic subject's free ownership and control of private property and the politically and legally guaranteed security of these rights. Around this one stable centre, all specific economic and social demands of liberalism can be modified — modified to the point of self-abolition.[3]

The new emphasis on individual rights — private property, freedom of speech, free competition, etc. — combined with laissez faire capitalism to create a new minority privileged class of capitalists which contrasted with the rapid growth of a great subordinate (wage-earning) class, widespread human misery among the urban poor and extreme social inequalities. Liberalism's central thesis was that freedom and individual rights need only be accorded to the individual economic subject in order for social justice to come about, as it were, automatically. In the pre-industrial society of small merchants and producers this had been largely true. But the process of industrialization produced a situation in which the numbers of small shopkeepers, artisans and independent professionals declined, while economic power tended to be increasingly concentrated in relatively fewer hands.

As the universal principles of the bourgeois revolutions thus came to vindicate and uphold *particular interests* during the eighteenth and nineteenth centuries, socialism arose as a reaction against liberalism and capitalism. Now the actual fundamental values proclaimed by socialism did not differ from those of liberalism. They were: liberty, equality, fraternity. The — crucial — difference lay in their relative emphasis. Where the freedom of the bourgeoisie originally meant freedom from arbitrary control of individual development, it came to mean freedom to amass property, exploit the subordinate classes and secure its own privileges with the instruments of the political, economic and legal systems. Reacting against these developments, the socialist Left saw freedom as a freedom from exploitation and capitalist economic fluctuations and as a universal extension of human dignity and individual economic security. In other words, the Left came to emphasize the elements of equality and fraternity as preconditions for the realization of liberty.

Many decades of liberalism-capitalism with its attendant economic concentration and inegalitarian tendencies increased the antagonism between socialism and liberalism. Socialism, the reaction against capitalism as the economic expression of liberalism, advocated nationalization of the means of production and distribution coupled with economic planning; it emphasized cooperation and egalitarianism at the expense of the profit motive and extreme individualism; it did this with the aim of ending human want and creating a new social order free from material distresses and economic exploitation. This motive frequently found its extreme expression in the notion of a New Man or the desire for a completely unstructured society devoid of authority and coercion. Classical socialism was indeed "a belief in the unlimited possibilities of the forging of social reforms on the strength of human reason".[4] Socialism — the Left therefore — is thus further connected with the notion of *utopia* in the sense of the mutability of an undesirable reality and the possibility of creating a better (but not necessarily "perfect" or "ideal") human order.

So long as bourgeois democracy or more or less constitutional monarchy remained the sole political systems in the industrialized nations, the characteristics of the Left mentioned above could apply to only one political movement: socialism. The political spectrum could be envisaged as a straight left-right continuum with conservatism on the right, liberalism in the centre and socialism on the left. The first of these, conservatism, was most closely associated with the status quo, an elitism, a belief that hierarchy was the natural and desirable order of things. Liberalism was the mid-point: the readiness to reform but without making any concessions which would interfere with the functioning of the capitalist order. And socialism was the extreme left pole of the continuum.

Both liberalism and conservatism came to support bourgeois democracy and capitalist relations of production and distribution. This mutuality of interest accounts to some extent for the liberals' and conservatives' ability to close ranks against the rising threat from "below" in modern times. Socialism in both its main variants — utopian socialism and "scientific" socialism — stood for common, cooperative or decentralized ownership and thus for the abolition of capitalism. This situation meant that the fundamental political cleavage now developed between Left on the one hand and Right and Centre on the other, rather than somewhere between the poles of left and right. This points to what is now perhaps the most important criterion of a definition of the Left in modern capitalism: it must be *anticapitalist*.

Under the conditions of advanced capitalism,[5] then, the Left must be *system-opposed*. If the movement or party under consideration is genuinely leftist than it must at some point arrive at an unbridgable gap vis-à-vis liberalism. For socialism cannot be implemented without at least temporarily setting aside *some* liberal rights: historically, the rights of the individual and the liberal creed have become "bourgeois" rights — as well as universal rights — guaranteeing among others the right to amass private property, to subordinate workers to the requirements of the profit motive and hence in some measure to exploit other human beings. Such uses of liberal rights are incompatible with the aims of the socialist Left. The Left, by definition and by nature, is intensely divided and fragmented into reformers and revolutionaries, socializers and syndicalizers, advocates of dictatorship or democracy, believers in a centralized or decentralized state, etc., but is, I submit, distinguishable and definable as any movement or party opposed to capitalism and in favour of socialism of some other form of common or communal ownership.

Liberal democracy has continued to exist into the late twentieth century, as will be discussed later, by absorbing on its own terms (i.e. without changing the fundamental power structure of the system, namely private ownership of the essential means of production) various programmatic features of the Left, or indeed leftist parties, *in toto*; or by suspending and transforming liberal political rights so as to retain the capitalist socio-economic system, as in 1922 in Italy or 1933 in Germany. Specifically, this meant in the first case the

creation of the modern all-embracing "classless" electoral party, the prototype
of which was developed by Dr Karl Lueger in his Christian Social People's
Party in Vienna at the turn of the century[6]; or in the second instance it meant
the transferral of political power to fascism.[7]

It was mentioned earlier that the Left exists in relation (i.e., opposition) to a
Right, and that the Left is therefore a dynamic concept. But in the context of
advanced capitalism a definition of what is "right" or "centre" has become
extremely problematic. Such phenomena as the broad social measures initiated
by the French Gaullists, the anti-trade union legislation proposed by the
British Labour Party Executive and the measures in support of small business
advocated by the German SPD serve to underline the general decline in
substantial differences between political parties in advanced capitalist
societies, especially in those in which the two-party system is prevalent.
Although space and scope do not permit an analysis of the causal relationships of these phenomena, two factors in particular stand out as contributing
to the decline in party political debate: a tendency to close ranks against the
potential rise of socialist and communist movements, and the growing
importance of technology which tends to impose its own conditions[8] if not
subjected to democratic control. It can thus be claimed that: "there is today
no longer *a* social problem, but rather many social problems . . . Social
problems have become problems of detail . . . Social questions have become
largely party-indifferent."[9] If the "great social problems" have been solved, if
in other words the political Millennium has been attained, then politics and
political debate must be *system-immanent*. The issues are now centred around
particular problems or individual personalities, not political directions or
alternative social systems ("the end of ideology"). This in any event is the
ideological position taken by most of the large western social democratic
parties and their advocates, and in this respect they have come closely to
resemble their liberal and conservative opponents.

Bipartisan debate during the nineteenth century was still largely dominated
by conservative (feudal) — liberal (bourgeois) debate, it is true, but the further
development of industrialization, the extension of the franchise and the
inevitable expansion of political democracy, had, by the twentieth century,
brought the socialist working-class party into serious competition with the old
parties. Whereas nineteenth century liberal and conservative parties had been
fundamentally cadre parties consisting of this or that group of representatives
of the ruling classes, the mass socialist party aimed at the recruitment and
active involvement of the (majority) lower classes. Socialist parties, deprived of
large-scale financial support and without access to the public coffers, depended
for their survival upon a large number of relatively small individual contributions. Their mass membership allowed them to provide facilities and opportunities for the workers' leisure time and to raise systematically the level of
their members' political education, while simultaneously enhancing intra-
party debate and democracy. Until at least the close of World War II, it
appeared that the socialist working-class party pointed the way which political
parties in bourgeois democracies would ultimately take. Certainly liberal,
conservative and christian democratic parties have adopted a number of
features of the socialist party.

Conversely, however, social democratic parties in the West, whose origins,
as has been demonstrated, lie in the once universal principles of the bourgeois

revolutions as well as in a reaction against these, have tended in recent decades to view the achievement of liberal rights (including the right of private property) and the establishment of parliamentary systems as the realization of their "socialist" programmes.[10]

Writing in the early 1950's, Maurice Duverger concluded from his now classic study of modern political parties that: "The vast centralized and disciplined parties of today . . . alone suit the structure of contemporary society."[11] A large, mass-based membership party espousing the needs and aims of a single class, he argued, provided opportunities for articulation, intra-party discussion and political training as well as a means of extending and developing the democratic idea among the party membership and through them outwardly to the general population and upwardly to the governments which were, after all, formed by parties. Duverger's conclusions were supported to a large degree by the seeming resurgence of socialist and social democratic parties throughout Europe after 1945.[12]

By the beginning of the 1950's, however, support for socialism appears to have reached its zenith in western Europe. The reasons for this — amelioration of the most wretched of postwar conditions, the onset of the economic boom and the rise of the new vested interests, the extensive restoration of former socio-economic relationships, the growth of the service, technical and white-collar classes together with the relative decline of the "classic" working classes, the negative example of communist "totalitarianism", the rise (in absolute if not relative terms) in the standards of the lower classes and their subsequent "embourgeoisement", the imperative rationale of technology — cannot be explored here. But developments in the West during the late 1950's and throughout the 1960's tend to bear out Epstein's thesis of a "levelling off" of European socialist parties: in those nations in which the socialist working-class party has failed to enlist the direct support of the trade union organizations, its share of the popular vote has frozen at about one-third or less in multi-party systems and at up to 40 per cent in two-party systems.[13] Every socialist party — in the United Kingdom, on the Continent or in the Scandinavian countries — which had succeeded in crossing these "levelling-off points", he demonstrates, has been connected with a large trade union movement.

Or, on the other hand, as Professor Miliband has pointed out, those socialist parties that have come to power in the West have, without exception, lacked the will or inclination to implement the socialist programmes or platforms upon which their bids for power were based,[14] and have transformed themselves into "enlightened liberal" parties. Is it true that: "it is now possible to argue that the socialist working-class party is a product of a fairly early stage of industrialization and of industrialization in specifically European socio-historical circumstances"?[15] Can socialist parties cast off their traditional socialist programmes and become instead "broad movements of social reform"?[16] Ought or must socialist parties "adapt" to modern circumstances and concentrate on gathering votes instead of attempting to "impose" a "rigid set of doctrines" upon an unwilling society?

These are some of the questions which have confronted socialist parties in the twentieth century. They can be answered, broadly speaking, by the adoption of one of two alternative strategies. The party may postpone its hopes for immediate electoral success and concentrate on inculcating into the "new" subordinate classes an awareness of their objective situation, while simultaneously calling attention to the numerous injustices and dysfunctions of advanced capitalism. Confident of its ultimate vindication by history, the party can then concentrate on preparing for the day when it is called upon to change society in the desired direction. This must remain an hypothesis, however, since no (nominally) socialist party in power has ever carried through this course in the context of advanced capitalism.

The alternative course chosen by Labour in Britain, the SFIO in France, the German SPD, the Austrian SPÖ, the Socialists in Italy and Sweden, to name a few, had been the adoption of what is usually called "liberal socialism". Liberal socialists argue that individual freedom, which is said to be more important than political ideology, has already been attained in liberal western democracies, and that such injustices as do remain can be remedied through the existing (capitalist) system.   D.C. Hodges writes that: "Since the liberal socialist is committed not only to the gradual extension of human rights, but also to the defense of existing ones, he finds unacceptable the revolutionary endeavour to substitute one set of rights for another." This is why for him liberal socialism "is a socialism in name only".[17] Certainly at some point the liberal right of private property must conflict with the socialist principle of communal or cooperative ownership.

But this is to obscure to some extent the actual starting point of liberal socialism. The transition from socialism to liberal socialism must rather be regarded as the abandonment by socialist political parties (or theorists) of their anticapitalist goals, and the gearing of those parties toward the pursuit of political power within the existing capitalist system. When a party abandons or makes ambiguous the aims toward which its pursuit of power is directed, it seems that a qualitative change in that party takes place. One view, Epstein's, argues that: "the consequence can be to free parties from members as well as programs, but to leave them no less effective in performing the electoral function *for which they have always existed.*"[18]   But the "electoral function" of socialist parties is only one side of their historical *raison d'être* (the other side being the implementation of a coherent programme or the realization of an idea). When the fulfillment of the "electoral function" (i.e., the striving for power based on an acceptance of the capitalist order) becomes the sole *raison d'être* of a left-wing political party, then that party

> . . . abdicates as a goal-setting political force and abandons the determination of political direction to the dominant social powers. Its policy is necessarily reactive and confirming; it is at the very least — in societies in which mass extraparliamentary movements of a large scope do not exist — conservative.[19]

This does not mean that there is (necessarily) no difference between political parties in advanced capitalist societies. Indeed, "problems of detail" can be very important questions involving vast sums of money, the utilization of massive resources or the material well-being of millions of people. But problems of detail are not (necessarily) problems of direction. This serves again to underline the fact that the conventional left-right continuum is inadequate to describe party political debate in advanced capitalism. The concept of the Left, as applied throughout this analysis, shall thus be confined to the system-opposed Left as defined above; the Right — if one would equate "Right" with "conservative" or "system-immanent" — must encompass all parties and movements, including "liberal socialist" ones, whose programmes and aims do not extend beyond existing socio-economic orders.[20]

The reaction of the Left, the alternatives available to it, its relationship with social democratic-cum-liberal socialist parties, the strategies, tactics and theories it develops in consequence of the evolution of "social capitalism" [21] and the integration of the social democratic parties into the capitalist state, is the subject of this book. It is concerned with the relationship between socialism and the German Social Democratic Party (SPD) since 1945. The thesis' subtitle is significant, for it implies that the story of the German Left is by no means identical with that of the SPD. Indeed, after 1959 these became almost two separate developments. But the very existence of the SPD, its policies, programmes, actions and reactions have affected the Left more profoundly than any other political factor in West Germany. For this reason alone it is essential to examine the evolution of the Left in the light of the evolution of the SPD. It will be demonstrated that each stage in the progression of the SPD toward liberalism and integration into the West German political system corresponds more or less with a different stage in leftist opposition.

And the kind of opposition a party generates, it will be argued here, can tell us a great deal about the nature of that party and the system in which it operates. This thesis is accordingly a study of the pressures toward conformity of the social democratic party in advanced capitalism, of the reaction of the Left when this occurs, and is thus *a study of opposition*. In the German Federal Republic, under the rule of the CDU/CSU government, this opposition evolved in four basic stages: so long as the SPD under Kurt Schumacher remained a party of fundamental socialist opposition, the Left's opposition was largely an (1) *opposition in detail* but agreement in principle. During the 1950's, however, with the SPD's rather uncoordinated drift away from its socialist programmes and aims, a definite (2) *inner-party opposition* began to crystallize which, after the SPD's Bad Godesberg Programme of 1959, developed into an (3) *extra-party opposition* aimed at achieving *inner-party results*. This form of opposition began to give way to an (4) *extra-party opposition* which sought to create an *alternative political force* during the mid-sixties and in particular following the SPD's entry into the Grand Coalition. The first two forms of socialist opposition evolved within an SPD that was, or was perceived to be an anticapitalist, and hence system-opposed opposition, and can therefore be described as an opposition within an opposition. The latter two forms, however, were a direct response to the SPD's formal and factual integration into the advanced capitalist system. With the transformation of the SPD into a "liberal socialist" party, the socialist Left was no longer represented in the parliamentary system, and was thus compelled to seek new forms and methods to bring its proposals to public attention.

Although all of the developments described above apply more or less to all western capitalist countries, their underlying causes, timing, socio-economic factors and power constellations vary considerably from country to country. This is a study of the German Left, and factors unique to West Germany must occupy the forefront. Some of these are: the authoritarian tradition in economy and society, the decimation of the Left under the fascist regime, the existence of total-authoritarian fascism before 1945 (the post-fascist society), total defeat and material distress after 1945, rule by four-power military governments, cession of territories in East and West, national division, the

Cold War, extreme anticommunism, the Economic Miracle and rapid recovery and the excessive influence of the Church.

Of course these factors have had a profound influence upon the development of the SPD and the Left. One can only agree with Gerard Sandoz' description of the difference between the SPD and the other European socialist parties: "c'est que les sociaux-démocrates allemands, contrairement aux 'partis frères,' sentent constamment poser sur eux le poids énorme de l'histoire malheureuse de leur pays."[22]

This should not, however, be taken as an apology for a strictly phenomenological approach applied here. Wherever purposeful, the historical (vertical) and comparative (horizontal) dimensions have been included. But these have very definite limitations. For example, the situation of both the SPD and the Left are quite different in the Federal Republic from in the Weimar Republic; then the SPD, at least in the early years, was cast in the role of the chief political defender of the Republic against attacks from the Right, while until December 1966 the West German SPD was not even accorded a share of the political power monopolized by the Right. Before 1933, there was always a leftist counterweight to any move to the right on the part of the SPD in the form of the KPD, USPD, or SAP; from 1945 to 1968 there was no really significant left-wing political party.

Similarly, the context on which the West German Left has existed is that of one of the most highly industrialized and rationalized, most prosperous advanced capitalist societies in the World, in this sense it has been subject to many of the same conditions as, and thus bears a number of similarities to, the Left in other Western European nations. This factor is particularly relevant to developments in the past decade. But the special factors mentioned above — total collapse in 1945, national division, position as the front line in the Cold War, etc. — place restrictions on the usefulness of the comparative approach, especially with respect to immediate postwar developments.

Thus this is very much a study of developments in Germany, of the western German Left and the SPD during a specific period: after Hitler. It is a study of a certain type of socialist opposition within a given political constellation. And as such it is also a study of socialist opposition in *a* modern capitalist state.

REFERENCES
Prologue
1 Prof. Jean A. Laponce, "In Search of the Stable Elements of the Left-Right Landscape", mimeographed draft, University of British Columbia, n.d. (1969) p.4.
2 Karl Marx, "Die Bourgeoisie und die Konterrevolution" in: *Marx-Engels Ausgewählte Schriften*, Vol.I, E. Berlin 1951, p.60 (italics in original).
3 Herbert Marcuse, *Negations. Essays in Critical Theory*, London 1968, p.9.
4 Albrecht Walz, *Vom Sozialismus zum Neosozialismus*, Freiburg (Switzerland). 1965, p.28.
5 For a definition of advanced capitalism, see Ralph Miliband, *The State in Capitalist Society*, London 1969, p.7 and ff.
6 On this see Kurt Skalnik, *Dr Karl Lueger — der Mann zwischen den Zeiten*, Vienna and Munich 1954. It is interesting that Hitler chose Lueger's all-party methods as a model for the NSDAP (see the numerous references in *Mein Kampf*).
7 The problems for political analysis arising from the rise of fascism and communism are not at issue here. It is sufficient to recall that fascism, even "fascism of the left", serves the primary purpose of defending the capitalist socio-economic system by

means of suspending or abolishing liberal political rights (cf. above all Reinhard Kühnl, *Die nationalsozialistische Linke*, Meisenheim/Glan 1965). Concerning communist practice in the countries in which the communist party has come to power, Ossip K. Flechtheim ("Sozialismus" in: Ernst Fraenkel, ed., *Staat und Politik. Fischer-Lexikon 2*, Frankfurt 1959, 4th ed., p.277) has argued that the "aggressive-totalitarian, universally institutionalized system of compulsion" which it had created precludes it from being able to lay claim to the attribute "socialist", since socialism represents an "optimal combination of freedom and equality".

8 This second factor is of course the central thesis of Marcuse's *One Dimensional Man*, London 1968.

9 Ralf Dahrendorf, "Links in der Bundesrepublik" in: Horst Kruger (ed.), *Was ist heute links? Thesen und Theorien zu einer politischen Position*, Munich 1963, p.8f.

10 Here cf. Arno Klönne, "Sozialdemokratie — Agentur kapitalistischer Interessen?" in: Reinhard Kühnl (ed.) *Der bürgerliche Staat der Gegenwart II*, Reinbek 1972, p.63f.

11 Maurice Duverger, *Political Parties: their Organization and Activity in the Modern State*, London 1964, p.58.

12 For a comprehensive discussion of developments in this period, see ch. 7 of Wolfgang Abendroth, *A Short History of the European Labour Movement*, London 1973; see also infra. ch.II (1).

13 Leon Epstein, *Political Parties in Western Democracies*, London 1967, p.162

14 Miliband, *op. cit.*, p.101 and *passim*.

15 Epstein, *op. cit.*, p.150.

16 Sydney Hook, "A New Ism for Socialism" in: W.J. Stankiewicz (ed.) *Political Thought Since World War II*, Glencoe, Ill. 1964, p.325.

17 D.C. Hodges, "Liberal Socialism: on the Horns of a Dilemma" in: *American Journal of Economics*, No.22 (oct. 1963), p.457 and 462.

18 Epstein, *op. cit.*, p.358 (my italics).

19 Bodo Zeuner, "Die SPD im Parteiensystem der Bundesrepublik" in: *Sozialdemokratie und Sozialismus heute*, W. Berlin 1968, p.199.

20 However, this classification scheme by no means implies a simplistic right-or-left choice. Indeed, as will be shown, Left and Right are extremely heterogeneous and represent a whole spectrum of interests within their respective spheres with regard to strategy, tactics and even theory. The point is that in advanced capitalism the essential criterion of classification is the party's or movement's position toward the capitalist system.

21 A term coined by Flechtheim in "Sozialismus", *op. cit.*, p.280.

22 Gérard Sandoz, *La Gauche Allemande. De Karl Marx à Willy Brandt*, Paris 1970, p.87 (This statement also applies *mutatis mutandis* to the Left outside the SPD).

PART A

ERSATZ REVOLUTION AND COUNTER-REVOLUTION 1945-1948

II. Between Total Defeat and Occupation Statute: Prospects and Limitations of the Second German Republic

1. The Significance of the Postwar Period

The collapse of the Third Reich bequeathed to Germany what has often been termed a social, political and economic vacuum. And indeed, the scale of physical damage and dislocation is, at first glance, enormous. About six million were dead (including military losses, civilians and *Volksdeutsche* in Eastern Europe), one and one-half million crippled, a further two million orphaned and the fate of some three million inhabitants of the former eastern domains was unknown. Between four and six million men were still interned in prisoner-of-war camps. The highways and railroads were crowded with millions of forced-labourers who had been brought into Germany during the war, and returning soldiers and refugees from the East and the Soviet Occupation Zone. Twenty-five million had lost their homes or were facing expulsion: more than 23 per cent of the housing units extant in the U.S. and British Zones in 1939 were now destroyed, and the urban areas were especially hard-hit (e.g., in Düsseldorf between 40 and 42 per cent of the 1939 housing units were destroyed; on average 10 Germans were now living in quarters in which four had lived in 1939). Starvation or near-starvation, overcrowding, disease and extreme hardship were everywhere.[1]

Industrial production, too, was at a standstill. Plants and factories were inoperative (in July 1945 only 1200 of the 12,000 plants in the American Zone were in limited production); the lines of transport and communication had been severed, so that in western zones less than ten per cent of the 1939 railway lines were usable, all the Rhine bridges had been demolished and the roads were clogged with the vast movements of displaced persons and ex-soldiers. Reparations in the forms of dismantlings of machinery and entire plants accounted for even greater losses, especially in the East Zone. These, and the many other statistics which could be cited, underline the general paralysis of German economic and social life in 1945.[2]

This extensive physical destruction and dislocation and human distress brought with it cataclysmic social changes. At a time when several thousand marks were needed to buy a single loaf of bread, when thousands were starving and millions perpetually hungry, when the forces of production and distribution were incapacitated, the only operative "vested interests" in Germany were the black marketeers and those small farmers who had been able to preserve some part of their productive acreage from the war's ravages.

The old elites in the former eastern territories had been driven from their lands, the East Prussian Junkers' properties had been expropriated and redistributed, and the military and business elites were thoroughly discredited by their association with the Third Reich. Wellmann has estimated that about two-thirds of the previous middle classes had been "proletarized" economically,[3] and their ranks were swollen by the influx of déclassé refugees from the East.[4]

Against this background of hardship and destruction, with its omnipresent reminders of the authoritarian fascist regime and total war, it is not surprising that there now developed a popular desire for radical social measures, a desire fostered by a far reaching anticapitalist mood which penetrated deeply into the bourgeois classes[5] and which was based on the realization on the part of most of the politically aware that the old ruling classes and the pre-war socio-economic system had produced (or at least failed to foresee, to resist) fascism and war.

Similar developments can be traced throughout Europe in this period. France, for example, had suffered moral collapse and a ruinous occupation. Czechoslovakia and Poland, who before 1939 had been abandoned by the western "liberal democracies", had been pillaged mercilessly by the National Socialist military governments. And in Britain, "because of the many sacrifices expected of the people during the war, it was inevitable that there should develop a desire to fuse the determination for victory with aspirations for a better life after victory."[6] The *Times* anticipated this postwar mood as early as 1940, shortly after Dunkirk:

> If we speak of democracy, we do not mean a democracy which maintains the right to vote but forgets the right to work and live. If we speak of freedom, we do not mean a rugged individualism which excludes social organization and economic planning. If we speak of equality we do not mean a political equality nullified by social and economic privilege. If we speak of economic re-construction, we think less of maximum production (though this too will be required) than of equitable distribution.[7]

And so social democratic governments came to, or remained in power in the United Kingdom, Sweden, Denmark, Norway, and communists supplied the undisputed leadership of Yugoslavia and Albania. In Finland, Austria, Switzerland, Belgium, the Netherlands, Italy and all the eastern European countries social democrats played prominent roles in coalition governments, frequently in collaboration with communists.[8] The new political constellations which emerged from the immediate post-war period have had important and in most cases permanent effects on the political systems of those countries.

But in Germany, where the social, political and economic system was more completely decimated than in other countries, and where prospects for even further-reaching changes initially appeared more favourable and indeed, in view of her support of the Third Reich, very necessary, this anticapitalist, socialist mood was inhibited by the presence of the four victor powers and their respective policies.

Certainly the indigenous leftward trend was at least as evident in Germany as elsewhere. Virtually all the party political pronouncements, social issues, major articles in the communications media (although these were under direct Allied control until 1947) and electoral platforms of the period revolved around proposals for expropriation, socialization and communal ownership. All the political parties originating in this time — save one — advocated a new socialist ordering of economy and society; only the LDP/FDP (liberal party) came out, guardedly, in favour of free competition and a "liberal" economy.

The Left, as well as a large number of former supporters of bourgeois parties, saw that the Third Reich had been a product of monopoly capitalism, drawing its mass base from the middle classes and its leadership from déclassé intellectuals and ex-soldiers, but serving the interests of the upper monopoly capitalist classes and forming a defensive bourgeois alliance against the working classes and their political and economic organizations.[9] Hence it was now evident that the capitalist system must be eliminated or at least drastically modified in a socialist direction in order to deprive a future form of fascist authoritarianism of its social and economic roots, since the very existence of capitalism — in whatever form — was thought to contain a fascist potential. The logical conclusion was to prevent the concentration of private ownership by adopting some form of communal, social or cooperative ownership. The communists, the radical wing of the SPD and other left-wing members of the labour movement had demonstrated by their opposition to the Third Reich that they had been the most consistent opponents of fascism. It was thus only natural that popular support for their organizations, initially the antifascist front, then the KPD, SPD and the trade unions, grew rapidly. The almost daily revelations of Nationalist Socialist crimes against humanity, the recollection that all the bourgeois parties had lent their support to Hitler's Enabling Law, the sequestration and denazification measures and the sheer extent of visible destruction and destitution compelled many classes who had formerly been ignorant of or impervious to socialist ideas — for example left-wing catholics or the "proletarized" middle classes — to reconsider their traditional antisocialist attitude.[10]

Yet it is all too easy to see in these developments a "great majority for socialism". When Wolfgang Abendroth speaks of the "brief heyday of socialist thought which without doubt temporarily won over the majority of this nation",[11] this is more indicative of the virtually total bankruptcy of the Right than of a broad acceptance of socialism on the part of the general population. The alternatives which presented themselves in this period arose from a concrete historical and material situation (redistribution, antifascism), not from a process of development of popular consciousness and theoretical training. On the contrary, the Wilhelmian Imperial regime, the Weimar Republic and the Third Reich, which had come and gone within four decades, had not been conducive to the development of a mass socialist following.

Part of the problem here was that Germany had been liberated from fascism not by any popular initiative from "below", but by a total victory of the Allies. Under National Socialism the German masses who, on hearing the Allied demand for a total surrender, had feared the worst, and who had certainly been at least vaguely aware of the Nazis' crimes against humanity (daily contact with forced labourers from many countries, round-ups of the Jews using brutal methods in all parts of Germany) had supported the war effort to the very end:

> The opportunities for far-reaching social reforms created by the liberation were not preceded — as would have been the case in a

normal and fully developed revolutionary situation — by a period of heightened revolutionary activity on the part of the masses, by political controversies and struggles which would have developed political consciousness and created clearly defined fronts.[12]

Indeed, all the evidence concerning the popular mood of this period points at least as much to one of shock, bewilderment and apathy as to political energy and fervour. A series of public-opinion polls carried out between 1945-1948 indicates a withdrawal from active politics, a disinterest in affairs not touching directly upon one's personal life and a desire to leave decision-making at higher levels to others.[13] One can only agree with Cornelia Koepcke's statement that: "The psychologist may speak of the suppression of, or a deficiency in coming to terms with mental conflicts; the lay observer must simply confirm the total abstinence of the postwar German vis-à-vis political questions."[14]

2. The Antifascist Coalition as Foundation of the New Political Order

If, however, the majority of the overall population was not actively socialist, a majority of the politically aware and the politically active undoubtedly was. This is particularly important in view of the virtual disappearance of the Right as a direct consequence of the Allied victory. The immediate tone of postwar politics was set largely by the minority of active anti-Nazis and, to a limited degree, by the so-called passive opponents of the Hitler regime. Who were these anti-Nazis? Subsequent war crimes trials and denazification proceedings would establish that they were not to be found among the former elites in the military, judiciary or civil services. Nor were they, with a few notable exceptions, from the Church hierarchy.

However much one might admire the courage and dedication of Count von Stauffenberg and his fellow "conspirators", it is nevertheless true that: "Perhaps the most important function of the July 20 affair is its use in propaganda and education as historic proof of the existence of the 'other Germany.'"[1] For the famous attempted coup was executed by isolated, conspiratorial and primarily upper-middle-class groups whose resistance stemmed not from an aversion to fascism based on principle or on a socio-political insight into the nature of fascist authoritarianism, but chiefly on a distaste for the crudest of Hitler's methods and his military failures. The movement enjoyed very little grass-roots support and, unlike the left wing resistance, "only in exceptional cases did it engage in propaganda or recruitment activities or attempt to create a mass basis."[2] Nor could it: it had no mass following, no formulated programme to rally the antifascist opposition, and presented no substantial alternative to the National Socialist government.

The principal opposition to fascism, it is clear, had come from the left: from the left-wing social democrats, the communists, members of socialist splinter groups and trade unionists who, during the early stages of the Third Reich, had recognized the nature of the fascist threat and who had consistently continued to oppose the fascist regime from inside and outside Germany.[3] At the height of the Nazi terror, the internal opposition often consisted of only token resistance in the form of furtively painted wall slogans, whisper campaigns or secret antifascist cells in plant and factory, usually at great peril to personal safety. From exile, the KPD and SPD opposition committees kept up a constant, if at times weak, barrage of anti-Nazi propaganda and activity.

Since "the Gestapo terror resulted in an internal selecting-out process of those unwilling to go the whole length of sacrificing comfort, security, family, property and life itself,[4] the anti-Nazi elite (to borrow Almond's term) that emerged from exile, the prisons and concentration camps and from the underground consisted predominantly of supporters of the labour movement who had indeed been prepared to make these sacrifices.[5]

The anti-Nazi elite was important to postwar political life for a number of reasons. It supplied the core of activists of the first hour, who arranged for the restoration of some semblance of order, emergency food and water supplies care for the ill and homeless and other essential services. It undertook the task of re-establishing local administration, occupying local Nazi offices and institutions and filling the "political vacuum" that now existed. In fact the conquering Allied troops were often met by delegations of leftist antifascists ready with lists of Nazis still in office, programmes for reconstruction, and their own nominees for posts in the new local administration.

By far the most important aspect of this antifascist elite was that it represented a spontaneous, popular, left-wing, grass-roots movement borne of time and place. In the ravaged cities and villages in all four occupation zones it organized antifascist committees or "antifas" consisting mainly of former KPD and left-wing SPD members and other leftist trade union and splinter groups, but also including many former bourgeois party supporters and representatives of the youth and Church resistance against Hitler.

The antifas consciously aimed at avoiding the mistakes made by the labour movement during the Weimar Republic, above all a repetition of the *Bruderkampf*, which had rent and weakened the Left and prevented it from making common cause against the National Socialist rise to power.

Not only the lessons of the Weimar Republic, then, lent an impetus to the formation of an antifascist, united socialist movement, but above all those acquired during the Third Reich. Seen from under the shadow of SS terror, from the desperate perspective of the concentration camp and from the lonely perch of foreign exile, the differences within the Left that had divided it and impaired its effectiveness diminished drastically. The years of isolation and internment, moreover, had precluded the working out of any real dissension-producing theoretical formulations and the conduct of lengthy discussions; only the will to survive and a deep-seated belief in socialism and democracy remained.

> 'Democratic socialism' or 'proletarian dictatorship'? To pose this question seemed futile, since the struggle for the state against the National Socialist system of terror could not be followed by a parliamentary epoch, but only by the radical reconstruction of the social order, the realization of socialism.[6]

The surviving members of the labour movement in the Buchenwald concentration camp, in their *Buchenwald Manifesto*[7] called for the establishment of a people's republic, the liberation of the working classes and the socialization of the economy. As the instrument for the fulfilment of their programme, they urged the creation of a unified, democratic socialist party, in anticipation of which they christened their own organization *Bund demokratischer Sozialisten* (League of Democratic Socialists). The Manifesto, today almost forgotten, is an eloquent and typical formulation of the principles and aspirations of the anti-fascist front for the achievement of a democratic-socialist Germany on the foundation of the lessons of the collapse of the Weimar Republic and the coming to power of the Third Reich. Though unfortunately little documentation is available today, we know that similar movements existed in a number of other concentration camps, under conditions of extreme oppression.

Since these antifas arose spontaneously at local levels, their theories and ends naturally varied, but not considerably. They all aimed at a more or less radical restructuring of society by means of the implementation of socialism. And this socialism was inextricably connected with democracy and the democraticization of economy and society as well as politics. The antifascists refused to have truck with not only former Nazis and fellow-travellers, but also with Weimar politicians who had no record of militant anti-Nazism, and former socialists who had capitulated to National Socialist pressure or persuasion.

In view of the anticommunist line later adopted by Kurt Schumacher and the SPD, it is notable that the initial impetus for a united front of the Left, at least in such urban centres as Berlin and Hamburg, originated in the SPD and was initially rejected by the communists. Nevertheless an *Aktionsgemein-schaft* (working committee) was formed between KPD and SPD members, at various levels, in Munich, South Baden, in Hesse, the Rhineland and Westphalia. In a conference held on 14th November 1945 in Bochum, the foremen of the Ruhr coal industry demanded the expropriation without compensation of the mine owners and the transferral of their holdings into the hands of the regional government.[8] The antifa movement was also active in individual firms. For example, the workers in the Krupp firm in Essen, in agreement with the civic administration (whose Lord Mayor was the communist, Heinz Renner), demanded in a memorandum delivered to the Military Governor on 16 November the expropriation of the properties owned by the war criminal Krupp and their re-tooling in the interests of peace.[9] Similar demands were put forward by the antifas workers in the Hoesch Concern in Dortmund, the Dortmunder Union, the Mannesmann industries in Duisburg and the Bochumer Verein.[10]

Then, in April (in the western occupation zones) and May (in the Soviet Zone) of 1945, the Military Governments of all four zones banned all political activity and dissolved the antifas. Although this action was completely within the provisions of the Potsdam Agreement and four-power agreements, it had the effect of wiping out virtually the only spontaneous, democratic-socialist movement, produced by the actual, immediate historical situation, in postwar Germany. No doubt the occupation powers were not fully aware of the potential of the antifas movements as a basis for the "new democratic order" in Germany, but subsequent developments indicate that other motives may have been operative as well. Thus Professor Abendroth writes that the Soviet Union "wanted to subjugate at least the communists to its discipline before they could permeate a united party."[11] When the ban was lifted in the Soviet Zone, only four parties were admitted, and the proposed KPD-SPD union was postponed for some months. In the western zones the Allies, in particular the Americans, were far from amenable to the antifa groups, which were dominated not only by the SPD-KPD, but in Munich, Leipzig, the Ruhr,

Bremen and Hamburg by more radical left-wing splinter groups.

The western occupation authorities' ban on political activity lasted several months longer than the Soviets' — thereby according the right-wing and conservative forces a necessary breathing spell — and by the time it was lifted the old party cleavages had been largely restored. The Allied policy, like the Soviet policy, was to appoint the party leaders from above, although the criteria of selection were different. Only four parties were "licensed" by the Military Governments: the SPD, KPD, CDU-CSU and LDP-FDP; this meant that no right-wing parties existed and the extreme rightists were forced to seek refuge in the two "bourgeois" parties (primarily the FDP), thus eventually drawing these parties and the whole political spectrum to the right. The Allies tended to select party leaders and local and regional administrative officials whose names were known to them, frequently on the basis of recommendations made by former political exiles or prominent clergy members.

Hence a substantial proportion of the initial leaders of the "new" Germany in the western zones were in substance very similar to, if not identical with the non- (or non-active) Nazi political elite of the Weimar Republic.[12] They owed their appointments to the goodwill of the Military Governments and, for the most part, endeavoured to adapt to the wishes of their benefactors. The western occupation authorities, who were suspicious of all socialist tendencies (and thus of the antifas), but who were as yet unable to rely on the compromised experts and officials from the Third Reich, tended to appoint persons who had been neither active opponents nor active supporters of the former regime. The result was not the formation of a proven anti-Nazi counter elite, as might have come to power, had the indigenous antifascists succeeded in overthrowing Hitler on their own strength, but an "elite coalition" of uncommitted or opportunistic politicians[13] in addition to convinced antifascists. It can be said of the post-1945 political leadership that it consisted largely of persons whose political consciousness and *Weltanschauung* had been formed prior to the advent of the National Socialist regime and whose concepts and theories in most cases had changed little during the intervening years.[14]

The leading members of the eastern political elite were of course older communists who for the most part had spent the war years in the Soviet Union: 13 of the 16 signatories of the first KPD proclamation had been in exile in Russia.[15]

But the effect of returning these old politicians and administrators to public office without reference to public opinion was largely the same in all zones: to exclude younger men and women with greater energy and new ideas from political life, to squander many of the hard-won lessons of the period 1933-45 and to impede political initiative from below. Still, such men at least represented either "the other Germany" or the "non-Nazi Germany" that had once been, and, in comparison with the ex-Nazis who would begin to regain top posts in economy, society and politics, in the late 1940's, were a positive democratic force.

Wolfgang Leonhard, who had arrived from the Soviet Union with the "Group Ulbricht" even before the fighting had stopped. and who was closely involved in the postwar reconstruction of Berlin, might be describing an event in any of the occupation zones when he relates his visit, on Ulbricht's orders, to an antifa group in Berlin-Charlottenberg. He has just informed its members that the cell is to be disolved:

> These people did not want to be administrative officials. Without respect to all the old ideologies they had found themselves engaged in a common struggle against Hitler and had formed a closely-knit community. Now, after Hitler's overthrow, they wanted to work together in an active antifascist organization for a new Germany. At this very moment when their primary aim, the destruction of fascism, had been attained, their organization was to be dissolved. Their disappointment was great. Mine too.[16]

The majority of this group, he continues, returned disillusioned into private life. When he later encountered others who had remained politically active, "there was not a trace left of their fire, their enthusiasm, their initiative." Leonhard also describes the political party formed in Thuringia by a group of former concentration camp inmates. It was a united socialist party called Party of the Working People and was also dissolved at this time. When the SPD and KPD were later reconstituted from above, only one-half of the previous members bothered to enlist in either of the two parties.[17] And although many former antifa members were to become prominent in East and West German politics, it seems probable that this process of eliminating a genuine democratic-socialist initiative was "the first victory of the machine over the independent movement of the antifascist, leftist-orientated classes of Germany."[18]

3. The Role of the Occupation Powers

The failure of the German Left to achieve political power in the western zones must be regarded primarily — but not exclusively — as a consequence of the occupation powers' policies and lack of policies. Let us immediately point out that here we are interested in the four powers' role in preventing a possible historical change in the direction of socialism from taking place (in the western zones) or in distorting it completely (in the Soviet Zone).[1] Given this focus, as well as space limitations, a comprehensive discussion of the foreign policies of the four powers and a social and diplomatic history of the Cold War cannot be undertaken here. Besides, a number of such works already exist.[2]

Postwar Military Government in Germany was established on the basis of the Big Three agreements concluded at Yalta and Potsdam. These provided for the extirpation of National Socialism; the proposals for accomplishing this aim reflected what was then jointly agreed to be the root causes of the Nazi dictatorship: disarmament and demilitarization, denazification and democratization at all levels, and the creation of a "new" Germany founded upon the principles of deconcentration and decartellization of the economy, elimination of social injustice and inequalities, and the reduction of war and industrial potential. Although Potsdam also contained provisions for the treatment of Germany as a single economic unit,[3] no arrangements had been made for a central administration. At the outset decisions were taken *ad hoc* by the various Military Governments in their zones, so that in time four quite different patterns of government and administration (and within these, varying and often conflicting interests) arose which, generally speaking, corresponded with the ideological, economic or diplomatic interests of the respective occupation powers.

The fact of the victors' assumption of sovereign power over the defeated enemy immediately following a bitter, protracted and costly war was bound to have adverse effects on the development of democracy in the defeated country:

> The demand for an unconditional surrender, the fact that it was met by the holders of power of the Third Reich, and the rejection of the idea of cooperation with the democratic forces in the German people as a partner capable of forming an alliance, placed the western democracies after the capitulation in the compulsory situation of ruling Germany in an authoritarian manner, against the principles which applied in their own countries. Democracy ought to be developed from the bottom upwards.[4]

Despite this situation, the conflict between the occupation powers and the indigenous political forces surviving the Third Reich was initially only latent. Both sides were agreed upon the need for the elimination of Nazism, the destruction of German war potential and the democratization of economy and society. This is why the Left was prepared at the outset to collaborate actively with the occupying powers (though participation in local administrative bodies without the prospect of gaining or exerting power responsibly and before having had time to prepare coherent programmes and platforms may well have absorbed much of the parties' will to change.) The first controversies arose from the occupation powers' view that the reduction of industrial production to a minimum was the way to eliminate Germany's war potential, while the political parties (including the bourgeois parties) saw a fundamental change in the distribution of social power and property as the guarantee for peace; crippling production could only create popular resentment and eliminate the essential precondition of democracy — prosperity.

The Western Allies' policy toward domestic political developments in their zones can be described in two basic stages. The first stage, prior to the intensification of the Cold War, was based both on considerations of the wartime alliance with the Soviet Union and the provisions of the Potsdam Agreement as well as on the requirements of the powers' respective foreign policies. What Professor Gimbel has said of American policy can be applied equally to British and French policy, namely that it was governed rather more by a "range of interests" than by any "attempt to democratize Germany." Whenever the two were in conflict, "Americans applied power where their highest priorities were."[5] Indeed:

> Besides wanting to denazify, demilitarize, decartelize, democratize and reorient Germans and Germany, Americans were also interested in seeing to their own security, bringing about the economic rehabilitation of Germany and Europe, and guaranteeing the continuance of free enterprise. They wanted to frustrate socialism, to forestall Communism, to spare American taxpayers' money, to counteract French plans to dismember Germany, and to contain the Soviet Union in Central Europe.[6]

In terms of domestic German politics, the western powers' initial role, during the first stage, in the frustration of the socialist trend in Germany was of a more indirect nature. It consisted of postponing or delaying important proposals or measures which would have led to fundamental political changes, with a view to stemming or checking the demand for the realization of social justice or social transformation until a more "moderate" climate could be restored in which free enterprise could flourish.

The most important step in this direction was the destruction of the socialist-antifacist movement. The basis of this policy was the well-known U.S. Directive J.C.S. 1067 which, among other things, advanced the theory of collective guilt. If all Germans had been equally guilty for the rise of the Third Reich, this theory went, then in the postwar reconstruction no political group could be given preference, not even the antifacists, socialists and communists who had been in the forefront of the struggle against Hitler. J.C.S. 1067 was the theoretical basis of the quarantine on political activities applied in occupied Germany. The way in which this ban, and the length of time for which it was imposed, affected grass-roots politics, has been described in the previous section. The subsequent reconstitution of the political parties from top-to-bottom with appointees (not necessarily active anti-Nazis) already active in the Weimar Republic, again as has been demonstrated, resulted in the recreation of the old ideological-political fronts in the western zones and the retreat of many of the most able and independent-minded from political life altogether. This policy, together with the fragmented and uncoordinated nature of interzonal administration, also increased the party leaders' power vis-à-vis the party members and supporters, for only the leaders were informed by the Military Governments, given a say in administrative appointments and permitted to participate in interzonal organizations.

The ban on political activities also affected the trade unions. Here the notion of an antifascist, socialist front was even more predominant than among the political parties. The trade unionists had not forgotten how the divided labour movement had been swallowed so comparatively easily into the National Socialist "Labour Front" in the first years of the Third Reich and how, on the other hand, social democratic, communist and christian trade unionists had shared experiences of exile, concentration camp and persecution. The first trade union proposals were aimed at the creation of a massive, centralized, single trade union (Einheitsgewerkschaft) which would not be subdivided into "ideological" trade unions, as in the Weimar Republic, nor even into industrial trade unions, but which would be unified and centralised as well as socialist and democratic at every level. The purpose of the unified trade union would be to give labour a maximum amount of power and influence in reconstruction and the establishment of the new (socialist) society.[7]

These plans were also inhibited by the political quarantine. The unified trade union was disallowed, and three stages of development leading from local to national organization, all subject to Military Government approval, were prescribed. The new trade union leaders, again for the most part former leaders in the Weimar era, now between 50-70 years old, were appointed by the occupation powers in their zone,[8] and such appointments were of course increasingly biased against communists, works' council leaders and the radical Left. More than three years would lapse before the American and British occupation authorities were prepared to permit the establishment of the German Trade Union Federation (DGB), by which time, as will be demonstrated in the next chapter, the once radical socialist trade union movement had been transformed into another "pluralist" institution of capitalist society.

Similarly, the economic principles of the Potsdam Agreement, which were based largely on American draft proposals, called for dismantlings, reparations,[9] the breakup of industrial concentration and the decentralization of German businesses. These principles reflected a general agreement that Germany must make good the vast damage caused by the war for which she was held responsible, that her war potential had to be effectively and permanently eliminated and that the classes who had financed and profited from the war should be made to pay for it. Thus when the Soviet Union, and later France, embarked on the unilateral exploitation of their occupation zones, with exports and requisitions vastly exceeding imports, they were acting completely in accord with the Potsdam principles. In view of the fact that, by 1952, the Soviet dismantlings exceeded 25 per cent of the total East German g.n.p., it would not be inaccurate to state that the Soviet Zone bore the overwhelming burden of reparations for all Germany.

By contrast, reparations in the British and American Zones never exceeded five per cent of industrial capacity and even when they did take place, were largely in industries which were already overequipped, so that the removal of such machinery merely cleared the way for the installation of modern equipment. But it would be premature to conclude from this that for the USA "a prosperous Europe would mean a Europe which did not need support, whereas to the Russians a destitute Europe would be all the readier to turn Communist."[10] The Soviet Union could hardly choose between a prosperous or destitute Europe, since it was itself vastly more impoverished and devastated than any other European nation in consequence of the war.[11] And the American policy of making (western) Germany a viable political unit was based less on an altruistic desire to alleviate the human suffering of the German people than on regaining a valuable trading partner for itself and, later on, guaranteeing the domestic stability of its "front line" in the Cold War. When the American Military Governor, Lucius D. Clay, finally halted the dismantlings in May 1946, he based his action on his objections to financing reparations to the Soviet Union without being able to obtain corresponding benefits. America and Britain were never against reparations in principle; the stoppages were motivated by national interests.

Britain and America's opposition to an effective decartellization law in 1946 may be seen in the light of this policy. As Professor Balfour has written elsewhere:

> It was commonly agreed in Britain and America during the war that the Ruhr and Rhineland industrialists had had as much to do with German militarism as the Prussian Junkers and must be treated equally firmly. But, whereas the Russian land reform struck effectively at the roots of the Junkers' power, and created a class ready to resist any attempt at putting the clock back, it would be idle to pretend that the Nuremberg prosecutions, decartellization and the other measures taken against the industrialists have done much to curb them.[12]

When decartellization was finally begun in March 1947, it affected only 25 firms primarily in the Ruhr, and was abandoned after twelve months. And in any case, unlike nationalization, decartellization was no threat to the capitalist system; on the contrary, the decentralization of German industry would have reduced Germany's ability to compete against international monopoly capital, and thus would have been entirely compatible with British and American interests.

Some evidence of the popular acceptance of the extensive land reforms and the expropriation of leading financial and industrial institutions and of persons who had profited from the war, Nazi war criminals and active Nazis was provided by a poll held in Saxony on 30 June 1946: these measures were approved by a majority of 77.6 per cent.[13] The far-reaching reforms carried out in the Soviet Zone, according to the Potsdam treaties, ought to have been complemented by the expropriation of industry in the western zones. Otherwise the post-fascist society would come more and more to resemble the pre-fascist society.

Another important factor in the prevention of the turn to socialism in the West was the victors' policy toward former National Socialists. The central criticisms of the western Allies' denazification methods may be summarized briefly as inadequacy of planning, brevity and insufficiency of execution and legalistic approach. The failure to include representatives of "the other Germany" (anti-fascists, members of the labour movement or even survivors of the 20th July Conspiracy) in the conception and execution of the denazification programme ensured that the great majority of Germans would disassociate themselves from the measures taken, regarding them as a "foreign imposition", and that the most consistent opponents of fascism would be denied a commensurate influence in the elimination of the remnants of National Socialism. Secondly, there were a number of administrative problems: the absence of a long-range projection, arbitrary and uneven applications of ambiguous laws, lack of coordination between denazification and other Allied programmes and an absence of precedents or standards, to name a few.

Perhaps the most substantial criticism of denazification, finally, was that through it the Allies attempted to treat a basically social and political problem with legalistic methods, an approach which attacked the symptoms, at best, but came nowhere near the root. The denazification criteria of rank or length of service in the NSDAP, for example, proved to be entirely inadequate. A fairly large number of convinced antidemocrats and war propagators had for various reasons never joined the party but had nevertheless been left in office after 1933 due to their importance to the new regime or the "reliability" of their views. Such persons had occupied, among others, high positions in the state bureaucracy, in business, the judiciary or university chairs. After 1945 they could of course demonstrate that they had never been party members (often using the argument of "inner immigration"); while young or misguided "small fry" were forced to spend a number of years in internment or could not practice the professions or trades for which they had been trained.[14] Even where the formal criteria were sufficiently conceptualized so as to affect hard-core Nazis, these were frequently applied so arbitrarily and inconsistently that many former leading National Socialists, following a brief period of internment, were able rapidly to find their way back into positions of influence in the Federal Republic. Most of the 42 representatives of big business labelled by the American Kilgore Commission, in a list published in 1945, as war or Nazi criminals — e.g., Friedrich Flick, Alfred Krupp von Bohlen and Halbach, Robert Pferdemenges, Hermann Röchling, Hermann von Siemens — as well as persons in the judiciary, civil service, education system and military, were back in their old positions after 1947 or 1948.[15] Their stepping-stone was the thesis of "collective guilt" which held the entire German people responsible for the crimes and actions committed "in the name of the people" by the ruling classes of the Third Reich. Like its counterpart, the theory of "the sole responsibility of Hitler," this thesis had the effect of exonerating those individuals and classes who had actively assisted in Hitler's rise to power and the formulation and execution of his policies

> In the diffuse twilight zone between the two theses, 'collective guilt' and 're-education for democracy' the forces which had just been defeated were able to rise again, and those which wanted a new and different Germany had to founder. Instead of the necessary lucidity, a kind of obfuscation was created which has not been eliminated up to the present day.[16]

The next stage in the rehabilitation of key individuals with "brown" pasts was the Cold War, the split between the eastern and western occupation powers, the realization in the West that a strong and rearmed western Germany could be the forward defence against potential or perceived "communist aggression" and the logical deduction that the persons best equipped to man the ramparts and produce the weapons were those who had already proven their ability in these tasks — during the Third Reich. Closely connected with this was the desire to create prosperous economic conditions in the West for both propagandistic (ammunition in the Cold War) and political reasons (consolidation of the neo-liberal capitalist order). Here again there was an ample reservoir of men who had "competently" run society and economy under National Socialism.[17]

The most telling criticism of western denazification occurred in the form of the denazification results achieved in the eastern zone: "There was nothing legalistic about Eastern denazification; it was intended to be political. In one respect it was more effective than in the West, for it never attempted to deal judicially with a purely political evil."[18] In the Soviet Zone all the key positions in the police, judiciary, administration and economy were occupied by anti-fascists returning from exile, concentration camps or the underground, or who had at least refrained from political activity during the Third Reich. When the army of the German Democratic Republic (DDR) was reconstituted in the 1950's its officers were drawn from veterans of the Spanish Civil War (on the communist side) or from members of the *Nationalkomitee Freies Deutschland* (officers who had turned away from National Socialism during World War II, mostly while in Soviet p.o.w. camps). The elimination of fascist influences was not confined to top positions, however. In order to break completely with the old traditions, changes had to go much deeper. Thus the new persons appointed as judges, teachers, administrators, etc. were drawn from the working classes and the younger generations. Due to the urgency of the situation, the new personnel received only a brief period of training and preparation, but with possibilities for continuing education to ensure higher standards in the long term: "Yet a temporary decline in quality was inevitable; this was, however, taken consciously into account in order not to imperil the new political beginning."[19]

The Cold War began in earnest by early 1947, and its intensification coincided with a more active policy on the part of the western occupation powers aimed at direct intervention and the application of force to suppress socialism in the West and surpass communism in the East. Since by late 1946, American policy predominated in the western zones — France and Britain were not only no match for U.S. economic power, they themselves were dependent upon it — it is important to recall that American foreign policy was governed by an anticommunist strategy which found its expression in the "Truman Doctrine", the policy of "containment", and later "roll-back", and the aims of Marshall Plan Aid.

The creation of the Bizone on the basis of an Anglo-American fusion agreement of December 1946, which was revised and enlarged one year later, and the subsequent establishment of the Trizone — France was brought in by promises of Marshall Plan assistance — meant that effective power in the western zones passed definitively into American hands. One of the central aims in creating the Bizone was Clay's (and Washington's) fear of socialism and a centralized economy[19a] a fear which had a special ground in the election of the Marxist trade unionist, Viktor Agartz, to the Executive Committee for Economics (the chief agency of bizonal rehabilitation). Bizonal agencies were then subject to strict Military Government supervision at all levels, socialization measures were prohibited at the bizonal stage and as much autonomy as possible was accorded to the individual *Länder*.

During this active interventionist stage of Military Government control, Clay consistently vetoed or deferred proposals by German political parties or local governments for socialization in one form or another. One witness to Clay's actions in bipartite negotiations, Wolfgang Friedmann, wrote that officially the Americans regarded socialization as a *Land* affair, "but the bias of the U.S. authorities is as antisocialist as is compatible with this theory, or perhaps even greater than that."[20] This helps the explain Clay's opposition to the "socialization articles" — which proposed in varying degrees to nationalize key industries and major financial institutions — in the American Zone *Länder* of Hesse, Bremen and Württemberg-Baden. These regressive acts were complemented by the British Military Government's rejection of the constitution of the *Land* North Rhine-Westphalia on the basis of an almost identical objection, namely that: "The question of socialization must be considered by a German government, and not by a 'Land' government."[21] Thus too, Clay's rejection of a works-council law passed by a 70-14 majority in the Hesse Landtag, representing a coalition of CDU, SPD and KPD against the FDP, in May 1948. Here Clay explicitly opposed the bill's proposals for codetermination in firm and plant as well as any strengthening of trade union powers. In December he went so far as to appeal against the French Military Governor's acceptance of a similar works-council law in that zone.

Following the formation of the Bizone on an antisocialist and capitalist foundation, came American Secretary of State Marshall's famous speech of 5 June 1947, heralding the beginning of Marshall Plan Aid. Such assistance would be dependent upon certain free-trade conditions and would necessitate a currency reform. Not surprisingly, the Soviet Union and therefore all of eastern Europe except Yugoslavia, was not prepared to accept Marshall Aid under these conditions. The collapse of the Council of Foreign Ministers in London in December 1947 due to lack of agreement on the questions of reparations, Marshall Plan assistance and currency reform marked the end of efforts at achieving four-power agreement regarding the reunification of Germany. France subsequently brought her zone into Bizonia and the ensuing

Trizonia was incorporated into the OEEC (Organization for European Economic Cooperation, the body set up to administer the Marshall Plan). Some days later, Marshall Sokolovsky walked out of the Allied Control Council and, beginning in April 1948, increasing restrictions were placed on interzonal travel by the Soviet authorities. After repeated attempts to bring the Soviet Union into Trizonia (on western terms) had failed, the western powers unilaterally introduced a new currency into their zones in June 1948. With this single act, the western occupation powers cemented the already latent division of Germany and ensured the success of the subsequent restoration in society and economy.

Discussing Germany's postwar "Economic Miracle", Richard Hiscocks, author of several works on contemporary Germany, wrote that "it was made possible by the benevolent policy of the Western occupying powers, particularly by American generosity and foresight."[22] This is one view of the genesis of the *Wirtschaftswunder*. In section (1) of this chapter, it was mentioned that heavy industrial equipment had hardly been affected by the war, and that what had been lost through war of reparations was in any case largely obsolete and in need of replacement. Moreover, the ranks of big business and "expert" personnel, following a brief period of sequestration, were scarcely touched by denazification. Not only did East Germany *de facto* pay the reparations for all Germany, the loss of agricultural and relatively backward areas in the East amounted to a gain for the western German economy: "As soon as (West) Germany could find the exports with which to pay for substitute imports of food, she stood to gain by the switch."[23] Moreover, the presence of a large number of mobile (because rootless) refugees helped to keep wages low and to supply labour where it was required, and the nascent trade union movement was still relatively disorganized and preoccupied with the tasks of rebuilding. Add to these the traditional German industriousness and the urgent need for reconstruction and the provision of elementary services and goods, and one finds amid postwar destruction and dislocation all the pre-conditions for the subsequent Economic Miracle. What was needed was merely an injection of capital to start all this machinery in motion. This was supplied by Marshall Plan Aid.

Currency reform, the essential pre-condition to the implementation of the Marshall Plan, was instituted by a series of Military Government decrees published on and after 20 June 1948. Apart from the first 40 Marks which could be exchanged at the rate of 1:1, individual currency holdings were converted at the rate of 100 old Marks:6.5 new Marks. One important exception was debts which were paid off at the rate of 10:1, so that creditors and money-lenders came off comparatively well. Apart from these, the currency reform was particularly favourable to those who had hoarded goods and now gained huge profits form their resale.

The victims were of course those holding savings accounts or whose assets had been in liquid capital, as well as all those without earning potential, such as widows and orphans, the old and disabled, welfare recipients, pensioners and invalids on fixed incomes. Since shortly after the reform the worker's take-home pay was about equal to the pre-war level, while the actual cost of living had increased by about 50 per cent, wage earners (workers) were disadvantaged vis-à-vis those on fixed salaries. This situation has prompted Theo Pirker to write that: "in the history of German capitalism the class division of society was never more openly and more pitilessly made the foundation of a decision of economic policy than in the currency of reform of 1948."[24] Then prices began to outrun payrolls, despite increased output, so that the workers' share of the national product declined relative to gains made by business and agriculture.

(Again a comparison is instructive: the later currency reform in the Soviet Zone provided for conversion at 1:1 of the categories of personal holdings of up to 100 Marks, all credit balances of public authorities, nationalized enterprises and the Soviet military agencies. Personal savings of up to 1,000 Marks were exchanged at 5:1, insurance policies at 3:1 and most other monetary holdings and postwar credit balances at 10:1. It was a policy consciously aimed at redistribution.)

The Berlin Blockade of the next few months was the Soviet response to the western Allies' *de facto* decision to set up a separate West German state. After this it was a very short step to the formation of the German Federal Republic in September 1949 and, as a direct response, the German Democratic Republic in October of the same year.

History has shown that there are very few periods, and that these periods are comparatively short-lived when they do occur, in which far-reaching social and structural reforms can be carried out. To stifle or delay such reforms for a few weeks of months in these times can be to destroy them or at least defer them for an indefinite period. In instance upon instance American, and to a lesser degree, British and French policy in occupied Germany did just that, sometimes as part of, sometimes for lack of a deliberate plan, but always guided by the principles of antisocialism and anticommunism. For this reason it can be said that America carried out not her self-appointed role as saviour of the German people from Nazism and the guiding hand and mentor of the new (liberal-capitalist) democracy in Germany, but became instead the greatest single agent of the reaction.

But this does not imply agreement with Schwarz' notion of Germany as the "helpless object"[25] of four-power foreign policy, nor with Sigmund Neumann's thesis that the occupation relieved the German people of "the last direct responsibility"[26] for political developments. This theory of the omnipotence of the occupation authorities lends itself all to readily to the exoneration of West (as well as East) German political leaders from responsibility for the shortcomings and deficiencies of political life, and to the defamation of the antifascist movements as simply "exported versions" of the Soviet Revolution.

Now the presence and active intervention of the occupation powers, as Rolf Badstubner argues, were indeed "indispensable pre-requisites" to and a "condition of the success" of the prevention of the historical turn to socialism in the Federal Republic.[27] However:

> If (the imperialist bourgeoisie) had not been successful in re-creating, through its policies, a mass political base for its political line . . . , then the bayonettes of the imperialist occupation powers, however numerous, could not have prevented the success of the historical turn in all Germany for any length of time.[28]

Badstubner goes on to compare the role of the *Freikorps* in 1919 with that of the foreign military in 1945/46, an analogy which omits one important difference — in 1945 the foreign military was not merely the executor of policy, but the formulator of it as well; Noske, as is well known, was basically only the (zealous) administrator of Ebert's policies.

Nevertheless the western powers did need, and found, an executive agent to help implement their policies in post-Hitler Germany: the CDU/CSU, the bourgeois coalition and the old upper classes who supported it, who would actively assist in the formation of the Bizone, national division through commitment to the Western Alliance, unilateral currency reform, rearmament and the Restoration in economy and society.

By underlining the fact of German collaboration with the interests and policies of the occupation powers, however, Badstubner had forged a powerful two-edged weapon. For the most outright collaboration of all was carried on by the KPD-SED who owed its power position almost entirely to the Soviet Military Government, and who was subsequently willing to carry out its wishes without regard to popular opinion, national interest or the consequences to German socialism.

It is worth mentioning that all the important measures which ultimately resulted in the division of Germany were initiated by the western occupation authorities, particularly the American Military Government. This is as true of the formation of the Bi- and Trizones, the imposition of currency reform and the propagation of anticommunism as it is of the establishment of a separate western state and the NATO alliance.

There is now considerable evidence, much of it having come to light only in recent years,[29] that until at least 1955 the Soviet Union was not interested in the division of Germany. The USSR wanted, and needed, access to the Ruhr industrial regions, as historically there was a vital economic tie between the coal-mining and agricultural regions of East Germany and the industrial regions of the West.[30] We know, too, that the communist policy was initially one of co-operating with all parties in a bourgeois parliamentary system.[31] Moreover, in 1947 and 1948 there was some prospect of the Communist Parties in France and Italy gaining power, or at least an important share of it, and the Soviet Union certainly did not want a German capitalist wedge between it and these potential allies. When the SED came to power in the Soviet Zone, there were four separate zones and the east-west dimension had not yet become as decisive as it would after the formation of the Bi- and Trizone. It seems more probable, therefore, that Stalin was interested in initiating certain reforms designed to prepare the way for a future transition to communism in all of Germany, meanwhile creating a Germany which would be more amenable, or at least not hostile, to the Soviet Union. Only when the western powers, in collaboration with the bourgeois coalition, had effectively split Germany (and then begun to clamour for re-unification based on the absorption of the Soviet Zone) did the Soviet Union begin to see the existence of a communist DDR as being in its interest.

REFERENCES
1 The Significance of the Postwar Period

1 These statistics, and those in the paragraph following, are quoted in, variously: Presse — und Informationsamt der Bundesregierung, *10 Jahre Bundesrepublik*, 5th ed., Bonn 1959, p.31ff; Wolfgang Bleyer, et al., *Deutschland 1939-1945*, E. Berlin 1969, p.414ff; Rolf Badstubner, *Restauration in Westdeutschland 1945-1949*, E. Berlin 1965, p.19ff; Lewis J. Edinger, *Politics in Germany*, Boston 1968, p.73, Lucius D. Clay, *Decision in Germany*, London 1950, *passim*; Fred H. Sanderson, "Germany's Economic Situation and Prospects" in: G. Almond and W. Kraus, eds.,

The Struggle for Democracy in Germany, Chapel Hill, N. Carolina 1949, p.111; Michael Balfour, *Four-Power Control in Germany and Austria 1945-1946, I. Germany*, London 1956. For an eyewitness account, complete with photographs, see Victor Gollancz, *In Darkest Germany*, London 1947; and for an excellent artistic portrayal of the period, see Heinrich Böll, *Und sagte kein einziges Wort*, Cologne and Berlin 1969.

2 However — and this is extremely important in light of the Restoration which set in later — the war damage was largely of the "visible" kind: "It was primarily Germany's social capital which suffered; the long-term damage to her industrial equipment was not so great, though the confusion of defeat and the breakdown of communications made it seem larger." (Michael Balfour, *op.cit.*, p.12) Even in the Ruhr, which had been particularly hard-hit by Allied bombing raids, only about 30% of the plant machinery had been damaged beyond repair (*ibid.*, p.11). In the western zones the combination of war damage and dismantlings had reduced industrial capacity by only about 10-20%; heavy industry had hardly suffered at all. (Badstubner, *op.cit.*, p.176). Only 11.9% of West Germany's industrial capacity had been destroyed; not including the construction and armaments industries, the destruction amounted only to 7.3%. A further 8.1% was lost through Allied dismantlings. But these losses were more than offset by the 65% increase in production which took place between 1939-43 (taking 1936 as the base year) (cf. Kurt Pritzkoleit, *Wem gehört Deutschland? Eine Chronik von Besitz und Macht*, Vienna-Munich-Basel 1957, p.72 and ff.).
Thus the ownership or control of the remaining industry would be crucial to the development of postwar economic power; control of the machines clearly meant a considerable influence in society and economy. And, as the above indicates, "the obstacle to recovery lay more in dislocation than in destruction." (Balfour, *op.cit.*, p.141) In considering political developments in this period, however, the subjective impression of the "visible" destruction is the relevant fact. In Herbert J. Spiro's words, to state that actual destruction was not as great as it first seemed "makes about as much difference as the class struggle in the history of the United States. If your home and your factory are bombed out, later corrections of economic statistics will have no influence on your present attitude toward your job." (*The Politics of German Co-determination*, Cambridge (Mass.) 1958, p.23f).

3 Thomas Wellmann, "Die Soziologische Lage der Bundesrepublik" in: *Deutsche Rundschau*, LXXXIX (1953), p.591.

4 By contrast, the Church hierarchy had emerged relatively unscathed (the implications of which will be discussed in the next chapter) and, due to the decimation and levelling of the middle classes, the owners of industrial machinery and real property — though temporarily in discredit and disarray — were now in a relatively better position than they had been during the Third Reich, at least in the western occupation zones.

5 Gerhard Stuby, "Bürgerliche Demokratietheorien in der Bundesrepublik" in: Reinhard Kühnl, ed., *Der bürgerliche Staat der Gegenwart. Formen bürgerlicher Herrschaft II*, Reinbek 1972, p.91.

6 Hartmut Kopsch, *The Approach of the Conservative Party to Social Policy during World War II*, unpublished doctoral thesis, University of London (L.S.E.) 1970, p.77.

7 From a leading article of 1 July 1940, quoted in *ibid.*, p.77.

8 Concerning the increase in communist support, it is worth mentioning that, although the number of capitalist countries decreased — corresponding to the increase in the number of communist countries — communist party membership in capitalist countries rose from about 1.7 million before the war to about 5 million in 1946. Communists were represented in the governments of 12 capitalist countries between 1944-47. (Bleyer, *et al.*, *op.cit.*, p.418).

9 Space unfortunately precludes a discussion of the relationship between capitalism and fascism here. But see: O. Bauer, H. Marcuse, A. Rosenberg, *et al.*, *Faschismus und Kapitalismus*, Frankfurt 1967; Arthur Schweizer, *Big Business in the Third Reich*, London 1964; Eberhart Czichon, *Wer verhalf Hitler zur Macht?*, Cologne

1967; David Schoenbaum, *Hitler's Social Revolution*, New York 1966. Some of the most significant work in this field is being done, I believe, by Professor Reinhard Kühnl at the University of Marburg. See, e.g., his *Die nationalsozialistische Linke 1925-1930*, Meisenheim 1965; "Faschismus — Versuch einer Begriffsbestimmung" in: *Blätter fur deutsche und internationale Politik*, Vol.13 1968, p.1260ff; *Die NPD*, Frankfurt 1968; *Formen bürgerlicher Herrschaft* (2 vols.) Reinbek 1971; and his *Faschismusdiskussion I* Reinbek 1974.

10 Here see Wolfgang Abendroth, "Bilanz der sozialistischen Idee in der Bundes-republik Deutschland" in his *Antagonistische Gesellschaft und politische Demo-kratie*, W. Berlin 1967, p.442.

11 *Ibid.*, p.449.

12 Badstubner, *op.cit.*, p.37.

13 In March 1946 one-third of the respondents to a poll said they were no longer interested in politics and felt it safer to stay out, while fully three-quarters had no intention of joining a political party. (Lewis J. Edinger, *Kurt Schumacher. A Study in Personality and Political Behaviour*, Stanford 1965, p.76). Seventy per cent of the respondents to an OMGUS (i.e., Office of the Military Government of the United States) poll of October 1947 said they would refuse to assume responsible political office (*OMGUS Public Opinion Survey*, Series I, No.88, unpaginated), and between February 1947 and August 1949, six in ten Germans said they would choose a government offering economic security in preference to one guaranteeing civil liberties. (*OMGUS Public Opinion Survey*, Series I, No.175, p.6). In November 1945, 80% declared themselves not personally interested in political affairs and pre-ferred to leave them to others; by January 1949, however, this figure had declined to 60%. (*OMGUS Public Opinion Survey*, Series I, Nos. 100 (n.p.) and 175 (p.8). And finally, in polls taken between 1945 and 1950, about 50% of respondents felt that National Socialism was a good idea badly carried out. (*OMGUS Public Opinion Survey*, Series I, No. 100, unpaginated; Allensbach Institute, *Das Dritte Reich. Eine Studie über die Nachwirkungen des Nationalsozialismus*, 2nd ed. 1949).

14 Cornelia Koepke, *Sozialismus in Deutschland*, Munich and Vienna 1970, p.78.

2 The Antifascist Coalition as Foundation of the New Political Order

1 Gabriel A. Almond, "The Social Composition of the German Resistance" in: G. Almond and W. Kraus, eds., *The Struggle for Democracy in Germany*, Chapel Hill, N. Carolina 1949, p.107.

2 *Ibid.*, p.64.

3 "Apart from a few prominent writers and intellectuals . . . exiles not belonging to the left-wing groups played a very minor role in the anti-Nazi exile movement . . . The political life of the anti-Nazi movement thus revolved primarily around the various left-wing groups." Lewis J. Edinger, *German Exile Politics*, Berkeley 1956, p.xi.

4 Almond, *op.cit.*, p.64.

5 For example, at least 90% of all prison sentences handed down for political reasons between 1933 and the outbreak of World War II were to supporters of the labour movement (Abendroth, *Sozialgeschichte* . . . p.176). According to a Gestapo report of 10 April 1939, there was a total of 162,734 persons interred in concentration camps for political reasons, a further 27,369 awaiting trial for political crimes and 112,432 serving time in prisons and gaols, again for political offences. At least 86 mass trials had taken place against antifascist groups and, by the outbreak of war, the KPD had lost between 60 and 70% of its older and more experienced cadres (Erich Paterna et al., *Deutschland von 1933 bis 1939*, E. Berlin 1969, p.325 and 330).

6 Albrecht Kaden, *Einheit oder Freiheit? Die Wiedergründung der SPD 1945/46*, Hanover 1964, p.46.

7 The wording and history of which are given in Hermann Brill, *Gegen den Strom*, Offenbach 1946, p.69 and *passim*.

8 *Dokumente und Materialien zur Geschichte der Deutschen Arbeiterbewegung,* Series III, vol. 1, E. Berlin 1959, p.267.

9 Badstubner, *op.cit.*, p.118.

10 See G. Mannschatz and J. Seider, *Zum Kampf der KPD im Ruhrgebiet für die Einigung der Arbeiterklasse und die Entmachtung der Monopolherren 1945-1947*, E. Berlin 1962, p.57f.

11 Abendroth, *Sozialgeschichte* . . . p.176.

12 Cf. Edinger, "Post-totalitarian leadership . . . ,"

13 Here certain elements of the argument put forth by Ute Schmidt and Tilman Fischer (*Der erzwungene Kapitalismus. Klassenkämpfe in den Westzonen 1945-48*, Berlin 1972, p.121ff) have been incorporated into the analysis.

14 To take a particularly flagrant example, when the first *Land* government in the western zone was formed on 28 May 1945 in Bavaria, the U.S. Military Governor, acting on the recommendation of Cardinal Faulhaber of Munich, appointed Fritz Schäffer premier. Schäffer, the former leader of the Bavarian People's Party in the Weimar Republic, had been responsible for his party's agreeing to Hitler's Enabling Law. In this case a popular outcry forced the Military Governor to cancel the appointment and to nominate instead Wilhelm Hoegner of the SPD.

15 See the list of signatories to the *Gründungsaufruf* in: L. Berthold and E. Diehl, eds., *Revolutionäre Deutsche Parteiprogramme vom Kommunistischen Manifest zum Programm des Sozialismus*, E. Berlin 1967, p.200.

16 Wolfgang Leonhard, *Die Revolution entlässt ihre Kinder*, Cologne 1955, p.318.

17 *Ibid.*, p.319.

18 *Ibid.*, p.320.

3 The Role of the Occupation Powers

1 For a contrary view of these developments, see Terence Prittie, *Konrad Adenauer. A Study in Fortitude*, London 1972. On p.22 he writes: "All too many myths have been propagated in twentieth-century Germany. The myth that German 'democrats' should have been allowed, after the Second World War, to take over such tasks as adjudicating war-crimes, eliminating Nazism and creating a German democratic community from scratch, is one which should not be encouraged. Allied administration of post-1945 Germany was often muddled and inept; but it gave Germans time to think."

2 To name two of the most useful here: Hans-Peter Schwarz, *Vom Reich zur Bundesrepublik*, W. Berlin and Neuwied 1966; Philip Windsor, *German Reunification*, London 1969; see further references below.

3 Except, of course, the territories east of the Oder-Neisse Line, which were to be administered by the Soviet Union and Poland pending a final settlement in a peace treaty; all Germans living in Poland, Czechoslovakia and Hungary were to be transferred to the area west of the Oder-Niesse. Thus even before the shooting stopped, a great reactionary potential had been created, namely a large class of displaced refugees and the appropriation of German territories.

4 *Jahrbuch der SPD 1946*, Bonn, 1946, p.3.

5 John Gimbel, *The American Occupation of Germany. Politics and the Military 1945-1949*, Stanford 1968, p.249.

6 *Ibid.*, p.xiii.

7 These developments are discussed at greater length in Ch.III (2) below.

8 Eberhard Schmidt, *Die verhinderte Neuordnung*, Frankfurt 1970.

9 Which were to be made in kind, i.e., in the form of plant and industrial equipment, rather than from current output, in order to prevent the development of industries forming the basis of modern warfare (heavy engineering, chemicals, metallurgy, synthetic petroleum, ammonia, etc). The agreements proposed to reduce Germany's standard of living to 74% of the pre-war average — the standard attained in 1932,

one year before the Nazi seizure of power — and did not take into account the postwar population growth in West Germany or shifts in emphasis of industrial production.

10 Balfour, *West Germany*, p.148.

11 15-20 million dead, destruction of 15 large cities, 1710 towns, and 70,000 villages, 25 million homeless, the collapse of transportation and communication, etc., etc.

12 Balfour, *Four-Power Control*, p.257.

13 Reinhard Kühnl, "Die Auseinandersetzung mit dem Faschismus in BRD und DDR" in Gerhard Hess, ed., *BRD—DDR Vergleich der Gesellschaftssysteme*, Cologne 1971, p.266.

14 See Schmidt/Fichter, op.cit. Nicholas Ryschowsky, who in 1945 was employed by the U.S. Military Government to assist in denazification proceedings, relates the story of a Catholic professor whose works in "racial biology" helped to prepare the way for the Nuremberg Race Laws, and of a young natural scientist whose bravery earned him the Ritterkreuz, an order which automatically brought with it the rank of Sturmführer in the SS. The professor had never actually joined the NSDAP, however, while the scientist of course had. After 1945 the former, whose contribution to the Third Reich had been far more insidious than the latter's, was permitted to occupy his chair without interruption, while the scientist was no longer allowed to teach even the natural sciences. (As told in a private interview with the author).

15 The implications of this process of "renazification" are discussed further in Ch.IV (1) below.

16 Hans-Werner Richter, "Zwischen Freiheit und Quarantäne" in: Richter, ed., *Bestandsaufnahme. Eine Deutsche Bilanz 1962*, Munich-Vienna-Basel 1962, p.13.

17 Terence Prittie has recently suggested a number of further reasons for renazification: . . . "vast numbers of Nazi Party members were non-political', . . . the infant Federal Republic needed all the help that it could get from the best available administrators, and . . . Nazism would be 'bred out' of the German people by good government, intelligible aims and a democratic ideal. Adenauer believed in creating positive factors, as the best means to counteract the negative elements of a situation which he had inherited." (see his: *Adenauer* . . . , *op.cit.*, p.200.

18 J. P. Nettl, *The Eastern Zone and Soviet Policy in Germany 1945-1950*, London 1950, p.79.

19 Kühnl, "Die Auseinandersetzung . . . , " *op.cit.*, p.252. He discusses the East German denazification policies at some length here, p.251ff.

19a Gimbel, *op.cit.*, p.126; See esp. Clay's Memorandum of February 1947 concerning the Bizone, reproduced there p.119f.

20 Wolfgang Friedmann, *The Allied Military Government of Germany*, London 1947, p.145f. See also Zink, *op.cit.*, p.40f.

21 Cf. Arnold Heidenheimer, *Adenauer and the CDU. The Rise of the Leader and the Integration of the Party*, The Hague 1960, p.133.

22 Richard Hiscocks, *Democracy in Western Germany*, London 1957, p.1 A few pages later he writes: The political weakness of Germany has its roots not only in past history but also in fundamental qualities of the national character" (p.4).

23 Balfour, *West Germany*, p.175.

24 Theo Pirker, *Die blinde Macht. Die Gewerkschaftsbewegung in Westdeutschland* Vol.I, Munich 1960, p.98.

25 Schwarz, *op.cit.*, p.11

26 See Sigmund Neumann's introduction to: Max-Gustav Lange, ed., *Parteien in der Bundesrepublik*, Stuttgart and Düsseldorf 1955, p.xxiii.

27 Badstubner, *op.cit.*, p.88.

28 *Ibid.*, p.89.

29 Cf. Windsor, *op.cit.*, p.21ff.

30 See Wolfgang Abendroth, "Entkrämpfung oder Entspannung?" in: Leonard Froese, ed., *Was soll aus Deutschland werden?*, Munich 1968.

31 See Ch. III (2) below.

III. The SPD: One Socialist Party among Many?

1. Socialist Competition from Left and Right

In the previous chapter it was argued that the original tendency of post-war political life in Germany was toward socialism, a tendency which originated in the historical situation, material necessity, the failure of the Weimar Republic, the lessons of the fascist dictatorship and total war, and the desire to create a "new" and "better" Germany. The struggle to achieve the necessary radical reforms and overcome the mistakes of the past took on the form of the anti-fascist, socialist front. Postwar political trends were, however, arrested and ultimately reversed by a number of factors, the most important of which were the policies of the occupation powers, their concrete interests, their discords and disagreements and the nascent Cold War. Certainly political developments immediately after 1945 were unthinkable without the interventions of the occupation powers. In considering the formation of the two German states, as Wolfgang Abendroth has written, it is essential to bear in mind

> . . . that by no means only on the road from the Soviet Occupation Zone to the DDR, but, in some degree, on the road from the three western zones of occupation to the BRD, the intervention of the respective ruling occupation power determined the future structure of the two German states to a far greater extent than did the indigenous opinion of the German people and their relevant social organizations which had been able to develop anew after the fall of the Third Reich. The Restoration in the BRD would have been just as impossible as the development of a bureaucratic form of socialist society in the DDR.[1]

The way in which the occupation powers' ban on political activities affected the antifascist and socialist popular front movement has also been described. This policy led directly to the reconstitution of the old political parties in accordance with the main directions of political party divisions in the Weimar Republic: on the bourgeois side, the Christian Democrats and Free or Liberal Democrats, and on the socialist side the Communists and Social Democrats. Similarly, the unified trade union was reduced to a system of industrial trade unions, all dependent upon approval by the Military Governments. Although the "new" parties' and trade unions' leaders were largely appointed by the Military Governments and their programmes and organizations approved by them at every stage, all the political parties and labour organizations retained to an almost remarkable degree the principles and policies of the antifascist front. The initial postwar desire for radical social measures found expression in the programmes of all the parties (except the liberal parties) and local and zonal trade union organizations originating in this period. For this reason, the German "Left" immediately after 1945 consisted, prima facie, of all the political parties (again, excepting the liberals) and all the trade unions then active. The subject of this chapter is an examination of this "Left", the pressure to which it was subjected, the programmes and strategies which it developed, the controversies within it, and its ultimate dissolution — all within a brief four-year period.

a. Communist popular front

At almost the precise moment when the last *Wehrmacht* squad capitulated in Berlin, the "Group Ulbricht" arrived in that city[2] It, and the other two groups which followed it, consisted of well-trained, selected communist party members who had spent the war years in the Soviet Union (Walter Ulbricht, Wilhelm Pieck, Anton Ackerman, Fritz Apelt, Wilhelm Florin, Fred Oelssner, Otto Winzer and Hermann Matern, to name a few). Although other communists were to return from elsewhere abroad, such as France (Franz Dahlem, Paul Merker, Wilhelm Bertz), Holland (Erich Gentsch) and Switzerland, the USSR group played by far the most important role within the KPD, especially since the leading cadres that had remained in Germany after 1933 (Ernst Thälmann, Anton Saefkow, Franz Jacob, Bernhard Bastlein) had for the most part not survived the Third Reich.

The KPD's initial aims, as laid down in its Gründungsaufruf[3] of 11 June 1945 (one day after the promulgation by the Soviet Military Government — SMAD — of Command No. 2 admitting political parties in the Soviet Zone), and as stated in speeches by party leaders, in brochures, broadcasts, etc, might be summarized as: for the people, peace and national recovery. This programme was far less "radical" than the SPD platforms drawn up at this time, and was chiefly concerned with economic recovery. It called for the expropriation of assets held by the "Nazi bosses" and war criminals, the liquidation of large estates belonging to the old nobility and the Junkers, and the nationalization of vital services, such as the water and gas supplies, electricity system, etc., and their control by local and regional governments. But these are the only points in the KPD's Call to Action which can be said to be expressly socialist in character.

The document went on to propose, indeed, was itself intended to serve as the basis of "the creation of a bloc of antifascist, democratic parties composed of the KPD, SPD, Centre and others."[4] The communists' postwar popular front policy traces back to resolutions passed at its Brussels (1935) and Bern (1939) Party Conventions. It was completely in line with the Comintern notion of an antifascist, democratic transformation of the foundation of a united front of all the organizations of labour. The popular front policy was applied throughout eastern Europe as well as in Italy and France where the communist parties had a share in coalition governments. Furthermore:

> The KPD now assumed that the class consciousness of many workers had been largely destroyed, and that large sectors among the petit-bourgeosie and bourgeoisie — influenced by National Socialist propaganda — would be negatively disposed toward any cooperation with the communists. Thus joint actions of the workers in the struggle for the socialization of key industries, for land reform and denazification were to create the preconditions for the establishment of a unified labour party.[5]

By way of concession to this united front, the KPD was prepared to make certain compromises: reconstruction was to take place according to the principle of the "completely unrestricted development of free trade and private entrepreneurial initiative on the basis of private ownership." And although the huge estates and properties of the Nazis and former nobility were to be expropriated and redistributed, "it is self-evident that these measures will not affect land ownership and the economy of the large farmers."[6]

Shortly after the founding of the SPD in the East Zone on 17 June 1945, steps were taken to establish a "working group" between it and the KPD, in order to prepare the way for the unification of the two parties at a later date. This was followed, almost a month later, by the establishment of an antifascist, democratic front between the KPD, SPD, CDU and LDP in Berlin (the process would take longer in the *Länder*). Yet a final merger of the two principal working-class parties, SPD and KPD — although the existence of a separate KPD directly contradicted the Bern Convention Resolution — was postponed for some time. The KPD, it was evident, now hoped to enhance its bargaining position before entering into the merger, in addition to having to cope with the massive resistance of the SPD in the western zones.

There were excellent tactical reasons for this delaying policy on the part of the KPD. Its initial advantages in the Soviet Zone were twofold: it was favoured by material, financial and moral support from the occupying power, and it had won for itself a positive association in the popular consciousness through its well known efforts in the resistance and its role in supplying the activists of the first hour. It was widely recognized that: "The fascist terror had been directed primarily against the KPD in order to destroy its most consistent and implacable opponent . . . The KPD was the only party whose functionaries and groups fought according to uniform political directions for the downfall of the Hitler dictatorship."[7] And it is also true that: "as the only party in Germany the KPD opposed Hitler-fascism with organized resistance from the first to the last day.[8]

The KPD's advocacy of the all-party antifascist front and its claim that it first wanted to see Germany finally complete the abortive revolution of 1848 before the establishment of socialism was surely effective in some measure in adding to its popular support. In both the eastern and western zones, the KPD was comparatively successful in the first postwar communal, regional and *Land* elections.[9] Between August and December 1945, the Soviet Union carried out a thoroughgoing programme of land reform and redistribution. This, Peter Nettl believes, represented "the ruthless exploitation for Communist purposes of the prevalent anti-Nazi feeling,"[10] because it was used to eliminate unwanted possessors from desirable property or simply undesirable opponents. One could, however, argue plausibly that the communists, at this stage, were simply carrying out what was undoubtedly a very popular, and perhaps necessary, policy at that time, in eliminating the excessive power of the Prussian Junkers, industrialists and military classes.

Against these positive factors, there had developed a considerable reservoir of anticommunist sentiment. There was, firstly, the legacy of Hitler's radical "antibolshevism" and a completely justified fear that the Soviet Union might seek revenge for the Nazis' unwarranted attack on Russia in 1941 and their subsequent pillage of the country and extermination of great numbers of civilians and prisoners-of-war. To these must be added the excesses of the Soviet troops in occupied Germany and the continued (frequently ruinous) dismantlings of industry in the Soviet Zone. The German population began to perceive the KPD as the executor of this Soviet policy.

Then two events occurred which lent particular urgency to the Communists' desire to merge with the Social Democrats. The first was a speech by Otto Grotewohl, the SPD leader in the Soviet Zone, on 11 November 1945. In it he called for the immediate implementation of socialism, indicated his — veiled — opposition to the dismantlings and hinted that the SPD's proper place was somewhere between the extremes of the bourgeois parties and the communists. The second event was the disastrous communist showings in the Austrian elections: while the Austrian People's Party (ÖVP) had attained 85 seats in the new Austrian parliament and the Social Democrats (SPÖ) 76, the KPÖ had won only four seats.

Suddenly the creation of a united socialist party became the order of the day. Now it might well have been necessary, as Pieck stated, to proceed with reunification "with all urgency" in order to avoid the "reaction's" increasing attempts to seize power, and to alleviate "the great destitution of our people,"[11] both valid enough reasons, but evidence suggests that the move was guided more by expediency than by such considerations. About this time the KPD began to play up a policy of "the special German road to socialism". For: "It would also be wrong to think that the development would occur uniformly in all countries. We in Germany must take the road that corresponds to developmental conditions in Germany, and that will not be precisely the same road as in other countries."[12]

"The Special German Road to Socialism" is indeed the title of an article by Anton Ackermann which appeared in the party journal, *Einheit*, in February 1946, and which played an extremely important role in communist policy for a time. There could never be a truly "peaceful" growth to socialism," Acker mann wrote, but in certain situations — e.g., when the bourgeoisie was not in control of the military, bureaucracy and the state, and thus in no position to suppress forcibly the rising proletarian socialist movement — there could be a "relatively peaceful" transition to socialism. The situation in Germany, unlike that in the Soviet Union in 1917, now allowed for this peaceful transition. In other words, different socio-historical situations called for different solutions and the German solution was now an antifascist union of the labour parties. This thesis found the support of Ulbricht, Pieck and of most KPD members.[13]

Following the "Conference of the Sixty" of the Soviet Zonal SPD and KPD in December 1945 ("Our goal is the realization of socialism in social democracy; the unified party will be an independent German socialist party" . . . organized according to "democratic principles."[14]) and the Second Joint Conference of February 1946, the stage was set for the official merger of the two parties into the Socialist Unity Party of Germany (SED) in April 1946.

The new party's aims, as declared in the "Principles and Aims of the Socialist Unity Party of Germany,"[15] (the resolution passed at the convention of unification), were quite straightforward. The united party was necessary to prevent a recurrence of the cleavage within the Left that allowed fascism to gain the upper hand. All "fascist remnants" and monopoly capitalist organizations were to be extirpated, large estates redistributed and business grouped into chambers in which the trade unions and people's cooperatives would have an equal voice. Profits were to be limited, exploitation eliminated and cooperatives encouraged. There would be comprehensive social legislation, including educational reform and an end to denominational schools. All this was to serve the new party's goal of "liberation from all exploitation and oppression, from economic crises, poverty, unemployment and imperialist threats of war."[16]

Though the SPD under Grotewohl in the Soviet Zone appeared content with these arrangements — the degree of pressure applied by the Soviet Military Government is uncertain — the SPD-West, under Schumacher's leadership, opposed the merger vehemently,[17] and its convention in Hanover one month later declared membership in, or activity on behalf of the SED to be irreconcilable with membership of the SPD. A plebiscite which had been held in March among members of the SPD in the western sectors of Berlin — those in the Soviet sector were denied a plebiscite — had shown that 2,937 favoured an immediate merger, 14,763 were in favour of an association "assuring cooperation and eliminating the *Bruderkampf*", and 5,559 were against any form of cooperation.[18]

The SED was able to achieve some 76.2 per cent of the popular vote (82 per cent if the "mass organizations" are included) in the municipal elections of 1946, and also emerged from the October *Land* elections in the Soviet Zone with a majority (again including the mass organizations),[19] it is true, but much of its success must be put down to the political and material support it received from the Soviet occupation authority. Had the KPD and SPD entered these elections separately, however, the two parties' total share of the vote might well have been higher and the SPD would have been the main beneficiary. There is some evidence of this in the Berlin elections of 10 October. The SPD's share of the popular vote here was 48.7 per cent (50.8 per cent in W.Berlin), the CDU's 22.1 (25.9), the SED's 19.8 (12.4) and the LDP's 9.4 (10.9).[20] These were the last relatively "free" elections in which the SED was to take part.

Then began the series of events — the failure of the *Länder* premiers' conference in Munich, the mounting Cold War, the Yugoslavian controversy, the continued Soviet dismantlings despite earlier assurances that they would stop, the luxuries (pajoks), special benefits and villas (guarded by Russian troops!) accorded to higher communist functionaries — which increasingly isolated the SED-KPD elite and brought about a gradual development toward Stalinism. The IInd Party Convention of the SED from 20-23 September 1947 was lavish in its praise of Stalin and the Soviet Union, and attempted to justify the dismantlings. The "Cominform Resolution Concerning Yugoslavia and the Lessons for the SED" of 16 September 1948,[21] passed by the Party Executive Committee (*Vorstand*), marked the final repudiation of the "special road to socialism" by the SED. It was now said to be necessary to learn from the history and experiences of the CPSU, especially in view of the "militarist and imperialist threats" made by the West against the USSR and the People's Republics. The "leading role of the party" (the "party of a new type", i.e., organized according to the principle of "democratic centralism") was affirmed, and measures were to be taken to extend the scale of public and state ownership of the means of production.

It is indicative of the progression of the process of Stalinization that Ackermann was compelled to recant his old thesis of the special German road to socialism. This he did in an article in the party organ, *Neues Deutschland*, of 9 September 1940. "This theory," he wrote, " . . . has proven to be unconditionally wrong and dangerous." Instead, a "specific situation" had originated in a number of countries following World War II, and this situation had been precipitated by the Red Army. Since the formulation of the original thesis, a considerable anticommunist sentiment, serving imperialist interests, had arisen, and it was now clear that the theory had been conducive to the development of anticommunism, rather than dampening it. Furthermore, " . . . for all revolutionary workers' parties, regardless of which country, the doctrines not only of Marx and Engels, but especially of Lenin and Stalin, are the guiding principles for practical action." Thus the CPSU had become the model for all Marxist-Leninist parties in the world, including the SED.

Despite the efforts to maintain a common policy made by the two parties concerned, one must speak of a separate development of the KPD in the western zones, at the latest on the establishment of the Socialist Unity Party. In the West, as in the East, the KPD had been active in the work of reconstruction, its officials had been appointed to local offices and the editorial boards of the "licensed" newspapers and its members were represented in local and regional parliamentary bodies. Following the formation of the SED in April 1946, the western KPD also made a number of overtures to a — considerably more hostile — SPD under Kurt Schumacher's leadership, but its successes were limited to cooperation in a few local administrative bodies. In February 1947, the Working Group formed between the SPD and KPD in the Soviet Zone was extended into the West, but, it was soon evident, consisted almost exclusively of KPD members. When the merger was officially proposed, the U.S. Military Government refused to admit the SED in Bavaria and Hesse, and the British authorities rejected a similar request in North Rhine-Westphalia. By this time, "the political guidance of the KPD in the western zones lay without doubt in the hands of the Party Executive Committee of the SED, of which the representatives of the West Zone KPD were also members.[22] The Allies' motives in refusing to admit the SED in the West were clear: the combination of SED-East and KPD-West would have been the largest — in terms of membership — political party in Germany. Toward the end of 1947 and the beginning of 1948, the KPD then found itself gradually being pushed out of the remaining offices which it still held in the western zones,[23] and its application to re-christen itself the "Socialist People's Party of Germany" was also rejected out of hand by the western Allied occupation authorities in June and July 1948.

During this period the western KPD's policies were undermined by the actions of the Soviet occupation power in the East. The USSR's annexations of the Baltic countries, eastern Poland and parts of Czechoslovakia and Rumania made the KPD's campaign against the French proposals for annexing the Saar seem hypocritical. Similarly, the extensive dismantlings in the East gave the lie to the KPD's campaign against the far fewer dismantlings in the West. These developments were reinforced by the beginning systematic efforts of the American Military Government after 1946 aimed at reducing the KPD's support in the field in which it was traditionally strongest: in the works' councils. For example, in the mining industry the percentage of communists in the works' councils declined from 71 per cent in 1946-48 to 32 per cent in 1949 and 25 per cent in 1950.[24]

Thus isolated from political power and mass following — in November 1946 a sample of the population in the U.S. Zone, asked to make an hypothetical choice between a Communist or National Socialist government, declared themselves nine per cent for the communists, 17 per cent for the Nazis, with the remainder choosing neither; in February 1949, 43 per cent chose the Nazis, two per cent the communists and 55 per cent neither[25] — the KPD-West came more and more under the influence of the SED. "We unconditionally support the policy of the Soviet Union," declared the Party Executive Committee, "because we are Marxist-Leninists, because the Soviet Union, under the leadership of the CPSU, has consistently taken the road of Marxism-Leninism, the road of proletarian internationalism . . ."[26] The communique of the 8th Session of the Party Executive Committee of the KPD, dated 3 January 1949, asserted that, although the SED and KPD were separate organizational entities, full agreement existed on the basic problems of German politics.[27]

The stage was now set for the almost total isolation of the Communist Party from the realities of political life, for the internal purges and painful self-criticism that would characterize it until its demise in 1956.

b. Christian socialism

In the first months following the collapse of the Third Reich many Germans saw their condition not as the outcome of an economic and historical development, but as the manifestation of God's wrath at their abandoning Him for the Führer, and therefore believed that the Church must play a central role in the new Germany. Others, seeking antifascist elements with which to begin again, hit upon the well-publicized conflicts between the churches and the National Socialist regime in the closing phase of the Third Reich. The power of christian faith was seen as an alternative to the "pagan" and "nihilistic" spirit of fascism. This power, it was thought, must be harnessed in the service of political democracy. But precisely the inter-denominational conflicts of the Weimar era must be avoided if the Church was to be an effective counterweight to any recurrence of fascism.

Hence the idea of a supradenominational christian "popular front", like the antifascist coalition, arose more or less spontaneously in various places. The new christian movement would eliminate the old cleavage between labour and bourgeoisie; as a party of the "progressive middle" it would express the new spirit by calling itself not a party but a "union."[1] And it would have to be socialist to some degree, since the material distress of Germany left no other choice, and since socialism (or at least social concern and welfare measures) was seen as a manifestation of the christian spirit.

The first and most important centres of this attempt to combine christian principles with socialist aims in a political programme were located in Berlin, Frankfurt and Cologne. The Berlin and Frankfurt centres were initially more influential because they determined the CDU's originally socialist profile and coined for it the leftist political currency so necessary to purchase popular support at this time. But the Cologne party, with Konrad Adenauer at its head, would ultimately provide the leadership and praxis of the federal party.

The Berlin group was directly connected with the 20th July Conspiracy and the old christian trade union movement before 1933 through its leader, Jakob Kaiser, and with the Hirsch-Duncker (liberal) trade unions of the Weimar era through its co-leader, Ernst Lemmer. Its central theme, "socialism based on christian responsibility," originated with the group's theorist, Otto Heinrich von der Gablentz.

In Frankfurt the idea of christian socialism was propounded by a group of Catholic intellectuals who had once belonged to the Centre Party. They were former publicists like Walter Dirks, Karl-Heinrich Knappstein, Josef Wirth and Paul Löbe, and professors such as Eugon Kogon. These contributed to the *Frankfurter Hefte*, a semi-scholarly periodical edited by Kogon and Dirks, the two major figures in the Frankfurt movement. Their central aim was to bring about a synthesis of the SPD and the former Centre parties as a kind of socialist but anti-communist alliance. In order to forestall the christian centrists and social democrats from establishing separate political organizations,² they founded the "Christian Democratic Party" on 15 September 1945 in Frankfurt and nominated Knappstein chairman. But the nomination was rejected by the U.S. Military Government who instead appointed Jakob Husch, an old Centre man with little sympathy for socialist intellectuals. This meant that the intellectuals were manoeuvred out on to the party perimeter and from the outset were unable to play a determining role in party affairs.

If there is a single theme running through the works of the christian socialists, it is that socialism, although necessary and even desirable, must not "go too far"; there is an omnipresent and curious admixture of acute concrete analysis surrounded by woolly and intangible articles of faith and unsupported rationalizations.

Gablentz, for example, discussing the need to go "beyond Marx", conceded the validity of the power of technology and the class struggle in the materialist view of history, but later went on to state that not class, not Mind, was the motive force of history, but "Jesus Christ . . . is the centre of history." From this it followed that:

> Only the christian view is realistic in the truest sense of the word . . .
> Christian politics are free from hatred and resentment . . . Because
> (the christian) has a view of the whole profusion and depth of the
> world, he knows that there are no unbridgable contradictions, either
> between people or between peoples. All have their God-appointed
> tasks, and . . . must be able to find the limitations which have been set
> between them.³

Similarly, Gablentz made an excellent case for the primacy of personal freedom in the formulation of modern socialist theories, but then proposed that the reorganization of state and society be undertaken on the basis of the old natural basic order of family and profession.⁴ Indeed, this is almost a classic expression of the old Catholic social doctrine which viewed society as a kind of organism with each individual fulfilling his divinely-appointed function within the order willed by God.⁵

The Frankfurt christian socialists correctly saw Germany as being at a great historical turning-point. Kogon wrote: "The socialists of freedom are no longer confronted by a firmly entrenched big industrialist-capitalist-large agrarian class rule in Germany, but only by a rubble-heap of profiteering remnants."⁶ For Dirks this situation approximated a revolution. But "when one plans, prepares, suffers through, fights out and finally wins a revolution, one usually knows what one wants."⁷ Just as in 1919, German socialists were said not to know what they wanted. What was needed was a "productive utopia"⁸ as a guide to action.

Now the two parties which had historically represented socialism in Germany, Dirks continued, were either too completely or at least partly atheistic, materialistic and doctrinaire Marxist to be able to realize socialism, and in any case the christian union could include only those who had understood both the nature of the times and the "political mission" of christians. After all, Dirks wrote, "before the gallows they were all equal, the nobles, the christians and the communists."[9] Elswhere Dirks managed to exceed even this degree of obfuscation — for what was the "political mission" of christians? Certainly christians, communists and murderers were all equal on the scaffold, but how many and what percentage of each group actually reached the gallows? — when he proposed a synthesis in christian socialism of what was best in Left and Right:

> The West is the knowledge of what we are; socialism is the will to do what is necessary . . . The concern of the Right is attitude and wisdom, the concern of the Left is the deed . . . One must have the virtues of the Right (reverence, discipline, fidelity) . . . and do the acts of the Left. *Or in short: be right and act left.*[10]

Of the various christian socialist theories put forward in the postwar period, perhaps Jakob Kaiser's version must be taken more seriously than most, for not only were his ideas relatively consistent (despite the influence of von der Gablentz) and realistic, but he also had a substantial prospect — prior to the division of Germany — of achieving the leadership of the new party and thus of realizing his theories. Kaiser spoke of the end of bourgeois society; the bourgeoisie's capitulation to the Third Reich represented its last attempt to prevent its decline as an historical force. Now bourgeois society had gone the way of feudalism and an "age of the working peoples" had begun. The CDU, he believed, ought by no means to be merely a continuation of the old-style bourgeois party because it contained workers, farmers and persons from all walks of life.

Socialism for Kaiser was not to be merely a question of good conscience or platitudes about brotherly love: "Intention and good will are not enough; we need action which reaches into the roots of the social and economic order if we are to be in a position to begin with reconstruction.[11] Thus action must be taken in the christian spirit, which pre-supposed the "immutable significance and dignity of the person". Christianity was the moral basis upon which freedom and socialism could be established and its acceptance the reason why the dictatorship of the proletariat was no longer necessary.

If socialism were realized on the basis of christian responsibility, if politicians could be made aware of the great historical changes taking place, then Germany could be a bridge, a synthesis between East and West, between Soviet socialism and western (bourgeois) democracy. "We must be a bridge between East and West, but at the same time let us seek out our own way to a new socialist organization.[12] This was the basis of Kaiser's "bridge" theory or notion of a Third Way which played an important role in postwar Germany. Yet Kaiser's insistence upon the central importance of human freedom above and beyond all else without defining what he meant by this, his belief in the regulation of private property only when it conferred power over other human beings upon its owners and his aversion to centralism and excessive state control must give rise to the question as to whether he intended not a synthesis between East and West, but simply a further development of western bourgeois democracy into a kind of reform capitalism.

But the most important — because ultimately predominant — centre of christian socialist activity was Cologne and the Rhineland. It never produced theorists and publicists like von der Gablentz, Kogon or Dirks, nor — with the exception of Karl Arnold — socialist leaders like Kaiser and Lemmer, but it did supply the party's future leader, Konrad Adenauer, and its future praxis: extreme doctrinal flexibility in the service of the acquisition and retention of power.

From the very outset, the Cologne wing's socialism was based less on a desire to implement socialism than the will to gain power by anticipating the popular mood. Thus the party's "Appeal to the German People"[13] and its "Guiding Principles of Cologne"[14] of 1945 called for state ownership of natural resources and "key monopoly industries," as well as for the elimination of large-scale capitalist enterprises. But the "Guiding Principles" also stressed the importance of private property and the need to encourage small- and medium-scale operations. Concepts such as "community," "*Volk*" and "nation" appeared frequently.[15] The Basic Programme of 1946 underlined the growing lower middle-class bias of the Rhineland CDU: "We reject the planned economy as the culmination of a collective theory." Special mention was made of rights of private property and the central position of the Church, including a rejection of the separation of church and state and the need for denominational schools.

Nevertheless, the socialist idea survived in the CDU as long as 1947 and the promulgation of its famous "Ahlen Programme" which demanded, among others, the abolition of the capitalist economic system because it had not been "adequate for the vital national and social interests of the German people" and the creation of a "new social and economic order" guaranteed by constitution, co-determination for the worker in industry, expropriation of large landed or industrial properties and an ongoing policy of social progress based on economic and social planning.[16] On the other hand these radical-sounding proposals were tempered at every stage by checks: the repeated use of the notion of *Gemeinschaft* implying as it did in Catholic social doctrine a diffuse control of industry, the central importance of private property in non-vital industries and resources, and the idea of a minimum amount of direction and central planning. Thus, as Arnold Heidenheimer has written: "The Ahlen Program was clearly a program of the Left, but it could rally the workers without alienating the propertied elements, to whom it offered broader protection than any other major party programme."[17]

Even prior to Ahlen, however, Adenauer had set the tone of CDU policy for more "normal" times in a speech held in March 1946. He declared that capitalism in Germany was dead after 1945. There were no more big capitalists and hence no class differences and, above all, no class struggle. Instead of class struggle, the time had come for a "social partnership" comprising a community of all former classes and professions.[18] If capitalism was dead, so too was socialism as the negation of capitalism. To observers on the left, there were more than a few similarities between "social partnership" and the fascist notion of *Volksgemeinschaft* (or organic community of all the people), each with his God — (or *Führer*-appointed function and duty to maintain the organism-state at the cost of his own personal liberty.

Following the Berlin group's loss of independence in the eastern zone and

the resignations of Kaiser and Lemmer under pressure from the Soviet
occupation authority — the Kogon-Dirks faction was of course no longer
influential within the party[19] — the Rhineland wing, with the support of the
Bavarian Christian Social Union (CSU),[20] inevitably came to determine the
whole party's programme and strategy. Guided by flexible opportunism and
the desire for political power. Adenauer was able to enrol christian socialism
in the service of an increasingly conservative policy.

In mid-1949, just in time for the first federal elections, the CDU, in its
Düsseldorf Programme of that year, cast off virtually all its socialist principles
from Ahlen and before, propounding instead Erhard's slogan of the "social
market economy" and the importance of "private initiative." "Probably none
of the large parties," Schutz says, commenting on this programme, "went into
the decisive electoral struggle for the first parliament of the West German
Federal Republic with a more imprecisely formulated and hastily put together
programme than did the CDU."[21]

The critique of German christian socialism after 1945, as argued here, is
threefold. Christian socialism must be rejected as a leftist movement for
reasons of historical accuracy, the contemporary alignment of political forces
and the ultimate doctrinal irreconcilability of ecclesiastic and socialist
thought. The union of secular and ecclesiastic forces brought with it a number
of problems. It introduced — or rather reintroduced — the principle of a
combination of church and state at an historical juncture when the separation
of these two institutions had otherwise gained near-universal acceptance in
the more advanced western nations. Beyond this, and above all in Germany, it
rested on a number of false assumptions, namely that the Church was a
progressive and democratic social force, and that it had been a genuinely
antifascist community.

During the Second Reich, the Lutheran Church had been subordinate to
the secular power and had come to share the *Weltanschauung* and way of life
of the ruling classes; indeed it was itself a part of the ruling class.[22] Socially it
had sided with Bismarck and his Anti-Socialist Laws, and during the Weimar
Republic became extremely anticommunist. Politically it had consistently
urged the faithful to return conservative and authoritarian governments and
had been associated with the Prussian bureaucracy. The Catholic Church had
also been closely identified with the status quo and had lent its support to
anti-labour measures as well.[23] It had occasionally attacked the National
Socialist regime before 1933, it is true, but the Vatican had been the first to
conclude a Concordat with Hitler in the spring of 1933, and this heralded a
period of truce between the Third Reich and the Catholic Church which
would be broken only because of actions initiated by the Nazis. This truce, as
is well known, prevented the Catholic Church both in Rome and in Germany
from placing its moral authority behind efforts to stop the deportations and
extermination of the Jews during World War II, and even before.

In the early stages of the Third Reich, in fact, the churches supported and
actively assisted National Socialism, and indeed had been one of the major
factors in the "socialization" of the German people under the Third Reich.[24]
In this way the churches acquired a vested interest in the maintenance of the
fascist regime, particularly with respect to the perceived "bolshevist threat"
from the East or even from within the Reich. Only later, when the total-
authoritarian nature of the Third Reich became apparent, and it aspired to

achieve a "total" control of society including the allegiances hitherto claimed by the churches, did the Church react against it, and then mostly in self-defence. Even the *Bekennende* (Confessing) Church did not organize a systematic resistance based on principle,[25] but opted instead for the role of anvil to the National Socialist hammer.[26] The Niemöllers and the Bonhoeffers were (admirable) exceptions to the overall rule.

Because the churches had co-existed with the Nazi regime, and indeed had benefited considerably from it, for so long, they were relatively prosperous and intact in 1945 and surrounded by an aura of antifascism which then enabled them to exert a disproportionate influence on politics and society. This moral authority was reinforced by the responsibilities accruing to the churches in consequence of material conditions after 1945. In the absence of the traditional administrative agencies, they often assumed the roles of food distributor, finder of shelter, reunifier of families, employment agency and, not least of all, protector and rehabilitator of "small-fry" former Nazis.[27] Thus any political party founded on the ostensibly antifascist, democratic or even socialist character of the churches, and drawing moral inspiration, as well as mass support, from them, rested on a fallacious interpretation of historical reality, or worse, laid itself open to a charge of opportunism.

However much Kaiser and Gablentz, Kogon and Dirks, Lemmer and Arnold might subjectively have espoused socialism, their objective role thus came to be one of providing a demagogic counterweight for the Right against the Left on the latter's own ground. In this task it could count on the cynicism and resignation of a post-fascist society weary of political controversy and prepared to place its trust in God, or His perceived representatives on earth. In the historical upheaval that followed upon the collapse, moreover, at a time when the Right had ceased to exist in an organized form, christian socialism, despite its egalitarian facade, was still the right wing of the leftward-biased political spectrum and as such bound to attract the support of those who in "normal" times — which sooner or later would have to return — would have been on the right. With returning prosperity and the re-establishment of economic interests, such a party would be the first to be drawn back into a conservative position.

The Church itself, or at least the Catholic Church, never espoused any of the forms of christian socialism in postwar Germany. The Papal Bull of 1931, the *Quadragesimo Anno*, had declared that: "Christian socialism is a contradiction in itself, it is impossible to be simultaneously a good catholic and a real socialist."[28] By 1947 it was evident that the Church's position had not changed substantially. Considerable Jesuit pressure was applied to Jakob Kaiser and other christian socialists to abandon their views. The Church's attitude was summed up by Paul Berkenkopf in the authoritative Jesuit journal, *Stimmen der Zeit*, in October 1947:

> The demand for a Christian socialism is, in its consequences and practical potential, in contradiction to the teaching of the Church in regard to property . . . One must repeatedly ask oneself just what christian socialism really wants. Does it want to socialize the whole economy, or at least all its decisive parts? Or will it be satisfied with the nationalization or socialization of certain limited areas of the economy, above all the basic industries? The first would be in clear contradiction to the teaching of the Church as well as economic

common sense. But if christian socialism wants only the second, well then it is just no longer socialism.[29]

We have considered at length the early programmatical development of the CDU because, according to its own initial pronouncements and self-image, it was at least until 1947 a left wing party. However, not only was it the least socialist of the major parties, the prefix "christian" was spurious and regressive. In the words of the then mayor of Mönchen-Gladbach, Wilhelm Elfes: "It seems inappropriate to call a good soap factory a christian soap factory."[30] (Elfes was later expelled from the CDU for "leftist deviations.") By 1949 christian socialism as an effective political force — as opposed to ideological power which it undoubtedly continued to be — was at an end within the CDU and Germany. Admittedly the vestigial "labour" wing (*Arbeiterflügel*) carried on under the leadership of Arnold, Kaiser and Lemmer, but only as a party minority and only because "the forces of the Restoration in the CDU were forced to accept that [the leaders of the party's left wing] (the guarantors of its electoral success in industrial regions) would continue to avail themselves of the formula of christian socialism."[31] In any case the CDU "Left" has never posed a socialist threat within the party. In virtually every important question, its votes have always been cast in support of party policy, even when this has conflicted with labour's interests[32] (rearmament, KPD ban, "reprivatization" of industry, etc.).

c. The unified trade union

Early developments in the trade union movement, like those in the antifascist front and the political parties, were conditioned by a desire to avoid the "mistakes" of the past, a hope for a socialist future (implying a new organizational form) and, in particular, the material distress left by the war.

The immediate concern of the trade unionists had to be the provision of food and clothing and shelter for the destitute, measures for reconstruction and rebuilding, and the restoration of elementary communal services. Since such tasks were far removed from the traditional trade union functions of advocating workers' rights, higher wages, reduced working hours, etc., the trade unions quickly obtained a position as one of the "pillars" of society as a whole. (The other two pillars were the Church and the Military Governments.) This position was enhanced by the elimination of the National Socialist political elite, the sequestration, imprisonment or at least discrediting of the former elites in business, justice, the army, the police and the state bureaucracy. The work of clearing the rubble and providing basic amenities was undertaken in collaboration with the Military Goverments who came to rely upon the trade unions to the point of delegating some important social tasks to them, e.g. in denazification or the re-establishment of local government and administration. Large sectors of the population, including members of the former bourgeoisie, also supported the trade unions' efforts in this period.

This support and respect was of course derived in large measure from the situation of a "power vacuum" which the trade unions now filled. Preoccupied with pressing day-to-day tasks, they did not have the time or the resources to develop an overall strategy or organizational form to prepare for a new ordering of economy and society. In so far as goals were defined at all, they were based largely on concepts current during the Weimar era. Particularly important in this connection was the idea of "economic democracy" as developed by the labour theorist, Fritz Naphtali, toward the end of the 1920's, which stressed the importance of democracy at the lower levels of the economy (in firm and plant) as pre-requisite to the democratization of society as a whole, and of socialization aimed at eliminating the concentration of economic power.[1]

Organization first developed on the local level, especially around the plant or factory. The centres of such organizations were the works' councils of the respective enterprises. In the first months after May 1945, most of the large plants on the Rhine and Ruhr were occupied by works' councils, many of whom had existed illegally throughout the Third Reich. Elsewhere whole firms were taken over by the workers through their democratically elected representative bodies as the bearers of their spontaneous[2] will. Among their first actions were the removal of former NSDAP members or supporters from prominent positions, the repeal of all Labour Front institutions from the Third Reich, the provision of social welfare measures for workers and cooperation in the work of reconstruction. Such moves were facilitated by the absence of resistance on the owners' side, especially because, according to the Potsdam Agreements, all trusts, cartels and monopoly holdings were to be dissolved; the future of large enterprises was uncertain, except that the western Military Governments had pledged that the firms would not be returned to their former owners — a promise which would not be kept. It must be stressed, however, that in the development of the works' council system at the lower levels, the German workers were by no means embarking on an original course. The institution of the works' council grew out of the "revolution" of 1918-19 and was anchored in the Works' Council Law (*Betriebsrätegesetz*) in force between 1920-1933. It was far removed from any soviet or syndicalist system.

With regard to the all-important organizational form which would eventually succeed the local works' councils, there was a surprising degree of unanimity among German trade unionists in 1945. The concept of the unified trade union (*Einheitsgewerkschaft*), encompassing all sectors and groupings within the general population who were dependent for their living upon wages or salaries, was a true product of the historical situation and the exceptional postwar conditions. Plans for a unified trade union were worked out by exiles in the USA, the UK, Switzerland and Sweden, to name a few,[3] and all were aimed at overcoming the ideological divisions of the Weimar Republic into social democratic, christian and liberal trade unions which had kept the labour movement divided and weakened its resistance to Hitler. Memories were still fresh of the ease with which the NSDAP had incorporated the old trade unions into the Labour Front under Robert Ley, of how all Marxist elements were purged with the assistance of trade union functionaries and of how the wage stop (based on the post-Depression wage-scale) was maintained for the duration of the Third Reich.[4]

Yet — and this aspect is seldom mentioned in the trade union literature today — the experiences of the Labour Front were undoubtedly in some measure decisively influential in the development of the unified trade union idea. Not only had the National Socialists succeeded for the first time in uniting the disparate factions of the labour movement, the conditions which they imposed — labour discipline, work-productivity intensification, a system of improvisation geared toward productivity increases, a large scope for individual initiative in production, the destruction of class-consciousness and collective initiative — certainly facilitated the fusing of the labour movement after 1945 and, beyond this were qualities much needed to enlist the full power of German labour in the work of reconstruction.[5]

The unified trade union, which actually developed spontaneously on the local level in many instances, especially in industrial regions such as Lower Saxony and around Düsseldorf, was intended to overcome not only divisions based on ideology (social democrats, liberals, christians, communists) but also those based on occupation (civil servants, employees, workers). Presenting his Five-Point-Programme for the new trade union system, Hans Böckler, who later became the First Chairman of the DGB, said on 12 June 1945:

> We reject the division into three pillars. We want *one* federation, naturally subdivided according to occupational groups. And locally the organization will be structured in the same way; that is, *one* organization comprising workers, clerks and civil servants in the respective group in which they are employed.[6]

The obvious purpose of this broad, united labour front was to combat any resurgence of monopoly capitalism or fascism, to coordinate policies on behalf of the wage-dependent classes, to put forward the claims and rights of labour in the organs of state and society and, perhaps, to develop a force with suficient strength to oppose the antisocialist policies of the occupation powers.[7] The question of a subdivision of the unified trade union into professional or industrial classifications was postponed, but whichever form would be chosen, it would be part of the unified trade union and financially dependent upon it. This centralized organization would be subject to democratic control "from below" at all levels. It would further be an important factor in the education of the worker for political democracy: the effects of National Socialism and the authoritarian tradition in Germany now appeared to fortify the working man's traditional distrust of politics and political parties; but the trade unions, whose existence had a direct and practical relation to his actual life and upon whom he was dependent for his material well-being, could be the agency to re-politicize him in the direction of social democracy.[8]

Implicit in the idea of a supra-factional, unified trade union was party political neutrality. This is not to say that the new trade union was to be politically neutral, however. As the representative of the employed classes, it could hardly remain above politics; the basic idea of the unified trade union was to improve its members' conditions in such political areas as social and economic decisions of the state, the government and administration, to increase the wages and rights of the worker, or even to elect deputies to the Bundestag whose views most closely coincided with trade union goals. In actual practice, as will be discussed in the next chapter, it was extremely difficult to maintain party political neutrality. Well over three-quarters of DGB members have always been simultaneously SPD members, and the SPD's goals have most frequently coincided with those of the trade unions. As a result the trade unions have consistently been more or less identified with the SPD, although the forms which the former's support for the latter have taken have had to be indirect (declarations supporting the SPD's aims but not the party itself, expenditures for advertising in SPD periodicals rather than outright contributions, etc.).

An interesting document from the year 1946, in the form of instructions to DGB functionaries, which had been kept secret until recently, survives in the DGB archives. Concerning the DGB's policy toward SPD-organized works' councils, the instructions state that although the SPD's political proposals most closely matched the DGB's (socialization of large concerns, thorough denazification, social welfare measures, etc.) and although the SPD members were best suited for leadership of these works' councils, the official policy of neutrality prevented any overt DGB intervention on behalf of the SPD.[9]

Viktor Agartz has argued plausibly against political party neutrality from the standpoint that the class struggle itself was a unified, closed and total struggle which could not be separated into a political side and an economic side.[10] The working-class party's task, he wrote, was to prepare theoretically the workers' struggle for emancipation, to represent them before the tribune of parliament and to further the socialist cause. The trade unions were supposed to carry on the same struggle directly from actual working conditions and to channel it into an anticapitalist and socialist direction. It was also a mistake to seek support for labour's cause in the CDU or other bourgeois parties because in their essence, social composition, programmes and actions they were anti-labour. "Labour party and trade union are two sides of one and the same cause," he wrote, "they are organizations which frequently march separately in order to be able to strike in unison."[11]

The way in which the Allied Military Governments' suspension of political activities affected the trade unions was demonstrated, in the previous chapter, to be part of an overall antisocialist policy. More than in the case of political party development, this policy destroyed a great part of the grass-roots initiative toward a works' council system in western Germany. When the trade unions were reconstituted after 1945[12] (with local delays occasionally exceeding a year), many of the ideological differences of the old trade unions from the pre-fascist era were also reconstituted. Certainly the delay placed severe impediments in the way of the works' councils system and the idea of the unified trade union. The new leaders, appointed from above without reference to rank and file opinion, were all between 50-70 years old and tended to be drawn from the right wing of the old SPD.[13] A three-phase sequence toward the re-establishment of the trade unions was prescribed, all subject to Military Government approval. The first stage, which involved application for permission to create local organizations and hold meetings, was particularly crucial because: "From the beginning the trade unions were forced to regard all problems concerning the development of political and economic structures as secondary, because the natural trend was firstly concentrated on the establishment of the trade union organization."[14] This tendency was of course reinforced by the trade unions' necessarily overriding concern with the daily tasks of rebuilding and reconstruction.

It is difficult to establish a direct connection between these developments and the Military Governments' policies at this time. But it is sufficient to recall that both Britain and the United States were apprehensive of any communist advantages accruing from the postwar situation, and that from the outset the US occupation power was extremely suspicious of works' councils.[15] Most of the first measures emanated from the British Military

Government, since the important heavy industries were located in its zone. Thus instead of allowing the works' councils in iron and steel to develop a form of labour administration, the British occupying power created in summer 1946 the North German Iron and Steel Corporation (NGISC) which then established a German Steel Trusteeship *(Stahltreuhandverwaltung)*, headed by the former industrialist Heinrich Dinkelbach. The latter institution then assumed ownership rights over all the works; this measure did not affect the rights of former owners at all; the question of ownership was simply put into abeyance. Then the struggle for socialization was made practically impossible by the confiscation of all properties in which the Allies were particularly interested, for example IG Farben, Krupp, Henschel, NSDAP possessions and, in August 1946, the entire iron and steel industries. These measures facilitated the continuation of "business as usual." In fact most of the managers and leading employees engaged by the Trusteeship had occupied identical or similar positions during the Third Reich and, in many cases, had been actively associated with the National Socialist bureaucracy.[16] There were further interventions by the UK authorities to prevent the establishment of the unified trade union (which was described as "too ambitious") in their zone, including a visit by a TUC delegation whose main purpose was to convince Hans Böckler that the industrial trade union system was more desirable.

At the first stage of trade union "rehabilitation" gave way to the second and third stages (permission to levy membership contributions, formation of supra-local and supra-regional mergers) the leadership came into an increasingly dichotomous position. On the one hand, pressure from "below" for socialization and social transformation continued unabatedly; this desire was expressed, among others, at the first interzonal conference in Hanover at the end of 1946, which advocated such measures as parity co-determination in all branches of the economy, the break-up of trusts and monopolies, the implementation of a planned economy based on the socialization of key industries and fiscal institutions, sweeping land reforms and immediate economic, then political reunification.[17] But on the other hand, daily pressures and close collaboration with the occupation powers led the trade union leadership to dampen all actions aimed at stopping dismantlings, achieving higher wages, organizing strikes and effecting the socialization of basic industries; the result of such pressures was the genesis of the notion of "social partnership" which would continue into the German Federal Republic.[18]

Organization proceeded apace, and by April 1947 the DGB for the British Zone, and in September a Trade Union Council in Frankfurt, were established, both under the leadership of Hans Böckler. As the organization was extended and enlarged — coinciding with the active stage of western Military Government intervention against German socialism — local initiatives became less relevant to DGB policy. Thus the DGB could now completely dissociate itself from the Soviet Zonal FDGB (Free German Trade Union Federation) without any notable concern for members' wishes.

By this time, early 1947, it was slowly becoming evident that the original socialist goals of the labour movement would not be attained in the foreseeable future. Rather than attempting to exploit their position at the centre of society by means of, say, strikes, work stoppages or threats of mass actions, the trade union leadership decided to attempt to gain as many concessions as possible from the Military Governments on the basis of services rendered or mutual interests. The example par excellence of this policy was the issue of co-determination (*Mitbestimmung*). As originally conceived, co-determination was only one element in a comprehensive programme of socialization and social justice: the workers were intended to have equal representation in the managing, supervisory and executive boards of all firms, whether communally or privately owned.[19]

When co-determination was first introduced into the iron and steel industries in the Ruhr (*Montanmitbestimmung*), it diverged considerably from the goals which labour had originally set for it. Far from obtaining at least an equal share in the running of the plant and overall economy, labour was conceded parity only in internal plant situations — meaning the exclusion of national or regional trade union representatives — through equal representation in the Supervisory Council (*Aufsichtsrat*) and one of three seats on the Executive Committee (*Vorstand*), confined to the iron and steel industries in the Ruhr.

The implementation of co-determination in this form coincided in many respects with the interests of the occupying powers and former owners. In agreeing to "limited" co-determination as a preliminary step toward a more comprehensive system of worker participation,[20] the trade union leaders had placed a great deal of faith in the ostensible solidarity of the British Labour Government with the German working classes, a trust which proved to be somewhat misguided, since the UK was too dependent upon American pressure,[21] especially financial pressure to be able to permit extensive socialization; and besides this, the British Military Government did not always pursue the same ends as the Labour Government.

One of the primary aims of the British Military Government was to ensure the continuation and increase of production; this was part of the policy of restoring German self-sufficiency as quickly as possible to ease the pressure on the British national budget. A convenient way of accomplishing this was by means of granting official recognition to the status the German labour organization had already de facto attained, vis-à-vis the owners and managers, as partners and near-equals in the joint tasks of reconstruction and resumption of production. Moreover, the works' councils would be useful, it was thought, in filling the power vacuum which would arise when decartellization was carried out in accordance with the Potsdam Agreements, which was still considered possible at this time. And finally, co-determination would contain the growing power of the works' councils which were thought to be more radical than the trade unions. In his report of 11 July 1947 on co-determination in the iron and steel industries, Harris-Burland, head of the NGISC, formulated the British policy rather precisely:

> In the separate steel works the Works' Councils who, in general, are more Left Wing and less responsible than the trades unions, were pressing the managements of the owner concerns for far reaching concessions, many of which were of an anarchical and impractical nature. Before our control was instituted the industrialists were making concessions to the Works' Councils in fear of being attacked and denounced as the nazis and reactionaries which, in most cases, they were. The result was a confused and disorganized relation between the

industrialist management on the one side and the workers represented by their Works' Councils which in many cases defied the more responsible trades unions. This increasingly disorganized state of labour relations was threatening the productive capacity of the steel works. Many of the Works' Councils were claiming rights of interference in the conduct of the works without assuming corresponding responsibilities. Giving the workers and the trades unions a share in these responsibilities of management should go a long way towards forestalling labour trouble in industry.[22]

This too was a source of the future policy of social partnership between employer and employee. In the iron and steel industries, at this time, owners were frequently forced into a temporary alliance with labour to forestall Allied dismantlings and decentralization proposals. This was at first entirely advantageous to the owners' side, as the labour organizations had become a central force in the community and had established a brief pattern of active cooperation with former owners in the resumption of production. Labour's motives in entering into such an alliance were less evident: probably its overriding concern with day-to-day work and a feeling that the power of socialism was too strong to be checked, as it indeed appeared immediately after 1945. Labour's reasons for accepting codetermination in its 1947 form, on the other had, can be found in the idea of the unified trade union. Codetermination was entirely compatible with the Catholic minority's concept of social peace and social partnership within individual firms, based on a "natural" and harmonious relationship between capital and labour, while Catholic trade unionists would never have agreed to co-determination as an integral part of a comprehensive programme of socialization.[23]

The achievement of limited co-determination in iron and steel marked the end of the owner-labour alliance. The Cold War, the changing Allied priories and the increase in the predominance of American policy provided the foundation for another alliance: between the bourgeois coalition and the occupation powers. At the same time, the trade union leadership was increasingly integrated into the re-emergent capitalist system. These developments first became evident in connection with Marshall Plan Aid in late 1947. The DGB Federal Executive Committee saw correctly that Marshall credits were conditional upon the abandonment or postponement of trade union plans for the socialization of key industries in the western zones. But it failed to develop an active strategy against the Marshall Plan's implementation; on the contrary, Hans Böckler termed the Plan a great assistance from America. Although he conceded that it could be used in the service of American imperialist ends, he argued for its complete acceptance in view of the desperate conditions which then prevailed.[24] But Böckler neglected to add ". . . that it was precisely the western Allies who, through their regimentation and production and confiscation and compulsory export of raw materials, prevented an improvement in the standard of living."[25] As Theo Pirker has pointed out, the issue of Marshall Plan Aid was forced through the DGB conventions without any substantial discussion, and oppositional trade unionists in Munich were compelled to resign their posts.[26]

After this, the trade unions found themselves increasingly removed from the centres of the important decisions which would determine the shape of the second German republic, the state which had once been "their" state. But now domestic power had shifted drastically: the interests of the re-emergent capitalist classes were entirely in agreement with those of the western occupation powers. The trade unions had only a minor influence in the deliberations of the Economic Council (*Wirtschaftsrat*), especially after 1948 when Ludwig Erhard became its chairman. They were also not represented in the most important social and economic committees and had virtually no say in the 1948 currency reform. After the currency reform, the struggle for higher wages replaced socialization as the central concern of the trade unions, while the pressure of reconstruction tended to restrict the possibilities of strikes or stoppages.

The DGB leadership continued to regard itself as the representative of labour in the system of social partnership. Thus when in January 1948 the works' councillors in the Rhine-Ruhr region, supported by a majority of the membership, came out in favour of a general strike in protest against living conditions and the antisocialist measures of the Military Governments, they were dissuaded by Hans Böckler and the trade union executive.[27] The DGB also failed to act when in November almost nine million workers called a work stoppage to protest against rising costs. Nor did it protest effectively against the suspension of the "socialist articles" in the Länder constitutions in North Rhine-Westphalia and Hesse. To be sure the DGB was faced with a number of technical problems with respect to any industrial actions which it might have undertaken. Among these were the large number of unemployed, limited strike fund reserves, a centralized form of organization at the zonal and supra-zonal level which ecouraged negotiations with public and private organizations at higher levels without reference to members' collective opinions, the internal pressures arising from the requirements of the various factions within the unified trade unions, and overriding all others, the prospect of Military Government intervention. But these need not have prevented an active trade union policy of resistance to the really crucial measures — Marshall Plan, currency reform, composition of the Economic Council and other bi- or trizonal agencies — which ultimately had to lead to the restoration of the capitalist social and economic system and to the loss of the trade unions' predominant position in society and economy.

In time the unified trade union also came to operate to the disadvantage of the labour movement, for it prevented the DGB from placing its full weight behind the political party which most nearly represented its aims. Thus in the election campaign of 1948 the trade unions declared their expectations of political parties deserving of their support to be a policy of full employment, a comprehensive housing programme, the democratization of the economy and the socialization of key economic branches. All of these points were included in the SPD's platforms and confirmed in the Bad Durkheim Resolution. Nevertheless, the DGB maintained its political party neutrality, while at the same time the Catholic Church and the business community overwhelmingly placed their support behind the bourgeois coalition, primarily the CDU/CSU. When some individual trade unionists declared their support for particular SPD candidates, this was countered by a great protest from the CDU's "labour wing."

This policy of neutrality in partisan politics also led an important grouping within the DGB to the illusion of complete neutrality. In a talk prepared for the Bavarian Radio and presented in September 1949, Max Wörner felt compelled to defend the trade unions' occasional entry into day-to-day politics:

> If we are [politically active] then it is of course primarily because upon our effectiveness depends whether the working man, as he eats his otherwise so thin soup, is able to discover a few more blobs of fat in it. To increase the number of his fat blobs is our most fervent endeavour.[28]

By the time the DGB came into being in the Federal Republic, then, its original aims and proposals had been diluted considerably. Consistent forebearance with respect to industrial action and wage demands had the effect of facilitating the re-establishment of capitalism.[29] Socialization and the "new ordering of society and economy" had become nearly impossible. Co-determination was "watered down" and confined to the iron and steel industry. The leadership was firmly entrenched and hardly needed recourse to the membership's opinions. The great power potential of the first postwar years was diminished to the extent that the trade unions could no longer compete on equal terms with business and the bourgeois coalition. The final form of organization had little in common with the concept of the unified-trade union: in accordance with the wishes of the British Military Government, sixteen industrial trade unions were grouped around the DGB, each with considerable autonomy, and the old division between civil servants, white collar workers and workers had been restored. Political party neutrality had robbed the DGB of much of its direct political influence. To be sure, the programme promulgated at the DGB Founding Congress of 1949 still contained four basic socialist demands, namely full employment assuring human dignity, optimum utilization of productive capacity, co-determination, the socialization of key industries and increased social services (wages, pensions, compensation). And trade union representatives sat in various committees and advisory bodies (social security panels, labour attaches in embassies abroad, broadcasting councils, etc.) But integration into the capitalist second German republic, though by no means complete, was now practically inevitable.

2. Social Democracy: Socialism plus Democracy

The postwar development of the SPD reflected the changed political constellation in Germany. On the surface, at least, it now appeared that it was only one of several parties aiming at the achievement of socialism by combining antifascist and anticapitalist sentiments into a popular socialist political front. After 1945, therefore, the SPD was compelled to define its principles of democratic socialism in terms of two poles: authoritarian or "totalitarian" communism and bourgeois or fascist capitalism. This problem of identification and self-image was particularly problematic in the postwar situation of fluid political fronts, rule by Military Governments, the unfolding Cold War and the popular desire for a socialist, antifascist coalition.

The most urgent problem facing the SPD after 1945 was its future relationship with the KPD, a problem which was implicit in the antifascist front and which was aggravated by the occupation powers' diverging policies. In the western zones party organization and policy centred around the *Büro Dr Schumacher* in Hanover (Kurt Schumacher, Alfred Nau, Fritz Heine and later

Erich Ollenhauer) while in the Soviet Zone the SPD was grouped around Otto Grotewohl and his associates Erich Gniffke, Gustav Dahrendorf, *et al.* The Berlin Group benefitted from the earlier moratorium on the political quarantine decreed by the Soviet Military Government. Within a few days, on 15 June 1945, the East Berlin SPD published its provisional aims,[1] which included the elimination of fascist or militarist remnants, the break-up of large estates, the expropriation of banks, insurance companies and all natural resources, the abolition of unearned income and inheritance and, significantly, the creation of an all-party antifascist front. When in October (December in the French Zone) the western SPD was permitted to resume political activities, then, the Grotewohl group had already established a solid political organization, based on a terse minimal programme, throughout the Soviet Zone. It had also acquired ample office space and funds as well as a party newspaper from the Soviet authority, and had achieved a membership of between three and four thousand.[2] Although the Schumacher group at first enjoyed none of these advantages from the western occupation powers, it was also able to reestablish itself rather rapidly, thanks in no small part to the dedication of party members at lower levels and the impetus of the antifascist movement. The first organizational convention, held in Wennigsen near Hanover in the same month, left open the question of the election of an Executive Committee and the promulgation of a basic programme until a further convention of an all-German SPD.[2a]

Because social and political conditions at this time were in an extreme state of flux, neither "branch" of the SPD was in a position to set out a political programme containing binding, long-term goals. As the theoretical bases of the parties' strategies one must therefore turn to two contemporary policy statements: Otto Grotewohl's speech of 14 September 1945 in Berlin, entitled "Where do we stand — Where do we go from here?"[3] and Kurt Schumacher's brochure "Political Guidelines for the SPD in its Relationship with the Other Political factors"[4] of August 1945.

The two embryonic "programmes" have more in common than many historians of the period in both East and West have suggested. Both Schumacher and Grotewohl agreed that monopoly capitalism had been the real cause of the growth of fascism, but that National Socialism had found in all too receptive mass basis among the middle classes. Now, while rebuilding and providing the vital elementary services it was necessary to take decisive steps to prevent monopoly capitalism from regaining a stranglehold on economy and society. This must be accomplished by means of nationalizing key industries and resources and implementing a planned economy. Both agreed further that the new order must be as democratic as it would be socialist; individual rights would be respected and a just legal, administrative and bureaucratic system would be established. But this would not mean a "dictatorship of the proletariat" or single-class rule; the middle classes, confronted with the catastrophic results of their support of Hitler, and now sharing a common lot with the working classes, could and must be educated to see where their "true" interests lay and to cooperate in the tasks of reconstruction and the implementation of socialism.

In the end, however, Grotewohl and Schumacher were irreconcilably divided over the question of a fusion of KPD and SPD, and this controversy was rooted both in power politics and the interpretation of the concept of democratic socialism.

Grotewohl, sensing the great popularity of the "antifas," and the desire for a common socialist front, felt certain that the SPD would dominate the proposed coalition. He declared that "the organizational unification of the German labour movement and the creation of a social democratic society are our fixed aims." He saw that, in the West, the KPD could never become the sole representative of the new Germany in the eyes of the occupation powers, just as the "bourgeois" parties would never be accepted in the same capacity in the Soviet Zone. Thus the leading role in (a united) Germany must fall to the SPD, in particular an SPD which incorporated the KPD.[5] But subsequent events would prove that here Grotewohl underestimated the extent to which the Soviet Union was prepared to intervene in the politics of its zone, while at the same time he overestimated the SPD's strength as an independent political force.

Schumacher, on the other hand, was prepared to work with the KPD only in the resolution of social questions and the extirpation of Nazism. He rejected all supra-party organizations, including the antifas, as "simply a communist attempt to employ non-communists and to train them for the Communist Party." Though, he claimed, he did not want the SPD policy to appear to be anticommunist or anti-Soviet:

> The slogan of the 'united party' is a tactical manoeuvre which until now has not even been attempted in the eastern zone because the communists know that they in fact no longer have the basis for a genuine mass party. Indeed, they are probably already by far the weakest party in Germany.[6]

Before the SPD would conclude any form of alliance with the KPD, Schumacher declared, a number of preconditions would have to be met: the KPD would have to cease cooperating in dismantlings and "selling out" to the Soviet Union, it would have to desist in its methods of force and denunciation, to declare openly its policy with respect to the lands cast of the Oder-Neisse Line and refrain from signing a separate peace treaty with any other states.[7] In such formulations Schumacher was able to articulate most of the basic apprehensions of SPD members in entering into an alliance with the KPD. The antifascist, socialist front was after all founded equally upon socialism, democracy and self-determination. "For every German Social Democrat," Schumacher wrote, "a socialism without democracy, without humanity and without respect for human personality is not conceivable."[8] This view was supported by a large sector of the party membership, and not only by those on the "right." In particular, many SPD members who had been in exile returned with negative attitudes toward KPD policies as they had experienced directly in, for example, the Spanish Civil War[9] or Moscow exile (purges, denunciations, unnecessary sacrifices to the exigencies of Soviet foreign policy, etc.).

Yet in both East and West popular enthusiasm for a united socialist party was still high. Against Schumacher's objections, a number of local groups (notably in Bremen, Hamburg, Brunswick, Wiesbaden, Munich and Ludwigsburg) had founded united antifascist labour fronts composed of SPD and KPD members. In greater Berlin there was initially a high degree of mutual sympathy between the two parties.[10] But in the Soviet Zone such desires were more and more tempered by a reluctance to become too closely identified with or under the control of the USSR. In the western zones a large number of SPD members, probably a majority, were at the outset in favour of the united labour front. In the eastern zone popular opinion, influenced by the negative aspects of Soviet policy (dismantlings, virtually absolute control over the KPD, etc.), increasingly demanded a socialist policy taking greater account of the national interest. Thus the SPD party leaderships in both East and West were in some measure isolated from their followers — both parties had been reconstituted from top-to-bottom following the lifting of the prohibition on political activities — and party members were increasingly called upon to choose between the rather simplified alternatives of unity (with the KPD) or freedom (from Soviet influence). It was an extremely problematical alternative, since the achievement of *both* unity and freedom represented the dominant mood among Social Democrats.

In the Soviet Zone the SPD's manoeuvrability was not as great as in the West. In addition to growing Soviet pressure and the increasing hostility of Schumacher and the western SPD, there is some evidence that had Grotewohl and the Berlin group refused to bring the SPD into a merger with the KPD, or even had they attempted to dissolve the party, the fusion would have taken place at the lower levels, either where there was a genuine enthusiasm for the united party or where the KPD would have arbitrarily incorporated the SPD. A development of this nature would of course have robbed the SPD of any influence whatever over events. And on any case most of the SPD executive in the Soviet Zone believed in the necessity of the union.[11]

All such questions were resolved with the formation of the SED in the Soviet Zone in April 1946. In the following month the western SPD — henceforth the only German SPD — held its long deferred elections to the Executive Committee at its Hanover Party Convention.

If the establishment of the SED put paid to the idea of a greater united proletarian front, a kind of democratic-socialist coalition in miniature was founded with the establishment of the separate western SPD. Leading representatives of breakaway factions during the Weimar era (Otto Brenner, Willy Brandt, Fritz Lamm, Arno Behrisch of the SAP or Socialist Workers' Party) or of left-wing exile groupings (Waldemar von Knoeringen, Erwin Schoettle and Richard Löwenthal of the New Beginning; Erich Ollenhauer and Fritz Heine of the exiled SPD Executive or SOPADE; Willi Eichler of the ISK or International Socialist Militant League),[12] together with the former Sudeten German Social Democratic Party under Wenzel Jaksch, the German Labour Delegation in New York headed by Max Brauer, independent Marxists (Viktor Agartz, Gerhard Gleissberg, Wolfgang Abendroth), many trade union leaders, some humanists (Carlo Schmid) and a few religious socialists (Adolf Grimme) — all agreed to combine forces to overcome postwar distress and begin the task of rebuilding. The extremely heterogeneous character of this combination of political forces precluded the working out of a co-ordinated programme. Instead the new SPD was held together by the firm leadership of Kurt Schumacher, a common disillusionment with the SPD's "social reformist" policies in the Weimar Republic, a desire to eliminate the capitalist roots of fascism and, above all, an agreement on the need for an equally democratic and socialist transformation of German society and economy.

These policies and the concrete historical and material situation in which they were rooted ensured that at the outset the SPD possessed a stronger inner-party left wing than it had during the Weimar era. The Hanover convention re-emphasized political democracy as prerequisite to the achievement of socialism and socialism as essential to the maintenance of democracy. Policy formulations were now terse, concrete and binding. The SPD's position toward the economic aspect of socialism was outlined in some detail by Viktor Agartz, at this stage the party's spokesmen on economic policy. Monopoly capitalism, he said, had eliminated economic competition, increased the product's cost to workers and consumers had hampered production. The situation had developed so far that it was impossible to achieve economic progress and individual economic freedom by simply adjusting the distributive apparatus:

> These injustices and errors are primarily bound up with the capitalist organization of production. Thus without a fundamental reorganization of production the existing errors cannot be eliminated. For this reason it is necessary to achieve a certain central influence over the scope and direction of production.[13]

This central influence, he continued, was the democratic *Rechtstaat*[14] which would plan and regulate the new economic system and replace the old profit motive of capitalism.

> State planning cannot be replaced or made unnecessary — a view which frequently predominates — by means of a workers' right of co-determination, however far-reaching, in the plants. In the plants only individual and partial economic plans can come about, but never an overall plan involving the entire economy. Overcoming the errors in the capitalist system, however, depends upon such an overall plan. The capitalist entrepreneur must therefore be replaced in the leadership of the economy. He cannot be replaced by single groups of economically committed workers' representatives in the plants, but only by representatives of the whole society committed to the state, representatives chosen by universal, equal and secret elections.[15]

The Convention's "Political Guidelines" went on to propose a total transformation of economy and society toward socialism. The greatest obstacle to socialism was said to be private enterprise. But "only the interest of the whole may decide the scope, direction and distribution of production." The socialization of the means of production was not an end in itself, however, and would be accomplished in various ways:

> For socialism there is no single form and no unfreedom, no command barracks socialism, no uniformity. There is no socialist society without the most manifold kinds of plants and forms of production. Socialism desires as much economic autonomy as possible and the greatest possible degree of participation of the worker and consumer.[16]

The immediate steps to be taken included the encouragement of cooperatives and communal enterprises, land redistribution and the expropriation of large estates, an all-encompassing finance and currency reform to eliminate the growing gap between owners and non-owners of property, and the socialization of natural resources, basic industries and monopoly or semi-monopoly enterprises. Socialism was no longer a distant goal, it was "a task for today."

The SPD now also began to regard itself as a *Volkspartei*, a party of all the people, capable of achieving an electoral majority and representing the interests of all the wage- or salary-dependent classes. Unlike in 1918, it was now thought that the aftermath of the Third Reich permitted the SPD to gain support from sectors of the population formerly bound to the bourgeois or even fascist parties, without sacrificing its socialist principles nor indeed without offering specific concessions to these middle classes;[17] this belief was of course eclipsed by the later policy which eventually culminated in the Bad Godesberg Programme of 1959. The great social upheavals of the war, Schumacher believed, had altered the fundamental class composition of Germany.[18] Many former members of the bourgeoisie, now "proletarized", had rejected capitalism and could and must be won over to Social Democracy, for: "A democratically orientated middle class is a precondition for the stability of the new order." However,

> . . . the anticapitalism of many Germans is not socialist and progressive. Their desires and longings are directed toward the past. Some would even like to see precapitalist relationships of production. Most want of the new Germany only to be restored to their former positions; they would like to get back what they have lost.[19]

The SPD must therefore devote a great deal of effort to instilling a class consciousness into this "proletarized" bourgeoisie; it must undertake a programme of education and enlightenment.

It was generally believed that the antagonistic nature of the class struggle and postwar conditions had brought about a semi-revolutionary situation which was prevented from developing only by the presence and intervention of the various Military Governments. Without them the unpropertied classes would overthrow the propertied classes who bore the responsibility for Hitler's coming to power (the SPD rejected outright the notion of collective guilt). The collapse of the Third Reich thus symbolized the bankruptcy of the propertied classes and the military. Despite the SPD's large membership and its positive results in the *Land* elections of 1946-1947, the changing economic and social conditions and the developing Cold War were bound to strengthen the forces of the Right and thus detract from the SPD's voter reserves. For this reason it was essential for the party (a) to gain political power as quickly as possible, (b) in order to attract support from the still "proletarized" middle classes and above all from the young.

The SPD was able to show some success in its efforts at winning over the middle classes: where in 1930 salaried employees had constituted only about ten per cent of the party's membership, by 1952 they made up 17 per cent. During the same period the self-employed, pensioners, housewives and farmers increased from 31 to 38 per cent of party membership. Against this, however, the percentage of manual workers dropped from 60 to 45 per cent and overall membership declined from over one million to not quite 630,000.[20]

But the SPD was less successful in increasing its support among the young. In 1946 about two-thirds of party members had also belonged to the party before 1933, a percentage which would remain constant until the second federal elections. And a poll taken in September 1950 revealed that only 32 per cent of SPD members were under 45 years old (cf. 53.4 per cent of the population as a whole), while 68 per cent were over 45.[21] This meant that the party profile was defined and policy set by men whose ideas and experiences had been formed during the Weimar era, a fact which is underlined by the composition of the first Executive Committee elected at Hanover. The five salaried members (Schumacher, Ollenhauer, Nau, Heine, Kreidemann) had also been salaried members of the pre-1933 Executive Committee, and all 25 elected members had been party members before the advent of the Third Reich.

Not only did these "old fighters" naturally tend to delegate authority and important positions to those with whom they had shared experiences in the underground, concentration camp or exile, they also failed to provide the approximately 30 per cent new members entering the SPD after 1945 with any real share in the party's tasks. To be sure, many of these new members were opportunists and "band-wagon" climbers, and many more were to arrive from prisoner-of-war camps too late to have a say in the re-establishment of the party. And the recruitment of youth that ought to have taken place between 1933 and 1945 was of course lost forever. Many potential members who had survived the holocaust either could not identify with a "top-heavy" party of old functionaries, or had grown too bitter and cynical to be able to commit themselves to any political movement.

Considering that by 1945 at the latest Kurt Schumacher was the undisputed leader of the SPD — at the Hanover Convention he was elected Chairman by 244 of the 255 valid ballots cast — and that "he was undoubtedly the most prominent German political leader . . ."[22] in the first postwar years, his role in the formulation and execution of the SPD's policies has been remarkably misunderstood and misinterpreted.[23] Although this is not the place to undertake a revision of established historical opinion, this, or any, consideration of the SPD's theory and praxis is the postwar period must relate these to Kurt Schumacher's belief system and person.

As an SPD *Reichstag* deputy and member of the party militant organization, the *Reichsbanner*, before 1933, Schumacher opposed, and was widely seen and heard to oppose, the Third Reich and all concessions to it. Rather than compromise the Social Democratic Party (like the "right" wing SPD) or diminish his effectiveness by fleeing abroad (like the SPD Executive Committee in exile), he adopted a position of unyielding opposition, and as a result spent almost all the years of the Third Reich in concentration camps, often under conditions of extreme hardship. After 1945 he was one of the few unblemished" SPD members with parliamentary experience and was seen as a representative of the "best" (or left) groups within the SPD. As such he was a natural candidate for the leadership of the "new" party.

Although Kurt Schumacher rejected Marxism as a "catechism" or "dogma", he felt that Marxist categories and methods were both applicable and necessary, and frequently employed Marxist ideas in his policies. "In both its main forms, the economic interpretation of history and the class struggle, Marxism is not obsolete," he said at the 1948 Party Convention.[24] "We have to understand," he declared in 1945, "that the Left in Germany has provided the theory, but the Right the practice, of the class struggle." [25]

Much of the confusion that has surrounded Schumacher's politics arises from a misunderstanding of his so-called nationalism. Fortunately one observer, at least, has placed it in the context in which it belongs — as a component of his view of socialism. G.S. Vardys has argued that for Schumacher the nation, not the class, was the primary moving force in history and society, and that he therefore saw the restoration of an intact German state, rather than the creation of a classless society, as the order of the day.[26] Now it would be more accurate to say that, in Schumacher's view, the classes *within* the nation were the primary moving force, i.e., although the factors of nation and class were interconnected, national unity had to have priority, and that national unity was therefore the precondition to the classless society. This view had of course three concrete historical references: the example of the superior force of nationalism and patriotism over international proletarian solidarity so evident in the issue of labour support for the war effort in 1914, the ability of the National Socialists to win over large sectors of the working classes with nationalist slogans, and the current paralysis of the labour movement under the Military Governments and the developing Cold War. Nevertheless, what is important — and this follows from both interpretations — is that, since a true internationalism for Schumacher was not synonymous with proletarian internationalism, but was something which could be achieved only via the sovereign national state, the workers' interests were, under present conditions, identical with those of the nation. Of this policy, which Vardys terms "democratic nationalism", Schwarz has said: "If the designation were not encumbered from the outset with its association with the Hitler movement, the term 'national socialism' would best characterize (Schumacher's) point of view."[27]

Bearing in mind Schumacher's belief in the indivisibility of democracy and socialism — "In Germany democracy will be socialist or it will be nothing!" — it is understandable that he should advocate a nationalism based upon the assumption that the German people should be able to control its own destiny. As he declared in a speech in 1946 in Berlin: "We do not want nationalism, we want Europe. But we want to feel ourselves respectable Europeans in Europe . . . Let us be subjects and not objects. The unity of Germany means the unity of Europe. A torn Germany would only result in a disunited Europe."[28]

Given this view of Schumacher's nationalism, then his subsequent denunciations of the KPD and CDU, of the occupation powers and of German integration into western Europe follow logically. The SPD, Schumacher believed, had a superior claim to national leadership as the only party which had (1) consistently resisted fascism, (2) upheld democratic principles and (3) enjoyed majority or near-majority support. As the KPD on the one hand and the CDU on the other lent increasing support to the eastern and western occupation powers, i.e. for Schumacher became "patriots of other states", this moral claim was extended to encompass the SPD as the only party interested on preserving the "true" national interest and as such entitled to above-class support. Patriotism, it seemed, " was the common denominator that could unify the diverse elements among the German people behind his campaign for a socialist democracy."[29]

Schumacher's belief in the superior moral position of the SPD included its relations with the occupation powers: "We were sitting in the concentration camps while the other peoples were still forming alliances with the Hitler government."[30] The Allies were only in control because of their superior might, he believed, and must necessarily rule not in the interests of the German people but according to their own ends. Any policy of appeasement would have disastrous results for Germany, just as it had had for Ebert in the first years of the Weimar Republic. Allied policy had to be resisted and the SPD under Schumacher was the party with the strength and will to do so. Thus, "the antifascist of the first hour assumed for himself the right to speak as an equal partner with the Hitler opponents of the wartime coalition."[31]

Schumacher's initial objections to the occupation powers consisted of protests against the dismantlings, territorial losses, reparations, the separation of the Ruhr and Saar areas and the like, but with the passage of time and the development of the Cold War, his opposition took on an increasingly fundamental character. He came to believe that the West's efforts to use Germany as a bastion against communism could not be reconciled with Germany's and the SPD's interests. The conflict with the USA in particular, was unresolvable: the new Germany could not be fashioned after the American capitalist system, since the political, social and economic situations of the two countries were fundamentally different. American aid to Germany was not based on altruistic motives, he rightly saw, but represented an attempt to subordinate western Germany to its national ends. He saw that US policy was leading to the irrevocable division of Germany and was heightening the real danger of another war on German soil. All this went against the beliefs and political prospects of the SPD.

Commenting that "in the end the relationship became so polarized that most American policy-makers judged it necessary to frustrate Schumacher's drive for power if the United States' interests were to be protected," Lewis J. Edinger writes: "Whether this view was justified is irrelevant for our purposes."[32] But Schumacher's assessment of the American role in postwar Germany is by no means irrelevant for *our* purposes. As has been demonstrated (in the previous chapter), the USA did have a not inconsiderable share in the frustration of German socialism in the years 1945-49 and, in terms of the SPD's policies and strategy for achieving power, Schumacher's analysis was extremely important. Unsuccessfully, he opposed the superimposition of federalism into German politics saying — with reason — that it would encourage particularist sentiments and unequal distribution of the national wealth; besides, the demands of reconstruction and socialist transformation would require a strong central (but democratic at all levels) state. He went on to oppose the Petersburg Agreement for an international Ruhr authority, participation in the European Coal and Steel Community, proposals for West German rearmament within the European Defence Community, the Marshall Plan and the Schumann Plan, arguing that these measures, taken before the question of reunification was resolved, must deepen the division of Germany. Reunification and independence were thus for him prerequisite to German participation in supra-national organizations.

But this policy does not mean that Schumacher saw Germany's role as a "third" or "middle" way between East and West. Although there is some evidence of an embryonic conception of a European equilibrium with Germany neutral amid a non-allied Europe, by 1947 at the latest Schumacher was rejecting neutrality, saying that "Germany must not be neutralized but Europeanized." He was thus able to dismiss the "bridge" or neutrality theory of Jakob Kaiser and the Berlin CDU with these words:

> German Social Democracy has often warned the heedless and, in their policies, downright primitive elements in our own country against the disastrous illusion the Germans have an opportunity of choosing between East and West. This illusion, in our opinion, means opting for the East and against the West . . .[33]

Schumacher was in fact hostile to what he saw as the "state capitalism"

and "oriental despotism" of the Soviet Union. Gemany's place was not with
Russia or even mid-way between East and West, but solely and exclusively
within the western tradition; Germany could now become an equal *socialist*
partner within a *socialist* (western) European federation independent of
both Russia and America, a European Third Force. The ideal partner for
Germany in her socialist reconstruction, and the natural leader of the
movement toward a socialist Europe, Schumacher thought, was Labour
Britain.

But what if the Labour Party declined to take up the role of Germany's
partner and European socialist leader? What if Europe, after all, failed to
take the turn to socialism?

What, in particular, of the SPD found itself in a situation in which it could
not acquire power on its own strength, but only via a coalition? By rejecting
all cooperation with the "socialist wing" of the CDU, calling the party as a
whole the chief instrument of the Reaction, the "party of the occupation
powers," the "party for the defence of property" and of "clerical reaction" on
the one hand, and with the KPD as "the instrument of Soviet exploitation and
totalitarianism" on the other hand, Schumacher was to drive the CDU/CSU
into the arms of the FDP and the other bourgeois parties, an alliance that
would survive for more than two decades, and to destroy the possibility of a
united labour front with the KPD once and for all. Not that Schumacher's
objections to the SPD's political competition from "left and right" were
unfounded: the CDU/CSU indeed became in time the chief instrument of the
Reaction and Restoration; and the SED did eventually create a Stalinist
bureaucratic regime in the Soviet Zone. But surely Schumacher's tactics of
uncompromising opposition — which is our main criticism of his actions in
the immediate postwar period — played to some extent the role of a
self-fulfilling prophecy with respect to his ideology; or in other words, his
absolute refusal to co-operate or collaborate with the other parties helped to
drive them into alliances or postures which he believed they had already
adopted.

Kurt Schumacher's opposition to the churches, especially the churches as a
pervasive political force, was founded not only on the — today widely
accepted — belief in the separation of church and state, but also on his actual
experience of the churches' complicity in the establishment and maintenance
of the Third Reich. This implacable opposition to the Church and "its" party,
the CDU/CSU, served mainly to prevent the SPD from detaching the CDU's
christian socialist wing, in centres like Berlin and Frankfurt, from the main
party when the Restoration set in and the CDU moved considerably toward
the right.

Similarly, Schumacher's anticommunism was successful in preventing a
merger of the two parties in the West, an accomplishment which a number of
observers believe to have been his greatest service.[34] Yet his at times excessive
anticommunism was in many ways regressive. It recalled the days of the
Bruderkampf in the Weimer Republic and helped to prevent the popular
labour front idea from being realized. More than this, it directly served the
ends of those interested in turning anticommunist resentments to their own
ends — namely the re-emergent capitalist classes, who saw in anticommunism
a way of deflecting attention from their own complicity in the Third Reich,
and the western powers who used it to enlist popular support in Germany for

their propaganda offensive in the Cold War. Hard-won experience during the Weimar Republic had shown that anticommunism had a way of developing into antisocialism and thus detracting from the SPD's popular support. The KPD for Schumacher was a monolithic, antidemocratic organization; his perspective may be contrasted with that of Wolfgang Leonhard who, after visiting a spontaneously establised communist cell in postwar Berlin, asked himself:

> Were there not really two kinds of communists? Until then I had had dealings mostly with functionaries who, with few exceptions, were distinguished by a hard, impersonal manner and constant repetition of party slogans. How different, it seemed to me, was the contrast with the lively, devoted and enthusiastic communists, bound to reality and to the "ordinary" people, whom I met that evening in Berlin.[35]

It seems that Schumacher greatly overestimated the communists' strength. The KPD was a not inconsiderable political force, to be sure, as its electoral successes in 1946-47 and its seizure of power in the Soviet Zone demonstrated. But its dominant position in the eastern zone was founded entirely on the support it received there from the occupation power; no such support would have been forthcoming in the western zones. Furthermore, since communist support was traditionally concentrated heavily in the East, it could not possibly have posed a "threat" to Germany as a whole.

The central point here is that Schumacher's emphaisis on the inseparability of democracy and socialism need not have prevented him from enlisting the support of "demcratic" communists on the one hand and "christian" socialists on the other. That he did choose to fight this war on two fronts, however, does not negate his position as the most influential figure in the German Left in the postwar period.

3. The Socialist Idea in the Postwar Period

It is significant that after 1945 virtually all the groups and organizations of what is usually termed the independent or nonconformist Left tended in greater or lesser degree to support the SPD. This fact lends some credence to Schumacher's theory, put forward in May 1945, of the SPD as a "magnet" beside which there was no room for other democratic socialist parties. In the exceptional political constellation of the period, however, there was in fact little scope for splinter groups and independent socialists: following the repeal of the ban on political activities, the Military Governments were unwilling to grant party "licences" to other than the old established parties. Besides this, there was a universal desire to get on with reconstruction and the provision of elementary services. Because of the intellectual isolation imposed by the Nazi regime and the restrictions of Military Government rule (which included a dearth of paper and controlled access to the mass media), the independent Left could neither propagate its theories and proposals nor was it in a position to incorporate contemporary innovations in European socialist thought into its own frame of reference, as for example French and Italian Marxist theory, the Marxist discussion in European Catholicism, the English socialist debates or even French existentialism.

By mid-1946 the more perspicacious among the independent Leftists realized that the top-heavy political parties were becoming increasingly less responsive to members' opinions, dogmatic and structurally ossified. For them the KPD had become too dependent upon the Soviet Military Government and too removed from its following, the CDU/CSU less concerned with socialism or even christianity than with achieving power within a restored socio-economic system and in collaboration with the western occupation authorities, and the SPD too extreme in its anticommunism and too inflexible in its policies.

Yet the SPD was more than the lesser of several evils; it was still the party which advocated both democracy and socialism in terms of concrete goals. Consequently most of the immediate postwar thought of the independent Left remained well within the orbit of the SPD, while advocating certain forms of strategy or tactics, e.g. a firmer stand against monopoly capitalism (the group around the periodical *Die Weltbühne*) or a more flexible foreign policy (Carlo Schmid[1]), or a more "liberal" approach to socialism (Willi Eichler's *Geist und Tat* and Otto Suhr's *Das Sozialistische Jahrhundert*). Even members of the Fourth International (Jungclass, Boepple, Wischnewski) were firmly committed to the SPD at this time. In a speech of 9 May 1949, Willy Brandt could thus rightly claim that: "Present-day Social Democracy in Germany is the trustee of the intellectual heritage of the 'Left' in the German and international socialist movement."[2]

Where inner-party opposition existed at all, it operated largely on the periphery of the party. This was true, e.g., of the *Marxistischer Arbeitskreis* in Berlin: in an address to it, Willy Huhn argued that, with party organization now complete, it was necessary to undertake an "intellectual-spiritual" (*geistige*) regeneration" of the SPD, "and so long as the old skeleton of our society is still capitalist, Marxism will be the theoretical foundation of revolutionary Social Democracy."[3] Similarly, Fritz Lamm, returning from Cuban exile in 1948, found that the SPD was not conducting a forceful enough campaign against private property and economic concentration — though this was largely the fault of the occupation powers' policies — and that too many functionaries were being absorbed into the state machine and neglecting the socialist goals of 1945.[4] As a counterweight to these developments he was able to assemble a few former SAP members and other oppositional SPD circles, the result of which efforts would be the periodical *Funken* during the 1950's.[5]

An important contribution to German postwar socialist thought emanated from the former chief theoretician of the New Beginning (which was considered to be the "New Left" among the exiled SPD groups during the Third Reich), Richard Löwenthal. His *Jenseits des Kapitalismus* (Beyond Capitalism), written in 1946 under the pseudonym of Paul Sering, stands today as perhaps the most eloquent and consistent expression of the socialist, anticapitalist mood in postwar Germany. In a differentiated and plausible analysis of modern capitalism Löwenthal demonstrated that it had created a very small and powerful class at the top levels of the economy and a great mass of dependent or subordinate classes which, however, were so divided according to the division of labour that they had no sense of common exploitation or solidarity.[6] But, contrary to Marx's predictions, modern capitalism had proven to be extremely adaptable and would not wither away without active intervention from the Left. For example the Great Depression had made evident the need for capitalist planning in both Germany and America. Under Hitler this planning was effected with the active assistance of big business ("the plan was their plan"), but under Roosevelt the New Deal — with its creation of mass purchasing power, its encouragement of the trade unions and its granting of wage increases at the expense of profit — though ultimately beneficial to the maintenance of the capitalist system, had to be carried out over big business' opposition.[7]

Though the planned economy was inevitable in whatever system, the leadership of socialists in the development of the planned economy or in the transition to socialist planning was not. Socialists must take the lead in bringing about a plan in their interests. the historical situation emerging from the war, Löwenthal believed, had obviated the old division of the labour movement into a communist wing with its theory that capitalist economic crises were synonymous with violent revolution. and a social democratic wing with its belief in the primacy of maintaining the working classes' hard-won gains within the existing system. Now both wings were thrown together in a common desire to achieve political power and use it to rebuild and establish socialism. "One hundred years after the Communist Manifesto," he wrote, "in the age of the realization of socialism, the restoration of the totality of the Marxist vision of reality and the unity of socialist strategy has once more become possible." [8] On the other hand, however, there could be no alliance between democratic socialists and communists because

... as an organization for instilling a contempt for democracy, a belief in authority, a utilization of alternating demagogic methods in the service of the constant aims of the Russian state, they are a foreign body in the labour movement, and indeed in many critical situations a destructive and contaminating foreign body.[9]

Socialism and democracy were also inseparable for Löwenthal. The precondition for the fulfilment of the socialist movement's goals was more than a class aim, it was a human aim. The starting point of modern socialism was "the demand for the liberation of man — liberation from all forms of political and social bondage, liberation too from the anonymous compelling laws of the capitalist economy . . ."[10]

Meanwhile in Heidelberg the efforts of an "Action Group for Free Socialism" had culminated in the publication of the book, *Freier Sozialismus*, by the movement's leaders, Alexander Mitscherlich and Alfred Weber (Max's brother). This was a group of socialists, "but socialists who want freedom above all in socialism and through socialism."[11] Their central thesis was that the new historical situation was no longer the class struggle but the preservation of freedom in the (capitalist or socialist) "monopolist, totalitarian and bureaucratic state."[12]

The fundamental fact of modern society, as Mitscherlich perceived it (in anticipation of Marcuse, it would seem), was the advancement of technology which had created an entirely new distribution of power. It had developed in such a way that production was now governed not by the needs of the consumer but by armaments. Human skills were no longer essential in the productive process, as increasing rationalization had reduced man to an automaton. The only control over the machines was exercised by their owners who, however, could only be motivated by profits. It had thus become impossible to eliminate the means of production without simultaneously eliminating their owners.

Technology had thus acquired its own rationale beyond man's needs or well-being. It determined the relationships among men and the direction of their efforts: "Commodities rule! They rule not only the individual, they rule not only the classes, they will soon also rule the state."[13]

Through a process which Mitscherlich called the "loss of society in the state," the increasing interdependence of big business and the state machinery was seen to proceed at the expense of society and the individual. The one class cleavage which retained any significance under monopoly capitalism was that of the minuscule group of entrepreneurs on the one side and on the other the mass of subordinate classes for whom it was a matter of indifference whether they were employed by private or state firms, since both subjected them to the same division of labour, the same inhuman rationalization, the same lack of influence over their product and working conditions.

This was why the "burning question" of the age was not the relationship between employer and employee, but the relationship of the individual to the "monopolist, totalitarian and bureaucratic state." "In a word", Mitscherlich concluded, "it is no longer a matter of the economic freedom of the socially weak, it is a matter of human freedom *per se* in the state which takes precedence over any other just balance of interests."[14]

Weber attempted to take such considerations into his programmatical formulations of a "free socialism." For him each act of socialization deprived the individual of a portion of his freedom because it increased the totalitarian potential of the state. Thus outright state socialization was a necessary evil to be employed when there was no other solution (e.g. railways, postal system, heavy and key industries, natural resources). Otherwise alternative forms of socialist property relationships must be found which eliminated the class struggle and human exploitation while simultaneously preserving spontaneity and free initiative. The alternative of free play of market forces and state socialism was a false one; there were intermediate forms, such as cooperatives, corporations of public law, semi-cooperative bodies, foundation enterprises (*Stiftungsunternehmen*), or even the break-up of monopoly holdings into small units subject to workers' codetermination and financial participation, where possible, at all levels.

Both the Heidelberg free socialists and Richard Löwenthal proposed nothing which went beyond the SPD's policies in this period. Their contribution was to emphasize and articulate what many social democrats felt to be the necessary course for the new Germany. This was particularly true of the desire for socialism, which was based on concrete historical experience and humanitarian motives, and of the stress on the primacy of the rights of the individual, which had been largely abolished during the Third Reich and were seen to be threatened by Stalinist communism. Their "failure" and the failure of many democratic socialists inside and outside the SPD was not to have seen that liberalism and socialism are, at certain crucial points in any liberal-capitalist system, mutually exclusive, despite their common origins and their nominally identical goals.[15] Their analysis ought to have contained proposals for the necessary suspension of the liberal right of e.g., private property in the transition to socialism. Without this qualification, the emphasis on individual rights — although completely justified and necessary — lent itself to being used as a pretext for the postponement or even rejection of radical socialization measures, especially after the return of "normal" conditions. On the other hand the idea of the primacy of individual freedom was important in the struggle against authoritarian communism which would have suspended a whole series of liberal rights, as it did in fact in the DDR.

All of the decisive developments in postwar politics, from the destruction of the socialist, antifascist front to the reconstitution of the old political parties and the nascent Cold War, had taken place in the absence of an important sector of the population: the young soldiers who at war's end had been left stranded on foreign fronts or interned for months in Allied p.o.w. camps, and who on returning home found themselves in a social and political system which they had no hand in creating. Many, perhaps the majority, renounced politics altogether and retreated into private life. Others joined existing political parties in hopes of transforming them from within. And some found the articulation of the critical views toward the political system in the fortnightly periodical, *Der Ruf der jungen Generation*, or popularly, *Der Ruf*, which appeared in Munich in the autumn of 1946 under the joint editorship of Alfred Andersch and Hans-Werner Richter.

In its appeal to youth, its rejection of the political system, its diffuseness, its informed openness to influences and theories from abroad and its interest in the arts and literature, *Der Ruf* was the forerunner of what, almost two decades later, would become the German "New Left." But the *Ruf* group was not and could not become a genuinely "new" Left. Its main appeal was to demobilizing and not-yet-reintegrated soliders; sooner or later its supporters would have to become clerks, workers, civil servants, etc., with quite different subjective social roles. *Der Ruf*'s ideas and proposals rarely went beyond or "transcended" those already espoused by the existing political parties; indeed much of its political debate revolved around SPD policies, and a great deal tended to be apolitical or unfounded. And finally it never attempted to formulate a coherent programme or even goals, nor did it attempt to constitute a movement or organization.

The *Ruf* group saw itself as an entire generation graduated from the Hitler Youth into the *Wehrmacht*, having suffered through and fought on the European fronts and now homeward bound, a generation which "(owned) nothing and never will own anything," and thus had "nothing to lose but its freedom and (had) nothing to gain but its freedom."[16] It was thought to be not unlike the generation of soldiers returning from the Napoleonic Wars in 1815. Then the young generation wanted national unity and victory of liberalism over feudalism; now it wanted European unity and the triumph of socialism over liberalism. The parallel continued: the reaction was omnipresent — in 1815 in the form of Metternich and the Concert of Europe, in 1945 as "other statesmen." But the Reaction of 1815 was seen as only a holding action, the maintenance of the status quo; applied to the 1945 situation it would be regressive and would set Germany's historical development back 100 years. [17]

To bring about the necessary historical transition, realism above all was thought to be necessary: "A generation which has lost its belief sees more realistically than those who live their beliefs and would like to convert others to them. It notices discrepancies in every word it reads and hears."[18] This applied in particular to the political parties. Heinz-Dietrich Ortlieb argued that in christian and liberal political parties the concept of socialism was losing — if it ever really had had — its anticapitalist character. The parties were merely biding their time, waiting for better material conditions before reverting to their old platforms and policies. As such they were potential agents of the Restoration who abused the idea of socialism for their own demagogic ends.[19] Erich Kuby took issue with the torpidity of political parties and advocated a new form of opposition:

> It is high time that in Germany a genuine socialist opposition rallied together far from the party groupings. On the one hand this opposition would be conducted by an uncompromising, unbourgeois feeling of vitality — rather than by ideologically woolly party programmes that say nothing — and on the other hand by the sober criticism of a healthy human understanding of accumulated, unprecedented misconceptions.[20]

If necessary, this opposition must be prepared to take direct action when warranted and perhaps to transform itself into an "extraparliamentary opposition."[21] This concept was not too far removed from Andersch's idea of a "new left" (his term) led by "homeless intellectuals" who were unable to find a place in the established political parties,[22] an idea which he unfortunately did not develop further.

But what was socialism and how as it to be accomplished? One of the periodical's most consistent themes was the call for a "united socialist Europe. The editors of *Der Ruf*, like Jakob Kaiser, saw Germany as a bridge between East and West. As they wrote in the first issue: "The developmental tendency in the large democracies of the West points the way to socialism, the desire for the democratization of public life in the Soviet Union the way to democracy."[23] The synthesis between democracy and socialism was to attain a higher stage than the mere combination of nineteenth century liberal democracy and totalitarian socialism; Germany had to "democratize socialism" and "socialize democracy" in equal measure so that, with the assistance of the young generation as a bridge, a "dialectical creation" — socialist democracy — could develop.[24] Dietrich Warnesius hoped for a new form of social democracy:

> But by this I mean neither a Russian nor an American nor an English nor a French democracy. I mean democracy. It will and must develop here from the special conditions of our mentality, our geographic position and the complete chaos in which the people and the country presently exists.[25]

As Richter himself conceded, the young generation's socialism was frequently "purely intuitive" but nonetheless a real force.[26]

Ultimately *Der Ruf's* radical ideas, its opposition to the existing political parties — which had of course been appointed by the Military Governments — and to the occupation authorities, its insistence upon the primacy of German unity and a specifically German road to democracy, and its occasional advocacy of the use of "revolutionary means" had to bring it into conflict with the occupation powers. This led to the dismissal of Andersch and Richter from the periodical's editorship[27] and their replacement by Erich Kuby and later Walter von Cube.[28] By this time the integration or reintegration of many of its readers had taken place, and *Der Ruf* folded in early 1948. More than most initiatives from the independent Left, *Der Ruf* was a genuine product of its time and place. As Richter suggested fifteen years later, "the great hopes of those first postwar years were never fulfilled. But perhaps it is good to know that they existed".[29]

If the movement around *Der Ruf* was a precursor of the German New Left, then the People's Congress for Unity and a Just Peace was the forerunner of a typically German kind of single-purpose movement which has appeared intermittently in the Federal Republic since 1945. The Congress was constituted in 1947 after the failure of the *Länder* premiers' conference, held to discuss ways and means of achieving reunification, in Munich in that year. This movement aimed at the restoration of German unity and the conclusion of a peace treaty with the occupying powers. It was founded on the basis of proposals put forward by the communist leadership in the Soviet Zone, and was thus hampered from the outset by western suspicion. Among those attending were Pieck and Grotewohl from the SED, prominent members of a number of western zone parties (such as Paul Löbe of the SPD and Friedensburg and Selzer of the CDU) and liberal intellectuals not attached to any political party (Alfred Weber and Martin Niemöller).

The Congress' characteristics were the absence of any formal organization and any mass basis of support; it was a kind of "rally" movement aimed at arousing popular opinion in support of delimited issues by means of meetings, marches, demonstrations, resolutions, pamphlets and mass petitions. In this case it was relatively unsuccessful because of the suspicions of collaboration to which it was susceptible and because it was largely ignored by the western press.[30] Its significance, however, was its role as the first extra-parliamentary action in postwar Germany, as well as the first single-purpose, supra-party movement in that country.

If considerable space has been devoted to the various currents of socialist thought in the immediate postwar period, this is because the period's influence on the development of the Left in the Federal Republic can scarcely be underestimated. The upsurge of socialism and socialist proposals in this period may be attributed to four basic historical factors. (1) An understanding, or at least intuitive perception, of the socio-economic and political factors leading up the fascist seizure of power and the support for the Third Reich laid bare the need to take radical measures in order to eliminate the economic and social roots of fascism. Since capitalism was widely seen to be the pre-condition and source of fascism, the transition to socialism was thought to be the most certain and necessary foundation for a new democratic order. (2) Material distress and economic necessity were widespread; what was available had to be redistributed, and rebuilding and reconstruction would have to be undertaken with the equal participation of all. (3) Connected with these was the desire for the inalienable right of freedom — freedom from arbitrary control as well as freedom to participate in all the organizations and decision-making processes not only in politics but also in society and economy. Free, emancipated and liberated human beings, it was thought, would never support another Hitler's bid for power and would cooperate creatively in the tasks of reconstruction. (4) And finally, the traditional elites in politics, the administration, justice, business and elsewhere were either in flight or totally discredited. Leading positions thus fell largely by default to members of what — rightly or wrongly — was felt to be the anti-Nazi elite.

Though it is futile to attempt to isolate the "socialist" vote in the local and regional elections of 1946 and 1947 — because at this time a vote for even the CDU/CSU could be considered as a (subjective) vote for the Left — it is worth noting that in five of the eight West Zone *Länder* in which elections were held in 1946-47, a combination of SPD and KPD would have attained a majority, and in the three remaining would have been the largest political force.[31]

Evidence of this leftist tendency in the postwar period is provided not only by electoral statistics and the predominance in local administrative bodies of Social Democrats and Communists, but strikingly, as Wolfgang Abendroth has pointed out, by constitutional developments as well. In all the *Länder* constitutions that originated — regardless of the zone of occupation — through popular initiative prior to the promulgation of the Basic Law in 1949,[32] extensive socialization and expropriation measures are anchored. [33]

Nor did popular support for these constitutions diminish when the western occupying powers subsequently requested that "the people" expressly ratify their socialization articles. A plebiscite held in Saxony indicated that 70 per cent of the population agreed that the properties of businessmen and industrialists who had been connected in any way with the NSDAP be expropriated.[34] The Hesse constitution was approved by a majority of more than two-thirds, and when the American Military Government insisted on a special plebiscite to confirm its socialization Article 41, a majority of 72 per cent did so.

Significantly, developments in those *Länder* in which the bourgeois coalition attained a majority did not differ in essence from those governed by the SPD. Thus the socialization articles in the constitutions of Bavaria, Rhineland — Palatinate, Saarland and Baden-Württemberg (the latter was then two separate *Länder*, Baden and Württemberg-Hohenzollern) came into effect under bourgeois coalition governments. Generally speaking, the socialization articles of this period empowered the governments to undertake the expropriation of large monopolistic industries, the break-up of large agrarian estates and the confiscation of all properties belonging to leading Nazis and war criminals. In almost every case they were promulgated on the basis of an agreement among the SPD, CDU and KPD, which usually provided them with majorities of 70 per cent and more — the real "socialist" majority of these years. In the case of Hesse, for example, the November 1946 constitution was passed by a coalition of SPD and CDU over the opposition of KPD and LDP.[35]

There are a number of further reasons for having considered at some length the various nuances and ramifications of political debate in this period. In comparison with the political spectrum before 1933 and again after 1949, politics immediately after 1945 revolved around socialism and socialist (or at least socialist-sounding) proposals. The question of right *or* left was no longer so important as the question of *how far left* the new system was to be. Moreover, the basic themes and platforms now put forward would, with very few alterations, dominate political debate on the Left for at least the next decade. The — crucial — difference was that the issues which after 1945 were at the centre of political debate were taken seriously in the German Federal Republic only by what would become the *extreme Left*.

While it was undoubtedly true that the degree of political participation and involvement was now far less than in 1918-19 — it has been demonstrated that the predominant political mood was one of apathy and resignation — the essential difference was that in 1945 there was virtually no powerful, organized Right to check the trend to the left. With the Right decimated and discredited, the political sphere was dominated, by default, by the Left. Among the politically aware and active — though admittedly and emphatically not among the population as a whole — there was now a clear leftist majority, as the previous chapters should demonstrate.

Given the pressing need for reconstruction and the fulfilment of the most basic human requirements, as well as the mass feeling of resignation, in the postwar period, one could argue plausibly that an all- or several-party leftist popular front *could have* taken the lead in the transition to socialism in Germany at the very least one could have expected the rise of a welfare state constructed on the British model. That this development did not come about, it may be argued further, is attributable to two central factors: the interventions of the occupation powers and the readiness of the indigenous political parties, the CDU/CSU and the KPD/SED, to collaborate with the respective occupation authorities in bringing about the restoration of the old socio-economic relationships in the West and the discrediting of socialism in the East.

That the "other Germany" did exist during and after the Third Reich in the form of a series of socialist and antifascist groupings should by now be beyond dispute. That this other Germany was a minority was also unquestionable. But the force which it generated, combined with the lack of resistance from the Right, might well have made it a catalyst to motivate, e.g., former Nazis who had originally joined the NSDAP out of misguided idealism or even revolutionary elan, the now "proletarized" bourgeoisie and large numbers of formerly apolitical persons. The antifascist front was after 1945 the only indigenous and genuine democratic force, and as such *could have* constituted the basis of the "new" Germany. The interventions of the four Military Governments prevented the realization of the principles and goals of the socialist and antifascist movement. In the East this movement was perverted almost beyond recognition and in the West was harnessed by means of the theses of collective guilt, political activity quarantine, free enterprise and the like into the service of a state whose social, economic and political system became very much like that which gave rise to National Socialism.

Seen in this light, the version of the strength of a great left-wing potential after 1945, as frequently put forward by the Left today, is entirely credible, provided that one also bears in mind that any "revolution" or transition to socialism would have had a unique and problematical character. The preliminary struggles would have been fought without the active participation — and hence without a corresponding development of consciousness — of the masses: what Heinrich Böll has called the *geschenkte Revolution*.[36] Or, as Isaac Deutscher has formulated it:

> Germany did not merely invent the *ersatz* industrially, it produced it socio-politically as well: the *ersatz*-revolution of a Bismarck, the *ersatz*-revolution of 1918 and the *ersatz*-revolution of 1945 — none of them were made by Germans, but by conquering foreign armies. That is the tragedy, the guilt and the misfortune of Germany.[37]

Thus although the socialist transition itself might well have been peaceful, the problem of relapse or reaction among a people lacking a socialist consciousness would have to be dealt with following the inevitable return to prosperity. This, coupled with the fragile democratic tradition in Germany, would certainly have heightened the possibility of the development of some form of leftist authoritarianism or "totalitarianism" on the one hand, or a relapse into rightist reaction on the other.

REFERENCES
1 Socialist Competition from Left and Right
a. Communist popular front

1 Wolfgang Abendroth in his foreword to Eberhard Schmidt, *Die verhinderte Neuordnung 1945-1952*, Frankfurt 1970, p.6.
2 Interview with Wolfgang Leonhard in: Albert Wucher, ed., *Wie kam es zur Bundesrepublik? Politische Gespräche mit Männern der ersten Stunde*, Freiburg 1968, p.38.
3 Text reproduced in: L. Berthold and E. Diehl, eds., *Revolutionäre Deutsche Parteiprogramme vom Kommunistischen Manifest zum Programm des Sozialismus*, E.Berlin 1967, p.191ff.
4 *Ibid.*, p.320.
5 Ute Schmidt/Tilman Fischer, *Der erzwungene Kapitalismus. Klassenkämpfe in den Westzonen 1945-1948*, W.Berlin 1972, p.58.
6 Berthold and Diehl, *op.cit.*, p.198.
7 Erich Paterna, et al., *Deutschland von 1933 bis 1939*, E.Berlin 1969, p.326.
8 According to communist estimates, approximately 150,000 (of a 1933 membership of 300,000) KPD members were prosecuted, imprisoned or interred in concentration camps; "tens of thousands" of functionaries and members were murdered. (Wolfgang Bleyer, et al., *Deutschland 1939-1945*, E.Berlin 1965, p.416). Cf. further Renate Riemick, "Das Verbot der KPD — historisch-politische gesehen" in W. Abendroth, H. Ridder, O. Schonfeldt, eds., *KPD-Verbot oder mit den Kommunisten leben?* Reinbek 1967, p.47.
9 See the data given in Richard Schachtner, *Die deutschen Nachkriegswahlen*, Munich 1956, *passim*.
And in the *Landtag* elections taking place between 1946-1948, the overall KPD vote was 9.6%; in the federal elections of 1949 it declined to 5.7%, and to 3.5% in the *Land* elections held between 1949-52, and 2.2% in the 1953 federal elections. (Conveniently summarized in Werner Kaltfleiter, *Wirtschaft und Politik in Deutschland, Konjunktur als Bestimmungsfaktor des Parteiensystems* Cologne und Opladen 1966, p.102.
10 J.P. Nettl, *The Eastern Zone and Soviet Policy in Germany 1945-50*, London 1951, p.76.
11 Wilhelm Pieck, *Probleme der Vereinigung von KPD und SPD*, E. Berlin 1945, p.8 and 32.
12 Walter Ulbricht in a speech of 25 June 1945 in: *Zur Geschichte der deutschen Arbeiterbewegung. Aus Reden und Aufsätzen*, E.Berlin 1955, vol. II, 1st half-volume.
13 Hans Kluth, *Die KPD in der Bundesrepublik. Ihre politische Tätigkeit und Organization 1945-1956*, Cologne und Opladen 1959, p.31.
14 Wolfgang Leonhard, *Die Revolution entlässt ihre Kinder*, Cologne 1955, p.351.
15 The text of which is printed in Berthold and Diehl, *op.cit.*, p.201ff.
16 *Ibid.*, p.205.
17 The SPD's opposition to the formation of the SED is abundantly documented in: SPD Vorstand, ed., *Acht Jahre sozialdemokratischer Kampf um Einheit, Frieden und Freiheit*, Bonn 1954 (mimeographed)
18 Leonhard, *op.cit.*, p.356.
19 Bundesinnenministerium für Gesamtdeutsche Fragen, ed., *Wahlen in der SBZ*, Bonn 1959, *passim*.
20 Senat of Berlin, ed., *Kampf um Freiheit und Selbstverwaltung 1945-1946*, Berlin 1961, p.38f and esp. 558ff.
21 Text in Ossip Flechtheim, ed., *Dokumente zur parteipolitischen Entwicklung in Deutschland.* Vol. III, W.Berlin 1962-1968, p.360ff.
22 Kluth, *op.cit.*, p.25.

23 Abendroth, *Sozialgeschichte der europäischen Arbeiterbewegung*, Frankfurt 4th ed. 1968, p.177f.
24 Harold Zink, *The United States in Germany 1944-1955*, Princeton-Toronto-London-New York 1957, p.285.
25 OMGUS Public Opinion Surveys, Series 1, No. 175, p.6.
26 KPD Party Vorstand, ed., "Die ideologisch-politische Festung unserer Partei auf der Grundlage des Marxismus-Leninismus" in: *Materialien der 14. PV-Tagung* Frankfurt n.d., p.85
27 See Kluth, *op.cit.*, p.25f.

b. Christian socialism

1 Interview with Jakob Lemmer in Wucher, ed., *op.cit.*, p.61
2 According to Gerhard Schütz, "Die CDU-Merkmale ihres Aufbaues" in: Max Gustav Lange, ed., *Parteien in der Bundesrepublik*, Stuttgart and Düsseldorf 1955, p.46.
3 Cf. Otto Heinrich von der Gablentz, *über Marx hinaus*, Berlin 1946, p.29 and 14f.
4 Ibid., p.7f, p.29 and 30.
5 On the subject of Catholic social doctrine, see Ralph Henry Bowen, *German Theories of the Corporative State*, New York 1947, ch.3 "Social Catholicism".
6 Eugon Kogon, *Die unvollendete Erneuerung. Deutschland im Kraftfeld 1945-1963*, Frankfurt 1964, p.42. This work is a convenient collection of Kogon's most important contributions to the *Frankfurter Hefte*.
7 Walter Dirks, *Die zweite Republik*, Frankfurt 1947, p.22. This volume is for Dirks what *ibid.* is for Kogon.
8 *Ibid.*, p.23.
9 *Ibid.*, p.170.
10 *Ibid.*, p.99ff (italics in original).
11 Jakob Kaiser, *Der soziale Staat. Reden und Gedanken*, Berlin 1946, p.10.
12 From Kaiser's famous "Bridge" speech in: *Neue Zeit*, No.39 (Feb. 14) 1946, p.2f.
13 See Flechtheim, *op.cit.*, Vol.II, p.32.
14 Leo Schwering, *Frühgeschichte der Christlich-Demokratischen Union*, Recklinghausen 1963, p.215ff.
15 Flechtheim, *op.cit.* . . . . Vol.II, p.32
16 Cf. mimeographed copy available from the CDU party headquarters in Bonn, n.d. In a letter to the author, Dr. Werner Brussau of the CDU writes: "This programme was at no time the binding economic programme of the CDU; it was merely the CDU's proposals of economic policy in the then British Zone of occupation."
17 Arnold J. Heidenheimer, Adenauer and the CDU. *The Rise of the Leader and the Integration of the Party*, The Hague 1960, p.128.
18 See "Rede des ersten Vorsitzenden der CDU der britischen Zone, Oberbürgermeister a.D. Konrad Adenauer" in: *Schriftenreihe der CDU des Rheinlandes*, Vol.8, Cologne n.d., p.17 and p.9.
19 "Basically too liberal to be political and Catholic in the usual sense, and receptive toward socialist ideas, it worked out a programmatical manifesto without, however, being certain of having the means to implement it in the day-to-day political struggle and to hold its own vis-à-vis other groups and forces." (Schutz, *op.cit.*, p.47).
20 The Bavarian CSU, from the outset the CDU's coalition partner, never really espoused the notion of christian socialism. The party's first chairman, Dr. Josef Müller was not in favour of firm programmatical commitment; the party's five-point provisory programme of May 1946 demanded the creation of a christian state, loyal cooperation with the occupation powers, etc. (Cf. Sekretariat der CSU in Bayern, ed., *10 Jahre CSU in Bayern*, Munich 1955, p.7ff). The Basic Programme of December 1946 rejected the idea of a planned economy, called for special support for artisans and the middle classes, and emphasized the right and the social obligation of ownership (reprinted in: Flechtheim, *Dokumente* . . . , Vol.II, p.213ff.
21 Schutz. *op.cit.*, p.60.

22 On this see Carl Meyer, "The Crisis of German Protestantism" in: *Social Research*, November 1945, p.397ff.

23 In his plea on behalf of the defence at the conclusion of Viktor Agartz' trial for subversion (q.v. Ch.IV (4) below), Gustav Heinemann discussed these developments from another viewpoint: "One of the tragic chapters in German history," he said, "is that our labour movement in the past century had no christian leaders. On the contrary, the churches were then against all that is today a matter of course, against banning child labour, etc. — I need not enumerate all that. This gave rise to a situation in which, in this country, political dissent overlapped into religious dissent with the result that Marxism became an ersatz religion." ("Plädoyer", reprinted as Appendix to Hans-Georg Hermann, *Verraten und verkauft*, Fulda 1959 (2nd ed.), p.238; *italic* in original not reproduced here.

24 Concerning the National Socialist policy toward the churches, see John S. Conway, *The Nazi Persecution of the Churches 1933-1945*; London 1968; for the churches' role vis-à-vis the Third Reich, see Friedrich Baumgartel, *Wider der Kirchenkampflegenden*, Neuendettlelsau 1959; Hans Müller, *Katholische Kirche und Nationalsozialismus*, Munich 1963; Gunter Lewy, *The Catholic Church and Nazi Germany*, London 1964; and Gordon Zahn, *German Catholics and Hitler's Wars*, New York 1962; for postwar developments see F. H. Littell, *The German Phoenix*, New York 1960.

25 Of the *Bekennende Kirche*, Heinrich Werner has written that: "Its resistance was directed almost exclusively against the 'neo-paganism' of Nazism — its (Nazism's) manic anticommunism was not called into question. Nor was its 'threat to peace.' " ("Europa-Idee und europäische Sicherheit" in: *Deutsche Volkszeitung*, 17 August 1972).

26 According to the "hammer and anvil" theory, repeated blows by the hammer would not affect the anvil, but eventually wear down the hammer itself.

27 The author is grateful to Mr. Heino Kopietz for calling to his attention these particular functions of the Church.

28 Heidenheimer, *op.cit.*, p.119

29 Quoted in *ibid.*, p.121.

30 See Johannes Albers, *et al.*, *Grundgedanken zum Thema: Christlicher Sozialismus*, Cologne 1946, p.5.

31 Wolfgang Abendroth, *Antagonistische Gesellschaft . . .* , p.444.

32 As emphasised by Peter Blachstein in private interview with the author.

c. *The unified trade union*

1 See Fritz Naphtall, *Wirtschaftsdemokratie. Ihr Wesen, Weg und Ziel*, new edition Frankfurt 1966.

2 Here see Bruno Broeker, "Wirtschaftliche Mitbestimmung der Betriebsräte? Eine Frage aus dem Bereich der Wirtschaftsdemokratie" in: *Die Neue Gesellschaft*, No.2 (Feb.) 1948, p.18f.

3 See Gunther Scholz, "*Ausserer und innerer Wandel der deutschen Gewerkschaftsbewegung in ihrer Entwicklung seit der Entstehungszeit bis zur Neugründung nach dem zweiten Weltkrieg*", unpublished Ph.D dissertation, law faculty, University of Marburg, 1955, where more details can be found.

4 August Enderle, *Die Einheitsgewerkschaften*, Vol.I, Düsseldorf, mimeographed manuscript of DGB Bundesvorstand, 1959, p.102ff.

5 Theo Pirker, *Die Blinde Macht. Die Gewerkschaftsbewegung in Westdeutschland*, Vol.I, p.114 and ff.

6 Quoted in *ibid.*, p.39 (italics in original).

7 According to Viktor Agartz, *Gewerkschaft und Arbeiterklasse*, Munich 1971, p.69ff.

8 This is essentially the argument put forth in Wolfgang Abendroth, *Die deutschen Gewerkschaften. Weg demokratischer Integration*, Heidelberg 1954, p.50.

9 "Referenten-Material—Warum sozialdemokratische Betriebsgruppen?" 6 April 1946 (unpaginated, mimeographed).

10 Agartz, *op.cit.*, p.31
11 *Ibid.*, p.116ff.
12 The Soviet zonal Free German Trade Union Federation (FDGB), by contrast, was established in June 1945.
13 However, in view of the large tasks confronting the trade unions, it was probably advantageous to have some experienced men in control who had not been pro-Nazi, indeed in most cases were anti-Nazis. Cf. Abendroth, *op.cit.*, p.35.
14 Agartz, *op.cit.*, p.70.
15 Zink, *op.cit.*, p.282 and 294; Schmidt, *op.cit.*, p.32; Agartz, *ibid.*, p.44ff.
16 Justus von Fürstenau, *Entnazifizierung*, Neuwied 1969, p.44.
17 Pirker, *op.cit.*, p.70ff.
18 Here see Agartz, *op.cit.*, p.45.
19 Wolfgang Hirsch-Weber, *Gewerkschaften in der Politik*, Cologne & Opladen 1959, p.73ff.
20 See the *Protokoll* of the DGB Founding Congress in the British Zone from 22 to 25 April, in Bielefeld, Düsseldorf n.d., p.28.
21 Herbert J. Spiro, *The Politics of German Co-determination*, Cambridge Mass. 1958, p.46.
22 Quoted in Spiro, *op.cit.*, p.33
23 Here see Pirker, *op.cit.*, p.154ff; *ibid.*, p.46f.
24 *Protokoll*, DGB British Zone, p.31ff.
25 Schmidt/Fichtner, *op.cit.*, p.39.
26 Pirker, *op.cit.*, p.93ff.
27 Hirsch-Weber, *op.cit.*, p.63.
28 Bayrischer Rundfunk, Program of 14.9.1949, 19:45 hours, typewritten copy available in DGB Archives, Düsseldorf.
29 Eberhard Schmidt, *Ordnungsfaktor oder Gegenmacht? Die politische Rolle der Gewerkschaften*, Frankfurt 1971, p.79.

2 Social Democracy: Socialism plus Democracy

1 In its: "Aufruf zum Neuaufbau der Organisation," reproduced in: Flechtheim, *Dokumente* . . . , Vol.III, p.2ff.
2 Lewis J. Edinger, *Kurt Schumacher. A Study in Personality and Political Behaviour*, Stanford 1965, p.98.
2a See *Jahrbuch der SPD 1946*, Bonn n.d. (1946), p.14
3 "Wo stehen wir—wohin gehen wir?" reproduced in: Flechtheim, *Dokumente* . . . , Vol.II.
4 "Politische Richtlinien fur die SPD in ihrem Verhaltnis zu den anderen politischen Faktoren," Hannover 1945; printed in slightly abridged form as "Sozialismus und Demokratie! (Richtlinien fur die Arbeit der SPD)" in: Kurt Schumacher, *Nach dem Zusammenbruch*, Hamburg 1948, p.48ff, which is the version used here.
5 Cf. Albrecht Kaden, *Einheit oder Freheit? Die Wiedergründung der SPD 1945/46* Hanover 1964, p.83ff, and the reference there to unpublished documents, in particular the text of Zhukov's speech to the Grotewohl group in June 1945.
6 Schumacher, "Sozialismus und Demokratie", *op.cit.*, p.70.
7 "Wir wollen keine neue Herrenschicht," speech delivered 18.3.1947, reprinted in: *Der Sozialdemokrat*, 19 March 1947.
8 From an article by Schumacher in: *Der Tagesspiegel*, 27 March 1946, reproduced in Klaus-Peter Schulz, *Auftakt zum Kalten Krieg. Der Freiheitskampf der SPD in Berlin 1945/46*, W. Berlin 1965, p.356.
9 As told to the author in private interview with Peter Blachstein, who supports this view completely.
10 As described by a witness and participant in postwar developments there, Reinhold Walz, in interview with the author.

11 See Kaden, *op.cit.*, p.233ff. Following his journey into the US Zone in November 1945, Dahrendorf urged the establishment of a committee to examine the question of collaboration with the KPD, for the reason that " . . . the unity of the labour movement is a political necessity". (Quoted in Schmidt/Fichtner *op.cit.*, p.57.

12 Here see SOPADE, *Querschnitt durch Politik und Wirtschaft*, Bonn, Aug. 1954, p.75.

13 *Protokoll* of the Hanover Convention, p.61

14 The concept of *Rechtsstaat* is not readily translatable. It refers, broadly, to a state whose institutions are constructed upon a common legal order, usually defined by a constitution, in which individual rights are secured against arbitrary state power. It is thus characterized by, above all, due process of law, as well as equality of all citizens before the courts, an independent judiciary, right of appeal against government or bureaucratic decisions, responsible government and separation of powers. The nearest English equivalent would thus be "constitutional state", although this does not convey all of the original meaning.; cf. Glenn Schramm, "Ideology and Politics. The Rechtsstaat Idea in West Germany" in: *Journal of Politics*, Vol.33 (Feb. 1971), p.133ff.

15 *Protokoll* of the Hanover Convention, p.61f.

16 "Politische Leitsätze", reproduced in: Flechtheim, *Dokumente* . . . , Vol.III, p.1.

17 *Protokoll* of the Hanover Convention, p.36.

18 He estimated that about 35% of the population had lost nothing or even profited from the war, 25% had almost nothing and 40% had literally nothing. See Kurt Schumacher, *Turmwächter der Demokratie*, Vol.II, W. Berlin-Grunewald 1953, p.86.

19 Flechtheim, *Dokumente* . . . , Vol.III, p.4 and 6.

20 See Edinger, *Kurt Schumacher*, p.107. The SPD-KPD merger had of course particularly affected the SPD. About one half the party's membership and millions of potential voters were lost through the separation of eastern Germany, a traditional reserve of SPD support, from the western zones. Indeed, the membership of the SPD-East has been estimated at between 619,000 and 631,000 (of which about 65,000 were in West Berlin and subsequently joined the western SPD). In view of these developments, the SPD's membership of 875,479 in December 1947 represented a fairly considerable accomplishment, since a simple addition of the eastern and western memberships (less the West Berliners) would leave a number exceeding the prewar total by at least 400,000. Viktor Agartz, among others, saw this middle-class influx as hampering the party's socialist goals, since for him too many joined out of an unfounded anti-Nazism, especially "bourgeois intellectuals" motivated by social, humanitarian or religious reasons. (Agartz, *op.cit.*, p.75ff).

21 Klaus Schutz, "Die Sozialdemokratie im Nachkriegsdeutschland" in: Lange, ed., *op.cit.*, p.205.

22 Edinger, *Kurt Schumacher*, p.72.

23 For example, Lewis Edinger has written that Schumacher ". . . brought to the image of the post-totalitarian leader the mystique of the concentrationnaire elite, the cream of the anti-Nazis, whose fate, voluntarily incurred, stood in sharp moral contrast in Schumacher's mind to that of men who had either profited under the Nazi system, or at least not suffered any great discomfort. Even underground fighters and exiles could not claim to have made so great a sacrifice." (*Ibid.*, p.86) Here, he is quite right in stating that Schumacher's considerable sacrifices invested him with a certain ascriptive moral claim to leadership after 1945. But the statement that underground fighters who had been tortured and murdered or exiles who had been terrorized and hunted down had paid a lesser price for their opposition, or indeed that Schumacher felt his position superior to theirs, requires far more evidence.

24 See the *Protokoll* of the 1948 Convention.

25 From his "Programmatische Erklärungen" of 1945, in: Flechtheim, *Dokumente*, Vol.III, p.4.

26 "Germany's Postwar Socialism. Nationalism and Kurt Schumacher" in: *Review of Politics*, Vol.27, April 1965, p.236.

27 Schwarz, *op.cit.*, p.488.
28 SPD Party Vorstand, *Acht Jahre Kampf* . . . , p.18.
29 Edinger, *Kurt Schumacher*, p.186.
30 *Turmwächter der Demokratie*, Vol.I, p.44.
31 Schwarz, *op.cit.*, p.522.
32 Edinger, *Kurt Schumacher*, p.186.
33 Schwarz, *op.cit.*, p.527.
34 Thus Kaden, *op.cit.*, p.286; Richard Hiscocks, *Democracy in Western Germany*, London 1957, p.83f; Edinger, *Kurt Schumacher*, p.138.
35 Leonhard, *Die Revolution entlässt ihre Kinder*, p.289.

3 The Socialist Idea in the Postwar Period

1 Cf. his essays: "Kampf um die Freiheit. Zwei Reden aus geschichtlichem Anlass," Hamburg 1948 (brochure); "Das deutsch-französische Verhältnis und der Dritte Partner" in: *Merkur*, No. 2 (Feb.) 1948, p.649ff; "Europa — nur als Bund Möglich" in: *Neues Europa*, Vol.9, 1948, p.14ff.
2 Willy Brandt, "Programmatische Grundlagen des demokratischen Sozialismus," speech delivered to 6th *Land* Party Convention of the Berlin SPD, mimeographed reprint, n.p., n.d. (Berlin 1949), p.16.
3 Willy Huhn, "Bausteine zu einem neuen Parteiprogramm," speech delivered to the Marxistischer Arbeitskreis in the August Bebel Institute, Berlin-Wannsee, 20 November 1949, leaflet, p.3.
4 As stated in private interview with the author.
5 Cf. Ch.VI below.
6 Paul Sering (=Richard Löwenthal), *Jenseits des Kapitalismus. Ein Beitrag zur sozialistischen Neuorientierung*, Nuremberg 1946, Ch.II, III and p.73ff.
7 *Ibid.*, p.106.
8 *Ibid.*, p.215; see also p.85.
9 *Ibid.*, p.176f.
10 *Ibid.*, p.183 (and p.9).
11 From the Introduction to: Alexander Mitscherlich and Alfred Weber, *Freier Sozialismus*, Heidelberg 1946, p.6.
12 Mitscherlich, "Entwicklungsgrundlagen eines freien Sozialismus" in: *ibid.*, p.17.
13 *Ibid.*, p.17ff.
14 *Ibid.*, p.26.
15 Cf. Ch.I, Prologue.
16 Anonymous (but most likely Richter or Andersch), "Die Wandlung des Sozialismus — und die junge Generation" in: *Der Ruf*, 1 Nov. 1946. It must be recalled that this was written prior to the advent of the Economic Miracle.
17 Anonymous (Andersch/Richter), "Churchill und die europäische Einheit" in: *Der Ruf*, 1 March 1947.
18 Anonymous (Andersch/Richter), "Deutschland — Brücke zwischen Ost und West" in: *Der Ruf*, 1 Oct. 1946.
19 "Sozialismus — gestern, heute und morgen" in: *Der Ruf*, 1 November 1946.
20 "Kritik oder Kampf" in: *Der Ruf*, 1 May 1947.
21 *Ibid.* Cf. also Kuby's "Die Krise der Demokratie" in: *Der Ruf*, 15 Jan. 1948.
22 "Die sozialistische Situation" in: *Der Ruf*, 15 March 1947.
23 "Deutschland — Brücke . . . ," *op.cit.*
24 *Ibid.*
25 "Bekenntnis eines jungen Deutschen," reprinted in: Hans Schwab Felisch, ed., *Der Ruf. Eine deutsche Nachkriegszeitschrift*, Munich 1962, p.169.
26 Hans-Werner Richter, "Der Sieg des Opportunismus" in: *Der Ruf* (Schwab-Felisch, ed.), p.293.
27 The exact circumstances of Andersch's and Richter's departure from the editorship of *Der Ruf* are still not certain. For many years the legend, fostered by Richter himself, prevailed that the *Ruf* had had its licence revoked by the American Military Governor in consultation with his Soviet counterpart (a claim accepted by, e.g.,

86 The German Left Since 1945

Abendroth, *Antagonistische Gesellschaft* . . . , p.440f) on the grounds that it had become too uncomfortable for the occupation authorities in both East and West. The retrospective selection from *Der Ruf*, edited by Schwab-Felisch (*op.cit.*), seems to support this thesis by ending with the last articles by Richter and Andersch. The claim that *Der Ruf* terminated with the "dismissal" of its founding co-editors has been maintained until very recently, by, e.g., Volker Wehdeking (*Der Nullpunkt. Über die Konstituierung der deutschen Nachkriegsliteratur (1945-48) in den amerikanischen Kriegsgefangenlägern*, Stuttgart 1971). But this was not the case. *Der Ruf* never had had a licence; it had only been "tolerated" by the Military Governments; it was impossible to revoke a licence which had never been issued in the first place. And Richter's and Andersch's departures were based formally upon their resignations, which had been submitted with the intention of securing certain changes in their contracts (increased salary? more liberties in the preparation of articles?). That the publisher did accept their resignations is probably attributable to internal political and economic differences between the editors and publisher on the one hand, and the publisher and the American Military Government on the other. (Cf. Jerome Vaillant, "Der Ruf der Gruppe 47" in: *Frankfurter Rundschau*, 30 Aug. 1972). That Andersch and Richter then went on to found the probably most influential literary circle in postwar Germany, the Group 47, is well known. The question as to the origin of the notion that *Der Ruf* was officially banned by the U.S. Military Government remains unanswered.

28 Under Kuby's editorship policy and standards remained at least as high, if not actually higher, than they had been under Richter and Andersch. But under von Cube, the readers, who had come to expect penetrating analysis and critical thought, found instead such bland editorials as: "There are no longer any classes and definite categories of ideas. We have all become unpropertied and there are holes in our robe of dogmas. Marxism is conservative, christianity liberal. Poverty can be made neither socialist nor capitalist . . . Our confusion is complete. The leftists want to be more nationalist than the rightists, the rightists more socialist than the leftists" (Walter von Cube, "Die Phönixe von 1945" in *Der Ruf*, 1 Feb. 1948). And, discussing the concept of "Europe," von Cube went on to even greater heights of obfuscation: "Although Russia must be rejected as a fundamentally non-European country", the United States was "a legitimate child of Europe." This argument was then used to urge Germany's dissociation from the Soviet Union and her acceptance of Marshall Plan Aid ("Es gibt noch ein Europa" in *Der Ruf*, 15 Feb. 1948). It was a rather sad and ignominious end to what had been a vital and genuinely radical left-wing periodical.

29 Richter, "Beim Wiederlesen des Ruf" in: Schwab-Felisch, ed., *op.cit.*, p.9
30 Here cf. Ernst Richert, *Die radikale Linke*, W. Berlin 1969.
31 See the data presented in: Richard Schachtner, *op.cit.*, *passim*.
32 I.e. in Rhineland-Palatinate (Art. 61), in Bavaria (Art. 160), in the Saarland (Art. 52), in Hesse (Art. 39,40,41), in Bremen (Art. 41-44) and in all the *Länder* in the Soviet Zone.
33 Wolfgang Abendroth, *Wirtschaft, Gesellschaft und Demokratie in der Bundesrepublik*, Frankfurt 1965, p.13.
34 Wolfgang Abendroth, *Das Grundgesetz*, Pfüllingen 1966, p.26 and 62.
35 Schutz,*op.cit.*, p.89. For a detailed discussion of constitutional developments in Hesse, which may be taken more or less as typical for developments in the U.S. Zone, see: Alexander Borosnjak, "Der Kampf um Artikel 41 der Verfassung Hessens in den Jahren 1946/47" in: *Beiträge zur Geschichte der deutschen Arbeiterbewegung*, E. Berlin 1962, Vol.3, p.711ff.
36 Heinrich Böll, "Deutsche Meisterschaft" in: Altmann, Böll, Flechtheim, *etal.*, *Zensuren nach 20 Jahren Bundesrepublik*, Cologne 1970, p.30.
37 Isaac Deutscher, "Germany and Marxism" in: *The New Left Review*, No.4 (Jan.-Feb.) 1968, p.63.

PART B

INTEGRATION OF THE WORKING CLASS ORGANIZATIONS 1949-1959

IV. DIMINISHING ALTERNATIVES ON THE LEFT

1. The Establishment of the CDU State

Possibly the greatest single factor in the development of the postwar German Left has been the success of the Right. During the two decades following the formation of the German Federal Republic, developments in politics, economy and society were determined by the CDU/CSU at the head of a bourgeois political coalition primarily serving the interests of the upper social and economic classes. In this sense West Germany was — and in many respects still is — a "CDU State."[1]

a. Political factors

The antecedents of the CDU State can be traced back to well before the establishment of the separate West German state. The bourgeois coalition emerged from the supra-zonal Economic Council of early 1948, which had been constituted by the Allies to promote German initiatives for economic recovery in the Trizone. The Council was from the outset weighted in favour of the bourgeois parties.[2] The SPD refused to participate after its demands for the key portfolios of economics and finance were not met by the bourgeois parties. The council's five-man directorate, controlled by the CDU, which became *ipso facto* the first CDU-led cabinet on an interzonal level, rested on a combination of CDU/CSU-DP-FDP. By June 1948, Ludwig Erhard, the council's "economics Minister," had laid down the basic proposals of what would become the "social market economy."[3] While America began pouring in Marshall Aid — which would total $1,389 million by 1952 — Erhard introduced a series of measures involving the removal of all but a minimal number of controls on prices, wages and supplies, and the stimulation of economic expansion on the basis of a "free" interplay of market forces. Prices were determined by supply and demand, and taxation was eased so that profits could be ploughed back into business expansion. The results of this policy could be foreseen: the concentration and thus ready availability of large amounts of investment capital and the growth in inequalities of income. Nevertheless, initial results were effective: the black market and the destitution of the first postwar years disappeared and industrial production rose astoundingly rapidly.[4]

Subsequent steps, culminating in the promulgation of the new constitution, were similarly dominated by the bourgeois coalition with the support of the western Military Governments. In July 1948, shortly after the Berlin Blockade, the *Länder* premiers were commissioned by the western Allies to form a Parliamentary Council for purposes of preparing a constitution. The premiers' objections that such a body ought not to be constituted before national unity had been achieved were overridden by the Allies. The basic principles and drafts for the Council's deliberations were furnished by the "Herrenchiemsee Convention," an appointed body which did not reflect the makeup of the population as a whole, and indeed a large number of its members had held important positions during the Third Reich.[5]

Nor was the composition of the Parliamentary Council itself much more representative.[6] Since the SPD and CDU/CSU delegations were identical in size at 27 members each, again the minor bourgeois parties were able to exercise a disproportionate influence[7] in the Council's deliberations. The Council's intentions were undermined by several Allied interventions aimed at weakening the power of the central government and bolstering the *Länder* governments' powers in finance and administration. Initially all the political parties opposed these interventions, but ultimately, in order to "avoid an impasse," the CDU/CSU agreed to comply with the Allied objections — thereby prompting Schumacher's charge that Adenauer was the "Chancellor of the Allies."

When the Basic Law was promulgated in the summer of 1949 as a "provisional" constitution until the achievement of reunification, it was the constitution of a bourgeois democracy much like any other. Nevertheless there remained a residue of the immediate postwar desire for socialism, as had been anchored in, e.g., the socialization articles of several *Länder* constitutions. This desire found expression in Articles 14, 15 and 20 of the Basic Law, which allowed for a possible transferral of land, natural resources and the means of production into public ownership, subject to the payment of compensation "determined upon a just consideration of the public interest and of the interests of the persons affected," and which declared the Federal Republic to be a "democratic and social federal state."[8]

These three articles, particularly Article 15, have since 1949 always been the starting point of any left-wing proposals for a constitutional or "legal" transition to socialism. For they can be interpreted to mean (a) that the state has a mandate to socialize all industries and firms exercising undue power in society, (b) that, in addition to the industries specified, the articles' provisions can be extended to include insurance, shipping, commercial organizations, etc., and (b) that compensation "determined upon a just consideration of the public interest" need by no means be the full value of the expropriated properties, since the whole purpose of nationalization would be to remove the concentration of power in the economy; to repay the full value of such properties would basically be merely to perpetuate this concentration of power in the form of money or credits rather than property or plants.

Perhaps the most significant and enduring decision to emerge from the constitutional deliberations was the complex of legislation which gave rise to the so-called "Chancellor Democracy." This legislation was the product of an effort to come to terms with a number of problems arising from the recent past and contemporary situation. First and foremost, the western occupation powers' objections had to be accounted for, which meant substantially the restoration of liberal democracy and capitalism. But this occurred at a time when it was widely thought that political democracy alone was no longer adequate to solve the social and economic problems thrown up by fascism and war.[9]

The dualist system of presidial and parliamentary powers of the Weimar Republic was also overcome, negatively, by simply reducing the President's powers and having him elected directly by Parliament, and positively, by greatly increasing the executive's (and especially the Chancellor's) powers vis-à-vis Parliament. This was accomplished by the so-called "constructive vote of censure" which made practically impossible the Chancellor's overthrow by vote of parliament. The possibility of a proliferation of minor parties was limited by the "Five per cent Clause," which denied parliamentary representation (and hence financing from federal funds) to parties obtaining less than five per cent of the overall vote. Any expression of popular will by means of plebiscite was virtually excluded. The effect of all this legislation was to invest the Chancellor and the Executive with a great deal of power. It, combined with Adenauer's forceful style of leadership and his ability to accumulate and exercise power, and reinforced by the growing importance of international policy decisions[10] (which were taken by the Executive), the Economic Miracle which set in shortly afterward, and the tense atmosphere of the Cold War, constituted the fundamental elements of Chancellor Democracy in postwar western Germany.

It would be a serious mistake to regard the CDU/CSU as merely a continuation of one or another of the old bourgeois parties from the Weimar Republic as, say, the spokesman for the Catholic Church like the old Zentrum, or the representative of business like Hugenburg's former DNVP. This simplistic view, to which the KPD and some factions of the German Left have occasionally succumbed, completely overlooks the fact that the CDU/CSU which emerged between 1945 and 1949 was a qualitatively new kind of political party in Germany.

Firstly, the CDU/CSU, more than any other West German political party, was a product of its time. The negative precedent of the fragmentation of the bourgeois camp, during the Weimar Republic, the strong apolitical-authoritarian tradition of modern German history and the success of the NSDAP in attracting support from all classes and strata — albeit disproportionately from the middle classes — surely played an important role in the postwar organization of the CDU.[11] Secondly, the creation of an all-christian front and the inclusion of both major religious denominations within a single political party had never before been achieved.[12]

Ideologically, thirdly, the party has never committeed itself to a single consistent and logical ideology; instead it has employed a series of simplified concepts and platitudes and adapted its platforms to suit the changing socioeconomic situation. Fourthly, support for the party came from all classes: at election time roughly all occupational and income groups voted in almost equal proportions for the CDU or CSU.[13] In other words, the CDU/CSU, the *Volkspartei* par excellence, "play(ed) a mediating and integrating role between the social partners which (was) hardly different from that of the state itself." [14]

Indeed, what was really "new" about the CDU, as Professor Narr has written, was that it is a conglomerating party, "a *Volkspartei* of a new type which does not in some way qualitatively comprise the people, but adapts to it and guides it in and through this adaptation."[15] But at the same time it was not a movement demanding a concerted effort from its members in order to achieve well-defined goals; its only goal was the retention of the socio-economic status quo of which it was an integral part and main beneficiary. Therefore it must also be seen as an "interest" or "aggregation" party. For example, the basically conservative and pro-business attitude of the CDU regime did not prevent it from making limited concessions to a number of trade union, refugee or pensioners' demands, such as the codetermination laws of 1951/52, home construction assistance or social welfare measures. The social committees and "labour wing" of the CDU continued to function as party minorities, but the social reform they aimed at was no longer the creation of a new social order and the elimination of class cleavages; they now wanted a share of economic prosperity, a stake in the burgeoning liberal-capitalist economy and increased social security benefits.

Ralph Miliband's comments are most illuminating in this context:

> . . . conservatism, however pronounced, does not entail the rejection of all measures of reform, but lives on the contrary by the endorsement and promulgation of reform at the least possible cost to the existing structure of power and privilege.
>
> Nevertheless, the conservative parties, for all their acceptance of piecemeal reform and their rhetoric of classlessness, remain primarily the defence organizations, in the political field, of business and property. What they really 'aggregate' are the different interests of the dominant classes.[16]

Thus the CDU/CSU was able to present itself as reformist, progressive, representative of the General Will, religious, modern, above-party, anti-communist, or whatever the exigencies of the current situation demanded, and this it could do with some justification, for it was simultaneously all and — with the possible exception of anticommunist — none of these.

b. Socio-economic factors

Following some initial reverses, the massive upswing of economic prosperity throughout the 1950's played a substantial role in politics: in the consolidation of the CDU State, the rise of business and the restoration of the old social and economic relationships. The structural weaknesses in Ludwig Erhard's neoliberal economic policy — low wages and pensions, excessive burden of taxation borne by the broad masses, high (nine per cent) unemployment and a disproportionate gap between the incomes of the upper and lower classes[16a] — were ameliorated by the Korean conflict, which increased the gross national product and promoted the vital export drive.

There was indeed an element of fortuitousness about the *Wirtschaftswunder*, based as it was upon trade and industrial exports. The economic factors which conspired, as it were, to encourage German economic expansion were: the world market's high rate of demand at a time when Germany had spare industrial capacity and the right products, a high rate of unemployment and great reserves of skilled labour created by the influx of refugees from the East which resulted in low costs, restraint on the part of the trade unions and organized labour, the absence of military expenditures, relatively low public expenditure and low consumer demand. This situation was exploited fully through the government's policies, within the framework of the "social market economy," of granting generous tax exemptions to export industries and removing or reducing tariffs to encourage exports and eliminate inefficiency [17]

— interventions which of course in themselves give the lie to claims that the West German economy was based on laissez-faire or liberal capitalism.[18]

Nevertheless, some very impressive economic gains were made during the reconstruction or extensive phase[19] of the Economic Miracle throughout the 1950's and into the intensive phase of the early 'sixties. Between 1950-1963, the gross national product quadrupled, signifying a growth rate of 11 per cent annually. And taking 1950 as a base year (= 100), the index of industrial production reached 225 in 1959.[20] Domestic production increased more rapidly in West Germany than anywhere else in western Europe and was second globally only to Japan: the average rate of growth between 1950-1959 was 7.5 per cent per annum.[21] Shortages in housing, living standards and social benefits which had been considered impossible to overcome within thirty or forty years were eliminated within a decade.

A most important (in terms of domestic politics) effect of the *Wirtschafts-wunder* was a strengthening of the relative wealth — and hence power — of the upper classes vis-à-vis the subordinate classes. In the decade between 1949 and 1959, it can be said that the rapid rise of income took the place of redistribution. Here it must be recalled that any number of statistics exist for the economic boom in postwar Germany, as for any other large-scale economic trend, and these statistics can be employed in a variety of ways, depending upon the purposes or interests of the economist or social scientist. The essential point here is that the greatest beneficiaries of the *Wirtschaftswunder* were the business elite and the CDU-led bourgeois coalition with whom the "Miracle" was identified.

To be sure, the working classes also gained materially from the rapid rise in prosperity. If real wages were 100 in 1950, they had risen to 143 in 1958,[22] which meant that the working classes also had a vital stake in, and felt a certain degree of identification with, the capitalist economy. Conversely, the process of concentration continued unabatedly during the same period, with the result that the percentage of the gross national product used for private consumption actually declined as that devoted to investment or channeled into profits increased.[23] According to Viktor Agartz, by 1954 a process of "capitalist expropriation" had taken place and created an "absolute identity of state and business."[24] While the claims of the invalid and destitute, the necessary concessions made to the CDU "labour wing," the provision of social security measures and the bourgeois coalition's need to retain supporters from a variety of social classes precluded this identity from becoming absolute, there can be no doubt that the influence of business "was probably greater in the Federal Republic than at any other time in German history."[25]

The concentration of economic power and the rapid rise of business concerns would have been inconceivable without an active state policy biased heavily in favour of these groups. Enormous subventions, tax benefits and generous write-offs, legislation favouring industrial exports to, in particular, the Common Market partner countries, state economic planning, investments and interventions, declining amounts of social security payments as a percentage of the overall national budget, the low ceiling on progressive taxation (50% maximum; cf. USA 80%, U.K. 90%) — all these are evidence of the CDU State's promotion and encouragement of business in postwar West Germany. No wonder Gabriel Almond found a "high degree of satisfaction" among businessmen with the policies of Konrad Adenauer.[26]

Broadly speaking, this excessive influence of business in the CDU State was exercised in three ways: through the party, through public opinion and through direct contacts with the cabinet and administration. Now the all-class reservoir from which the CDU/CSU drew its electoral support did in fact prevent it from becoming entirely the party of business, as explained above, but the vast sums of money donated by business,[27] not only to the CDU/CSU but also to the executive and administration,[28] ensured its ascendancy within the "party of all the people," while the support of "all the people" ensured the party's success at the polls. Hence the pre-eminence in Federal German politics of the interest group and lobby. In Bonn there are more than 300 offices of various organizations, associations and interest groups whose main task is to promote contacts with or extract favours from the parties or government.[29]

Since 1949 the business community has proven to be extremely efficient at organization, publicity and negotiation in defence of its interests. For these purposes, it is organized into three principal agencies, the Federation of German Industry (BDI), Federation of German Employers' Associations (BDA), and the German Chamber of Industry and Commerce (DIHT). [30] Among these organizations there was and is a considerable degree of consultation, cooperation and indeed cooptation. They sponsor jointly the German Institute of Industry which coordinates their work to some degree and arranges meetings, conferences and luncheons for members. Thus, despite the high degree of "heterogeneity" which Lewis Edinger purports to have found in the business community, western German business was and is rather more characterized by a high degree of cohesion, cooperation and concentration. All these developments were encouraged by Adenauer's well-known preference for bypassing parliament and entering into direct negotiations with the representatives of business.[31] Lobbies and pressure groups unable to achieve their ends through influence on parliamentary committees and ministries would turn to the Chancellor's office, where their demands would then usually be met. [32]

Two of the leading observers of contemporary Germany, Ralf Dahrendorf and Lewis J. Edinger, have argued at length against the thesis of the primacy of business in the Federal Republic. Edinger believes that the "countervailing power" of government and non-government elements is too strong and that business is too divided according to "competition" and "specialization" to be completely dominant.[33] Dahrendorf discusses the existence of a non-cohesive "abstract elite" and argues that "nobody governs Germany; Germany is governed."[34] Both Dahrendorf and Edinger, whose works cannot be ignored, continue to employ categories and concepts applicable in the nineteenth and early twentieth centuries in analysing — in Reinhard Kühnl's words (discussing Dahrendorf) —

> . . . the completely different situation of modern mass democracy in which political power (*Staatsgewalt*) is at least partially legitimated, while at the same time the advanced capitalist, oligopolistic 'economy', characterized by concentrated economic power, only represents a small minority of the people. [35]

For even if one accepts that a great variety of social groups — ranging from old-age pensioners to independent professionals, from some sectors of the working class to the remnants of the old aristocracy — support the CDU/

CSU, that business is to some extent "heterogeneous" (that is, except when threats to its basic controlling position are posed from the side of labour or the lower classes), and that neither business nor its political representatives are in a position of absolute control of economy and society (it has been attempted to demonstrate above that the manner in which its power is exercised is much more subtle and indirect) — despite these objections, business still remains the most powerful single social economic group in West Germany.

To repeat: by far the greatest beneficiary of the CDU State is, and always has been, business, a fact which is underlined by the existence of the vast body of legislation favouring business, the ever-increasing degree of concentration in industry which now exceeds that attained during the Weimar Republic and Third Reich, and the growing personal wealth, in relative as well as absolute terms, of a smaller and smaller percentage of the population.[36]

Did a Restoration of the old — pre-1933 or pre-1945 — socio-economic relationships in fact take place in postwar western Germany? Certainly the vast social changes effected by the war and the creation of two German states (expropriation of the Junkers, influx of masses of refugees into the West, the total discrediting of the Nazi political elite, etc.) precluded a total reversion to the prewar situation. But if the discussion is in terms of the restoration of a certain climate, about the *basic* continuity of the old social and economic system and about the fact that "in the West no fundamental political reforms have taken place,"[37] then the theory of a Restoration takes on considerable validity. The principal effect of the elimination of the Junkers, the old aristocracy and the excessive power of the Prussian military caste was to eliminate the vestigial remnants of the feudal system (except for the Church), and hence to make the capitalist system more functional by increasing business' relative ascendancy in society and economy.

This fact may be what Professor Ortlieb had in mind in discussing the "disintegrating effect" of the market economy or the "hedonistic happiness" afforded by it,[38] or what Lewis Edinger has referred to as "the climate of hedonistic materialism, pragmatic egocentrism and ruthless competitiveness which seems to characterize the spirit of the new mass-consumption and achievement oriented society."[39]

In the absence of a desire to effect fundamental reforms or to change the educational, press, judicial, administrative or political structures, the need for changing the old elites was non-existent. On the contrary, replacing them would have been dysfunctional; they had after all already proven their ability to do the jobs required of them. Thus there is an extremely high degree of continuity in the military, ecclesiastical and administrative elites. Although not quite half of the economic elite occupied the same positions as they had between 1940-44, the overwhelming majority had been born into the upper classes.[40] And where Dahrendorf has pointed out that no cabinet ministers has the same position in 1955 as they had had between 1940-44,[41] on the other hand not more than eleven per cent of the 1956 political elite could be said to have been part of the anti-Nazi counter-elite, and of these at least half were SPD supporters.[42]

Similarly, the old elitist educational system remains virtually unchanged: the former three-class school system, operating on a denominational basis, has ensured that access to higher education has remained a privilege of the upper classes. And press concentration has even increased in scale in comparison with the Weimar press. [43]

In the previous chapter it was argued that the churches emerged relatively powerful after World War II and acquired more influence in government and society than they had had either in the Third Reich or the Weimar Republic. Since 1949, the actual number of laws promulgated directly on behalf of the churches has not been great, it is true, but those few laws — the child subsidy law of 1954, for example, or the 1961 supplementary law on divorce — have always been, in Rudolf Augstein's words, "contrary to good sense."[44] On 26 March 1957, the Federal Constitutional Court ruled that the Concordat signed between the Vatican and the rulers of the Third Reich was still binding on the Federal Republic.

The churches' role, however, has been far less one of active participation in the formulation and propagation of new laws than of opposition to any amendments to existing laws and resistance to the promulgation of "progressive" legislation. On the one hand the Church has established itself as a "guardian" of the constitution, democracy and social market economy, as well as the implacable foe of communism, socialism and permissiveness. And on the other hand it has actively attempted to resist proposed legislation, or the repeal of existing legislation, concerning a wide range of "morality laws" such as: divorce laws, equal rights for illegitimate children, artificial insemination, the notorious *Kuppeleigesetze* (co-habitation laws), and birth control, sterilization, abortion and homosexuality legislation. In the first case the Churches' policy is probably best described as conservative; in the second case positively reactionary.

In postwar West Germany, with the population about equally divided between Catholic and Protestant and only about three per cent of the overall population not registered as members of one of the two major churches, the churches' influence on society is obviously not inconsiderable. This is especially so in consequence of the CDU State's decision to reintroduce the old *Kirchensteuer* (percentage of wages collected by the government and paid, tax-free, to the church of the donor's "choice"). These monies, which increase annually with the overall rise in prosperity, together with the churches' vast income from properties and investments — which need not be accounted for either to any public authority or to the churches' membership — enable them to exert an influence on public life on a scale very large in comparison with other advanced capitalist countries. Some of the activities which the churches carry on are youth clubs, social services, educational and political tasks, denominational schools, family counselling, delegation of representatives to educational and radio-television advisory boards, etc.

And finally, the involvement of the Church in party politics has always been considerable, and this involvement has almost invariably been on the side of the bourgeois coalition, predominantly the CDU/CSU, and in any case against the Left. The Church has been in fact one of the most influential subscribers to anticommunism (as described in the next section) in the Federal Republic and, until very recently, a decided and decisive opponent of the SPD.[45]

By far the most striking and ominous aspect of the Restoration was the return of former Nazis, beginning in the early 1950's, to prominent positions in public and civil life. The western occupation powers' role in the instigation of this process has been outlined in Chapter II. For David Childs, the "Restoration" was simply a "massive reinstatement of former officials of the Third Reich and pensions for those who could not be given their old jobs back."[46] But Ossip Flechtheim's term "renazification"[47] is more useful here because it implies (a) that at least an attempt at denazification preceded it, and (b) the renazification was only one of a number of symptoms of the overall Restoration in society, economy and politics.

Konrad Adenauer himself, of whom it can be said that he was neither pro-nor anti-Nazi, seemed to have a curiously "blind spot" when it came to appointing former National Socialists to important political posts. Thus Dr. Hans Globke, Adenauer's Secretary of State for the Chancellery and close confidant, had not only helped to write the authoritative commentary to the Nuremberg Race Laws, he had also been instrumental in drafting these laws. Indeed former Nazis were represented in Adenauer's first cabinets: Theodor Oberlander, Minister of Refugees; Gerhard Schröder, Minister of the Interior; Hans-Christoph Seebohm, Minister of Transportation — a full one-third of Adenauer's first cabinet in all. Many more Nazis found their way into the diplomatic service, the judiciary (where at least two-thirds and probably about three-quarters of all judges serving in the 1950's had also served the National Socialist regime), the *Länder* governments, the Bundeswehr, top positions in business and government service.[48] And it is estimated that in the three years between 1949 and 1952, more than 70 "significant" right-wing organizations were established in the German Federal Republic.[49] In Professor Kühnl's words, since

> . . . important positions of leadership are in the hands of groups who consorted with fascism, who profited from fascism and were intellectually affected by it, it is not surprising that authoritarian and fascist tendencies are at work here in a variety of forms.[50]

Nor is it surprising that during the 1960's even the highest representatives of the Federal Republic, President Lübke and Chancellor Kiesinger, were both nominated by "groups who had had important functions in the fascist period",[51] indeed had both been closely involved with National Socialism, Kiesinger as party member and functionary in Goebbels' Propaganda Ministry and Lübke as builder and alleged (but not definitively proven) constructor of concentration camps.

A new quality was introduced into the Restoration, beginning in 1959, with the so-called "reprivatization," or return to private ownership, of the Preussische Bergwerks- und Hütten-A.G., followed by similar actions in 1961 with Volkswagen and in 1965 with the Vereinigte Elektrizitäts- und Bergwerks-A.G. The predictable result of this process was a further strengthening of management's power vis-à-vis the now atomized and uninformed shareholders on the one hand and the firms' employees on the other, and thus a further stage in the Restoration.[52]

c. Supra-national factors

It is difficult to overestimate the part that armaments production and the armaments economy has played in the entrenchment of the CDU State. The question of rearming the Federal Republic first occurred in late 1947, in connection with the policy of "roll-back," and gained further impetus with the outbreak of the Korean War. Due to popular opposition,[52] however, rearmament did not begin until after the Treaty of Brussels came into effect in May 1955. This was followed by a series of laws throughout 1955 and 1956 providing for voluntary military service, production of war materials and universal conscription. About this time rumours began to circulate, fed by a rather imprudent declaration by Defence Minister Strauss, that the government had decided to acquire atomic weapons.[53]

Of a large number of writings and speeches which appeared in connection with German rearmament in this period, two in particular, an anonymous article in Viktor Agartz' *WISO-Korrespondenz*[54] and a pamphlet by the trade unionist Theo Pirker,[55] pointed out that a number of groups stood to gain from rearmament. Taken together, the two articles designated the beneficiaries as: (a) the three western occupation powers: Britain, France and the USA, (b) the CDU/CSU and the bourgeois coalition, (c) the upper classes, above all big business, and (d) the military.

The *occupation powers* stood to gain collectively by a corresponding decline in the occupation costs as the West Germans assumed an increasing share of the defence burden, as well as by the reduction of Germany's competitive industrial strength through the diversion of large sums of money and a considerable percentage of her productive capacity into arms production. England in particular, but France as well, were threatened by German competition in manufacturing exports. American industry also initially profited from many exports of war materials to Germany, especially since weapons and weapons systems were manufactured according to American standards. For all three a rearmed West Germany would be a buffer in case of war with the USSR and would absorb the initial impact.

The *ruling political parties*, it is evident, desired rearmament in order to stabilize both the domestic and export economy upon whose success their own fortunes as guardians and beneficiaries of the status quo depended. Moreover, the new military could be used, if necessary, to quell any serious domestic uprising.

The *upper classes* were of course also interested in preserving the existing system. This included, broadly, the civil service, diplomatic corps, and the military and business elites. The state could safeguard the entire economy as a reliable and large-scale customer protecting the economy against crises and fluctuations. For:

> Under the banner of 'surplus' armaments in the West today have acquired a new function: where they formerly increased the scarcity of goods, today they facilitate the flourishing of an economy which, in the western industrial states, is constantly in the shadow of the danger of overproduction and underconsumption . . . Without armaments our partial welfare society would be scarcely conceivable; we would then only have this choice: either mass unemployment and poverty, or total welfare and social society.[56]

When Professor Flechtheim elsewhere concludes that "our welfare state is thus also a military state, our social capitalism also armaments capitalism,"[57] he is further underlining the fact that armaments and arms production have become the most stable element, and as such a principal support of advanced capitalism in West Germany.

Just as the Economic Miracle restored much of the lost prestige of business, so rearmament helped immensely to make the *military* more respectable again. As already mentioned, many generals who had fought against the Weimar Republic and served the Third Reich faithfully — including assisting in the round-up of Jews and the shootings of hostages[58] — were accorded high positions in the Federal Army. But the new military was even further handicapped: it lacked the participants of the 20th July Conspiracy who represented the "morally strongest" and "politically most valuable"[59] elements in the Wehrmacht.

There was, incidentally, one further beneficiary who was not considered at the time: Walter Ulbricht, who represented the other status quo:

> . . . in going ahead with West German rearmament, the Western allies had now done more: they had ensured that East Germany became the front line of Soviet security, and they correspondingly increased Ulbricht's importance in the Eastern bloc. At the same time they made him and his government even more subject to Soviet supervision and control.[60]

As will be discussed below, the existence of a strong and uncompromising East German state was entirely compatible with Adenauer's purposes. In any event, if until 1956 there had been any prospect of German reunification, following the rearming of the Federal Republic national unity could practically be achieved only by an act of war.

Thus armaments expenditures rose dramatically: from ten per cent of the federal budget in 1956 to 32% in 1964, from a non-existent force to over 600,000 men (446,000 of whom were soldiers, the remainder civilians), so that by the early 1960's Federal Germany's forces had exceeded those of France and Britain and were second only to the USA within NATO.[61] The military was now a force to be reckoned with in economy and society.

By the time of currency revaluation, at the latest, West Germany had embarked on a unilateral process of integration into the West. The formation of a separate western state, the rejection of all Soviet attempts to attain a modus vivendi — e.g. the 1951 overtures prior to the Korean War or Stalin's note of March 1952 — with West Germany, entry into the European Coal and Steel Community, the European Defence Community (EDC), the Organization for Economic Cooperation and Development (OECD), later the customs union, the Council of Europe and the World Bank and Monetary Fund were all steps leading toward the integration of the western partial state into the (capitalist) West. The crowning act, through which the Federal Republic recovered its autonomy by cooperating with the western Allies, came with German entry into NATO in 1955. In exchange for assigning all her military forces to a European command, West Germany was granted full independence and the repeal of the Occupation Statute. This meant, on the one hand, that:

> Instead of Germany's recovery becoming again a threat to the stability of Europe or leading to a disruption of the international system, it became an inseparable part of the process of western integration, and as such helped to make the international order more stable.[62]

But on the other hand, the CDU's continued policy of reunification on the basis of the absorption of the DDR into the Federal Republic was logically more contradictory with each successive step toward western integration. The Soviet Union could not permit its sphere of influence in Germany to be incorporated into a state which was a leading member of a coalition founded upon implacable opposition to it. The twin aim which the West German policy implied, namely the re-creation of a Gross-Deutschland and the dissolution of the East German Communist state — to say nothing of the regaining of lands since incorporated into Poland or the USSR— could be attained by one method only — force.

Adenauer himself was under no illusions concerning the direction this policy would lead West Germany. In a famous remark made in 1954 to the French High Commissioner, François-Poncet, he declared: "Don't forget that I am the only German Chancellor who has preferred the unity of Europe over the unity of his own country." In this sense, there is no doubt that Adenauer was a "good European." And Adenauer was able to turn to his own ends the current wave of pro-Europeanism. This pro-West sentiment now evident in the Federal Republic, as Gabriel Almond has suggested, [63] was rooted in a number of factors: (a) a genuine current based on religious, cultural, economic or political considerations, (b) a desire to achieve political and economic dominance through integration, and (c) an attempt to "escape into Europe," which may have been the most important:

> As we know, Hitler had committed the greater part of his crimes in the east — against the 'Slavonic and Jewish sub-humans.' Clearly, the whole people had carried out these crimes, but equally clearly only a part of the people were to bear the consequences: all those, that is, who remained under communist domination. It was to be expected that the western part of the population would wish to seek refuge in an alliance with the United States, or in any European or Atlantic sanctuary which would preserve it from the danger of having to pay part of the bill even now. Any agreement on Germany with the Soviets would have forced the West Germans to bear an indirect share of reparations, to conduct an active and unremitting struggle against the remnants of the SED regime, and to make their neutrality acceptable to the Western countries. [64]

The central point about West German integration into the West — and this point was largely ignored or misunderstood by the contemporary Left [65] — is that it coincided with a new stage in monopoly capitalism, with what might be termed "internationalized" advanced capitalism. Postwar capitalism had to be qualitatively different from its predecessor for a number of historical reasons: the discrediting of "national" monopoly capitalism by the rise of fascism and the results of the war; geographical limitations imposed upon old-style imperialism by the existence of communist or socialist states and the growing trends in the Third World toward the rejection of capitalist forms of development; all-out competition between the capitalist and communist states; and, in Elsner's words, "the tendency toward internationalization of economic life under the pressure of the scientific-technological revolution. [66]

All these factors combined to create a great drive toward efficiency, maximum utilization of capital and natural resources, intensification of production and increased rationalization — which in turn brought about an increased degree of concentration and monopolization extending beyond national boundaries. As foreign trade thus came to take on a greater and greater share of the national product and as international corporations and capital pools arose in response to these pressures, it became incumbent upon the state as guardian and representative of capitalist interests to create the supra-national framework to facilitate these developments and to increase the capitalist state's competitive ability vis-à-vis the communist states. This it has accomplished through the agencies of economic integration: OECD, currency and customs union and above all ECM. The supra-national agencies so created then elude national control because they operate largely outside the indigenous legal system, but at the same time benefit from special supra-national regulations (tax write-offs, subsidies designed to increase their competitive ability); the reciprocal effect of this process has been to increase the capital reserves and power concentration of the large monopolies who alone have the resources to exploit fully new technological findings and achieve the required degree of rationalization.

These developments are not only economic; they are also highly political. They tend, firstly, to enhance the power and influence of large capital within each country. And secondly, they lend themselves readily to an international capitalist strategy, e.g. NATO, "roll-back" of communism or a "policy of strength," in so far as they (a) wage the "war of statistics" of domestic production and economic development, and (b) supply the required arms and armament technology for the event of a "defensive" war.

And finally, the growth of supra-national organizations has been an effective weapon of the upper classes against labour. Not only, as just stated, do they increase monopoly capitalism's power within the respective country, but the ECM, for example, as an organization created by capitalists for capitalists, is necessarily directed against labour. The Council of the Common Market and its respective organs are far removed from popular control: labour has only 35 of 107 members in the Economic and Social Committee, which in any case is appointed by the Council of Ministers.[67] And, until 1969, the Italian and French Communist Parties were denied representation in the Council, while delegates from minuscule liberal parties were admitted. Capital, once internationalized in this way, has then been in an even better position to ignore the workers' social demands, or to put down strikes, since it can move funds or resources to the most favourable regions or countries, as changing circumstances should require.[68]

Thus integration into the West meant for West German business the creation of a new dimension of power based on internationalization, while labour's scope and influence were still confined to the national level. This development was reinforced, indeed facilitated, by rearmament and arms production, and would not have been possible without the Restoration in society and economy and the dominant position of business, which in turn were favoured by the establishment of Chancellor Democracy and the CDU State. By 1960, West Germany had become one of the most efficient and effective advanced capitalist countries in the world. This was the CDU State. The CDU/CSU was so successful in gaining popular support — in 1957 it obtained the only absolute majority ever given any party in "free" elections in German history — and in fashioning "its" state that it determined the whole pattern and issues of postwar politics. The consequencies of this to the Left, as will be demonstrated below, were disastrous.

2. The Ideology of Clerical Anticommunism

To return for a moment to the previous section, it has been argued that a large part of the CDU/CSU's strength can be attributed to its success in propagating a popular image of itself as the guardian of the national interest, standing above particular, sectional and class interests and embodying the General Will. Since the CDU/CSU has never aspired to effect fundamental changes, or even extensive reforms, but aimed instead at retaining power within and as part of the existing socio-economic system, its "ideology," on closer examination, proves to be basically a glorification of the status quo. Thus the "social market economy" is a useful euphemism for advanced capitalism. "Freedom and security in foreign policy" meant virtually unqualified support for the West and the conduct of the Cold War, which signified anything but freedom and security. The "national interest" in particular signified reunification on terms extremely perilous to the "maintenance of peace." The personalization of politics in the form of Adenauer, or later Erhard, Strauss and Kiesinger, points further to a lack of basic policy. The emphasis on success and accomplishment veil the fact that only a small minority obtained "success" or acquired substantial wealth.

So far, none of these elements differs essentially from the ruling "ideologies" in other western nations. What was distinctive about the prevailing ideology of the CDU State, however, can be summed up in the formula "clerical anticommunism" — a combination of a clericalism which, running through the polity, does not exist to the same degree in any other advanced capitalist country, and an irrational form — but with very rational goals — of anticommunism comparable only to American McCarthyism, with the important difference that the West German anticommunists were not attempting to expose or undermine the government; they were part of it.[1]

We have already criticized at length the immanent contradictions of christian socialism and the churches' conservative role in postwar western Germany. Here it remains only to state that this political christianity — the invocation of God, "the West," or "christian civilization" to justify the restoration of the old socio-economic relationships, the failure to effect fundamental reforms and the perpetuation of the division of Germany — was employed in the CDU State to a far greater degree, and with far greater effectiveness, than it had been either in the Weimar Republic or the early stages of the Third Reich.

Clericalism and anticommunism were closely interrelated. An essential part of the struggle for the West against the "anti-christian" forces was the fight against communism. Heinrich Werner has demonstrated how the basic anticommunist orientation of the christian churches has, with some outward modifications, continued from the Second Reich through the Weimar Republic and the Third Reich into the Federal Republic. For example, the notion of a decisive battle (*Entscheidungskampf*) between the "christian" West and "Asian Bolshevism" has always been an integral part of the churches' political *Weltanschauung*.[2] And even when the churches have not actively propagated anticommunist ideas or emotions, the basic ideological predisposition which they have helped to produce has frequently lent itself to application in the service of reactionary anticommunism. Let one example stand for many: when extreme right-wing circles began calling for atomic

weapons for the Federal Republic in 1956, they were able to declare, among
other things, that the choice for the atom bomb was more than a military
decision, that it was also a christian decision; the soldiers supporting this
policy were said to "believe that the destruction of physical existence is little
against the ravage of the soul and conscience by an absolute ideology. They
have already learned how dead one can be while one's body still lives."[3] Such
statements were almost never challenged by the churches as such, but at most
by individual clergymen.

The well-known words: "A specter is haunting Europe — the specter of
Communism. All the powers of old Europe have entered into a holy alliance to
exorcise this specter," recall that anticommunism has existed as long as
communism itself. In Germany it has been used to vindicate ideologically the
semi-feudal Wilhelmian regime and the monopoly capitalist order of the
Weimar Republic. And "antibolshevism," as is well-known, was, next to anti-
semitism, one of the most salient features of the National Socialist ideology.
After 1945 it was only necessary to take up and propagate a latent feeling
already firmly imbedded in the popular consciousness.

This popular anticommunist feeling was strengthened after Stalingrad by
the military victories of the USSR against the Wehrmacht, the expulsions of
German minorities from the eastern European nations and the well-
publicized excesses of the Red Army on German territory (which conveniently
overlooked the outrages committed by German troops and the SS in the East).
The CDU State then knew how to use the Stalinist dictatorship under Walter
Ulbricht, the reparations it was forced to pay to the Soviet Union and its
consequent retarded economic development as a "bogey," as the black-and-
white alternative to the West German partial state which the bourgeois
coalition had been instrumental in establishing. A further impetus to this anticommunist mood came with the increasing integration of West Germany into
the western economic-military system, and especially as a result of her
position as the "front-line" against the "Iron Curtain" and the "forward
bastion of democracy."

The anticommunism prevalent in the immediate postwar period was at least
partly rational, and communist proposals were for a time discussed (if only to
be refuted) in party political debates. So long as the other parties offered
alternative proposals and programmes, the level of debate was comparatively
high. But in time, perhaps as early as the end of 1947, anticommunism began
to take on a different quality. Elements of irrationalism and emotionalism
were increasingly evident. Returning from a visit to Moscow in 1955, for
example, Adenauer declared:

> I learned at first hand that the Kremlin leaders are firmly convinced
> that Communism under Moscow leadership will one day rule the
> world. And . . . although I only travelled a few kilometers through the
> country, I could see on the faces of the men I met that they had lost
> their souls. People in Russia can no longer laugh or cry. They are
> without souls. Such a regime, I am more than ever convinced, is fatal
> to mankind.[4]

By the early 1950's anticommunism had gone from more or less objective
critique to *Weltanschauung* to irrational resentment. Such a development
cannot occur spontaneously; it must be promoted and encouraged. The one
new element in postwar anticommunism was the concept of totalitarianism,

which ignored the different starting points and developmental conditions of communism and fascism and regarded the two systems as essentially identical. "In this way the apologists of capital were relieved of the necessity of seriously analysing fascism, above all its roots in the capitalist system." [5]

Indeed, West German clerical anticommunism fulfilled, and was intended to fulfil a definite social function: what Reiche and Gäng have termed the "externalization of the class struggle"[6] or, in the words of the late Werner Hofmann, "the transposition of vertical intra-societal conflicts on to the horizontal level."[7] By means of diverting popular resentment away from socio-economic contradictions in domestic politics on to the foreign or external enemy, the bourgeois coalition and the dominant classes supporting it were able to support ideologically the continuation of the existing power structure and their own pre-eminent position within it. This exonerating or apologetic function of anticommunism vis-à-vis discredited capitalism and the old elites then lent itself, after 1949, to the vindication of the policies and omissions of the CDU State, from the western alliance which made peaceful reunification impossible to armament and arms production, to the Restoration, the ascendancy of business and the failure to effect fundamental domestic reforms.

More than this, the exaggeration of the "bolshevist threat" or the "communist conspiracy" on to a comprehensive emotional plane, beyond the bounds of normal credibility, transformed ideological anticommunism into an article of faith. The invocation of this faith then became a test of one's own loyalty to one's country, its "national interest" and even "the West." Thus any challenge to the existing constellation of power and possession — such as wage demands, advocacy of a neutral foreign policy or political protest — could be attacked as disloyal, communist-inspired or, even worse, treasonable. This is how anticommunism in West Germany has come to be used as a form of "social discipline,"[8] a negative method of enforcing social cohesion. The greater the "threat" was perceived to be, the more drastic the methods that could be used against it: the arrest of a high-school student for sending for materials from the DDR to use in a school essay, widespread detentions of suspected communists, public campaigns against the communist "Anti-Christ," etc.

Heinrich Hannover has outlined in some detail the basic methods of West German anticommunism.[9] These are worth discussing here — with some modification — since they reveal a great deal about the quality and effects of anticommunism and about the organizations and persons responsible for its execution.

The first method, *guilt by association*, or on the strength of contacts of any kind with communists, is probably best known. This technique consciously omits the purpose of the "accused's" visit to a communist country or talk with a communist functionary, and mentions only the fact of the visit or the name of the "contact."

A more insidious form is accusing an individual, organization, party, etc. of being *objectively in agreement with communist designs*. For example, although the Stockholm Appeal against atomic rearmament of 1950 was signed by a large number of prominent persons from many political persuasions, the fact that Max Reimann, the KPD leader, had also signed it was used to demonstrate that the other signatories were in agreement with communist goals. Or in many instances, merely proposing negotiations with the DDR brought charges of treason upon well-meaning persons. Attacks on the ex-Nazi Globke[10] were equated with support for communist policies, while at the same time support for him was made into a test of patriotic loyalty against the communist enemy.

The conditions of the Cold War were then exploited to create a united ideological front against this enemy by means of an outright *one-sided, polemical propaganda*. Every war was said to require the ideological solidarity of the whole population against the opponent, and those who declined to participate were branded as traitors to their own side. Any criticism of one's own government, for whatever reasons, was tantamount to betrayal. Alternatives were simplified: if one was against rearmament then one was against the state, the government and the West. Any critique of government policy, when attempted, must be matched with an equally strong criticism of the eastern regimes; but such criticism, directed with equal vehemence and lack of differentiation against both sides, was deprived of the power of specific criticism and was therefore ineffectual. "Freedom and human dignity," Hannover wrote, "have become for us relative concepts; the Cold War contains its own value which blinds us to the principles for which it is being waged."[11]

Instead of judging a political act by asking whom it benefited, the *cui bono* method asked only: does it benefit the Soviets (DDR, KPD)? This method was employed effectively in attacking the "Action Unatoned Nazi Justice"[12] on the grounds that the Action's supporting material originated in the DDR, and indeed in attacking the judges who confirmed the material's authenticity as "useful idiots" in the communists' service. This of course completely obfuscated the real issue, namely that large numbers of former National Socialists were in fact active in the judiciary.

The next stage, the method of *moral discrimination*, contained several elements of a total-authoritarian terror ideology. For example, opponents against atomic armaments were accused of an overriding opportunism in so far as they were said to hope that coming victory of communism would give them certain advantages and benefits. Furthermore, it was immoral to partake of economic prosperity and to attack it at the same time; if one was against the Federal Republic's social order, then one ought to go to live in East Germany. Or, when a scapegoat was needed, it could be found on the Left: when in August 1961 a scheduled public meeting was cancelled by a tear-gas bomb being thrown into the hall, Franz-Josef Strauss, acting upon not a shred of evidence, immediately placed the blame upon the German Peace Union (DFU) and the "draft dodgers."

The — desired and intended — result of the application of such methods was a great pressure toward social conformity. Accusations of anticommunism needed only to be levelled, not supported; the onus of proof then automatically went over to the accused who, even if he could prove his innocence, was "tainted" by the charge. Political proposals or policies were not judged according to their intrinsic value but by the degree to which they were associated with communist objectives or by the number of "eastern contacts" which their proposers were said to have had. Such defamation almost invariably meant the neutralization of independent-minded persons, particularly those on the Left. Professors, Nobel Prize winners, former anti-Nazis, distinguished public personalities, whole parties and organizations — all saw their influence diminished through the application of the techniques of anticommunism.

These developments also found their way into the legal system. Where once the publication and dissemination of political materials and tracts had been permitted, and indeed cited in evidence of the liberal nature of the CDU State, after the early 1950's even to subscribe to the SED organ, *Neues Deutschland*, or to write to it became a criminal offence. It was also illegal to "import" publications sponsored by the SED or FDGB and to distribute these in West Germany. This represented a serious infringement upon the right of information (about the "enemy"). Laws such as these then constituted a precedent which could be applied against the activities of the legal opposition, as e.g. in the "Spiegel Affair" of 1962.[13]

The actual practice of anticommunism in the Federal Republic, almost incidentally, infringed considerably upon the liberal rights of freedom of information and expression, and upon the ideals of peace and coexistence which it was supposed to be upholding. Freedom tended to be defined negatively, in terms of the state's relationship to communism: the *defence* of "freedom and democracy" became itself "freedom." Similarly, advocating peace and coexistence was equated with supporting communism. According to the extreme right-wing *Rotbuch*, peace for the communists meant world revolution, and hence those in the West desiring peace were "fighters for the world revolution."

Thus considered, clerical anticommunism was an integral component of the CDU as perhaps its major ideological support. Even though the actual "threat" of communism declined in time, it had to be perpetuated subjectively in order to uphold the order which it vindicated. This meant, however, that there was "a connection between business interests, anticommunism and the heightening of the international conflict,"[14] since:

> Beyond all subjective claims of the ruler and ruled, one can establish objectively a connection between the class and power structure within a society and the antagonism of the established system of power. The antagonism of the system contributes to the maintenance of the hierarchical order within the group, while the internal stratification contributes to the consolidation of the external contradictions.[15]

One of the central reasons for the continued ascendancy of the CDU/CSU was its ability to equate the government it formed with the state and society in the popular consciousness, and the principal method by which it achieved this was clerical anticommunism. The converse of this identification of party with state and society was the equation of opposition with the disloyal, "communist-inspired forces of darkness." This is not an exaggeration. Witness Adenauer's claim in the 1953 election campaign that SPD candidates had received financial support from the DDR (which charge proved to be based on falsified documents), or the effectual 1957 campaign slogan: "Remember Hungary — Vote Adenauer!" The ostensibly total offensive against the "communist threat" was by no means aimed exclusively or even primarily against communism. For by the early 1950's the communists were no longer a serious domestic political force, and until the erection of the "Wall" in August 1961, there was always a possibility of achieving reunification through negotiations and concessions. Clerical anticommunism was pre-eminently intended to discredit and neutralize the "legal" political opposition, particularly any opposition that threatened the CDU State, the advanced capitalist order and the upper classes. In this it was immensely successful, and this success and its repercussions on the Left is the subject of the remainder of this chapter and most of those beyond.

3. The Isolation and Euthanasia of the KPD and the Problem of a Third Way

In attempting to ascertain the reasons for the success of clerical anti-communism in the German Federal Republic, as manifest in the isolation, lack of popular support for, and virtually uncontested legal ban on the Communist Party of Germany, one must turn repeatedly to the residual anticommunist feelings from the Third Reich,[1] the psychological force of the Cold War which equated the KPD with the SED and the latter with the Soviet "enemy," and the weight of the western occupation powers' policies. These are some of the more salient external factors. And the KPD itself exacerbated popular anticommunist sentiment through its uncritical identification with the SED and the CPSU, while the CDU-led bourgeois coalition was able to strengthen its power position through an adroit application of clerical anti-communism. All of these developments have been discussed in previous sections.

After 1946 the SED and KPD were officially two separate parties; the 8th Session of the KPD Executive Committee (*Vorstand*) of 3 January 1949 determined that "special conditions of struggle" necessitated the organizational division, which would represent "the first step toward an independent policy of the KPD."[2] But they, KPD and SED, remained, for various reasons, in quite close theoretical and organizational proximity. It was emphasized that full agreement existed on the "basic questions of German politics," including national unification and self-determination, the conclusion of a peace treaty, the unity of the labour movement and "the struggle against the transformation of West Germany into a protectorate of western imperialism."[3] Such a relationship, which after 1949 was compelled to overcome the two quite different national contexts created by the Cold War and the evolution of diametrically opposed social and economic systems, was bound to work to the disadvantage of the partner who did not enjoy political supremacy, mass popular support or the protection of the occupation powers. Following the formation of the separate East and West German states, the KPD thus found itself basically in the role of the adherent and executor of theories and policies which had been formulated under conditions quite different from those prevailing in the German Federal Republic.

This situation was one part of a *circus vitiosus* whose ultimate result was the decline of the KPD to a negligible political factor: excessive identification with the SED lost the party a great deal of popular support; and as contact with the masses receded, the party's structure and organization tended to ossify; which in turn prevented any new and necessary breakthroughs in theory, strategy or tactics; and this further contributed to the party's dwindling support.

Even after the currency reform and the promulgation of the Basic Law, the KPD still enjoyed sufficient popular support — which largely rested upon its role in the Resistance and the antifascist front after 1945 — to achieve 5.7 per cent of the popular vote in the first federal elections in 1949, although even this represented a substantial drop in the ten per cent and greater percentages the party had achieved in initial postwar *Länder* and local elections. But in the wake of the intensifying Cold War, the Czech coup, the Berlin Blockade, the Soviet offensive against "Titoism" and the East German campaign against proponents of the "German road to socialism," the KPD was caught up in a wave of purges, self-criticism and expulsions that could only impair its effectiveness in western Germany. When in mid-September 1949 a number of local cells submitted resolutions to the 13th Session of the Party Executive Committee, blaming a too great adherence to the policies of the USSR for the KPD's disappointing results in the elections, the Chairman, Max Reimann, called such proposals opportunistic and an expression of ideological weakness on the part of the KPD, and declared:

> Any dissociation from the policy of the Soviet Union, any toleration of evasions of our commitment to the Soviet Union and its policies leads inevitably to a nationalism of a Titoist character, to a betrayal of proletarian internationalism and thus to a slide into the camp of the enemies of democracy and socialism, leads inevitably into the camp of imperialism.[4]

A series of purges between 1949-51 saw the expulsion of a number of prominent secretaries of the Party Executive Committee, party organ editors and deputy chairman Kurt Müller who was kidnapped into the DDR and sentenced to a prison term of 25 years (but released in 1955). By September 1950, expulsion proceedings were pending against over 700 functionaries and members,[5] mostly on pretexts that they had maintained contacts with the CIA, the SPD's *Ostbüro*, Titoists, Trotskyists, or had become opportunists. But in retrospect it appears that the expulsions were directed primarily against the proponents of a more independent communist policy in the West and less dependence upon policies and directives formulated in East Berlin or Moscow. It is difficult to disagree with Hans Kluth's statement that: "Many functionaries of the KPD owed the fact that they did not share the same fate as so many of their comrades in the satellite states solely to the existence and institutions of the Federal Republic which they had so often called down."[6]

At the same time, the stricter organization of the party in the direction of "democratic centralism" proceeded apace with a correspondingly tighter discipline at all levels and the centralization of decision-making processes. This meant, e.g., that less recourse was made to rank and file opinion. The KPD held only two conventions during the years 1948-56: in Weimar in 1951 and in Hamburg in 1954. The less reference to members' opinions, the more the party structure grew rigid and bureaucratic, eventually employing one full-time secretary or clerk for every 40-50 party members (cf. the SPD with a ratio of 1:1500).[7]

Of course this extensive party machine increased the KPD's reliance on funds from the communist countries and restricted even further any potential development toward some form of "national" communism. Until 1956, the KPD had no Central Committee, Politburo or Executive Committee Secretariat of its own, and was required to submit a monthly report to the SED Executive Committee, on whom it was utterly financially dependent.[8]

This gradual isolation of the KPD leadership from the rank and file was matched by the growing dissociation of the other organizations of the labour movement from the party. Under Schumacher the SPD had rejected all proposals for a united labour front of KPD and SPD largely because of the undemocratic internal structure and political dependence of the KPD; after Schumacher the SPD, aiming at winning over voters from the bourgeois parties and basing a substantial part of its bid for power on an anticommunist appeal (cf. Ch. V below) was not interested in any kind of association with the communists, and indeed began more and more to define its own position by stressing the differences and contrasts between the two parties. And by the early 1950's the DGB was also not only concerned with gaining concessions from the existing socio-economic system rather than transforming it, it was also bound by the terms of its establishment to party political neutrality. Besides, by this time, most communist elements had been removed from the trade union organizations, and its (largely Social Democratic) leadership was growing increasingly anticommunist.

Party membership and electoral statistics provide telling evidence of the decline in popular support for the KPD. Where in 1947 it had had a membership of approximately 300,000, by 1956 (prior to the party's being banned) the figure had dropped to 70,000 and its percentage of the 1953 federal vote went down to 2.2. Even when allowances are made for the fact that membership figures were to some extent conditioned by the threatened ban of the party after 1951 and the social pressures of clerical anticommunism, and that the 1953 elections took place while the impression of the forcible suppression of the 1953 workers' rising in East Berlin was still vivid in the popular consciousness, there would nevertheless appear to be a positive correlation between decline in support for the KPD and the party's growing dependence on outside powers. By 1956 the West German KPD was smaller and less significant than any western European C.P., save that in Great Britain.

Nevertheless the KPD was not entirely insignificant in Federal German political life up to the time of the ban. It still had some influence in individual firms and factories, as well as on the local level, areas in which it had always been relatively strong. Although no longer an important force in the trade unions, the communists still maintained much of their former strength in works' councils and local cells. In 1954 the party was publishing thirteen daily newspapers with circulation figures of between 18,000 and 60,000 each, four weeklies, one fortnightly and three monthlies (of which *Wissen und Tat* and *Unser Weg* were the most important),[9] in addition to hundreds of leaflets and intra-firm or -factory newspapers. Though much of the content of these publications was shrill, insipid or repetitive, their propaganda value must have been considerable.

And in its role as the representative of the SED and CPSU in western Germany, the KPD was in a position to present some political alternatives not advocated by the other parties. Until at least 1956 it perpetuated the idea of a socialist and antifascist front but, after 1949, no longer on the basis of a formal merger of the two parties SPD and KPD; now the national front policy as contained in the 1949 and 1953 election programmes and confirmed at party conventions and Executive Committee sessions, was a patriotic "National Front of all Germans which is not bound to party barriers, differences of *Weltanschauung* or religious beliefs, but which includes all honest Germans who love their people and homeland,"[10] aiming at the establishment of a coalition government "of all German patriots acting on behalf of the German people."[11] Since the other parties were seen to have abandoned the national interest in agreeing to the Basic Law, rearmament, the continued occupation and the Western Alliance, the KPD proclaimed itself "more than a party": "We are the national consciousness, we are the real patriots who are showing the whole people the only possible way to its final salvation and who are fighting for this."[12]

An essential element in the national patriotic front was intended to be the conscious sectors among the SPD membership, who were supposed to see that their "right-wing" or "reactionary" leaders, such as Kurt Schumacher, Erich Ollenhauer or Carlo Schmid, were playing ". . . in reality the role of agents of American and English imperialists in the labour organizations of West Germany and (were) endeavouring to bring the German worker to an agreement with American-English Imperialism, the most malicious enemy of the working people of Germany and the entire world."[13] The fusion into a united labour front under KPD leadership must therefore take place on the lower levels in order to circumvent the "social fascist" SPD leadership.

As the political spokesman for West Germans opposed to Adenauer's and the western Military Government's policy of unilateral integration into the West, implying as it did the permanent division of Germany and a heightened threat of war, the KPD had appropriated for itself a potentially very powerful issue, particularly after Schumacher's death and the increasing integration of the SPD into the western partial state. For apart from the KPD, no other party officially represented such views, though these were certainly shared by a large number of West Germans, particularly among the independent Left. But, for reasons discussed above, the KPD was not in a position to sustain such policies credibly nor to form the vanguard of an opposition based on them. With its unremitting uncritical praise of Stalin and even of the excessive and occasionally brutal methods of expropriation employed in the people's democracies, its unfailing adaptation to all exigencies of Soviet foreign policy and its purges and internal discipline, the KPD alienated potential supporters among the independent Left whom its policies of national independence and self-determination should otherwise have gained for it. Its appeal to critically minded patriots was undermined by its ready agreement to the cession of former eastern territories and the establishment of the Oder-Neisse Line as Germany's eastern frontier. And finally, the KPD's opposition to the creation of the separate western state, beginning with its rejection of the Basic Law and extending to the Ruhr and Occupation statutes and the Paris Treaties, lost much of its weight by the simple fact that it was advanced by the KPD in precise reflection of what was the Soviet Line until 1955![14]

There is some evidence that the KPD never fully understood these immanent contradictions which prevented it from becoming the centre of a popular front aimed at regaining national unity. Among the reasons which the party gave for its losses in the 1949 elections were the success of misleading bourgeois propaganda, an undemocratic electoral system[15] and the SPD's strong anti-communist campaign. Certainly the KPD has always been the victim of misleading propaganda and the electoral system was to some extent undemocratic with the barriers placed upon the representation of small parties in parliament. But communist policies and platforms were sufficiently known and disseminated so as to have justified a better election result than 5.7 per cent of the vote. In its attacks on the KPD's lack of internal democracy and independent policies the SPD merely struck upon some of the real weaknesses of the postwar KPD. On the other hand the KPD more nearly approximated the real problem in stating that ". . . it did not come into the masses' consciousness that they decided against the interests of the nation, against life and the future of the people" and that the party's main error lay in its failure to convince the masses of the rightness of its own policies.[16] The KPD rightly saw that it had been forced into a defensive position with respect to its stand on the Soviet Union, the Soviet Zone and Oder-Neisse Line, that it had not directed its attacks against the main enemy, namely "foreign and German capitalists," and that "the party, in its praxis, did not carry out a concrete policy of daily struggle for the interests of the workers and working people in the firms, trade unions and mass organizations and did not combine these with the national struggle."[17] Rather than adopting a more independent policy, providing a greater resonance for members' opinions and incorporating a more "liberal" view of state and society, as these deficiencies would seem to suggest, the party opted for "greater ideological clarity, political firmness and iron discipline",[18] measures which were bound to increase its isolation and diminish its popular appeal even further.

After 1949 the KPD's particular strength was to have been the consistent articulator of the political ends of a large number of persons. Its continued advocacy of a socialist and antifascist front, its opposition to rearmament and remilitarization, to economic and political integration with the West as a bulwark against the East, its support for peace and cooperation with the communist countries, its resistance to authoritarian trends such as electoral laws aimed at barring smaller political parties from parliamentary representation and restrictions on free speech, and its demands for greater participation of the working class in economic decision-making were aims shared by members of pacifist, independent socialist, neutralist and even radical bourgeois groups. On the other hand, the KPD's fundamental weakness was its lack of popular support, even from many or most of the groups whose aims coincided in some measure with its own. It was evident that the discrediting of the KPD would also mean the discrediting of such oppositional groups, and that the successful defamation or even "criminalization" of the communist party could be extended to all groups who shared any of its aims, which were necessarily in opposition to the direction that the CDU State had taken.

In any event a definite temporal connection can be demonstrated between the CDU-led government's attempts to ban the KPD and the stages of rearmament of the Federal Republic. When the question of rearmament first arose in 1950, public opinion was largely negative: an EMNID poll in that year revealed that 74.6 per cent of respondents would have rejected a call to arms or into the military.[19] At the same time the KPD and SED launched a nation-wide campaign to carry out a plebiscite which asked the question: "Are you against the remilitarization of Germany and for the conclusion of a treaty of peace for Germany in the years 1951?" Though this plebiscite was banned by the Adenauer government as unconstitutional, at least nine million West Germans answered it positively, and a further eleven million DDR citizens also approved it.[20] In August 1950, Adenauer's secret plans for West German rearmament became known, and led to a minor inner-party crisis and the resignation of the government's Minister of the Interior, Gustav

Heinemann. During the first half of 1951, as the Federal Government continued its negotiations toward rearmament over growing opposition, the first legal persecutions of communist organizations began: in June the Free German Youth (FDJ) and in July the Union of Persons Persecuted by the Nazi Regime (VVNR) were banned in West Germany. On 14 September a communique of the three western occupation powers' Washington Foreign Ministers' Conference was made public, which cleared the way for the incorporation of the Federal Republic into the European Defence Community; and on 22 September the Adenauer government made formal application for the official ban of the Communist Party of Germany. When subsequently the question of a West German contribution to European defence was put into abeyance, so too were proceedings against the KPD.

Then in November 1954, after the London Nine Power Conference had come to an impasse over the issues of German rearmament and entry into NATO, and domestic opposition against rearmament had begun to increase again, particularly on the part of the DGB and SPD, the trial against the KPD was resumed and exposed to widespread publicity. During 1956, Adenauer began to make renewed efforts at rearming the Federal Republic: in April he announced his "policy of strength" at the CDU's Stuttgart Convention and demanded universal conscription; in June certain repressive measures were taken against the *Sozialistische Aktion* group, an ostensibly communist sponsored organization[21] and a number of KPD Executive Committee members were made to stand trial for treason;[22] and June also saw the passing of the Law of Military Obligation (*Wehrpflichtgesetz*). Meanwhile the popular antimilitarist movement, which had begun in 1955 with the St. Paul's Church movement and anticonscription groups, was growing and beginning to develop into a semi-organizational form.[23] On 17 August 1956 the official suspension of the KPD, as decreed by the Federal Constitutional Court, came into force.

The contemporary institutional or "official" Left failed to comprehend the full significance of the suspension of the KPD. The SPD, although it did not actively support the ban, also did not oppose it actively and appeared to accept it without protest. The Trade Union Federation went even further, claiming that the KPD had itself provoked the ban because of its isolated position from the working masses, its undemocratic methods and its disruptive influence on firm and factory.[24] Many members of the leftist opposition seemed to share the view of an anonymous author, writing in the *WISO-Korrespondenz*, who declared that the KPD was itself to blame because of its close identification with Stalin's "rule of terror" in the Soviet Union, and its blind acclamation of every step taken by the SED; through such policies the KPD was said to have " . . . isolated itself so far from the decisive sectors of the proletariat that all, even the most modest, acts of solidarity did not come about."[25]

This absence of solidarity on the part of the Left is indicative of its somewhat myopic attitude which seemed to prevail at this time. In so far as the application for the ban, the extensive and well-publicized trial, the years of existence under the threat of a ban and ultimately the legally sanctioned verdict were directed against a party whose policies and goals brought it into fundamental opposition against the bourgeois coalition, the advanced capitalist system and the government of the CDU State,[26] all these measures affected all opposition to the ruling power structure. Not only was the KPD itself banned *de jure*, so too were *de facto* opponents of rearmament, western integration and the North Atlantic Alliance, as well as the socialist opposition and even some bourgeois oppositional groups. The KPD ban was the symbol and ultimate expression of clerical anticommunism and as such was a broader and further-reaching political and social act. As the KPD later pointed out:

> . . . it is essential to understand that the ban of the KPD is not an isolated political act but an important part of the assault, carried out on the broadest level, of the imperialist camp under the leadership of the USA against the camp of peace, democracy and socialism. The Karlsruhe verdict is an integral component of Bonn's NATO and remilitarization policy.[27]

The wider implications of the KPD ban must be examined in several respects. On the first level, the outlawing of the party was certainly successful in reducing its popular appeal and in deterring its supporters and adherents. The fact of its having been labelled "criminal" was then used to brand as illegal all its subsequent actions and policies, however objectively right or necessary these may have been. This stigma, the risk of continuing to adhere to the party or any policy which it represented, and the official sanction given to an essentially political act were bound to set off an exodus of the more "moderate" members from the party who either believed the "evidence" presented, or feared the consequences of continuing their membership. This left only the more determined members[28] to carry on the party's work, members who, because of persecution and threats of persecution, and the need for solidarity under extremely adverse conditions, tended to adhere even more tenaciously to accepted doctrines and tactics, i.e., became "radicalized" or "intransigent." Moreover the reduced KPD's dependence on members' opinions and financial contributions had to decline as their reliance on the SED or CPSU for moral and financial support increased. The radical and determined members who then remained could be attacked, extirpated and punished as the "undemocratic," "Moscow-trained fanatics" which they had been alleged to have been in the first place, but which they had only become in consequence of the process of persecution.[29]

Secondly, not only the ban itself, but the way in which it was applied had grave consequences to the system of liberal rights which the Federal Republic had embodied in the Basic Law. After 1956 party functionaries and members were the victims of a wave of arrests, interrogations and trials. These applied not only to party members but also to their families, so-called "substitute organizations" and persons or groups suspected of sympathizing with or sharing communist views. According to the lawyer, Dr. Ammann, speaking at the 10th meeting of the Initiative Committee of Defence Lawyers in Political Cases for an Amnesty, in 1963 there were then more than 200,000 "preliminary investigations" taking place or completed, and these involved searches, confiscations, interrogations, arrests, dismissals from jobs and black lists. In view of the application of such methods to families, colleagues and neighbours, as well as to individuals actually accused, he argued, "a number exceeding half a million people" had been affected by political persecution methods.[30]

In the extension of surveillance to other "communist front" organizations, such as voters' association, political groups, atomic armaments opponents, pacifists, social democrats, theologians, professors, trade unionists, works' councillors, publishers, journalists, etc., a number of other methods came into use, including police spying, preparations of lists of "suspects," defamation, use of agents and secret lists in industry which allowed politicians or businessmen to determine who was communist and who was not.[31] The legal mandate which the ban had bestowed upon the government was interpreted as a licence to persecute and prosecute real or perceived communists without recourse to due process of law, inasmuch as preparations for *possible* high treason were used as grounds for prosecution and conviction. West German anticommunism here exceeded even American McCarthyism: the US Supreme Court's verdict on "Yates versus the United States" did away with similar "flagrant abuses" of due process.[32]

In the face of such methods, the KPD in fact found itself with a vital interest in retaining the system of liberal rights which the CDU State was now abusing in its persecution of communists. For the KPD was, by its existence, opposed to the manifestations of "political justice" which the ban represented; it was against further legislation in this direction, in particular the so-called emergency laws, and it sought to prevent the undermining of basic rights such as freedom of speech, freedom from arbitrary arrest and punishment and freedom of coalition or association. Indeed, the Federal Constitutional Court had been forced to suspend certain liberal rights in order to ban the KPD. In its verdict the Court found that statements which levelled criticism at the current concrete state decisions and acts which contradicted the overall aim of the state were not protected by the system of constitutional rights.[33] Loyalty to the constitution and the socio-economic order which it represented, it was now evident, took precedence over individual "liberal" rights.

And thirdly, the ban of the KPD represented a decisive blow against the socialist Left. Not only did it result in the suppression of criticism of specific government policies (rearmament, western integration) as propounded by the Left, it virtually precluded any kind of criticism based on a questioning of the socio-economic order. If the KPD's programmes for socialization and redistribution were "criminal" so too, by implication, were those of the SPD and DGB. One of the reasons for the ban, the official KPD explanation reads, was ". . . in order to facilitate the SPD leadership's road to the right, toward open cooperation with the party of the big monopolies and militarism."[34] Certainly the ban eliminated any competition from the left of the SPD and did coincide with the SPD's adaptation to the CDU State, as the following three chapters will demonstrate. For Wolfgang Abendroth:

> The criminalization of a party which from the first to the last day of the Third Reich had played a leading role in the resistance struggle was . . . suited to removing from public observation the de facto liquidation of denazification and, taking place at the same time, the integration of former members of the NSDAP into the state machine and soon into the leaderships of the political parties as well.[35]

The KPD ban also marked the completion of the Restoration, as a kind of formal confirmation of the campaign against the Left which had been waged since late 1947. It vindicated and rehabilitated anew the military and bourgeois classes, and opened the way for the re-emergence of all varieties of traditionalist organizations, military clubs, revanchist organizations and neo-Nazi associations. When the banning of the Social Reich Party (SRP), a neo-fascist formation, of 1952 is cited as evidence that the Federal Government was attempting to eliminate extremists of both persuasions, then it must be recalled that, unlike the KPD, the SRP was permitted to develop successor organizations (e.g. former SS members' clubs) which were not subject to the same degree of persecution as "communist front" organizations. And where former Nazis could be members of other political parties, the very existence of former communists in a party frequently meant that the party was designated as "communist infiltrated" and prosecuted or banned.[36]

After 1956, as after 1933, the legal restrictions placed on the KPD could not eliminate it from all political influence. On both occasions the result was to reduce membership, drive the party into the underground, force it to engage in other forms of political activity, radicalize it and increase its reliance on communist organizations outside the indigenous political system. Many communists affected by the 1956 ban had already experienced illegality, exile, imprisonment, torture, concentration camp confinement, murder of family members, colleagues, etc. — all of which made the Adenauer government's sanctions appear mild by comparison. For the ban was merely a further proof of the authoritarian nature of the Federal Republic and an added reinforcement of their belief system. The communist attitude was epitomized in the then popular inner-party slogan:

Die Hitler kamen und gingen — aber die Kommunisten sind geblieben
Die Adenauer kommen und gehen — aber die Kommunisten werden
bleiben!

The KPD saw in the ban a confirmation of the rightness of its political position and was convinced furthermore that history was on its side. According to the Central Committee, the epoch of transition from capitalism to socialism was at hand and the victory of socialism was ultimately inevitable, as the course of history could not be stopped. But since in West Germany the preconditions for the realization of socialism were not now at hand, "the whole task of the party in the present period is to secure peace and a parliamentary democratic order in the Federal Republic".[37]From the underground or from exile in the DDR or elsewhere, KPD members continued to play a role in the Federal Republic's political life. In a session of the Central Committee of 1956, some of the methods of the party's future mode of operations were outlined, including a greater development of individual initiative in, e.g., the firm, municipality, works' council or "wherever the masses are", in a combination of illegal methods with the possibilities of legal work; agitation for social security and improvement in the lot of the working people; entry into organizations opposing atomic armaments, militarism or national division; election of works' councils members; publication of illicit newspapers; holding illegal party conventions in the DDR, etc. These would have to be supplemented by a restriction of some aspects of inner-party democracy, " . . . for the safety of the party," including suspension of elections to party offices, "iron discipline," absolute public silence on party affairs and strict centralism.[38]

During the decade after 1956, the KPD could be described as a small but dedicated party of radical or determined members, forced to operate in the underground or in exile and subject to official persecution. This situation tended to make it dogmatic and inflexible and lead it to support all aspects of DDR or Soviet Union policies, including the erection of the Berlin Wall in

1961. This policy lost for the KPD most prospects of adding new or critically independent members so that in time it came to resemble a club of old fighters, with its social composition, strategy and political theory remaining virtually static.[39]

After the establishment of the Federal Republic and the Democratic Republic and the hardening of the division in Germany in consequence of the Cold War, many West German socialists gradually came to advocate a return to some version of the antifascist front based on an independent approach to socialism and reunification, and opposed to the ruling political parties in East and West. Hence the notion of a Third Way between capitalism and communism, as had been widely popular in the immediate postwar period, once again gained some support.

This desire found its first expression in the only serious attempt to create a new political party in West Germany during the 1950's: the Independent Workers' Party of Germany or UAPD. The genesis of the new party can be found in the wave of expulsions from the KPD in the years between 1949 and 1951, together with leftist disillusionment at the increasing integration of the SPD and DGB into the CDU State. Of the 144 voting delegates attending the UAPD's founding convention in December 1950 in Worms, 21 were or had been SPD members, 75 had been KPD members and 23 members of other socialist groups; and of these 100 were also members of a trade union.[40] According to Wolfgang Geese, writing in the party organ, *Freie Tribüne*, these delegates were people " . . . who within their party have warned against both the pernicious road of revisionism and embourgeoisement of the SPD, and the road of the KPD toward a party of a Stalinist character and thus toward becoming an instrument without a will of its own of Soviet foreign policy.[41] The new party was supposed to have had 5,000 members and approximately 25,000 sympathizers in western Germany,[42] though no corroborating evidence is available today of such extensive support.

In its social composition, its attitude toward the other political parties, its theory and its practice, the UAPD was almost an archetypical expression of the Third Way in Germany. Although its leaders were largely ex-communists (Chairman Georg Fischer, expelled from the Bavarian CP; General Secretary Wolfgang Geese, former member of the KPD *Land* Executive Committee of Lower Saxony; Jupp Schappe, former editor of *Freies Volk*; and Wolfgang Leonhard, former member of the Group Ulbricht and refugee from the DDR), the party was also joined by disillusioned SPD and DGB members, former supporters of the *Falken* and a number of Trotskyists.[43] The KPD, through its blind adherence to foreign directives, was seen as a hindrance to the labour cause and this fact was revealed in the miserable electoral results of a party which in Germany once had had over six million supporters. In the DDR all reforms in land ownership, the school system, currency, etc. were not the work of the German working classes, they had been achieved by "the commands of a Soviet general."[44] The UAPD's form of anticommunism was far more effective than the Adenauer government's clerical anticommunism, however, because it rested upon a solid knowledge of communist theory and praxis:

> The bourgeois combats what is *still revolutionary* in the KPD. By contrast we criticize the KPD because, through its disastrous policies, it is prolonging capitalism's life span, because it has stopped being

consistently revolutionary. Our criticism of the KPD is thus subordinate to the struggle against the capitalist system. Our main enemy is and remains the capitalist system, and we oppose the KPD only because it is waging the struggle against capitalism on the wrong basis, i.e. in practice sabotaging it.[45]

Criticism of the SPD, on the other hand, was not nearly as strident as that reserved for the KPD. Though the SPD was considered too vacillating and in constant danger of going over to the bourgeois camp, as it had after 1918, [46] the SPD under Schumacher nevertheless shared a number of priorities with the UAPD, including the primacy of national unification and the importance of democratic socialism, which brought the two parties into occasionally very close proximity. The UAPD pledged to support the SPD in "positive measures in the interests of the workers," because the SPD was seen as " . . . at present the strongest political factor in Germany by whom the greatest sector by far of the German working class is directly or indirectly influenced. For this reason the UAPD rejects any destructive policy toward the SPD."[47]

In its organizational structure, the UAPD rejected the idea of becoming a cadre party and opted instead for a centralized but democratic structure based on the model of the Yugoslavian CP.[48] This decision, together with the fact that a number of individual party members were positively inclined toward Yugoslavian communism,[49] and that the party was at least partially dependent upon the CPY for funds,[50] has led a number of contemporary observers to call the party "Titoist." Certainly it was a neutralist and social democratic party, but seems to have been more concerned with the achievement of socialism under specifically German conditions than with following the political line of Josip Broz Tito.

The exact causes of the decline of the UAPD remain obscure. Nicholas Ryschkowsky mentions the controversy over the expulsion of the Trotskyist faction in August 1951 and the withdrawal of Yugoslavian fiscal sponsorship of the *Freie Tribüne* a short while thereafter. [51] The last issue of the party organ in December 1951 listed a lack of revenues due to an absence of advertisements and subsidies as well as an increasing slander campaign directed against the movement.[52] In any case — and this is decisive — Georg Fischer was correct in saying that the UAPD was not able to attract members of the "homeless Left" and in particular the masses of the working classes.[53]

Today the UAPD is scarcely a footnote in the political history of the German Federal Republic. But its fate is in many respects illustrative of the failure of the idea and fact of the Third Way in the postwar situation. The oppressive atmosphere of the Cold War tended to reduce politics to single-choice alternatives with little middle ground. After 1950 the great majority of Germans, including sectors among the labour movement and working classes, were far more concerned with returning prosperity and stability than with what were perceived to be esoteric political arguments. Without the compelling conditions of economic crisis or social upheaval, popular support for new socialist movements was practically non-existent. On the contrary, the success of the Economic Miracle tended to cause political questions to recede from the popular consciousness. Moreover, at this time the SPD was still the party to which most independent socialists were attracted, advocating as it then did the importance of democracy and socialism and the need for national unity before western integration. And the SPD had one asset which neither the KPD nor the UAPD was able to obtain: a mass following. It is indicative of this situation that Fischer and most of the UAPD leaders subsequently went over to the SPD while, so far as is known, none joined the KPD.[54] The lesson of the UAPD was that prospects for the success of the Third Way in Germany were now effectively at an end.

4 The Absorption of the Trade Unions

Following the establishment of the CDU State the trade unions found their social and economic position greatly diminished from what it had been. If after 1945 they had been one of the pillars of society essential to rebuilding, reconstruction and the provision of vital services, then once the decision had been taken in favour of a liberal-capitalist Second German Republic, organized labour gradually found itself a rather more tolerated institution in an ostensibly pluralist society. Indeed, in many respects the trade unions were viewed as an "undesirable" or "harmful" element in the CDU State: the capitalist state's *raison d'être* is the maintenance of the capitalist social and economic order (law and order, freedom of contract, private property); when the trade unions attempt to intervene on behalf of their interests in these spheres, as, e.g., in demanding higher wages, greater social security, codetermination, expropriation and redistribution measures — which the DGB's 1949 programme did — then they represent a potential source of fundamental opposition to the capitalist order. In so far as the state enacts measures to promote private enterprise and to restrict labour's anticapitalist demands — e.g. when in 1950 the bourgeois coalition and western Military Governments promulgated legislation controlling codetermination in coal and steel industries and providing for compensation to the former shareholders which would be fixed by the Allied High Commission[1] — it is therefore intervening on behalf of private capital. Such measures, which typically involve safeguards of private property, protective tariffs, tax write-offs, etc.,[2] in fact constitute an *active* antilabour policy because they help the beneficiaries (the upper classes in business and government) to attain and maintain social and political power over the other social classes.[3] Thus the trade unions' struggles for redistribution or social justice, even if only for higher wages or better working conditions, contain a basic anti-system tendency in a modern capitalist state.

But this tendency may become, in a prospering and economically dynamic capitalist state, merely an objective one. The DGB in the CDU State was subject to a great variety of intensive system-immanent pressures. Not only was the burgeoning Economic Miracle a subjective proof of the success of the new liberal capitalist system, the CDU State, once established and widely accepted, tended to preclude socialist alternatives. In the words of Wolfgang Hirsch-Weber:

> Those who defend the existing system almost always have it easier than those who would overcome it. That which exists, which is handed down, to which one has accustomed oneself, appears to people to be, if not always good, at least necessary. The existing relationships often appear, even to those who suffer under then, as willed by God or Nature ... The trade unions also discovered this fact. When the mental effects of the collapse began to ebb away and the tendency to persevere with the existing system or to restore what had been grew, so too did resistance to the demands put forward by the trade unions. The desire

of the entrepreneurs to retain the old economic order found a greater resonance among the social classes who were not directly concerned with the controversy than did the desire of the trade unions to change the foundation of society by means of workers' codetermination.[4]

Even the old alliance between business and labour, based on a joint need for economic recovery and resistance to dismantlings, was carried over into the CDU State and gave rise to the notion of a partnership or social community between capital and labour. Although under the changed balance of social power in the Federal Republic labour could at best be a junior partner in a state structured and run in the interests of the upper classes, the high degree of industrial peace which it brought with it subsequently made western Germany a European model of "successful industrial relations."

The identification of the trade unions and labour movement with the new political and economic structure proceeded in a number of ways. Firstly, labour leaders were co-opted directly into the state bureaucracy and business positions; but at the same time they were often allowed to retain their posts in works' councils or trade unions. This led to what Theo Pirker termed a pattern of "double thinking"[5] or conflict of loyalties on the part of the holders of dual posts. And the support of the rank and file was easily obtained as a result of the economic boom which satisfied most elementary needs, as well as by means of concessions which did not fundamentally alter the balance of economic power, such as limited codetermination, company housing, production bonuses, supplementary pensions, etc. In a very real sense German workers became "shareholders of the Chancellor Democracy"[6] during the 1950's.

The notion of social partnership is rooted in the assumption that the interests and ends of capital and labour are identical or can be made identical. But if the objective of the labour movement is concerned with the re-definition of social priorities, the redistribution of the social product and, above all, the intra-societal power conferred by the ownership or control of wealth and property, then the interests of these two groups must be ultimately antagonistic. The primary ends of the labour movement in capitalist society must thus include the extension of political democracy into the economic and social spheres; the minimum prerequisites for the achievement of such ends would be the democratization of the labour organizations, the politicization of the trade unions in the direction of partisan politics and a consistent struggle aimed at a redistribution of powers in the polity.

A democratic trade union structure is necessary for several reasons. Intra-organizational discussion and debate tend to promote a development of consciousness on the part of members, so that they are eventually able to understand where their interests lie. These interests are essentially democratic interests as they are necessarily concerned with equality, e.g., with income distribution, access to education, culture and leisure, and the abolition of particularist interests and privileges. This knowledge then helps to mobilize the organization on behalf of labour actions (strikes, demonstrations), and to channel these into political acts. Unlike the particular interests of big business, which cannot hope to gain a mass following and thus must proclaim its interests to be the "common good"[7] or the interests of society as a whole (free competition, labour peace, etc.), or must obtain a direct and relatively secret influence in the government bureaucracy, executive or agencies;[7a] the interests of labour are universal interests in so far as they are the interests of not only the actual union members — the DGB had almost five million members in 1949 — but also those of the more than eighty per cent of the population which is dependent upon wages or salaries for its living, whose objective interests the unions also represent. Lacking the concentrated resources or power positions of business, labour is thus dependent upon a high degree of publicity and open discussion to implement its demands. The incorporation of labour leaders into government and business institutions prevented a development of trade union democracy because many labour leaders were thereby made partners with a vested interest in the continuation of the capitalist system, while the rank and file were not consulted or informed. Social partnership subjectively makes the workers and owners of a given firm or plant into partners, and hence competitors against the workers and owners of other plants and firms, i.e., firm or corporation solidarity replaces class solidarity.[8]

In particular the precept of political party neutrality works to the disadvantage of the trade unions. The democratization of society and the change in social priorities and economic redistribution must, in a political democracy, take place through the mediation of a political party or parties; indeed one of the central functions of political parties in liberal capitalist democracies is the representation of their members' interests. Despite the fact that the DGB which was constituted in Munich in 1949 bore little resemblance to the original postwar concept of the *Einheitsgewerkschaft* — it was of course organized around sixteen industrial trade unions and the old divisions between civil service, clerical and blue-collar trade unions had been perpetuated[9] — the DGB continued to pursue an official policy of political party neutrality. The disadvantage that this policy placed labour into vis-à-vis the upper classes is evident: whereas the latter could contribute vast sums of money, propaganda and other forms of support to the bourgeois coalition, the DGB was prevented from providing outright moral or material support to the party whose policies most closely coincided with its interests at this time, namely the SPD. This is not to suggest that the DGB was robbed of all political influence; approximately 85 per cent of its leaders and about the same percentage of leaders of the individual industrial unions have always been simultaneously SPD members,[10] and a comparatively high number of Bundestag deputies have been trade union members.[11] But the absence of a direct parliamentary representation must have seriously restricted the trade unions' strength in the political system. (Where social democratic parties have come to power in postwar western Europe, it has almost always been as a result of a direct alliance with the trade union movement).

One of the most influential forces for trade union neutrality was the presence in the DGB and industrial trade unions of the "labour wing" of the CDU, represented by its "social committees" (*Sozialausschüsse*). The CDU regarded its social committees as a "bridge to labour which had become estranged from us on the one side, and to the good ideas and forces of the bourgeois world on the other"; this was the "historical mediating role" which the social committees were called upon to play. They were seen as being necessary "so that the christian workers (would) not be assimilated or neutralized" and their task was defined as "the social conscience, the social motor and the social barometer of the Union."[12] In other words the social committees were the "agent" of the CDU in the trade unions, fulfilling the primary role of preventing the labour movement from lending direct support to the Social Democrats, and, as Siggi Neumann, writing on behalf of the SPD Executive Committee in 1949, correctly saw, aiming at "waging the struggle against the political Left."[13] This struggle was carried on ideologically by the promotion of the Catholic social doctrine within the trade union, including the notions of the plant as a community or family subject to the same natural laws of hierarchy and division of labour as the latter social institutions,[14] and in practice by ensuring a non-socialist counterweight in important areas of trade union activity such as education, school, youth and social organizations.[15] That trade union political party neutrality operated to the satisfaction of the christian members is demonstrated by the fact that, unlike in the Weimar Republic, the trade union movement since 1945 has never produced any serious dissensions between its Social Democratic and Christian wings, apart from an unsuccessful separatist attempt in 1953 by a few ardent CDU trade unionists. The contribution of the SPD's election defeats of 1949 and 1953 to the reinforcement of the unified and neutral trade union is difficult to ascertain.

The changed situation of labour in comparison with the pre-1949 period became abundantly manifest in connection with the struggle for codetermination and the larger issues which it raised. When after 1949 the DGB began to return to priorities left in abeyance since the first postwar years, it was suddenly compelled to wage an extensive campaign involving publicity campaigns, hard negotiations and strike threats. Labour's forbearance with respect to wage claims and increased worker participation had indeed afforded the re-emergent capitalist classes time to reorganize and regroup. Organized labour had once been one of the acknowledged spokesmen and representatives of the nation in negotiations with the occupation powers; now it had to gain concessions from a West German capitalist state in which it no longer had a controlling interest.

In the early months of 1950, the DGB began to agitate in favour of the extension of limited codetermination, which had been achieved in 1948 in the coal and steel industries, into all economic spheres, from the firm or plant up to the federal level. Full codetermination was seen as the central element in labour's struggle to achieve equality by extending the liberal rights afforded by the political system into the social and economic spheres. The DGB attempted to carry on this struggle through the existing political machinery, viz. parliament. But given that this parliament and its government did not have a mandate to represent labour, it is evident that the struggle would have had to have taken place against the ruling political powers. For them to implement full codetermination and achieve redistribution amounted to revolutionary proposals.

The trade unions' demands for codetermination were, as might be expected, met with massive resistance on the part of business and the government. In initial negotiations with the DGB, the employers' representatives were prepared only to concede codetermination on the level of the individual plant, and then only in question of personnel and social matters. In a well-planned publicity campaign, business argued that labour's proposals would bring "foreign elements" into the firm in the form of DGB representatives, that a great bureaucratic web of functionaries would arise and that the way would be clear for "communist infiltration" into individual plants ("then we would be back precisely where we were and where we still are in the Soviet Union"). [17] Of course such propaganda neglected to add that the managers and executives of industry were themselves "foreign elements" within the corporation, and conveniently overlooked the fact that the DGB had already eliminated from its own ranks all functionaries and clerks who had been active on behalf of the communist party.[18]

During the early 1950's, codetermination proved to be an issue with a great deal of potential for mobilization of the trade union membership. General polls among the metal workers' and miners' unions in late 1950 indicated that almost 96 percent of the former and 93 per cent of the latter memberships were prepared to resort to strikes in support of increased worker participation in the running of firm and factory. Due largely to labour pressure, the Adenauer government conceded codetermination (but only in basic production) in the iron, coal and steel industries in April 1951. The corresponding legislation was approved in the Bundestag by the SPD and a majority of the CDU/CSU and Centre parties, over the opposition of the FDP and German Party (DP). This parliamentary alliance then appeared on the surface to vindicate the trade unions' policy of political neutrality. But in fact, as the subsequent struggle for general codetermination would demonstrate, coal and iron represented a special case in so far as the Allies and the government needed these industries to maintain economic progress.[19] In any event the actual concessions gained by labour were by no means equivalent to an equal share in the running of plants and firms. Parity codetermination (which provided for five representatives each of management and labour and a "neutral" eleventh man) was obtained only in the enterprises' supervisory board (*Aufsichtsrat*). Labour also gained the appointment of an *Arbeits-direktor* in the managing committee (*Vorstand*) and the right for works' councils to nominate candidates for this position.

Thus labour's main achievement in the 1951 codetermination law was rather more symbolic than effective. The conflict surrounding it did suggest that the trade unions, ". . . when they proceeded with sufficient determination, were in a position to influence legislation by means of extraparliamentary actions or a credible threat of such."[20] But in the ensuing struggle for universal parity codetermination, the trade unions were unwilling or unable to exploit their potential stength. Christian Fette succeeded to the chairmanship of the DGB following Hans Böckler's death in early 1951. The trade unions' leadership, already integrated to some extent into the CDU State by virtue of their connections with the government and business, and frequently intimidated by the growing anti-labour atmosphere in the Federal Republic, largely supported Fette's policies of "constructive cooperation" and conciliation with business and government, as well as his apparent preoccupation with organizational detail.

The trade unions' support for such policies, while at the same time they adhered to the notion of a "new ordering of society and economy" as symbolized in universal parity codetermination, resulted in a necessarily contradictory policy of attempting to employ system-immanent methods to achieve system-opposed goals. On the one hand the DGB's anticapitalist ends permitted Adenauer to reproach the DGB with operating outside parliament and thus attempting to be a "state within a state" advocating measures which coincided with communist purposes, and with hindering the government in difficult foreign policy decisions.[21]

And on the other hand, the DGB leadership, instead of adopting a strategy of opposition (strikes, anti-armaments demonstrations, partisan political actions), which could assist it in realizing its essentially anti-system ends, began to assert even more tenaciously its intention of achieving these goals within the limits of the existing system by maintaining political neutrality. Thus Fette and the DGB leadership waged the struggle for codetermination on the basis of trade union subordination to parliament, abandonment of all effective extraparliamentary pressure and an emphasis on the importance of influencing government policy through the electoral system. By this time: "The trade unions had completed their integration into the existing system which, although this was in keeping with the policy they had already been practising for some time, was not in accord with their continued claim to change the economic order as such."[22] Despite the fact that the SPD represented in parliament virtually all of the trade unions' demands with respect to codetermination — including its application to both the public and private sectors, the placing of trade union representatives on the boards of individual firms, the elimination of the distinctions between wage and salary earners and the introduction of codetermination into all but the smallest enterprises — and despite the increasingly active anti-labour policy of the Adenauer government (arousal of public opinion against the unions, deferment or dilution of codetermination legislation, etc.), culminating in the DGB's withdrawal of its representatives from various government economic committees in November 1951, the DGB nevertheless clung to its policy of political party neutrality, declaring that: "The DGB cannot allow itself to be misused as a coalition partner in the political sense. This is just as impossible as would be its becoming a part of the political opposition. The DGB is a separate organization with its separate character which is determined by its party political neutrality."[23] The DGB then urged its members during the 1953 election campaign to "elect a better Bundestag" by voting for trade union candidates or at least those with a proven record of trade union support.

Furthermore, while the SPD was carrying on a fundamental opposition to western integration, the DGB came to accept in principle the Schumann Plan and, in mid-1951, Fette was beginning to regard a German contribution to a western military alliance as a logical continuation of the DGB agreement with the Marshall and Schumann plans. That this ambivalent attitude toward a government policy which was directly opposed to the interests of the workers (guns before butter, postponement of social services, conscription, etc.) served to increase the distance between the DGB leadership and the rank and file, is demonstrated by the great popular protest from the latter following a speech supporting government policy delivered by the DGB member, Hans vom Hoff, in January 1952.[24] Demonstrations and strike threats, culminating in the militant two-day printers' strike of 28-29 May 1952, on behalf of codetermination were extremely well supported during 1952,[25] thereby contributing to heightened consciousness on the part of trade union members.

This propitious situation notwithstanding, DGB leaders eventually bent to "public opinion' and government persuasion in agreeing to suspend all trade union action which might have been construed as "political blackmail" during the period in which draft legislation on the subject of codetermination was before the Bundestag. This was a decisive concession on the part of the DGB as it signified the final commital of the vital interests of the trade unions to the decision of the bourgeois-controlled parliament with no further possibility of revision or veto. Not surprisingly, therefore, the codetermination legislation promulgated by the Bundestag in July 1952 fell far short of the trade unions' expectations. As labour was only given one-third of the seats in supervisory boards, and that only in firms of over 100 employees, effective intra-firm decision-making power rested, as always, in the hands of management. The works' councils were not allowed to engage in political party activity, nor could their members be appointed by labour organizations outside the firm (e.g. the DGB). Although workers' representatives obtained certain rights to information and discussion in social and personnel questions their influence in overall economic policy was negligible. For Wolfgang Hirsch-Weber there was no doubt that: "The substance of the law signifie(d) a victory for the entrepreneurs," i.e. the big industrialists.[26]

If the achievement of codetermination under conditions set by the bourgeois coalition signified the absorption of the trade union leadership and much of its organization into the CDU State, it by no means brought about the full integration of all trade union members. To integrate the German workers, as Urs Jaeggi has pointed out, would have had to involve " . . . the unfolding and development of their personalities in all spheres of the state, culture and the economy, the promotion of their self-responsibility through training, securing their basis of existence, property ownership, improvement of their opportunities for advancement."[27] This fact was also recognized by a number of DGB functionaries and members of the individual industrial trade unions, who began to take issue with Christian Fette's public acceptance of labour's reversals, as symbolized in his call for continued moderation and for a policy of waiting until the next federal elections to marshall trade union support behind individual Bundestag candidates "who support trade union demands."[28] This "backlash" movement then culminated initially in an endeavour to unseat the DGB leaders who were held to be responsible for the "capitulation." At the DGB's Berlin Congress in October of 1952, Christian Fette was replaced, through a general vote, by Walter Freitag, and both vom Hoff and Erich Buhrig were not re-elected to the Federal Executive Committee.[29] And the Congress' *Aktionsprogramm* was concerned primarily with advancing the trade unions' position within society through such measures as a reduction of working hours, increased social security, better living standards, full employment, job security and an extension of codetermination rights. It opposed the western alliance, rearmament and conscription as well. But gone already were the old aims of the transformation of society and economy and the achievement of socialism.

This brief resurgence of leftist activity in the DGB from 1952 up to perhaps 1955 originated in several complementary sources. Within the DGB, as has been mentioned above, there were a number of functionaries and members disappointed at the failure of the great hopes and prospects for socialism after 1945, and angered at the DGB's defeat in the issue of codetermination. Although such leftists could be found in many local and regional DGB organizations, they seemed to crystallize in the so-called "Circle of Ten" (*Zehner Kreis*), which was an informal, relatively unorganized group of leading functionaries endeavouring to return the DGB to its postwar goals and to gain key posts for themselves as a means to this end. Among these were Otto Brenner, probably the group's informal leader and chairman of the metal-workers' union, IG-Metall, the largest and most powerful industrial union; Siggi Neumann, a member of the SPD Executive Committee; the journalists Eduard Wald and Kuno Brandel; Hermann Beermann, the *Land* DGB chairman of Lower Saxony; Werner Hansen, DGB *Land* chairman of North Rhine-Westphalia and later a member of the Federal Executive Committee, and a number of others.[30] The Circle of Ten's strategy appears to have been to exert pressure and channel grievances in support of radical platforms involving concrete and readily definable issues affecting the direct interests of the working classes. It largely eschewed theory and binding programmes — which no doubt is one reason why today it is difficult to reconstruct the group's principles and goals — but on the other hand, by virtue of the positions of power and influence which its members enjoyed, it was certainly an important factor within the DGB.

Elsewhere a few regional DGB organizations evolved a similar type of inner-union opposition based on specific issues which touched upon larger questions, in particular that of rearmament. In the latter issue, the DGB regional group in Munich took the lead in advocating the use of "all legal means" to support the trade unions' resistance to rearmament. They argued that rearmament must increase political tensions, enhance the danger of war, act as an obstacle to national unity and hinder social and economic reforms; the group proposed, for example, to disseminate antimilitary propaganda among the whole people, to hold a plebiscite among trade union members, and to place pressure wherever possible on the government.[31] The influence of such groups was manifest in March 1953, when the European Defence Community was ratified by the Bundestag, giving rise to a broad popular movement at the lower levels which urged the DGB to proclaim a general strike or take other drastic opposition measures. Such thoughts were, however, suppressed by public statements of disavowal and internal pressure by the DGB leadership.

The third left wing grouping within the DGB was centred around the unions' theoretical organ, the *WWI-Mitteilungen*, edited by Viktor Agartz and his co-workers, Theo Pirker, Walter Horn and Bruno Gleitze. In it, an essentially Marxist interpretation of postwar developments, the bourgeois capitalist state and the role of the trade unions was eloquently expounded. Many of the articles in the *WWI-Mitteilungen* have been alluded to above. It advocated a policy of trade union socialism and labour action which implied that, as a result of the "embourgeoisement" of the SPD and the decline of the communist and independent Left, the trade unions themselves ought to fill the political vacuum and become a kind of interest party of workers' rights. Where Agartz had once represented and articulated the mainstream tendency in the Trade Union Federation, as well as in the SPD, however, he was now on the radical left wing of the labour movement.

For a brief historical moment, these various left wing factions in the DGB came together. This occurred at the DGB's Frankfurt Congress of 1954. The salient results of the Congress were a strongly-worded resolution opposing the Federal Government's attempts at rearmament, a decision to prepare an action programme embodying concrete demands on behalf of the working classes, and a well-received speech by Viktor Agartz attacking limited codetermination as a means of integrating the trade union leaders and officials and of apportioning to labour a share of responsibility for the operations of enterprises without however granting it any say in economic policy or the relations of ownership. Agartz' speech represented one of the last attempts at a theoretical assessment, from an inner-DGB left wing viewpoint, of the trade unions' position in the capitalist state. And the Congress itself could be said to have been the last major attempt by the DGB Left to obtain a controlling influence over the programmatical development of that organization.

Agartz' speech in particular, advocating as it did full codetermination, socialization of the key economic sectors and a drastic redistribution of wealth and power in society, made him the spokesman of the Marxist Left within the DGB and a symbol of labour opposition to the CDU State. It thus brought down widespread opposition on the part of the bourgeois press, members of the SPD parliamentary party, representatives of the Catholic Church, the CDU's labour wing and the CDU-led coalition.[32] As Pirker has written, "Precisely the greatness of his speech was the direct cause of his later fall."[33] For the applause which it received and the resonance which it found showed that Agartz' popularity threatened to rival that of the DGB bureaucracy, especially at a time when popular resentment against the latter was increasing after the DGB's capitulation in the issue of codetermination and its failure to take a firmer stand against rearmament. The massive opposition that Agartz invoked obviously posed a threat to those in the DGB concerned with gaining maximum concessions from within the existing system, including, on closer examination, the Circle of Ten, the DGB leadership and the others involved in preparing an action programme on the basis of the mandate accorded by the 1954 Congress. For the programme produced on the basis of the 1954 Congress, in its 1955 version,[34] called specifically only for such reforms as reduced working hours, increased social security and guarantees of the continuation of codetermination. It avoided controversial formulae such as socialization or nationalization, and referred instead to the "transferral of the key industries into common ownership." Finally, the programme advocated a more independent trade union policy following the electoral defeats of the SPD and the need for a more independent DGB policy going beyond parliamentary exigencies and present legislation. It was thus a compromise containing specific demands entirely compatible with the capitalist system and nebulous, long-range goals of achieving socialism at some future date, but lacking the strategy and tactics necessary to bring these about.

Following protests by the CDU/CSU and a large scale propaganda counter-offensive by its labour wing against the DGB Left, in the forefront of which were the polemical writings by the Jesuit scholars, Oswald von Nell-Bruening [35] and Peter Reichelt, Viktor Agartz was suspended indefinitely in October 1955 from the DGB's Institute for Economic Sciences (WWI) to which he had been attached, on the pretext of having used falsified documents to attack his co-worker, Bruno Gleitze.[36] Also dismissed were two other prominent members of the DGB Left, Theo Pirker and Walter Horn. The reasons given for Pirker's dismissal were (a) a speech which he had delivered in February 1955 in Göppingen arguing that the impulse for labour action passed by default to individual DGB members and functionaries when the Executive Committee

did not actively intervene in the Bundestag's deliberations in order to prevent
rearmament, (b) an article which he had written in *Die Andere Zeitung*
arguing that the right to strike was a basic right and that a strike must have
political ends, and (c) his contacts with the French socialist, Joseph Rovan.[37] And
Horn was suspended because of an article he had written in one of the trade
union organs defending Agartz against attacks by Nell-Bruening, and in
general opposing the reactionary influence of Catholic dogma in the trade
union organizations.[38]

The pretexts on the basis of which Agartz, Pirker and Horn were expelled
are in themselves evidence of the kind of opposition which they had aroused
from within the DGB. No doubt the expulsions served to placate the CDU
labour wing and the Adenauer government[39] as well as to entrench the
integrated DGB bureaucracy. And, according to Franz Altmann, the Circle of
Ten also agreed to sacrifice Agartz *et al.* in order to ensure support for "its"
1955 programme and to maintain Walter Freitag's position as chairman,
which could have been imperilled as a result of a possible counter-offensive
from the Right.[40] In any case, the upshot was the entrenchment of the
"maximizers" around Otto Brenner and Circle of Ten in an ascendant
ideological and an excellent tactical position within the DGB.

The maximizers' attitude toward Agartz' expulsion, when faced with massive
right wing protest, was entirely logical when viewed in perspective. Unlike
Agartz, the Circle of Ten and its adherents nowhere had presented a socialist
programme; their policies were essentially a glorified platform which presented
partial demands or concrete reforms as basic principles. The fulfilment of
such demands was not only entirely compatible with a functioning capitalist
system, it also signified the exhaustion of the maximalists' contribution to the
advancement of labour's cause, i.e. when the platform was realized or
perceived to have been realized, there was nothing left. Concerning this trade
union "activism," Theo Pirker has written that it

> . . . is a rhetorical propagandistic expedient to cover up the political
> defeats from 1949 to 1953. It is a form of adaptation by the trade
> unions to the relationships of political power in the Federal Republic
> — authoritarian democracy and the new capitalism — trimmed up
> with radicalist rhetoric. Both the trade union policy of a new ordering
> of state and economy, and trade union activism were only ostensibly in
> contradiction to circumstances, but the contradictions in their concep-
> tion, a collection of radical- and activist-sounding banalities, could not
> be overlooked. It was only a question of time as to when this trade union
> activism would overcome its internal contradiction by throwing its
> radicalist ballast overboard.[41]

At the Fourth Federal Congress of the DGB in Hamburg in October 1956,
one year after the expulsion of Horn, Pirker and Agartz, all discussion of
transforming capitalist society into socialism or of achieving full codetermination at all levels of the economy had been eliminated from the DGB's
public stance. Here too anticommunism came to be used as a negative form of
intra-organizational discipline. The Congress agreed that: "We decisively
reject everything which has occurred in respect to the suppression of freedom,
human dignity and the law in the Soviet occupied Zone since the division of
Germany."[42] An Executive Committee resolution of 1956 attacked the KPD as
a disruptive element in the labour movement and argued that it had itself

provoked the ban.[43] Similar developments occurred in various individual industrial trade unions, as, e.g., in the expulsion of over 100 communist functionaries from the construction workers' union (*IG-Bau*) in the course of the so-called *Leber-Aktion* of 1956.[44]

And, as mentioned in the previous section, the DGB did not oppose the KPD ban in any way; on the contrary, the ban removed the last potential organized opposition to the executive's policies. Now, when individual socialist DGB members contradicted the organization's official policies, they could be attacked and isolated as "communist agents" or "useful idiots" without fear of contradiction. Thus when Wolfgang Abendroth delivered a speech to youth participants at a DGB sponsored conference in Munich and Augsburg, and the conference subsequently passed a resolution opposing rearmament, the creation of a German army and conscription, the DGB press launched an attack against Professor Abendroth declaring that he was in this way "serving the propaganda of the Soviet Zone of Occupation," and attempted to have Abendroth barred from future trade union meetings or gatherings.[45]

Nor did the DGB effectively oppose the Law of Conscription (*Wehrpflicht-gesetz*) passed by the Bundestag in July 1956, other than through declamatory speeches by individual members, notably Otto Brenner. On the day before the ban was imposed on the KPD, Brenner and Freitag paid a visit to Adenauer for discussions on reduced working hours, a visit which " . . . at this point in time must have appeared as an act of solidarity of the trade unions with the policy of the Federal Government against the KPD."[46]

With the maximalists or activists now ascendant, the DGB leadership was henceforth primarily concerned with extracting concessions from the CDU State, of which it was now a subjective and objective part. The maximalists came to discover that it was more effective to negotiate in relative secrecy with the government or employers in order later to present the members with a *fait accompli* for their acclamation.[47] The "responsibility" for society as a whole, which the DGB saw itself as sharing with business and government, was of course a rationalization of the subordinate role that labour had assumed in society and economy. Between 1955 and 1961, West Germany enjoyed the highest European level of labour peace, with fewer strikes and workdays lost than any other country.[48] This fact would seem to indicate that, by the late 1950's, West German labour was more integrated into the liberal capitalist state than their fraternal organizations elsewhere in Europe. Siggi Neumann argued plausibly that there were now labour *organizations* but no labour *movement* because: "The broad mass of members and functionaries in party and trade union have as good as no factual internal share in the political aims and struggles of the party."[49] If the DGB was to be regarded as a pressure group for labour with an active interest in the functioning of the CDU State, then it no doubt fulfilled its role admirably. But if it was seen as an institution for the emancipation of labour and the transformation of the capitalist system in the workers' interests, then it had failed utterly.

REFERENCES

1 The Establishment of the CDU State
1 A term borrowed from the title of the excellent collection of essays edited by Gert
   Schäffer and Carl Nedelmann, *Der CDU-Staat. Studien zur Verfassungswirklichkeit
   der Bundesrepublik*, Munich 1967.
2 Representation by party was as follows (figures in brackets indicate no. of seats per
   party after the extensions of spring 1948):

SPD 20 (40)	CDU 20 (40)
KPD 3 (6)	Zentrum 2 (4)
	DP 2 (4)
	FPD 4 (8)
	WAV 1 (2)

3 Twenty-five years later both Clay and Erhard, in separate interviews, agreed that the
   conditions for the "free market" were created by Erhard on his own responsibility —
   in fact against the official opposition, but with the tacit approval of the U.S. Military
   Government. ("Das versilberte Wunder," television programme on ARD (1st
   Programme), 20.6.1973, 20:15hrs.).
4 From 54% of the 1936 level in June 1948 to 84% in February 1949 to over 100% by
   the end of 1949 (See H.C. Wallich, *Mainsprings of the German Revival*, New Haven
   1955).
5 On the social antecedents of the Convention's members, see Wolfgang Abendroth,
   Das Grundgesetz. Eine Einführung in seine politischen Probleme, Pfüllingen 1966,
   p.37.
6 Its 65 members were appointed or chosen by the various *Länder* governments —
   thereby ensuring a bias toward federalism, since any power the Council accorded to
   the Federal Government would be at the expense of the *Länder* — and among them
   were 43 civil servants, 50 members of *Land* assemblies and 12 ministers or state
   secretaries. (Richard Hiscocks, *Democracy in Western Germany*, London 1957,
   p.45; obviously these are overlapping categories).
7 The minor parties were represented as follows:

KPD 2	DP 2
	Zentrum 2
	FPD 5

8 The compensation clauses, it should be noted, were added at the express request of
   the western Allies.
9 A view expounded, among others, by Helmut Lindemann: "When after 1945 the
   Germans for the second time set about implementing parliamentary democracy in
   their country, they took over more or less uncritically a system whose functional
   difficulties had already become visible in the classic countries of western democracy.
   Representative democracy, as had been anchored in unadulterated form in the Basic
   Law, was based upon a social order which no longer existed in 1948." ("Daseins-
   verfehlung — Dritter Akt" in: Altmann, Böll, Flechtheim, *et al.*, *Zensuren nach 20
   Jahren Bundesrepublik*, Cologne 1969, p.134.
10 Which between 1949 and 1955 were taken largely by Adenauer, in spite of the
   Occupation Statute which went into effect simultaneously with the Basic Law and
   which reserved powers of disarmament and demilitarization, trade and foreign
   affairs, refugees and reparations to the occupying powers.
11 See Wolf-Dieter Narr, *CDU-SPD-Programm und Praxis seit 1945*, Stuttgart 1966,
   p.74.
12 Cf. Joseph Rovan. *Le Catholicisme Politique en Allemagne*, Paris 1956, p.253f.
13 See Uwe Kitzinger, *German Electoral Politics*, Oxford 1957, p.103; Gabriel
   Almond, *The Politics of German Business*, Santa Monica 1955, p.19f; and Rudolf
   Wildenmann, *Partei und Fraktion*, Frankfurt 1954, p.61.
14 Gerhard Schutz, "Die CDU — Markmale ihres Aufbaues" in: M.G. Lange, ed.,

Parteien in der Bundesrepublik, Stuttgart and Düsseldorf 1955, p.123.
15 Narr, *op. cit.*, p.75.
16 *The State in Capitalist Society*, London 1969, p.187.
16a See Karl W. Roskamp, "Distribution of the Tax Burden in a Rapidly Growing
Economy: West Germany in 1950" in: *National Tax Journal*, XVI (1963), p.31; and
see Wolfgang Stolper, *Germany between East and West*, Washington 1960, p.128.
17 Here see variously, Michael Balfour, *West Germany*, London 1968, p.180; Lewis J.
Edinger, *Politics in Germany*, Boston 1968, p.19ff; and esp. Henry Wallich, *op. cit.*,
ch. 1.
18 Thus when Ralf Dahrendorf (*Society and Democracy in Germany*, Garden City
1967, p.213) claims that postwar industrialization took place in "comparatively
liberal forms," he fails to recognize that the period in question represented nothing
more than a transition to advanced capitalist forms which had little in common with
liberalism, even in 1948. See also below. Harald Mey regards the social market
economy as an "integrating myth" similar to the "C" in CDU. ("Marktwirtschaft
und Demokratie. Betrachtungen zur Grundlegung der Bundesrepublik" in:
Vierteljahresschrift fur Zeitgeschichte, Vol.19 (1971), No. 2 (April), p.179 and 182).
19 The economic factors governing the extensive and intensive phases of the
Wirtschaftswunder and beyond are discussed in: Heiko Korner, "The Social Dimension of Political Economy" in: *The German Economic Review*, No. 3 1971, p.197ff.
20 "Wirtschaftskonjunkturbericht des Instituts für Wirtschaftsforschung." Munich,
March 1960, Supplement 1, p.5 (figure does not include the Saar region).
21 Cf. Italy 5.7%, USA 3.3%, France 4%, Sweden 3.3%, and the UK 2.5%. See
United Nations, *World Economic Survey 1960*, p.16.
22 *Handbook of Economic Statistics for the Federal Republic and the West Sector of
Berlin*, published by Economic Affairs Section of the American Embassy, Bonn,
1 Aug. 1959, p.49. It should be noted that Jürgen Kuczynski (*Darstellung der Lage
der Arbeiter in Westdeutschland seit 1945*, vol.I, E. Berlin 1963, p.385ff.) has made
an excellent case that during the 1950's the standards dropped, while at the same
time productivity rates rose. Unfortunately the statistics he presents in support of
these trends are extremely difficult to corroborate.
23 *Statistisches Jahrbuch für die BRD 1966*, table on p.553. The number of firms with
more than 1,000 employees increased more than fourfold compared with pre-1914
Germany (D. Claessens/A. Klönne/A. Tschoepe, *Sozialkunde der BRD*, Düsseldorf
1968, p.240f); in 1960 the 100 largest firms were responsible for almost 2/5 of
industrial turnover, employed 1/3 of the labour force and shipped 1/2 of all
manufacturing exports (Michael Kidron, *Western Capitalism since the War*,
Harmondsworth 1970 (revised ed.), p.27); and in 1964 two per cent of all enterprises
accounted for 37.8% of all industrial turnover, which figure does not include the de
facto dependence of small suppliers and service firms upon the larger concerns,
inter-firm agreements, capital inter-connections and personal and legal agreements
among the larger firms (see *Statistisches Jahrbuch . . . 1966, passim*). As a result of
this process of concentration, about 40 per cent of steel production is carried out by
two firms, the Thyssen-Phoenix-Rheinrohr amalgamation and Krupp (both firms
having been convicted of war crimes committed during the Third Reich), banking is
again dominated by the "big three", Dresdener Bank, Commerzbank and Deutsche
Bank; and the three successor firms to IG Farben control the chemical industry.
Similar trends, though not nearly so pronounced, are evident in the agricultural
sector as well.
24 Viktor Agartz, speech delivered to the Third Federal Congress of the DGB 1954 in
Frankfurt, quoted in: N.J. Ryschkowsky, *Die linke Linke*, Munich/Vienna 1968,
p.15f.
25 Ralf Dahrendorf, *op. cit.*, p.261. Almond, (*op. cit.*, p.iii) makes a similar statement.
26 Almond, *op. cit.*, esp. 217ff.
27 Arnold Heidenheimer has shown how dependent the CDU had been upon business
for financial support: two-fifths of party funds came from the so-called "sponsors'

associations," 1/5 from members (including many businessmen) and a final 2/5 from donations solicited by deputies, subscriptions, etc. (again largely backed by the business community) Cf. "German Party Finance. The CDU" in: *APSR* LI (June 1957), p.384f.

28 For example, of the BDI's expenditure between 1949-1958, on average 82.8% of all donations went to executive authorities; the Bundestag and Bundesrat received only 7%; and the remainder went to the Federal and Central Bank Council. (See H.-J. Blank/J. Hirsch, "Parlament und Verwaltung im Gesetzsgebungsprozess" in: Schäffer/Nedelmann, *op. cit.*, p.93.

29 Between 1953-1958 about 35% of CDU/CSU deputies were associated directly with interest groups (predominantly business), while about 25% of SPD deputies were also affiliated with such groups (but 84% of these were with trade unions). (See Viola Gräfin von Bethusy-Huc, *Die Soziologie wirtschaftspolitischer Entscheidungen*, Wiesbaden 1962, p.127).

30 On the BDI see Gerhard Braunthal, *The Federation of German Industry in Politics*, Ithaca, N.Y. 1965; for the BDA, Ronald F. Bunn, "The Federation of German Employers' Associations. A Political Interest Group" in: *Western Political Quarterly*, Vol. 13, Sept. 1960, p.653 and esp. p.667; and on the DIHT, Edinger, *Politics in Germany*, p.219f.

31 See K.D. Bracher, "Zwischen Stabilisierung und Stagnation. Die mittleren Jahren der Ära Adenauer (1956/57)" in: Heinz Maus, ed., *Gesellschaft, Recht und Politik. Wolfgang Abendroth zum 60. Geburtstag*, Neuwied and W. Berlin 1968, p.45ff. See also, and in greater detail, W. Besson, "Regierung und Opposition in der deutschen Politik" in: *Politische Vierteljahresschrift*, No. 3 1962, p.233f.

32 Rudolf Augstein, *Konrad Adenauer* (trans. W. Wallich), London 1964, p.106.

33 *Politics in Germany*, p.48.

34 *op. cit.*, p.276 and 278.

35 "Konstituierung und Regierungssystem der Bundesrepublik — übersicht über die Gesamtdarstellungen" in: *Politische Vierteljahresschrift*, No. 2 (June) 1967, p.345

36 These points are documented and expounded in far greater detail in quite all the works by Kurt Pritzkoleit (e.g. *Gott erhält die Mächtigen*, Düsseldorf 1963; *Wem gehört Deutschland?*, Vienna/Munich/Basel 1957; *Männer, Mächte, Monopole*, Düsseldorf 1953); see further Helmut Arndt, *Die Konzentration in der westdeutschen Wirtschaft*, Pfüllingen 1967; and Hermann Marcus, *Die Macht der Mächtigen*, Düsseldorf 1970.

37 K. Schultes, "German Politics and Political Theory" in: *The Political Quarterly*, Vol. 28, Jan. 1957, p.42.

38 H.-D. Ortlieb in: Hans-Werner Richter, ed., *Bestandesaufnahme. Eine deutsche Bilanz 1962*, Munich/Vienna/Basel 1962, p.288.

39 *Politics in Germany*, p.35.

40 Dahrendorf, *op. cit.*, p.227f; and W. Zapf, *Wandlungen der deutschen Elite*, Munich 1965, ch. 3.

41 Dahrendorf, *ibid.*, p.227f. The last figure quoted must not be taken to mean that many of the postwar cabinet members had not served the National Socialist regime in other capacities. Cf., e.g., Tetens, *The New Germany and the Old Nazis*, London, 1962, p.37ff; see also below.

42 Lewis J. Edinger, "Post-totalitarian Leadership. Elites in the German Federal Republic" in: *APSR* No. 1 (March) 1960, p.69.

43 88 per cent of the supra-regional daily and Sunday press belongs to one firm, Axel Springer, known for its (at times extreme) right-wing bias. Even the local press is to a great extent controlled by the provincial or district press, which means that, despite a semblance of independence, it is subject to control of the large news agencies, the advertisers' policies, etc. (cf. Reinhard Kühnl, *Das Dritte Reich in der Presse der Bundesrepublik. Kritik eines Geschichtsbildes*, Frankfurt 1966, p.180f.

44 Augstein, *op. cit.*, p.112f.

45 In the 1957 election campaign, for example, the Bishop of Munster made a public declaration to the effect that no Catholic could vote in good conscience for the SPD. And on the Sunday before the election a joint pastoral letter from the cardinals and bishops was read in all churches urging the faithful to support candidates "whose Christian faith is known and whose public acts correspond to it." (see S.K. Panter-Brick, "Adenauer's Victory in Munich" in: *Political Studies*, Vol. 7, No. 3 (Oct.) 1959, p.261f).

46 David Childs, *Germany Since 1918*, London 1971, p.146.

47 "Defizit der deutschen Demokratie" . . ., p.42.

48 The presence of former Nazis at all levels of West German society has been amply documented. The statements made here are supported by the following: Hannah Arendt, *Eichmann in Jerusalem*, New York 1967, p.16ff; Tetens, *op. cit.*, esp. ch. 5 and *passim*; Fritz Bauer, "Justiz als Symptom" in: Richter, ed., *op. cit.*, p.222ff; Reinhard Kühnl, *Die NPD*, W. Berlin 1968, *passim*; exhaustively, if not always credibly, Nationalrat der Nationalen Front des demokratischen Deutschland, ed., *Braunbuch: Kriegs- und Naziverbrecher in der Bundesrepublik und in Westberlin*, 3rd ed., E. Berlin 1968.

49 Kurt P. Tauber, "Aspects of Nationalist-Communist Collaboration in Postwar Germany" in: *Journal of Central European Affairs*, Vol. 20, April 1960, p.52. To be sure the author is arguing here for the existence of a communist-extremist right-wing conspiracy to bring down "western bourgeois democracy."

50 Reinhard Kühnl, "Die Auseinandersetaung mit dem Faschismus in BRD und DDR" in: Gerhard Hess, ed., *BRD-DDR. Vergleich der Gesellschaftssysteme*, Cologne 1971, p.269. Examples which he gives include school texts, the press, comic strips and illustrateds, murder-mysteries, political education in the Bundeswehr and the agitations of extremist refugee groups.

51 *Ibid.*, p.262f.

52 For a critique of the Volkswagen A.G., and by implication the other firms mentioned, after its return to private ownership, see Wolfgang Abendroth, *Wirtschaft, Gesellschaft und Demokratie in der Bundesrepublik*, Frankfurt 1965, p.34f.

53 From 45% of respondents opposed in the autumn of 1950, opposition increased to 50% in 1951, while only between 22-26% approved. See Edinger, *Kurt Schumacher*, p.229f.
See Hans-Karl Rupp, *Ausserparlamentarische Opposition in der Ära Adenauer*, Cologne 1970, p.33ff. See also *infra.*, ch. VI (3).

54 "Warum wir aufrüsten sollen" in *WISO-Korrespondenz*, No. 10 (31 July) 1956, p.108ff.

55 *Warum sind wir gegen die Remilitarisierung?*, Munich 1952.

56 Ossip K. Flechtheim, *Eine Welt oder keine?*, Frankfurt 1964, p.241f.

57 Ossip K. Flechtheim, "Widerstände gegen Abrüstung" in: *Frankfurter Hefte*, 1966, p.463.

58 Cf. Tetens, *op. cit.*, ch. 16.

59 Hans Speier, *German Rearmament and Atomic War*, Evanston Ill. 1957, p.150.

60 Phillip Windsor, *German Reunification*, London 1969, p.74.

61 Here see Fritz Vilmar, *Rüstung und Abrüstung im Spätkapitalismus*, Frankfurt 1965, p.81, 83 and 31.

62 Windsor, *op. cit.*, p.57.

63 Almond, *Politics* . . ., p.85f.

64 Augstein, *op. cit.*, p.84f.

65 Which is why the following analysis is based almost exclusively on recent sources, above all: Hans Matthöfer, "Internationale Kapitalkonzentration und gewerkschafts-bewegung" in: *Gewerkschaftliche Monatshefte*, No. 8 (Aug.) 1971, p.470ff; Wolfram Elsner, "Westeuropäische Integration und Arbeiterbewegung" in: *Blätter für deutsche und internationale Politik*, No. 12 (Dec.) 1971, p.1233ff; Authors' Collec-

tive, *Der Imperialismus in der BRD*, Frankfurt 1971; Ernest Mandel, *Europe versus America? Contradictions of Imperialism*, London 1970.
66 Elsner, *ibid.*, p.1233.
67 Here see Ulrich Teichmann, "Die Gewerkschaften in der Europäischen Wirtschaftsgemeinschaft (EWG)" in: *WISO-Korrespondenz*, No. 10 (Oct.) 1958, esp. p.244ff.
68 Cf. Mandel, *op. cit.*, p.100; Matthöfer, *op. cit.*, p.472.

2 The Ideology of Clerical Anticommunism

1 Heinrich Hannover, *Politische Diffamierung der Opposition im freiheitlichdemokratischen Rechtsstaat*, Dortmund-Barop 1962, p.2f.
2 "Europa-Idee und europäische Sicherheit" in: *Deutsche Volkszeitung*, 17 August 1973.
3 Major Mauer, writing in *Deutsche Monatshefte*, No. 3/1960, p.12.
4 Quoted in Augstein, *op. cit.*, p.39.
5 Gertrud Bienko, K.-J. Jockers, *et al.*, *Schulbücher auf dem Prüfstand. Antikommunismus, Antisowjetismus und Revanchismus in Lehrbüchern der Bundesrepublik*, Frankfurt 1972, p.8.
6 Reimut Reiche/Peter Gäng, "Vom antikapitalistischen Protest zur sozialistischen Politik" in: *Neue Kritik*, No. 41, April 1967, p.18.
7 Werner Hofmann, *Stalinismus und Anti-Kommunismus. Zur Soziologie des Ost-West Konflikts*, Frankfurt 1967, p.152f. See further Otwing Massing, "Recht als Korrelat der Macht" in: Schäffer/Nedelmann, *op. cit.*, p.141ff.
8 Hofmann, *op. cit.*, p.158.
9 Hannover, *op. cit.*, p.13ff
10 Adenauer's chief advisor in the 1950's and author of the authoritative commentary on the Nuremberg Race Laws.
11 Hannover, *op. cit.*, p.35.
12 See ch. VIII (2) below.
13 Hannover, *op. cit.*, p.116 and 93f.
14 K.O. Hondrich, *Die Ideologien von Interessenverbänden*, W. Berlin 1963, p.170.
15 Flechtheim, "Wiederstände gegen Abrüstung . . .", p.457.

3 The Isolation and Euthanasia of the KPD and the Problem of a Third Way

1 One of the perils of providing monocausal explanations for such complicated developments is evident in the contrasting situation of Italy, a country which was ruled by a fascist government for almost twice as long as Germany and in which the communist party became the second largest party in parliament after 1945.
2 "Kommunique der 8. Tagung des Parteivorstandes der KPD. 3 January 1949," reproduced in: *Dokumente der KPD 1945-56*, E. Berlin 1965, p.166f.
3 *Ibid., loc. cit.*
4 From a brochure of 1949, quoted in: Ute Schmidt/Tilman Fischer, *Der erzwungene Kapitalismus. Klassenkämpfe in den Westzonen 1945-48*, W. Berlin 1972, p.89.
5 As described in *Die Welt*, 29.8.1950.
6 Hans Kluth, *Die KPD in der Bundesrepublik. Ihre Politische Tätigkeit und Organisation 1945-1956*, Cologne & Opladen, 1959, p.35.
7 Ossip K. Flechtheim, *Die deutschen Parteien seit 1945*, W. Berlin 1965, p.102.
8 Kluth, *op. cit.*, p.37 and 106; and H. Toppe, *Der Kommunismus in Deutschland*, Munich 1962, p.76.
9 Helmut Rulke, *Die KPD — ihre Politik und ihre Organisation seit 1945*, unpublished *Diplom* thesis, Otto-Suhr-Institut (Free University of Berlin), 1959, p.68f lists all the KPD publications in this period.
10 "Einheit, Frieden, Wohlstand. Aus dem Wahlprogramm der KPD. Juli 1949" in: *Dokumente . . . 1945-56, op. cit.*, p.186 and ff.

11 "Das Programm aller deutschen Patrioten. Aus dem Wahlprogramm der KPD. 9.7.1953", in: *ibid.*, p.380.
12 "Einheit . . .", *op. cit.*, p.186.
13 "Die gegenwärtige Lage und die Aufgaben der KPD. Aus der Entschliessung des Parteitages der KPD. 3.-5. Marz 1951" in: *ibid.*, p.272.
14 In Ch. II (3) it has been argued that until at least 1955 the Soviet Union was interested in restoring German unity on the basis of neutrality and free all-German elections.
15 "Die Lehren der Wahlen vom 14. August 1949, Resolution des Parteivorstandes der KPD. 16 September 1949" in: *Dokumente der KPD . . . op. cit.*, p.198.
16 *Ibid.*, p.196 and 200.
17 *Ibid.*, p.200.
18 *Ibid.*, *loc. cit.* and f.
19 Max Reimann, *et al.*, *KPD-Verbot. Ursachen und Folgen 1956-71*, Frankfurt 1971, p.20.
20 *Ibid.*, p.20f.
21 Cf. SPD, ed., *Hochverratsprozess gegen getarnte Kommunisten. Eine Sozialdemokratische Darstellung über den Karlsruher Prozess gegen die 'sozialistische Aktion'*, Bonn 1956 (brochure).
22 Concerning these political trials of leading communists, see Tribunus (Wolfgang Abendroth?), "Vorbereitung zum Hochverrat?" in: *Funken* No. 8, 1955, p.113ff.
23 On this see *infra*. Ch. VI (3). On the chronological sequence of these events see: KPD Central Committee, ed., *Das Schandurteil von Karlsruhe. Ein Entscheid gegen Frieden, Freiheit, Einheit und Recht*, E. Berlin 1957, p.9ff.
24 Here see the text of the DGB Federal Executive Committee's position on the KPD ban, reproduced in: Theo Pirker, *Die blinde Macht. Die Gewerkschaftsbewegung in Westdeutschland*, Munich 1960, Vol. II, p.189f.
25 Anon. (but not Agartz), quoted in Gustav Heinemann's "Plädoyer" in: Hans-Georg Herrmann, *Verraten und verkauft*, Fulda 1959, p.242.
26 In this connection, Helmut Ridder has written that the main reason for the KPD's objectionableness to the ruling powers was that: "As a Marxist-Leninist Party it exercised . . . system-transcending criticism of the outdated bourgeois-constitutional democracy. It strove toward a socialist form of state and society without which, in its view, democratic freedom and equality could not be realized." See his "Einführung" in: Wolfgang Abendroth, *et al.*, *KP-Verbot oder mit den Kommunisten leben?*, Hamburg 1968, p.12.
27 KPD Central Committee, ed., *Das Schandurteil . . ., op. cit.*, p.6.
28 Shortly after the 1956 ban, the KPD membership dropped from approximately 70,000 to 7,000, and virtually no new members joined until 1968; see Rolf Ebbinghaus/Peter Kirchhof, "Der angepasste Klassenkampf. Organisation and Politik der DKP" in: *Politische Vierteljahresschrift*, 11th year, December 1970, p.558.
29 On these factors see KPD, ed., *Die KPD lebt und kämpft. Dokumente der KPD 1956-1962*, E. Berlin 1963, p.550ff; and Heinrich Hannover, *op. cit.*, p. 131ff.
30 Quoted in Reimann, *et al.*, *KPD-Verbot . . .*, p.34.
31 *Ibid.*, p.37ff.
32 See Ridder, *op. cit.*, p.14.
33 Cf. Bundesministerium für Gesamtdeutsche Fragen, ed., *Das Verbot der KPD. Das Urteil des Bundesverfassungsgerichts — Erster Senat — vom 17. August 1956*, Karlsruhe 1956, p.645.
34 Reimann, *et al.*, *op. cit.*, p.26.
35 Wolfgang Abendroth, "Einige Bemerkungen zur Analyse der politischen Funktion der KPD Verbotes" in: Abendroth, *et al.*, *op. cit.*, p.27.
36 Here cf. Renate Riemeck, "Das Verbot der KPD — historisch-politisch betrachtet" in: *Ibid.*, p.52f.

37 KPD Central Committee, *Die Lage in der Bundesrepublik und der Kampf um Frieden und Demokratie*, n.p. (E. Berlin), n.d. (1959) (brochure), p.60.
38 See the Central Committee Resolution of the 2nd Session, reproduced in: KPD, ed., *Die KPD lebt und kämpft . . . op. cit.*, p.18ff; See further KPD, ed., *KPD 1945-1965. Abriss, Dokumente, Zeittafel*, E. Berlin 1966, *passim*.
39 Here see Flechtheim, "Die KPD nach 1945" in: *Der Politolog*, Vol. 21, Oct. 1966, p.5.
40 "Gründung der UAPD" in: *Die Welt*, 27 March 1951.
41 "Freiheit, Unabhängigkeit, Sozialismus" in: *Freie Tribüne*, 6 April 1951, p.?
42 See dpa (Deutsche Presse-Agentur), reports for members of 11 December 1950 and 24 March 1951.
43 S. Bernhard, "Auf dem Wege zu einer unabhängigen Arbeiterpartei in Westdeutschland" in: *pro und contra*, No. 2 (February) 1951, p.20ff.
44 "Der Sozialismus ist stärker" in: *Freie Tribüne*, 12 August 1950.
45 B.L., "Der Antisowjetismus und wir" in: *Freie Tribune*, 9 September 1950.
46 Der Sozialismus ist stärker . . . ," *op. cit.*
47 Mimeographed communique of the Secretariat of the UAPD of 23 October 1951.
48 Cf. "Deutsche 'Titoisten-Partei' gegründet in: *Stuttgarter Nachrichten*, 27 March 1951.
49 In particular Wolfgang Leonhard. See, e.g., his "Die Arbeiterräte in Jugoslavien" in: *Freie Tribüne*, 16 September 1950.
50 Ryschkowsky, *Die linke Linke*, Munich and Vienna, 1968, p.20f. In a footnote on page 20, reiterated in a private interview with this author, Ryschkowsky claims that the UAPD was also the recipient of CIA funds donated for the purpose of promoting factionalism within the Left.
51 *Ibid., loc. cit.*
52 "An alle Leser" in: *Freie Tribüne*, 22 December 1951.
53 dpa report from Munich 20.10.1952.

4. The Absorption of the Trade Unions

1 When this legislation (Law 27 of 20 May 1950) was in fact executed, the members of the boards of directors of the firms to be liquidated were themselves appointed the liquidators. Cf. Eberhard Schmidt, *Die verhinderte Neuordnung 1945-1952*, Frankfurt 1970, p.176f.
2 As discussed in context in section (1) of this chapter.
3 As pointed out by Viktor Agartz, "Zur Situation der Gewerkschaften im liberal-kapitalistischen Staat" in: *WWI-Mitteilungen*, No.8 (Aug.) 1952, p.147ff.
4 Wolfgang Hirsch-Weber, *Gewerkschaften in der Politik*, Cologne & Opladen 1959, p.116.
5 "Neutralisierung der Gewerkschaften" in: *Die Andere Zeitung*, No.1 (Jan.) 1956,
6 Rüdiger Altmann, "Der Verdacht, ein Staat zu sein" in: Altmann, Böll, Flechtheim, *et al.*, *Zensuren nach 20 Jahren Bundesrepublik*, Cologne 1969, p.16.
7 On this see Hans See, *Volkspartei im Klassenstaat oder Das Dilemma der innerparteilichen Demokratie*, Reinbek 1972, p.88; and Herbert Sultan/Wolfgang Abendroth, *Bürokratischer Verwaltungsstaat und soziale Demokratie*, Hanover & Frankfurt, 1955, p.66f.
8 With whom they tend to have special priority, a relationship based on, among other things, "social provenance, personal ties and connections, class situation, self-interest, ideological inclinations, concepts of the 'national interest'." Cf. Ralph Miliband, *The State in Capitalist Society*, London 1969, p.161f.
Here cf. A. Offen, ''Die Mitbestimmung kränkt an der Partnerschaft-Ideologie" in: *Die Andere Zeitung*, No.1 (5 Jan.) 1956, p.8.
9 As described at length in Ch.III (1) above.
10 Gérard Sandoz, *La Gauche Allemande de Karl Marx à Willy Brandt*, Paris 1970, p.131.

11 The numbers in the first Bundestags were as follows:

	1949	1953	1957
Total no. of deputies	420	506	519
Total no. trade union members	89	172	198
Of these: CDU/CSU	22	44	43
SPD	67	129	154
other	—	—	1

Source: Kurt Hirsche, "Gewerkschaftler im Bundestag" in: *Gewerkschaftliche Monatshefte*, December 1957, p.707.

12 CDU brochure, *Die geistigen Richtlinien der Sozialausschüsse*, n.p., n.d. (1950?).

13 Mimeographed circular letter from SPD Party Exec. Committee, division Betriebsorganisation, to all regional chairman of the DGB, Hanover, 17 Nov. 1949, signed by S. Neumann.

14 On this see Viktor Agartz, "Kapital und Arbeit als Sozialpartner" in: *WISO-Korrespondenz*, No.12, 1 September 1956, p.134ff.

15 And on this see letter from Siggi Neumann (SPD Party executive Committee) to Hans Böckler, Hanover, 19 September 1949, available in DGB archives, Düsseldorf.

17 From a BDA statement, quoted in Hirsch-Weber, *op. cit.*, p.113.

18 For the genesis of this policy see *Protokoll des ausserordentlichen Bundeskongresses des DGB*, 1951, p.121f. KPD members' resignations were forced by the simple expedient of presenting them with the alternative: either pledge themselves to follow no directives from outside the trade unions, or resign their DGB offices. Since the KPD forbade its members to sign such a pledge, many KPD functionaries were expelled from the DGB beginning in 1952. Then the DGB began a campaign against functionaries' participation in any "communist-sponsored" movement or causes.

19 As pointed out in Herbert J. Spiro, *The Politics of German Co-determination*, Cambridge Mass. 1958, p.38.

20 Eberhard Schmidt, *Ordnungsfaktor oder Gegenmacht. Die politische Rolle der Gewerkschaften*, Frankfurt 1971, p.40.

21 Pirker, *Die blinde Macht . . .*, Vol.I, p.260ff, reproduces a letter to this effect from Adenauer to Fette of 16 May 1952.

22 Schmidt, *Die verhinderte Neuordnung . . .*, p.221.

23 From a DGB Federal Executive Committee resolution of 3 December 1951, quoted in Pirker, *Die blinde Macht . . .*, Vol.I, p.233.

24 See *ibid.*, p.235.

25 According to Schmidt (*Ordnungsfaktor . . .*, p.42) a majority of union members were prepared to support any strike actions at this time in support of increased codetermination.

26 Hirsch-Weber, *op. cit.*, p.110.

27 Urs Jaeggi, *Macht und Herrschaft in der Bundesrepublik*, Frankfurt 1971, p.66.

28 See, e.g. the text of his radio speech, reprinted in Pirker, *Die blinde Macht . . .*, Vol.I, p.284f.

29 August Enderle (with assistance of Bernt Heise), *Die Einheitsgewerkschaften*, Düsseldorf, mimeographed M/S of the DGB Bundesvorstand, 1959, p.584f.

30 Including Peter Michels, DGB district chairman in Cologne, later *Land* chairman of that city; Alfred Dannenberg, district leader of IG Metall in Hanover; Ludwig Linsert, first chairman of DGB Munich; and Karl Hanenschild, secretary of the DGB youth movement and later first chairman of IG-Chemie. In a private interview with the author, Professor von Oertzen kindly provided many details concerning the Circle of Ten, to whom he attaches a great importance in preserving socialist policies in the DGB and the Federal Republic in the early 1950's, a feeling which, despite his respect for Professor von Oertzen, this author does not share, for reasons given below.

31 According to Professor von Oertzen, the strength of the Bavarian movement was such that: "Only a few people knew how close the Federal Republic then missed a revolutionary strike movement." See Richard Petry (= Peter von Oertzen), "Die SPD und der Sozialismus" in: *Frankfurter Hefte*, October 1954, p.672.
32 See, e.g., H.H.Z., "Die Liquidierung des Frankfurter Kongresses" in: *Sozialistische Politik*, No.7 (July) 1955, p.3F.
33 Pirker, *Die blinde Macht* . . ., Vol.II, p.141.
34 Published by the DGB as a special brochure, *Aktionsprogramm des DGB*, Düsseldorf 1955.
35 See, e.g., Nell-Bruening's "Mitbestimmung und Partnerschaft auf der Ebene von Betrieb und Unternehmen" in: *Wege zum sozialen Frieden*, ed, by the Akademie für Gemeinwirtschaft, Hamburg, Stuttgart & Düsseldorf, 1954; and his: *Oswald von Nell-Bruening contra Viktor Agartz*, special publication of the *Gesellschaftspolitische Kommentäre*, 2nd year, 1 February 1955.
36 According to press accounts, Agartz had given to the DGB Executive Committee copies of letters allegedly written by Gleitze to important persons in the DDR. But these letters then proved to be forgeries, and it was assumed by the DGB that Agartz had himself produced the forgeries. See Gunter Treitsch, *Die Macht der Funktionäre*, Düsseldorf 1956, p.73.
37 Concerning the reasons for Pirker's dismissal, an interesting file has recently become available in the archives of the DGB. The information given here is based on the following documents: (1) Letter from Erich Potthoff to Pirker, Cologne, 7 November 1955, (2) Pirker's article, "Wilde Streiks und Streikrecht" in: *Die Andere Zeitung*, No.19, 1955 and (3) A letter from Joseph Rovan to Walter Freitag, Paris, 9 August 1955, in reply to the latter's request for further information on the events of a vacation which Pirker and Rovan had spent together. In it Rovan wrote of his surprise ". . . that ten years after the collapse of the Hitler regime the coworkers of your great movement find it necessary to present accounts to their superiors in this manner of how they spend their holidays."
38 Which was: Walter Horn, "Oswald von Nell-Bruening S.J. contra Oswald von Nell-Bruening S.J. Die Frankfurter Gewerkschaftskongress im Spiegel der katholischen Soziallehre," issued as supplement to *Gewerkschaftliche Monatshefte*, May 1955.
39 As pointed out by Anon., "Agartz und die 'marxistische Utopien'" in: *Sozialistische Politik*, No.11 (Nov.) 1955, p.1. A huge file in the DGB archives containing protests from local, regional and federal DGB organisations shows that the pretexts for the dismissals were not given much credence by many members and functionaries.
40 "Das Dilemma der Radikalen" in: *Die Andere Zeitung*, No.5 1956, p.8f.
41 Pirker, *Die blinde Macht* . . ., Vol.II, p.196f.
42 *Protokoll* of the DGB Bundeskongress 1-6 October 1956 in Hamburg, Manifest "Wiedervereinigung."
43 Text in Pirker, *Die blinde Macht* . . ., Vol.II, p.4.
44 See Theo Pirker, "Die IG Bau wird gerettet" in: *Die Andere Zeitung*, No.5 1956, p.8.
45 The text of Abendroth's speech has been printed in the DGB Youth-sponsored brochure, *Was können wir tun?*, Munich 1956. On these developments see Theo Pirker, "DGB Bundesvorstand verleumdet Professor Abendroth" in: *Die Andere Zeitung*, No.17 1956, p.9.
46 Pirker, *Die blinde Macht* . . ., Vol.II, p.189.
47 On this cf. Franz Altmann, "Wieder Arbeitsgemeinschaft" in: *Die Andere Zeitung*, No.10 1956, p.9.
48 According to Ralf Dahrendorf, *Society and Democracy in Germany*, Garden City 1967, p.165, comparative statistics were as follows:

Country	Employees involved (annual avg.)	Workdays lost (annual avg.)
W. Germany	137,000	637,000
France	1,523,000	2,196,000

Great Britain	762,000	4,154,000
Italy	1,761,000	6,202,000
Japan	1,255,000	5,102,000

49 S. Neumann, "Kritische Notizen" in: Willi Birkelbach, *Die Grosse Chance. Diskussionsbeiträge zum Thema 'Demokratischen Sozialismus',* Frankfurt n.d. (1956), p.69f.

V. CONTRADICTIONS AND CONFLICTS IN THE SPD

The isolation of the KPD and the Left's inability to organize an alternative political force left the SPD, apart from the (integrated) trade unions, the sole legal representative of the tradition, ideas and voting potential of the Left. This situation was in marked contrast to that which existed after World War I, when a number of rival left wing movements, such as the KPD, the Independent Socialist Party (USPD), the "free" trade unions and the works' council groups, challenged and opposed every tendency toward the right on the part of the SPD. Now the SPD was no longer forced to compete in the market place of socialist parties and movements. Its only competition now came from the Right. But, as the elections of 1953 and 1957 would clearly demonstrate, the bourgeois coalition enjoyed the support of roughly two-thirds of West Germans who went to the polls. In other words, the SPD, relying on its traditional socialist programme — albeit with a number of concessions and compromises which will be discussed here — and its traditional sources of mass support among the working classes, was able to attain only one-third of the popular vote in the decade following the establishment of the Federal Republic.

Two basic alternatives offered possible ways out of the "33 per cent ghetto." The SPD could: (a) adhere to the socialist principles contained in its Heidelberg Programme of 1925 and the course of democratic socialism set by Kurt Schumacher, deferring its prospects for gaining political power immediately while carrying on its efforts to develop the consciousness of the subordinate classes, above all the working class, or (b) alter or abandon its traditional socialist planks piecemeal in an endeavour to adapt to perceived changing voter expectations and social conditions, a process which would involve transforming the SPD into a modern "non-ideological" mass party employing the newest techniques in advertising and public relations and aiming at obtaining power on the basis of image-making and its leaders' personalities rather than concrete proposals or alternative programmes. Both proposals found their advocates within the SPD during the 1950's.

However, the SPD's receptiveness to the latter alternative was greatly enhanced by the fact of its being the opposition party during the periods of reconstruction and economic boom. The CDU/CSU's ability, by virtue of its position as the dominant ruling party, to satisfy a wide range of expectations and demands proved to be a powerful stabilizing agent against which the SPD could counter — if it adopted the first course just mentioned — (a) with an uncompromising alternative socialist programme, or — in the second instance — (b) with the simple negation of the bourgeois coalition's tangible achievements coupled with promises that, once in office, it would effect even greater

138

accomplishments (by implication within the capitalist system) than the CDU/ CSU had already brought about. In the first case the SPD left itself open to opposition charges of being "a band of nay-sayers" and in the second exposed itself to a strong "system-immanent pressure"[1] tending to bend it into acquiescence with the ground rules of the existing capitalist system and the CDU State.

1. The Legacy of Kurt Schumacher

Most of the programmatic inconsistencies and policy formulation problems with which the SPD had to come to terms during the 1950's had their roots in the party's development under Kurt Schumacher.

Now Schumacher's basic, inflexible proposals for the achievement of socialism only under the conditions of majority parliamentary vote, with special regard to the primacy of foreign policy (vis-à-vis the military governments) and in complete disassociation from communism, were after 1945 completely within the mainstream of political party debate. The SPD's 29 per cent of the popular vote in the 1949 elections showed it to be almost equally as popular as the CDU/CSU with the latter's 31%. The fact that Adenauer had been elected Chancellor by a one-vote margin in the Bundestag indicated that a socialist SPD, in the postwar political climate, had a realistic chance to achieve political power on the strength of its democratic and socialist pro- gramme as outlined at the Wennigsen/Hanover and Nuremberg party conventions of 1946 and 1947.

The SPD first became a party of "fundamental" or "categorical" opposition in its refusal to bend with changing socio-economic conditions and the Restoration. Where the socialist (or socialist-sounding) proposals of all the postwar political parties — except the FDP/LDP — might conceivably have formed a basis for cooperation or coalition with the SPD in the immediate postwar years, developments after 1948 — creation of the separate western state, formation of the bourgeois coalition, German involvement in the Cold War, onset of the Restoration — rendered any such policy impossible if the SPD were to maintain its basic socialist tenets.

The basis of this policy of "intransigent opposition" was laid down in a series of resolutions formulated by Schumacher, in collaboration with a number of "old guard" party members such as Carlo Schmid, Willi Eichler, Otto Suhr, Waldemar von Knoeringen and Erwin Schoettle, and presented to the Party Executive Committee (*Vorstand*) in Bad Dürkheim in August 1949, shortly after the first federal elections. The Dürkheim 16 Points, or the "Document of the Opposition," as Schumacher called it, outlined the party's "as-if" policy as the political opposition in the CDU State: proceeding as if it were already the government, operating as if it had already gained controlling political power, as if German reunification were going to be achieved and the occupation ended. Declaring that: "With any less forceful or firm position we shall allow Germany's development toward democracy to take the wrong turn and plunge into the abyss,"[2] Schumacher presented a series of specific policies from which the party would not deviate: abolition of unemployment, economic planning and rejection of the profit economy, large-scale social assistance, comprehensive codetermination, socialization of important industries and large property holdings, opposition to Allied intervention in

German domestic politics, strengthening of federal government powers over those of the *Länder*, and full sovereignty for both Germanies.

The inevitable effect of applying the Bad Dürkheim policies was to involve the SPD in a political struggle on several fronts — against all four Military Governments, the bourgeois coalition and the KPD-SED.

Schumacher understood, and his successors tended to overlook, that the division of Germany, the western alliance and the continuation of the Cold War represented perhaps the single most powerful source of the CDU State's strength, and that the feelings and resentments which this situation engendered tended to divert popular awareness away from social questions and problems of socialism. Given further that the eastern territories represented a traditional source of Social Democratic mass support, then in all probability in a reunited Germany the SPD would have had a far better chance of gaining power, or at least a vastly increased support.

Thus the SPD's stress on the primacy of national reunification challenged the basic policies (western integration), ideology (unification with the DDR would have eliminated the main object of clerical anticommunism) and voter reservoir of the CDU/CSU, and made the SPD a fundamental opponent of the bourgeois coalition. However, the SPD's efforts found little resonance among the broad sectors of the population, chiefly because: "The mere fact of the existence of two mutually exclusive regimes transforms any opposition into opposition between the two regimes, emptying strictly domestic conflict of much of its substance and meaning."[3]

The priority of reunification also explains to some degree the SPD's antagonism toward all four occupation powers whose presence and policies in Germany diminished prospects for reunification. And this antagonism was heightened by Schumacher's desire for a more centralized political and economic system, as well as by his policy of implacable anticommunism, in the case of the USSR.

When Theo Pirker accuses Schumacher of not objectively criticizing government policy, but instead "declaring principles" ("Parliament for Schumacher was not a place for debate, it was the platform from which he addressed the German people, the victor powers and the world"[4]), he is perhaps overlooking the fact that a policy of intransigent opposition toward virtually the entire political development of the Federal Republic after 1949 — the Basic Law, all foreign treaties, membership in supra-national associations, rearmament, etc. — as factors tending to make national division irreversible could be little more than a declaration of principles. But at least they were socialist principles.

Moreover, this policy brought with it a number of problems: the absolute oppositional party in the liberal capitalist state, by refusing to take part in committee work, consultations and the like, prevents its members from gaining actual political experience, deprives the party of at least a partial influence in passing legislation, restricts the opposition's democratic control function, increases the executive's power,[5] and encumbers the party in the public mind with a negative image.

This problem was compounded by the fact that, while the federal SPD was proclaiming its policy of opposition on principle, many local and *Länder* party organizations were active in the work of reconstruction — frequently in coalition governments — and policy formulation. Even the federal SPD's opposition in the first Bundestag was by no means completely negative, especially in the realm of domestic legislation where it often actively supported the CDU-controlled government. (Only foreign policy decisions had to be decisively accepted or rejected). The dichotomy between theory (absolute opposition) and practice (active participation in formulating legislation and in policy-making) which this situation created would plague the SPD for two decades.

If for Schumacher a consistent *socialism* came to mean opposition on principle, the second central tenet of his belief-system, *democracy*, became in the debates with communism a policy of *"Nur-Parlamentarismus"*: a total reliance on parliament and parliamentary methods and, in time, an inability to envision any other than strictly constitutional solutions to the problems — rearmament, NATO, renazification, etc. — which it opposed in principle and attacked in radically phrased and intransigent speeches and writings. Here Pirker's criticism is more telling: "The party almost completely overlooked the tasks and possibilities in the extraparliamentary realm."[6]

Strict parliamentarism, especially as practised by Schumacher's less determined successors, proved to be a tactical tightrope, as it gradually became apparent that the SPD's one-third of parliamentary votes was in itself insufficient to prevent the long series of developments during the 1950's tending to promote the Restoration, cement the division of Germany and place even greater obstacles in the way of the achievement of socialism in the Federal Republic. On the one hand, protracted verbal opposition reinforced the public image of the SPD as "undeserving" a "responsible" share in the government. And on the other, left wing members grew restless and discontent at the party's failure to employ or support the use of the traditional weapons of the labour movement — mass political strike, protests, demonstrations, etc. — in order to forestall these antisocialist developments. Schumacher's insistence on the importance of the state machinery and election by majority vote caused Willy Huhn to call him a "Lasalleaner" for whom the state was an "independent, supra-class institution, an organization which classes and parties struggled to gain control of."[7]

2. Criticism from the Left

From the Left's point of view, Schumacher's tenacious adherence — subject to a number of minor inconsistencies which will be explored further in this section — to the indivisible principles of democracy and socialism, and his policy of uncompromising opposition to the direction taken by the capitalist western state under the leadership of the bourgeois coalition meant that membership in the SPD was entirely compatible with a socialist commitment.

But following Schumacher's death in 1952, the party leadership came to be more and more undistinguished and indecisive. "With the death of Kurt Schumacher," Theo Pirker has written elsewhere, "the West German labour movement lost its tribune — just as it had lost its labour leader with the death of Böckler."[1] Schumacher's successor, Erich Ollenhauer, was not only, in Keith Panter-Brick's memorable phrase, "not a speaker to set the town on fire,"[2] he was in many ways the typical party functionary. As party chairman of the Exile-SPD during the Third Reich and Schumacher's chief executor and liaison man after 1945, he had grown accustomed to delegating authority and concentrating on organizational aspects. Under his leadership political policy was given over in large measure to specialists and experts, while Ollenhauer himself was concerned with "organizing" a consensus. Gerhard Gleissberg summarized this situation in his analysis of the SPD's defeat in the 1957 election:

> It was not Ollenhauer's face which was responsible for the SPD's electoral defeat, it was the ear which he lent to the "military expert" Erler, the "economic expert" Deist, the "constitutional law expert" Carlo Schmid, the "finance expert" Schoettle, the routine men of parliament, holders of *Länder* ministries and mayors and the Cold Warriors of the Ostbüro — and his weakness for party functionaries who see the "machine" as an end in itself and hunt down the Left as a substitute for socialist action.[3]

In a process of integration similar to that which occurred in the DGB, many SPD members were accorded posts in government bureaucracies or in big business — e.g. Alex Möller became General Manager of the large insurance corporation, Karlsruher Lebensversicherung, and Carlo Schmid was appointed to the supervisory board of MAN — and the acceptance of such posts diminished their holders' credibility as representatives of the working classes' interests. In Viktor Agartz' words: "Instead of power, they chose office."[4]

Together with the decline in leadership quality went a corresponding ossification of the party structure. The organization of the postwar SPD was necessarily centralist and authoritarian to some extent because of the urgency of the situation which demanded immediate political measures and decisions from the party, the absence of any state machinery and the need to meet the challenge of the KPD and forestall the absorption of the SPD into the SED.[5] But the result was the establishment of a rather centralist and rigid party hierarchy which derived much of its cohesiveness from a "narrow-minded and intolerant" (rather than objective or realistic) anticommunism and, unlike the pre-1933 SPD, a basic intolerance of all opposition and an unwillingness to discuss party decisions and policies. ("In the beginning was the Machine.")[6]

Intra-party discussion gradually declined. As Peter von Oertzen wrote, it was difficult but not impossible, to get a resolution passed which went against the party line, but it was entirely impossible to elect a new Executive Committee which would implement this line.

> Thus the inner-party opponent is faced with an insoluble dilemma: either he keeps his distance from the machine, thereby acquiring the reputation of an eternal grumbler who can only criticize and avoid work; or as an individual he enters the Executive Committee, an advisory body or committee — which he can do without difficulty if he is proficient — where he wears himself out at routine work without being able to change the overall picture in the least.[7]

The decline in party membership which had begun under Schumacher (from 875,479 in 1947 to 683,000 in 1950) continued to around the 600,000 mark by 1954, where it remained relatively constant for more than a decade. Although, as Pirker has stated, there have been no studies made of the "lost" members, it is probable that "in their majority they may have been new members and younger party members"[8] for whom the SPD had failed to provide a relevant role. And many may have been opportunists for whom membership in the SPD represented a quick route to positions in the new administration or a safeguard against denazification proceedings. Still others may have been those who had joined the party in 1945 as a token of their rejection of Nazism and who thus " . . . brought nothing more into the party than their rejection of the past."[9]

One of the primary effects of this "ascendancy of the machine" was the exaggeration of parliamentarism and the rules of formal democracy into an increasing tendency to overlook or neglect the party's ultimate socialist aims. But for the Left, outward democratic forms were not the ends of a socialist party: they were one means among many. The Left's "aim and goal (was) the socialist society."[10] Where Schumacher's concentration upon parliamentary methods had represented a component part of his conception of democracy, however, the new leaders' parliamentarism largely signified their inability to envision any other strategy. This attitude could be at least partly understood in the light of their political experience in the Weimar era and their fidelity to the postwar policy laid down by Schumacher. Any criticism from the Left of parliamentarism was increasingly met either by incomprehension or by references to "communist" or "syndicalist" tendencies."[11]

In virtually none of the major issues of West German politics, from reunification to defence, foreign policy and socialization, can it be said that the SPD adopted a firm and consistent stand during the decade after Schumacher's death. The literature of the Left between 1952 and 1962 is replete with exhortations and admonitions to the party to take a position one way or the other. Peter von Oertzen complained of the SPD's lack of consistency, failure to raise the question of socialization, inability to comprehend the class nature of society, increasing alienation from its mass basis in the working class and its confusion of social reform with socialism.[12]

Another problematical issue during the 1950's was that of the unity of the labour movement, the SPD's failure to act in concert with the other workers' organizations, especially the DGB, and its unwillingness to sponsor or even support extraparliamentary mass movements or demonstrations. For those who had advocated the unity of the working classes' representative organizations after the war, this proved that: "By its inaction the labour movement of West Germany has proven that it has not yet overcome the consequences of the fascist dictatorship and the military dictatorship after 1945."[13] The divisions within the workers's organizations were pointed out by the monthly *Funken* as early as 1951. For example, while the SPD and KPD opposed West Germany's entry into Council of Europe and participation in the Schumann Plan, the DGB and DAG (the white-collar workers' trade union) were in favour of both these steps — despite the fact that both parties and both trade unions were ostensibly representative of the working classes, with frequently overlapping memberships.[14] Similarly, while the SPD leadership was submitting proposals for a "people's army," between 80-90 per cent of the party's rank and file, as well as its youth arm, the *Falken*, were opposed to rearmament in any form.[15]

The fundamental cause of dissension between the SPD and the trade unions, as has been discussed above, was the two institutions' concepts of the role of labour in post-fascist Germany. Where the unified trade union after 1948/49 was more concerned with maintaining unity and extracting maximum concessions from the capitalist system, Schumacher saw the trade unions as a potential source of support and mobilization for the SPD, whose aim was the realization of socialism. For Schumacher a "trade union mentality" had no place in labour's primary struggle for political power.[16] After Schumacher's death the conflict became largely pragmatic, with the SPD aspiring to more, and more direct, support from the trade unions.

In a comparatively recent article commemorating the twentieth anniversary of Kurt Schumacher's death, Arno Behrisch argued that the SPD leader's anticommunism was at the root of the party's failures in the postwar era. Pointing to Schumacher's attacks on the DDR as "totalitarian state capitalism" and "slaves of the Soviet occupation power" and his reference to "Soviet fascism" and "communists as Nazis painted red," Behrisch emphasized one aspect of Schumacher's policy.[17] This problem was discussed in Chapter II. But there it was further argued that Schumacher's anticommunism ought to be considered as a part of his more central policies of national self-determination and democratic socialism.

Admittedly Schumacher's attacks on the KPD and Soviet Union were excessive and at times irrational — considerably more polemical than his attacks on Adenauer as the "Chancellor of the Allies," the CDU as the "agents of the reaction" and the western occupation powers as representatives of monopoly capital and the dividers of Germany — but the SPD's struggle to maintain a separate existence from the Soviet-dominated SED was also a bitter one. There were indeed fundamental points of difference between the SPD and KPD, for example the KPD's dependence on Moscow:

> Here lies the deepest cause of the moral and political corruption of the KPD: the suppression of all intra-socialist discussion, terror against socialists not faithful to the party line. For blind obedience toward a distant headquarters precludes objective argument, free discussion, tolerance and loyalty toward those comrades who think principally otherwise. So long as every communist party in the world is not as independent as Tito is today, so is any partnership impossible.[18]

In this connection two aspects of the antifascist popular front ought to be recalled, (a) that its initial spontaneous, democratic and indigenous quality was checked and perhaps destroyed by the Military Governments' ban on political activities and subsequent encouragement of the old political parties, and (b) that one of its central tenets was a thoroughgoing democratic organization and discussion "from bottom to top." The compulsory union of KPD and SPD to form the SED, and Anton Ackermann's reluctant recanting of his theory of "the special German road to socialism" demonstrated conclusively that the KPD-SED no longer *primarily* represented the interests of the German working classes. Kurt Schumacher's anticommunism was not solely, nor even principally responsible for the failure of the antifascist popular front — though after 1949 it must have reinforced the CDU/CSU's functional and emotion-invoking clerical anticommunism — but the policies of the occupation powers, Ulbricht's Stalinist communism, the bourgeois coalition's anticommunism, and the actions of the KPD itself.

Nevertheless, Schumacher and, in particular, his successors tended increasingly to define their policies or justify their acts simply by attacking the KPD, SED or CPSU. To be sure, once the separate western state had been formed and it had become obvious that the KPD no longer enjoyed the support of any large sectors of the working classes, this continued controversy was no longer objectively necessary — except perhaps as a disciplinary threat within the party. According to the pattern of Federal German anti-communism, as described in the previous chapter, however, this anticommunism grew more vehement and illogical as it became less and less relevant to the actual "threat."

Throughout the 1950's (and 1960's), the pronouncements of party leaders, the publications of the SPD' *Ostbüro* (Office for Eastern Affairs) and the party organs propagated a kind of anticommunism which was not essentially different from that of the CDU/CSU. Within the party, anticommunism was increasingly used to threaten dissident members with expulsion[19] and to ensure the loyalty of those who remained. The SPD's changing anticommunism was indicative of the decline in intra-party discussion, the party's increasing tendency to bend to the "system-immanent pressure" referred to above and its lack of original conceptions or strategies.

> With its anticommunism the SPD itself spoils any chance of becoming a real reform party, for the moment the CDU/CSU calls the reformers communist revolutionaries, the SPD shrinks away because the party itself surrounds communism with superstitious fear, because it is itself relentlessly cherishing and harbouring anticommunism, 'this source of all the world's misfortune.'[20]

The SPD failed to see that irrational, "total" anticommunism was primarily the ideology of the Restoration. By raising the anticommunist banner, the party was ultimately opposing itself, for:

> [The SPD] will never be in a position to represent the interests of big industry more plausibly than big industry itself, to echo the legends of the 'Christian West' and the 'Free West' better than the qualified authors of this ideology, the CDU. It cannot relate antibolshevist horror stories in a more gruesome manner than the professional antibolshevists of the stamp of Taubert and his consorts from the school of Herr Dr. Goebbels.[21]

From the Left came a twofold critique of the SPD's anticommunist line. On the one hand the SPD was said to be increasingly receptive to political agreements with "former active Nazis and extreme clerics," while on the other: "Whoever sits down to talk with communists is expelled from the party."[22] It was evident that the only peaceful means of achieving reunification was through negotiations with the DDR, in direct opposition to Adenauer's policy of non-recognition (Hallstein doctrine) and establishing a superior military force ("Policy of Strength"), but again the SPD, until 1959, failed to develop a firm foreign policy as an alternative. Taking up proposals put forward by Abendroth and Jenssen, Franz Neumann advocated discussion with the SED on the basis of Ulbricht's suggestions for the nationalization of big concerns, restriction of the powers of high finance, socialization of basic industries subject to a plebiscite, abolition of conscription and West German withdrawal from NATO.[23]

Here it must be recalled that reunification held out prospects of a considerable gain for the SPD and the Left within the SPD. Echoing Schumacher's policy, Peter von Oertzen declared that the political struggle for unification had to be fought on two fronts because " . . . the aim of a socialist policy for Germany is: elimination of the Adenauer *and* the Ulbricht regimes."[24] If by the mid-fifties there was still any realistic chance of national division being overcome, it was evident that a compromise formula would have to take place over the opposition of the leadership of the eastern as well as the western partial state, and would have to involve an attack on strong vested interests in both East and West.

In any event the SPD's increasingly hard-line anticommunism, coupled with its sporadic moves toward the right, could not bring about a rapprochement. What was needed, as the Left saw it, was a socialist critique of communism which would be qualitatively different from clerical anti-communism. In a letter to Ollenhauer, Arno Behrisch argued against primitive anti-bolshevism and declared: "We must overcome communism by recognizing its roots."[25] Where, for example, the CDU/CSU was opposed to nationalization, socialization and planning per se, the socialist ought to oppose the possible absence of democratic codetermination and workers' control which could occur under conditions of a communist takeover, while remaining basically in favour of such measures. Kurt Hiller, among others, argued for a differentiation in the independent socialists' view of communism. Although the two groupings had many differences, their points in common — a desire to aid the poor and oppressed, the goal of reunification, the hope for peace — could constitute the basis of a common front against the conservatives and clerics with whom neither had as much in common as with each other.[26]

Of the issues with which the SPD had to come to terms within the CDU State, none was more problematic than that of foreign policy and defence. Kurt Schumacher's policy of "national" socialism, of the primacy of foreign policy was an indication of the weight which this problem assumed in his thought. He said:

> The struggle for foreign policy is at the same time a struggle for domestic policy, for the social content of the democratic state. Foreign policy determines the bounds of the possibilities which remain to us in economic policy and especially in social policy.[27]

The priority which Schumacher accorded to national unity and his fundamental opposition to the CDU State compelled his rejection of the Schumann Plan, the Federal Government's Saar policy, the Pleven Plan for a European army, any German contribution to western defence, the Council of Europe and later the Coal and Steel Community.

Yet the pressure to gain at least some influence over events, which were rapidly and often irrevocably taking place without the SPD's participation, eventually produced a number of cracks in this oppositional facade. Thus Schumacher rejected any contribution to Adenauer's defence policy so long as West Germany's role would be merely that of a buffer, or the front line in a possible world war. But he indicated that he would consent to the establishment of a defence system provided that the West's striking power could be built up to such an extent that the first important battle in the event of war could be carried east of the Elbe.

Whether or not this policy ought to be interpreted as a "forward thrust" strategy in a war of liberation rather than as "blind anticommunism,"[28] it convinced many among the politically aware that he was not against war preparations in principle,[29] and objectively lent credence to Adenauer's "policy of strength." Similarly, Schumacher expressed his basic agreement with the establishment of soldiers' associations and the bearing of decorations, but without swastikas and the colours of the Third Reich. In fact, Kurt Schumacher's "Jein" policies in the issue of rearmament and national defences were the main source of left-wing opposition to him in the last two years of his life.[30]

After Schumacher, however, the SPD's defence and rearmament policies became even more confused. Already in 1955 the *Sozialistische Politik* noted a growing tendency toward a "joint foreign policy" with the CDU which was tending to draw the SPD into an alliance with the capitalist system. [31] Then in March 1956, the SPD parliamentary party supported a constitutional amendment in the Bundestag enabling the Federal Government to introduce military service. On this occasion only twenty SPD parliamentarians abstained; none opposed the bill. [32] The SPD's assent to this amendment was significant as the beginning of a pattern of cooperation between the SPD and the bourgeois coalition. The SPD also rejected universal conscription officially while at the same time the party's "military expert," Fritz Erler proposed the creation of a volunteer army, the so-called "citizen in uniform".

Searching for alternatives to Adenauer's foreign policy, and unwilling to oppose for the sake of opposition, some SPD members suggested the formation of an all-European security council, guaranteed by both the USA and USSR, in which a reunited Germany would be neutral. But such plans could not prevail against Ollenhauer's rejection of what Walter Möller called any "genuine neutrality," a rejection which was based on the fear of being reproached for having communist sympathies and of losing favour with the occupation powers.[33]

Not until 1959 did the SPD evolve in its *Deutschlandplan* an independent foreign policy — only to give it up again the following year. In the years after 1955 it did not even come out in favour of direct negotiations with the DDR, although this omission tended to make its foreign policy resemble even more that of the CDU/CSU, which *Die Andere Zeitung* described as:

> We are against the Oder-Neisse Line, we are against diplomatic relations with the East Block states, we are against negotiations, we are for NATO and for atomic arms — what more should we do to bring about a peaceful return to our homeland?[34]

The importance of these issues, concerning which the SPD was unable to develop an independent or consistent policy, as mobilizing and catalyzing factors for a popular oppositional movement will be discussed in the next chapter.

The most substantial charge, finally, levelled by the Left against the SPD was the abandonment of the latter's socialist principles and goals. So long as Schumacher was party leader, the Left might take issue with his exaggerated anticommunism or his strict parliamentarism, but it knew that with the Hanover Convention's *Politische Leitsätze* and Schumacher's *Politische Richtlinien*, as well as the Bad Dürkheim Resolutions, the SPD was bound to a *platform* of socialism and socialization.

But Kurt Schumacher had not left a comprehensive *programme* incorporating a thorough analysis of existing society, concrete proposals for changing it and long-term socialist goals. Due to the exigencies of the postwar situation — the need for a rapid reorganization of the party, the immediate pressures of rebuilding, participation in local and regional administrative bodies, etc. — Schumacher had deferred the formulation and discussion of such a programme until the return of a more "normal" situation. This omission enabled a less determined leadership to ignore or alter the early platform planks without reference to a binding socialist programme.

Thus the SPD's Dortmund *Aktionsprogramm* of 1952, resolved shortly after Schumacher's death, still placed the socialization of the mining and steel industries in the foreground of a socialist economic policy which included extensive social reforms.[35] But here the role of socialization was already perceptibly less prominent than it had been under Schumacher. More important, the *Aktionsprogramm*, together with other developments after the party's 1953 defeat at the polls, indicated a growing trend on the part of the SPD to present itself as a *Volkspartei* or "party of all the people," which in itself did not represent an essential departure from Schumacher's conception. The difference was that now, instead of attempting to show the great majority of the population — the subordinate or wage-dependent classes — that the SPD was best qualified to represent their interests, the party began simply to make promises of "more but better" of the same once it came to power. This was the beginning of the long process of "casting Marx overboard" which culminated in the Bad Godesberg Programme of 1959.

In 1954, the Party Executive Committee advocated for Germany the kind of social democracy which had already been established in Great Britain and the Scandinavian countries, and reiterated the party's continuing efforts at becoming a *Volkspartei* in the existing social system. The Berlin Convention of that year confirmed these points and, practically overnight, began to emphasize the importance of competition as against planning and socialization. At this point experienced observers — not only on the Left — were noting the demise of the SPD's former praxis and ideals, and its advocacy of the liberal market economy which was said to owe more in its conception to John M. Keynes than Karl Marx.[36] Fritz Lamm wrote: ". . . instead of drawing the masses to the Left, we turn after them to the right, then we are surprised when they go even further to the right."[37]

After the Munich Convention of 1956, the SPD leadership began to propound a qualitatively new criticism of the social market economy through the party's financial expert and "shadow" economics minister, Heinrich Deist. It was now occasionally argued that Erhard had violated the spirit of liberalism by not being liberal enough.[38] To be sure, this criticism was coupled with a demand for further-reaching social security measures, but the dominant line of economic debate in West German politics was gradually developing into a competition to convince the voters who could operate the market economy most efficiently. The SPD's election programme of the following year, entitled "Security for All," ignored all proposals for changing power and property relationships while at the same time advocating the protection and encouragement of "free competition."[39]

3. The Programme Discussion

This relentless, if uncoordinated, drift toward the right and a series of defeats at the polls which culminated in the absolute CDU/CSU majority of 1957 resulted in increasing intra-party dissension and made acute the need for a basic programme. The absence of a socialist critique of the existing state and society and SPD's inability to account for the changed nature of postwar capitalism in a socialist analysis produced within the party number of antagonistic policies and strategies.

Thus anticommunism, intended to draw a distinct line between the party and the KPD-SED, had the effect of reinforcing the CDU's reactionary anti-communism, which was then turned against the SPD, indeed was intended to be used against the SPD. In other words: "Attempting to present itself to the voters as being anticommunist but not entirely pro-Western, i.e., attempting to resist one ideological force without accepting the other [or offering an intelligible, coherent alternative (author)] the SPD became the butt of both."[1]

The SPD's gradual adaptation to the CDU State only served to make the party's former socialism popularly less credible and to convince the public that the CDU's politics had perhaps been right after all. Even the concessions made were not part of an overall strategy, but in large measure acts of desperation or opportunism. And in any case these were often accompanied by the old rhetoric on social justice or by standard clichés concerning the capitalist-clerical-reactionary CDU as the agent of the Restoration which, although true, lacked the conviction and persuasive force which a comprehensive programme and a plausible alternative, forcefully presented, might have had.

The impetus for the programme discussion of the mid-1950's stemmed directly from the SPD's electoral defeat of 1953, as well as the growing controversy surrounding the party's foreign and defence policies. These were followed by the rather heated discussion which developed in the course of the Berlin Convention of 1954, the founding of a theoretical party organ, *Die Neue Gesellschaft* under the editorship of Ulrich Lohmar in the same year, and the publication of the brochure by Willi Birkelbach, *Die Grosse Chance*.[2] As the discussion slowly gained momentum and extended into various party organs, the left wing press, academic publications and even the bourgeois press, the inner-party cleavages began to coalesce into a tentative Right and Left.

The SPD *Right*,[3] by far the largest group numerically, could be further divided into what might be termed (a) the traditionalists, and (b) the pragmatists.

The traditionalists, embodied by Ollenhauer himself, theorist Willi Eichler, treasurer Alfred Nau, and others, were the ruling group of party-minded functionaries who had helped to reorganize and rebuild the party under Schumacher and whose horizons, as has been demonstrated, scarcely extended beyond the machine. Although they generally advocated the precedence of the party over the parliamentary party, it was more often the party machine, rather than the party's socialist purpose, which they had in mind. Most of the preceding section has been devoted to a discussion of the traditionalists' policies and their contradictions.

Their contribution to the programme discussion was largely a defence of existing policies. In a brochure which they issued, the SPD was described as a "community of people who are struggling for social justice, for the liberation of man from exploitation and oppression and for intellectual and political freedom." Few political parties in western democracies would not advance a similar claim. But the traditionalists were willing to concede the value of action outside parliament, as complementary to parliamentary work, in e.g., preventing "undemocratic electoral laws," the "coordination of the trade unions" or the "establishment of a propaganda ministry by the government. Symbols of party solidarity such as the greeting "comrade" (*Genosse*) and the red flag were to be retained. Concerning the latter, the brochure stated that for the SPD.

> . . . the red flag is the emblem of the power of the faith of liberal democratic socialism. In times of political oppression millions have derived from it the strength to fight for freedom at the risk of their person and their life. Our renunciation of the red flag would be interpreted as the surrender of our international goals. The red flag is, for traditional, political and human reasons, inextricably bound to socialism.[4]

The *pragmatic party Right* was less concerned with the party or with socialism than with achieving political power. For it the party was primarily a vehicle to power, while its activities centred chiefly around the parliamentary party or regional and municipal governments. In the forefront of this group were the largely younger deputies such as Heinrich Deist, Fritz Erler, Karl Schiller and Helmut Schmidt, prominent local and municipal office holders such as the mayors Willy Brandt (Berlin), Wilhelm Kaisen (Bremen) and Max Brauer (Hamburg), most of the parliamentary party in the Bundestag, and a younger group of intellectuals who, according to David Childs, were more likely to be economists and sociologists rather than writers or artists, who had begun their careers during the Third Reich and had completed the transition to Federal Germany without any essential discontinuity in the progression of their lives.[5] Such men were Klaus-Peter Schulz, Fritz Baade, Bruno Gleitze and Heinz-Dietrich Ortlieb.

This group was by no means opposed to party reform in the sense of reorganization. In a brochure probably published in late 1953, which may be considered the first substantial manifestation of the existence of a reform-minded Right, "a group of SPD and SDS members"[6] expressed their discontent at the excessive power of the party machine and proposed more democracy and inner-party discussion and selection for office as well as the inclusion of more social groups — such as youth, the rank and file and other "prominent people" not necessarily within the party — in decision- and policy-making.

The brochure also marked the first significant intra-party challenge to Schumacher's notion of winning the wage- and salary-dependent classes for a Social Democratic policy. It argued that the SPD must now abandon its class character — including all references to Marx, the concept of a planned economy, the use of the red flag, the reference to fellow party members as comrade — and develop into a genuine *Volkspartei*. It advocated more cooperation with the Federal Government, industry and the churches, in order to lead the party out of its "isolation." Since Marxism was "outdated," the binding goals of the party could now be "personal freedom," a rise in general prosperity, and "social security and solidarity." The points in common which the SPD had with both the churches and the government, it continued, must be located and emphasized in order to create a spirit of mutualism and to attract badly needed votes in subsequent elections. This document was of not inconsiderable importance, since it represented a first outline of the course actually taken by the SPD after 1959.

Typical of the pragmatic reformists' view was a dual emphasis on the challenge of modern technology and the need for an increased empiricism and expertise to account of the new developments in society and economy on the one hand, and a stress upon the omnipresent danger of totalitarianism, especially communist totalitarianism, on the other. Thus Ulrich Lohmar argued that any socialist theory could not be a "permanently binding and intrinsically stable model"; it ought to be based on an ongoing "comparison between empirical analysis and the values appropriate to our practical work." Such a comparison enabled socialists to ascertain "the ways and means leading to the realization of socialist goals," or in other words, "science is the connecting link between the means and ends of a socialist policy."[7] Without this scientific approach, the party would tend to lapse into totalitarianism, to claim a monopoly of socialist theory.

These ideas were taken a step further by Fritz Erler. Any political party, he argued, can only be a part of the whole; a party identifying itself with the whole must deny other parties the right to exist and in doing so present a totalitarian claim to power; this was the significance of the "C-element" in the CDU. Since modern industry had reduced the relative percentage of actual blue-collar workers in the overall population, the SPD must "balance out the various group interests in such a way that the common interest of the liberal democratic society follows from this. Only thus will a large party be considered fit by public opinion, without which it cannot govern, for the work of governing."[8] However, this was not to say that the SPD must develop into a "totalitarian *Volkspartei*": its core mass social base remained the industrial workers and protestants (cf. the CDU's farmers and catholics). The renewed party political struggle must be for the support of the "middle" voters, the white-collar workers and the "new" middle classes.

To this end, Erler continued, the party must use modern analytical methods to recognize the direction of society's development, and must know how to incorporate changing conditions into its own theories and therefore set its tasks according to existing possibilities. Since universal suffrage had brought political parties into the position once occupied by the upper classes (*tragende Schicht*), "it is clear that we do not stand outside this state and this society, but that we share responsibility for them (*wir tragen sie mit*), even if we want to change them."[9] Sharing in the responsibility for state and society, but at the same time possessing the will to change them, the SPD had to use scientific methods to obtain an overall picture of society and having gained an understanding of developmental tendencies, to intervene purposefully with the aims of achieving "a human society, the correct relationship between freedom and obligation, social justice with personal freedom and complete development of man in dignity."[10]

The pragmatic reformers' emphasis on the dangers of authoritarianism or totalitarianism most certainly reflected the apprehensions of a people who had just emerged from the Third Reich and were witnessing the establishment of a Stalinist dictatorship in the eastern partial state. With the ideological pressures of the Cold War and the tangible successes of the capitalist economy, many came to regard "freedom" or the maintenance of liberal rights as a value in itself, rather than continuing the postwar policy of socialism and democracy as inseparable and equally important. And the greatest threat to democratic rights was seen to be totalitarianism, a concept which equated fascism with communism, and counterpoised both against liberal democracy, so that the struggle for political freedom now became less a class struggle than a struggle against totalitarianism:

> The class struggle has changed its nature and, from a struggle against feudal or bourgeois classes, has not become, e.g., a struggle against persons, but a struggle against systems. It is no longer a question of our opposing economic classes but political hierarchies and oligarchies, party machines and their dictators . . .[11]

The notion of liberating man or achieving the conditions necessary for human freedom were, as discussed in previous chapters, contained in the SPD's programmes and platforms after 1945; but then they were coupled with socialism as the precondition of liberation. In other words, where democracy for the SPD had once been both an end and a means — the means toward economic and political liberation of man in society; and the end of achieving personal and intellectual freedom in a social context — it now seemed to signify only the end, with the means simply omitted or glossed over. The party's new emphasis was on formal, liberal or constitutionally guaranteed freedom, *viz.* through economic liberation. This meant that the SPD's policy was now directed toward the realization of liberal democracy, which is what the CDU State had largely achieved already. The SPD could not hope, therefore, to achieve liberal democracy, but only to reform it. The espousal of such goals would signify the end of the SPD's self-image as the representative and advocate of historical change.

Moreover, as the upholder of liberal capitalist democracy, which the adoption of the pragmatic reformers' proposals would have made it, the SPD would come to be a defender of a social and economic order very similar to that which had given rise to fascism, and which all major political parties after 1945 had agreed must be extirpated. Since there no longer appeared to be an immediate threat of fascism, however, the full weight of the anti-totalitarian mood was directed against communism. And communism was the then only existing antithesis of capitalism, at least in the way in which the climate engendered by the Cold War made it seem. Ultimately, then, anti-communism on the part of the SPD served the same ends as it did for the CDU/CSU and the bourgeois coalition: the ideological support for the capitalist system.

On one level, the SPD's anticommunism became itself the party's own self-definition, in a strictly negative and essentially opportunistic sense:

> No modern socialist can escape the fact that the Marxist idea, as scarcely any other idea that has even existed in history, has been compromised by Bolshevism, and that it is no longer of any use to demonstrate that Bolshevism deviates from Marxist doctrine. If socialism does not want to surrender itself as a movement, then its first concern today must be not to permit any doubt to arise that it is precisely the opposite of Bolshevism."[12]

This quotation points to the apologetic function of anticommunism in the SPD, serving to make the party more "respectable" in the minds of the new voters it hoped to attract among the intellectuals, pensioners, clerks, etc. For the pragmatic reformers it was essential that these new voters ". . . must be convinced that we do not endanger economic progress, but that we shall continue it successfully and secure it against reverses."[13]

Given this motivation, the SPD's pragmatic reformers were not interested in distinguishing Marx' historical materialism, which was anything but inflexible and "totalitarian," from the rigid and opportunistic formulations and rationalizations to which Marxism was put by the Soviet Union and the DDR. The most expedient and purposeful course was simply to omit all reference to Marx and Marxism within the party, and, for the benefit of potential new voters, to join in the anticommunism which the bourgeois coalition had proven to be so successful. The SPD's criticism of communism, as has already been described in this section, was anything but a socialist critique. In the various party organs of the late 1950's and early 1960's, one finds an extremely unobjective, moralistic vocabulary, with communism accused of being unscrupulous, opportunistic, fanatical, slanderous, evil, hypocritical, etc. The SPD's position seems to justify the communist critique which states that the SPD's failure to oppose the ban on the KPD "shows where one must arrive at when one surrenders the principles of Marxism-Leninism and succumbs to petit-bourgeois illusions of the bourgeois state, its rights and its law."[14] Certainly in a negative sense anticommunism represented an integrating factor within the party and acted as a form of intra-party discipline, as well as a means of integrating the party into the capitalist system through the myth that any movement or party to the left of the SPD must surely be, or become, communist-inspired.

This process of de-emphasizing the party's socialist aims and tradition by means of unqualified anticommunism must of course bring with it a further development away from socialism. For if one considers communist and social democratic parties to be ". . . factors which, despite all their controversies, share an objectively close causal connection, then it is understandable that the decline of socialist theory in the left (communist) wing of the labour movement further increased the lack of theory in the right (social democratic) wing of the same movement."[15] The reverse must also apply: that the defamation by and animosity on the part of the right wing can only promote further dogmatization and ossification on the communist side. For if the two movements have a common origin, a common appeal to the same classes and common theoretical ends, then an open and continuous discussion on the appropriate means could only be beneficial to the labour movement.

In any case, an exclusive emphasis on personal freedom and liberal rights would signify the abandonment of socialism on the part of the SPD. This was abundantly evident in the writings of the pragmatic reformers. An article in the party theoretical organ declared that:

> In practice socialism today is thus nothing more than the sum of *actual decisions (Sachlösungen)* which the people who are part of the Social Democratic Party consider to be the right ones . . . here lies at present the only possibility of elucidating what socialism can believe and want. [16]

On this account, party differences are simply differences of actual decisions taken within the framework and limitations of the liberal capitalist order.

The *Left*, which may have represented between five and ten per cent of the SPD's membership, could also be further divided into (a) a group regarding itself as representative of the subordinate or working classes and aiming at either maximizing the benefits for these classes within the capitalist system or modifying — but not fundamentally transforming — this system[17] to their advantage, and (b) a group advocating the use of democratic means to effect fundamental anticapitalist structural reforms of society, economy and politics, again on behalf of the subordinate classes, in order to bring about a qualitative transformation of existing relationships. Since the substance of the next chapter is this Left and its divisions, factions and theories, it will be considered for the time being as a single unit.

The inner-party Left had in common with the pragmatic reformers a desire for the reform of the party organization, for both saw that: ". . . one thing is certain: if the SPD remains as it is, it will be just as incapable of realizing 'socialism' as it would if it turned itself into a *Volkspartei*."[18]

A rather precarious alliance of these two groups brought a modest success at the 1958 party convention in Stuttgart when Ollenhauer announced that he would not stand as the party's candidate for Chancellor in the subsequent elections. The difference was that the Left tended to emphasize the grassroots basis of the decision-making process more than the pragmatists, and to reject co-optation and reliance on experts.

On the other hand, the Left advocated the supremacy of the (reorganized) party — rather than the machine — over the ministry or parliamentary party, which in this respect brought it closer to the traditionalists, with this essential difference:

> The opponent is not just the state bureaucracy in the narrow sense, it is the comprehensive tendency toward the total bureaucratization of society. The party as form of organization, however, is fundamentally related to the state, is itself a piece of the 'state.' But socialism is only possible as a social movement . . . Paradoxically expressed: only a party which understands that it cannot realize socialism by itself is socialist. [19]

Intra-party struggles were, however, not fought in a clear-cut struggle between Left and Right. Indeed the real *power* struggle was between the traditionalists and the pragmatic reformers. The Left's battle was largely a rear-guard action, fought from isolated positions of power and with limited means; and even this narrow base was diminished, as the next chapter will demonstrate, by the systematic isolation and expulsion of the consistent socialist Left from the party. The real direction of the party was toward the right. The crucial struggle centred around how, and how far right, the party would go.

During the 1950's a struggle took place in the Berlin party organization which in almost every way was a microcosm of the larger controversy. There Willy Brandt (then President of the Chamber of Deputies or *Abgeordnetenhaus* and later Lord Mayor), backed by the Lord Mayor, Otto Suhr (himself Ernst Reuter's successor and disciple), was involved in an ideological dispute with Franz Neumann (then district chairman or *Landesvorsitzender*). In opposition to the Reuter-Suhr-Brandt policy of emotional anticommunism, cooperation with the bourgeois parties and, in particular, the partnership with the Berlin CDU in a "grand coalition," Neumann shared the Schumacher view of "against communism and against the reaction with equal severity." Neumann argued that negotiations must take place between the SPD and SED, especially after the relative liberalization of the DDR regime following Stalin's death, in order to achieve some measure of tension reduction and to draw the SPD away from the bourgeois coalition. He emphasized the points in common between the SPD and communists as being the desire for peace, the struggle against militarism and fascism, and the achievement of socialism.

But the opponents' relative strength was unequal. While Brandt and Suhr held important offices in the Berlin government, as well as having the majority within the party and public opinion on their side, Neumann's support was derived almost entirely from individual party members and minor sectors of the public. The conflict came to a climax following the demonstration of 5 November 1956 against the Soviet actions in Hungary. Neumann eventually fell into obscurity and isolation, while Willy Brandt's "victory" increased his status with the federal party as the champion of intra-party reform and pragmatic reformism, so that after Ollenhauer's announcement of 1958 it became increasingly probable that he would be the party's next Chancellor candidate.[20]

Similarly, in the federal SPD organization, few positions of importance were held by the Left; on the contrary, the traditionalists largely retained their party posts, but were increasingly forced to admit representatives of the pragmatic reformists following electoral defeats in 1953 and 1957. Thus Fritz Erler, who had been defeated at the Berlin Convention, was elected to the Party Executive Committee at the Munich Convention; and Willy Brandt was elected to the that body in Stuttgart in 1958.

The drift of the SPD to the right was probably the main focus of the growing opposition on the Left after 1953/54. To counteract this trend, the Left proposed, e.g., a renewal of socialist aims and principles, a return to the party's working-class roots, support for workers' councils in firm and factory and a resort to extraparliamentary campaigns or actions when necessary, in order to develop the subordinate classes' consciousness. [21] It was extremely dissatisfied with the main line of the programme discussion, claimed that there was no longer any scope for free discussion within the party on the substantial issues of political life, and that the party leadership had become too unresponsive to appeals or pressures from below.[22]

This situation prompted[23] Wolfgang Abendroth to outline in some detail the Left's conception of what the SPD's programme ought to be.[24] A political party, Abendroth wrote, "that stands within the existing social order, basically accepts the existing social power relationships and recognizes the fundamental features of the political order as expressed in the constitution of the state does not need a party programme." [25] To be sure, such a party needed a platform — if it existed in a democracy in which elections took place — in order to gain electoral support; but a programme was necessary only if the party aspired to change the system.

Despite its shortcomings, Abendroth continued, the SPD's Dortmund *Aktionsprogramm* demonstrated that the "preservation of democratic legitimacy and of the real function of political parties" fell almost entirely to the party "whose aims point beyond bourgeois democracy."[26] But election platforms were not adequate to cope with fundamental social changes, such as the confrontation with National Socialism in 1933. Then, the SPD, as well as the KPD, possessed a programme which took such possibilities into account, and as a result were the only parties (together with the Catholic Centre) whose voters did not go over to the Nazis.[27] The postwar SPD, however, had no such programme and was therefore in danger of capitulating to the totalitarian forces which were inherent in the capitalist system and which would be greatly strengthened at the first economic or social crisis.

Now the party desperately needed a basic programme as (a) a framework for the preparation of each individual election programme, which in turn had to be based on the current situation, (b) a central reference point to coordinate all partial programmes and policies prepared by various committees and groups, (c) a counterweight against bureaucratic tendencies, and (d) a point of orientation for party members in political life.

> The Social Democratic Party is, however, not only the party whose concern must be the maintenance of formal and bourgeois democracy, but, beyond this, in its essence and its tradition, is the party which is called upon to transform formal democracy into social democracy and to make possible the transition from the bourgeois society in its advanced capitalist phase to the socialist society. The *starting point* of its practical action must of course be the current extant society; this is why the action programme of the party must be formulated on the basis of the existing society. However, the *aim* of the Social Democratic Party points beyond bourgeois society; for this reason its theory must go beyond bourgeois society and must regard it as a mere historical transitional point in human development.[28]

The increasing contradictions of advanced capitalism lent urgency to the need for a basic programme, Abendroth went on, while new developments in science and the social sciences made possible a greater degree of concreteness and precision in platform formulation than was formerly possible. Moreover, the new programme ought not to be a *Weltanschauung* or even an abstract philosophy or theology; but "The party must be a unit in the questions of its social starting point and its historical and social function, in the question of the struggle for socialism."[29]

By this time, however, it was abundantly clear that the SPD had no intention of "going beyond existing society." The Left came to realize increasingly that at best it might prevent the SPD from going too far right. But in the absence of a major crisis or shift in the balance of power in society, it was apparent that the party would not "return to its socialist goals." This situation would ultimately confront the Left with a relatively simply choice: either adhere to the party line in hopes of effecting at least minor, system-immanent reforms from within, or leave the party to work from without. This conflict is the subject of the next chapter.

REFERENCES

1. The Legacy of Kurt Schumacher

1 A term coined by Walter Euchner, "Zur Lage des Parlamentarismus" in: Schäffer/Nedelmann, *Der CDU-Staat*, Munich 1967, p.72.
2 Kurt Schumacher, *Turmwächter der Demokratie*, Berlin-Grünewald 1953, Vol.II, p.167ff.
3 Otto Kirchheimer, "Germany. The Vanishing Opposition" in: Robert H. Dahl, ed., *Political Oppositions in Western Democracies*, New Haven 1956, p.249.
4 Theo Pirker, *Die SPD nach Hitler*, Munich 1965, p.118.
5 According to W. Kralewski and K.-H. Neunreither, *Oppositionelles Verhalten im ersten deutschen Bundestag 1949-53*, Cologne & Opladen 1963, p.219f.
6 Pirker, *op. cit.*, p.117.
7 From an unpublished paper, "Schumacher" in possession of Frau L. Huhn.

2. Criticism from the Left

1 Pirker, *Die blinde Macht. Die Gewerkschaftsbewegung in Westdeutschland*, Munich 1965, Vol.II, p.25.

2 S.K. Panter-Brick, "Adenauer's Victory in Munich" in: *Political Studies*, Vol.7, No.3 (Oct. 1959), p.256.

3 "Was lehrt die Niederlage?" in: *Die Andere Zeitung*, No.38/1957, p.1.

4 Viktor Agartz, *Gewerkschaft und Arbeiterklasse. Die ideologischen und soziologischen Wandlungen in der westdeutschen Arbeiterbewegung*, Munich 1971, p.80.

5 On this see the study by a contemporary member of the SPD Left, Peter von Oertzen, writing under the pseudonym Richard Petry, "Die SPD und der Sozialismus" in: *Frankfurter Hefte*, October 1954, p.663.

6 See *ibid.*, p.664. Further see Wolfgang Abendroth, "Die deutsche Sozialdemokratie zwischen Restauration und Demokratie" in: *links*, March 1956, p.4ff.

7 *Ibid.*, (Petry-Oertzen), p.665.

8 Pirker, *Die SPD . . .*, p.127.

9 Viktor Agartz, "Die ideologischen und soziologischen Wandlungen in der westdeutschen Arbeiterbewegung" in: *WISO-Korrespondenz*, No.11/1959, p.491.

10 See Hans Thies, "Was will die Linke?" in: *Die Andere Zeitung*, No.47/1956, p.5.

11 Cf. Pirker, *Die SPD . . .*, p.117. See also Thomas Munzer (=Fritz Lamm), "Die Linke — und die Linke der Linken" in: *Funken*, January 1955, p.4.

12 "Beginn einer echten Diskussion" in: *Sozialistische Politik*. May-June/1956, last two pages (unpaginated).

13 T.P. (Theo Pirker), "SPD- und DGB-Führung demobilisieren die Massen" in: *Sozialistische Politik*, March/1955, p.2.

14 Fritz Lamm, "Dilemma der Demokratie" in: *Funken*, June/1951, p.9f.

15 Ludwig Rohrbach, "Der Sozialist und die Rüstung" in: *ibid.*, p.13f.

16 Cf. Schumacher, *Turmwächter . . .*, Vol.II, p.127.

17 "Warum Kurt Schumacher scheitern musste" in: *Deutsche Volkszeitung*, No.35/1972 p.8.

18 Peter von Oertzen, "Weder Bonn noch Pankow" in: *Die Andere Zeitung*, No.6/1956, p.4.

19 On the subject of expulsions for alleged "contacts with the East," see Peter Peters, "Warum wurden sie ausgeschlossen?" in: *Die Andere Zeitung*, No.15/1959, p.15.

20 Behrisch, *op. cit.*, p.8.

21 Wolfgang Abendroth, *Antagonistische Gesellschaft und politische Demokratie. Aufsätze zur politischen Soziologie*, W. Berlin 1967, p.76f.

22 Anon., "Entscheidung im Weltmassstab" in: *Die Andere Zeitung*, No.15/1956, p.6.

23 Franz Neumann, "Arbeiterbewegung und Wiedervereinigung" in: *Die Andere Zeitung*, No.15/1957, p.2.

24 Peter von Oertzen, "Weder Bonn noch Pankow . . .", p.4.

25 Reprinted in Hans Frederik, *Die Kandidaten*, Munich n.d. (ca. 1961), p.238ff.

26 "Die Kommunisten und wir" in: *Die Andere Zeitung*, No.24/1955, p.2. Cf. further his "Volksfront" in: *Die Andere Zeitung*, No.4/1956, p.5.

27 Quoted in Arno Behrisch, "Nun ruht der Mann, der niemals ruhte" in: *Die Andere Zeitung*, No.33/1962, p.5.

28 As Pirker (*Die SPD . . .*, p.134) argues.

29 This was the conclusion drawn by, among others, Fritz Lamm, "Offensive Verteidigung" in: *Funken*, October 1950, p.4f.

30 According to Gerhard Gleissberg in personal interview with the author. See also Ch.VI below.

31 Anon. "Gemeinsame Aussenpolitik — Flucht aus der Verantwortung" in: *Sozialistische Politik*, October 1955, p.1f.

32 Pirker, *Die SPD . . .*, p.220. As he mentions there, the SPD's vote amounted to a symbolic act, since all the bill would have been passed in any case on the strength of the bourgeois coalition. More important, this incident showed that the SPD was not

158   *The German Left Since 1945*

principally opposed to military preparations, which apparently surprised a number of leftist party members. Here cf. W. Boepple, "Die Partei vor der Wehrfrage" in: *Sozialistische Politik*, April 1956, p.2.

33 Walter Möller, "Die ungenutzte Chance" in: *Die Andere Zeitung*, No.2/1955, p.1f.
34 Unsigned quote in No.37/1960.
35 See *Protokoll der Verhandlungen des Parteitages der Sozialdemokratischen Partei Deutschlands vom 24. bis 28. September in Dortmund 1952*, Bonn 1952, p.103ff and especially 110ff.
36 See, e.g., Fritz Rene Allemann. *Bonn ist nicht Weimar*, Cologne 1956, p.320.
37 "Der Weg nach rechts — oder weg von rechts" in: *Funken*, December 1953, p.99.
38 Cf. Heinrich Deist, "Wirtschaftsdemokratie" in: *Die Neue Gesellschaft*, No.2 (March-April) 1957.
39 "Sicherheit für alle" in: *Jahrbuch der SPD 1956/57*, p.354f.

3. The Programme Discussion

1 H.K. Schellinger Jr., "The Social Democratic Party after World War II. The Conservatism of Power" in: *Western Political Quarterly*, No.19 (June) 1966, p.255.
2 Republished in book form: Will Birkelbach, *Die Grosse Chance. Diskussionsbeiträge zum Thema 'Demokratischer Sozialismus'* (With contributions by Siggi Neumann and Wolfgang Abendroth), Frankfurt n.d. (circa 1956).
3 Peter von Oertzen's analysis ("Wohin geht die Partei?" in: *Sozialistische Politic*, Aug.-Sept. 1959, p.1), upon which some of the following observations are based, distinguishes between a Right (my classification: pragmatic reformers), a middle (traditionalists) and a Left. If the Right is taken to mean the status quo, however, this classification is untenable. Similarly, there was no single Left, as he would seem to imply; even the distinction made here is inadequate to classify the many left wing factions and types. For Klaus-Peter Schulz, the pragmatists were the "Left" because they desired change; all others, traditionalists as well as consistent socialists, were the Right. (see his *Opposition als politisches Schicksal*, Cologne 1958, p.19).
4 SPD Party *Vorstand*, ed., *Zur Partei-Diskussion* (brochure), Bielefeld, n.d. (ca. 1954), 3rd page (unpaginated).
5 See David Childs, *The Development of Socialist Thought within the SPD 1945-1958*, doctoral thesis, London School of Economics, 1962, p.34.
6 Which included Otto Wenzel, Klaus Kundt, Hans-Karl Behrend, Hermann Schmitz, et al. Cf. *15 Thesen zur Erneuerung der Sozialdemokratischen Partei Deutschlands*, Bonn n.d. (1953).
7 See Ulrich Lohmar, "Das Experiment muss weitergehen" in: *Die Neue Gesellschaft*, No.6/1955, p.3f.
8 Fritz Erler, "Die Sozialdemokratie — eine Partei unter vielen?" in: *Die Neue Gesellschaft*, No.3/1956, p.203.
9 *Ibid.*, p.204f.
10 *Ibid.*, p.206.
11 Ernst Tillich, "Klassenkampf oder Volkspartei?" in: *Das Sozialistische Jahrhundert*, No.4/1949, p.169.
12 Prof. Hans-Dietrich Ortlieb, quoted by Johannes Gaitanides, "Der Sozialismus sucht neue Wege" in: *Frankfurter Allgemeine Zeitung*, 9 March 1954.
13 Willy Brandt, "Vordringliche Aufgaben sozialdemokratischer Politik" in: *Die Neue Gesellschaft*, No.3/1956, p.198.
14 KPD Central Committee, ed., *Das Schandurteil von Karlsruhe*, E. Berlin 1957, p.24.
15 Arno Klönne, "Sozialdemokratie — eine Agentur kapitalistischer Interessen?" in: Reinhard Kühnl, ed., *Der bürgerliche Staat der Gegenwart II*, Reinbeck, 1972, p.61.
16 L-r (Ulrich Lohmar?), "Aufbruch ins Ungewisse" in: *Die Neue Gesellschaft*, No.4/1956, p.300, italics in original.
17 For a fairly typical statement of this view, see Olaf Radke, "Reform oder Revolution" in: *links*, November 1953, p.3ff.

18 Petry-Oertzen, ''Der Sozialismus . . .,'' p.675

19 *Ibid.*, p.675.

20 On the developments in Berlin, see G.A., ''Was geht in der Berliner SPD vor?'' in *Die Andere Zeitung*, No.50/1956; Pirker, *Die SPD* . . ., p.410ff; numerous editions of *Die Berliner Stimme* (the organ of the Berlin SPD), 1954-1959; see also the two reproduced speeches of Neumann and Brandt from the year 1958 in Flechtheim, *Dokumente* . . ., Vol.VII, p.58ff. L.A. Jenssen summarized the controversy from the Left's point of view: ''The 'reform,' however, consists of a negation, namely the dispelling of socialist thought from the SPD. Not the slightest trace of a new political idea or conception can be found in (Brandt).'' See his ''Was tun'' in *Funken*, March 1958, p.39.

21 Here cf. Oertzen, ''Wohin geht die Partei . . .,'' p.2. Information supplemented in personal interview with the author.

22 See Gerhard Gleissberg, ''Ein Auftakt zur Diskussion'' in: *Die Andere Zeitung*, No.16/1956, p.6.

23 According to Wolfgang Abendroth in private interview with the author.

24 ''Warum Parteiprogramm?'' in: *Die Neue Gesellschaft*, No.4/1956, p.283ff.

25 *Ibid.*, p.283.

26 *Ibid.*, p.285.

27 Concerning this argument, Douglas Chalmers (*The Social Democratic Party of Germany: From Working-Class Movement to Modern Political Party*, New Haven 1964, p.284) writes that it ''. . . goes beyond the Marxian notion of equipping the workers with an understanding of their world in order to protect them from the ideologies of the bourgeoisie; dogma is here considered good in itself, no matter what the content, which seems to have been too great a step for most socialists, since it finds little echo in the writings of leading members of the party.'' However, a closer examination of the article would have revealed Abendroth's statement that all large German political parties arose as *Weltanschauung* parties, each with its objective historical necessity; thus the Catholic party was still ''objectively necessary so long as Catholicism still had to struggle for equality'' (Abendroth, p.284), a struggle which had carried into the Weimar era. The working classes were still struggling for equality and therefore the SPD, as their representative, was carrying on a struggle objectively historically necessary after 1945. Far from stating that dogma was good in itself, Abendroth argued for the primary importance of that dogma's content.

28 *Ibid.* (Abendroth), p.287 (italics in original).

29 *Ibid.*, p.291.

VI. THE RISE OF INNER-PARTY OPPOSITION

1. Hibernating in the party and trade union.

To understand the development of the Left within or near the SPD during the Adenauer era — and indeed up to the present — it is necessary to comprehend the extent and influence of the prevailing climate of clerical anticommunism. The CDU/CSU's success in establishing a popular image of itself as the bearer of western, christian values as against "atheistic bolshevism" or even "creeping socialism" was possibly the dominant factor in West German political life in this period.

All alternatives to the left of the SPD had of course been long eliminated. The KPD-West was by the early 1950's no longer a viable political force, and any attempt to form an alternative party or organization, as the fate of the UAPD demonstrated, was foredoomed. The few attempts to create an organ or circle for discussion, when they did not founder utterly, were constantly threatened with the "Damocles Sword" of anticommunism. The sword could be wielded in two ways: either by means of defamation and insinuation to deprive the organ/circle of all popular support, or by banning or threatening to ban it, thus forcing it to modify its line or compromise its ends.

Not only was West German anticommunism not fundamentally different in quality, content and tone from that employed by the Third Reich — which was indeed one reason for its success — it was also in many cases propagated by the same people, "the professional agitators and anticommunists who had served Goebbels' propaganda machine."[1] Anticommunism made virtually any opposition from the Left against the CDU State with its social system and foreign policy into a "crime" approaching treason. It became, for example, a more serious offence for SPD members to arrange discussions with former KPD and SED members on questions of reunification and socialism than for neo-Nazis to paint swastikas on memorials to victims of fascism, to judge by the respective sentences handed down to the persons convicted of these offences.[2]

This climate alone made the establishment of an independent left-wing political force extremely difficult, if not impossible. A second important factor was the absence of any kind of mass base for a political movement to the left of the SPD or DGB, a situation which could be attributed in part to the success of anticommunism and in part to the systematic destruction of all working class consciousness during the Third Reich ("co-ordination" of the trade unions, formation of the Labour Front, banning and persecution of labour parties) as well as in the Federal Republic (clerical anticommunism, ideology of social partnership, integration of the trade unions and SPD). And even if it had been possible to detach greater or lesser sectors of the working

160

classes for an independent organization, most socialists, recalling the days of the *Bruderkampf*, would have been reluctant to do so. "The unity of the class," Fritz Kief wrote in this connection, "is the precondition for the victory of socialism. The self-laceration of labour benefits the class opponent, not us."[3]

Thus the Left during the 1950's existed almost entirely within, or in close proximity to, the Social Democratic Party and the Trade Union Federation. No significant movement emanated from outside these organizations.

The "misery" of the postwar German Left was a direct reflection of the integration of the organizations of the working classes into the CDU State. By the mid-1950's the independent Left was so diminished that it became possible to classify it in terms of its relationship with the SPD: those who remained within the party and those who did not. Although these categories do not reflect all the important cleavages which still existed within the Left, they do reveal the importance of the SPD vis-à-vis the development of the Left, and do cast some light on the most important problematic for the Left in this period: to work toward its goals within a party that no longer represented its beliefs and interests, or to attempt to establish a new political force to the left of the SPD, an enterprise which offered very little prospect of success and which, even if successful, could divide the labour movement.

The strategy adopted by a large part of the Left, which came to be known popularly as "hibernating" in the party and trade union, was to work and agitate from within labour organizations, to act as a "motor"[4] to promote reforms and discussion on the one hand, and on the other to be a "brake" against further shifts to the right. To this end, the Left often attempted to promote theory and discussion in journals and periodicals, to maximize its strength at the grass-roots level through membership in and influence over various committees, works-councils, etc., and to propound the socialist idea in party meetings and conventions.[5]

The salient point about the strategy of "hibernating" was that it implicitly abandoned all ideas of changing and reforming the SPD or DGB; instead it represented a "holding action," an attempt to prevent the worst consequences, until the situation should become more favourable for a transition to socialism. Disappointed at the failure of their aspirations for social and economic reform of the late 1940's, angered at the "capitulation" of the SPD and DGB leaderships to the capitalist CDU State, seeing their ideas and proposals seemingly become irrelevant in the wake of the atmosphere of boom and prosperity that characterized the economic miracle, and defamed by the prevalent climate of anticommunism, the Left resorted to withdrawal, to "hibernation." And even this course was difficult to maintain under these conditions.

Viktor Agartz in 1954 compared the situation of the few academics, scientists and nonconformists who dared to persevere in their socialist convictions with that of quarantined individuals living in a vacuum.[6] Elsewhere he lamented: "Is it not deeply sad and perhaps also characteristic that today not the party and trade union are in motion, not in action, but intellectuals, professors, the free professionals and students?"[7]

Finding a *modus vivendi* within the party could take many forms. Many members of the Left tended to gather around individual members of the party hierarchy or parliamentary party who were perceived to be at least in sympathy with socialist goals. Of these individuals, some, such as Herbert Wehner (a former communist and an important voice in the party) and Hans-Jürgen Wischnewski (former Young Trotskyist and briefly a contributor to *Sozialistische Politik*) ultimately adapted outright to the changing party line. Beginning about 1956, with the growing popular opposition to rearmament and nuclear weapons, the Left briefly saw in Herbert Wehner its representative in the party hierarchy and supported his election to the Party Executive Committee. As late as the Stuttgart Convention in 1958, these hopes appeared to be justified when it appeared that Wehner would oppose the non-socialist proposals for the pending new programme. But his sudden *volte-face* with respect to the Godesberg Programme, and in particular his famous 1960 Bundestag speech renouncing any independent SPD foreign policy [8] indicated that such hopes had been misplaced.

Other deputies were, by virtue of personal conviction or the constituency they represented, naturally on the party Left. A kind of unorganized and vague movement developed around such individuals as Willi Birkelbach (South Hesse) and Peter Blachstein (Hamburg). Essentially this inner-party Left owed its first loyalty to the party. Peter Blachstein, for example, remembering the division and fragmentation of the labour movement before 1933, was determined to remain where the masses were.[9] As the SPD's policies and platforms became progressively more removed from socialism, such men could be used as evidence for the continued existence of a "socialist wing" within the party while at the same time posing no threat to the leadership's hegemony of organization and policy formulation.

It is nevertheless instructive to examine the source of their opposition, as this is indicative of the SPD's changing course. Thus Birkelbach's *Die Grosse Chance*, intended to revive leftist discussion in the 1950's, argued that the "torpidity" then affecting the SPD could be overcome by increasing the party's organizational strength and achieving broader intra-party democracy, to the point where it would become more than a mere organization and instead develop into an "organism".[10] And Blachstein first began to express his opposition in connection with the SPD's approval of the market economy at the Dortmund Convention of 1954 and after; in this respect he was against the proposals of Karl Schiller and Heinrich Deist. Later he rejected Erler's suggestions for a military policy increasingly in agreement with that of the CDU. And in a general way he opposed the growing power of the party machine and the lack of contact between trade union and party.[11]

Individuals like Blachstein and Birkelbach were in many respects unique and courageous in a party which was increasingly losing sight of its socialist past and perspectives. But their absolute loyalty to the party largely prevented them from developing an overall strategy and theory. There could be no question of their becoming an organizational focus for intra-party opposition. Thus Birkelbach postulated the "central question" of the struggle for political power as being the right to work which, he argued, must be raised to an equivalent level with the other "basic rights and basic freedoms."[12] And in order to avoid unemployment, he later wrote, socialization was necessary — "if there is no other way."[13] And Blachstein, in a speech to the *Falken* in Berlin, criticized the contradictory policies of the SPD leadership — omitting the CDU campaign funds contributed by big business, clerical anticommunism and the successes of the CDU State[14]— as responsible for the SPD's defeat at the polls.[15]

What this inner-party Left achieved was at least a questioning of specific policies and action on the part of the SPD. No doubt their efforts retarded somewhat the party's drift to the right. And equally certainly, by remaining within the party, they simultaneously retained a kind of direct contact with the working masses. But their criticism and opposition did not point to an alternative socialist course nor, given their view of the primacy of the party, did it ever threaten the dominant line the SPD was now pursuing.

Apart from these few deputies and party officials, the inner- as well as extra-party Left of the 1950's was largely centred around a number of periodicals and publications having a rather limited circulation and aimed at reviving socialist discussion within the SPD. When these periodicals were able to survive opposition by the party, persecution by the CDU State and their own chronic financial difficulties, they frequently produced interesting, provocative or important contributions to West German political life. As documents of the contemporary Left, or as critical views on government policy, social ills and and decline of socialism within the SPD, the best of them are still unsurpassed in quality and insight.

These periodicals typically reflected the issues of main concern to the Left in the period in which they were founded. Thus *pro und contra,* edited by Willy Huhn and Otto Schlomer in Berlin after 1950, was critical of the occupation powers' policies and tended toward a socialist Third Way. The *Thomas-Münzer-Briefe,*[16] edited by a small group around Fritz Lamm in Stuttgart beginning in 1949, aimed at "sounding out" independent socialist opinion in the western zones as a preliminary endeavour to overcome the SPD's rigid internal structure and to act as a spur to sustain socialism within the party. A merger in 1950 of the *Thomas-Münzer Briefe* and another minor periodical *Blätter für internationale Sozialisten,* which had been published by the *Neues Beginnen* group, resulted in the establishment of one of the most original and certainly one of the qualitatively best left wing periodicals of the 'fifties', the *Funken* ("Sparks"). Aimed at recruiting the so-called *heimatlose Linke* (or "homeless Left"), a term then fashionable for the politically disappointed who were unable to find a commitment to any of the existing political parties, and at establishing contact between otherwise isolated and ineffective left wing groups, *Funken* saw itself as a completely independent forum where the Left could gather, express its views and debate. In this it succeeded admirably in the years between 1951 and 1958. Some of its many articles on the lack of intra-party discussion, the decline of socialism within the SPD, on proposals for socialist changes and the dangers of the CDU State have already been cited in previous chapters.

A second important centre of the intra-party Left revolved around the twice-monthly publication, *Sozialistische Politik.* Founded in late 1954, *SoPo,* as it was popularly known, became "beside *Funken* surely the most important periodical of a leftist opposition in the SPD between 1955 and 1964."[17] It was primarily concerned with the question of the Left's proper relationship to the SPD and, like the *Funken,* attempted to provide a forum for broad range of socialist opinion.

Perhaps the most important organ of the independent Left in these years was *Die Andere Zeitung* ("The Other Newspaper"). Its genesis was the SPD's extremely equivocal attitude toward rearmament and conscription, which caused virtually the entire editorship of the party organ, *Neuer Vorwärts*, led by Gerhard Gleissberg and Rudolf Gottschalk, to resign their posts in early 1954.[18] In order to provide an expression of alternative policies and to counter the monotony and sterility they found in the West German press ("But the public keeps silent. It takes in passively what it is given to read as though there were nothing but the song of praise of the German Miracle and beyond that the sentimental entertainment of fables of empresses and princesses, the exciting stories of crime and murder, the pride of memoirs"[19]), Gleissberg and Gottschalk then founded the *Andere Zeitung* in May of the following year.

Its initial articles against the Restoration,[20] rearmament, renazification, authoritarian trends in government and society, political justice, *de facto* press censorship and blind anticommunism, as well as its advocacy of political neutrality for Germany, negotiations with the DDR and a firmer domestic and foreign policy on the part of the SPD instantaneously placed the periodical in the centre of left wing political debate. Indeed, its most important task, as seen by its editors, was to provide a mouthpiece for the Left which, although existing in all classes, denominations and political parties, had hitherto been largely unable to articulate its views.[21]

These left wing publications had a number of things in common. All were beset by chronic financial problems. Since advertising and subventions from business were, for obvious reasons, out of the question, they were largely thrown back on subscriptions and donations from dedicated followers. Very rarely were the contributions paid, and certainly those involved in editing the publication often carried on in the face of great personal sacrifice.[22] In general the highest item of overhead was postage, and a small rise in postal rates could mean the elimination of the periodical. By limiting editions to around 1,000 copies, an optimum balance between costs and income could be reached, as in the case of *Funken, Sozialistische Politik* and *pro und contra*; above that, a circulation of 10,000 or more was necessary, a figure which only the *Andere Zeitung* ever reached.

Editors and contributors were further harassed and threatened by the possibility of expulsion from the SPD and persecution by the federal anti-communist organizations. Thus Willy Huhn was expelled from the SPD in 1953 for allegedly advocating a system of works' councils and for his attacks on the western occupation powers.[23] And Gleissberg and a number of others were deprived of their SPD memberships in mid-May 1956, just slightly over a year after the founding of the *Andere Zeitung*, ostensibly for having opposed the SPD's foreign and defence policies.[24] None of these periodicals escaped investigation by federal agencies, though outright searches and seizures were seldom carried out. The one flagrant exception was the trial of Viktor Agartz, which will be described in the next section.

Also typically, the socialist periodicals were either one- or two-man efforts whose continuation depended on the fortitude of a few individuals, or they were published by editorial committees consisting of a number of persons with occasionally quite differing concepts of socialism and journalism. *Funken, pro und contra* and *Die Andere Zeitung* were examples of the former, *SoPo* of the latter.

In the case of *Sozialistische Politik*, the diverse political origins of its editors and contributors not only ensured an extraordinarily varied choice of topics (of extremely variable quality), but also represented in microcosm many of the problems of factiousness which the Left faced in this period. The periodical was sustained by two major factions, the supporters of the Fourth International (Trotskyists) and an extremely heterogeneous group of "independent socialists". But even these could be further subclassified. The Trotskyist group was dominated by those who saw their political possibilities within the SPD, such as Hans-Jürgen Wischnewski and Walther Boepple, but included a few former members of the UAPD[25] as well. The second major group, the independent Left, virtually consisted of as many different political shadings as there were individuals. Most of these were not associated in any way with the Trotskyists, indeed, were often opposed to them. The "ultra-left" KPD was represented by Erich Gerlach (a member of the SAP before 1933, a supporter of anarcho-syndicalism and perhaps the then foremost expert in Germany on Spanish socialism and the Civil War), as was the right wing of the KPD by Fritz Opel (an executive of the metal-workers' trade union). Direct connections between the *SoPo* and the trade unions were maintained by Sigfried Braun and Theo Pirker. A minority, above all Peter von Oertzen, was more closely allied with the SPD than the *SoPo* and tended to regard the periodical as a strictly intra-party spur to reform and action. A few independent Marxists, mainly Wolfgang Abendroth and, to a lesser degree, Viktor Agartz, could not be associated with any one faction and acted as arbitrators, conciliators and co-ordinators.[26]

Alone, none of these groups had the money, resources and appeal necessary to sustain a left-wing periodical — indeed, even the combined effort was chronically short of funds — and therefore the alliance was foreseeably a precarious one. Frequently articles written by one faction would be contradicted in subsequent issues by members of other factions. Never was *Sozialistische Politik* able to speak with a unanimous voice, nor could one consistent line be attributed to it.

However, this organizational and ideological unevenness brought with it the advantage of a great variety of articles on a number of relevant topics from many different points of view. At its best, *SoPo* could be more impassioned and polemic than, say, *Funken*, with occasional brilliant analyses and critiques; but at its worst it could lapse into petty factionalism, inconsistency and "nit-picking". In all these qualities it provided — and provides — a fairly accurate image of the Left in the 1950's.

By 1960, these factional disputes, heightened by the problem of the periodical's relationship to the SPD after the Godesberg Programme and Wehner's foreign policy speech, led to the departure of the independent socialist group, many of whom would join Peter von Oertzen in publishing the *Arbeitshefte* a few years later. *SoPo*, after 1960 until its demise in 1966, came under the editorship of the Trotskyist faction. During this time the standard of its content remained at a relatively high level, but it gradually lost the quality of immediacy which it had had, continuing, e.g., to urge the SPD back on to a socialist course long after it had become obvious that the SPD was primarily concerned with divesting itself of its socialist image and after the Left had begun to search for new forms and organizations.

Even in the smaller periodicals, factionalism could become a major problem. *Pro und contra* ceased publication in 1953 after a dispute between Willy Huhn and Otto Schlomer on the role that Trotskyism had to play in the periodical.[27]

But the greatest single problems of these minuscule publications were financing and the prevailing climate of anticommunism. These were the factors in *Funken's* demise. In its last issue of September 1959, shortly before the SPD's Bad Godesberg Convention, Fritz Lamm wrote:

> "The purpose, orientation and content of a socialist periodical goes against the current of a time in which socialism is discredited, dishonoured, distorted and renounced . . . by the politics and propaganda of the Stalinist epoch and by the factual, intellectual and formal amalgamation of the social democratic parties with modern capitalism."[28]

2. The Left-wing Spin-off

The term "extra-party Left" would be somewhat misleading here. Those individuals and organizations who broke with the SPD or DGB during the 1950's (apart from a small group of communists and anarchists who had never really identified with either organization), very seldom left the party or trade union on their own initiative or at their own wish. The beginnings of a pattern now became evident which would recur much more frequently after the Godesberg Programme of 1959: old party members, consistent socialists and frequently former concentration camp inmates or resistance fighters, who had taken seriously the SPD's post-1945 programmes — indeed had helped to draft and pass them — continued to advocate the same kind of socialist transformation and anticapitalist reforms which they had always supported. Refusing to modify their largely uncompromising stand in the light of changed conditions following the establishment of the CDU State and the SPD's progressive adaptation to it, they found themselves gradually more isolated from the mainstream of political debate and, almost as a matter of course, defamed as communist agents or traitors. At the end of this process came their expulsion from the SPD for reasons of "anti-party behaviour" — although almost invariably they were proposing nothing more radical than what the SPD itself under Kurt Schumacher or the DGB under Hans Böckler had promoted as official policy.

Once the tie to the party or trade union had been severed, however, the almost inevitable result was isolation and often ultimate resignation. In a period in which even an increasingly concessionist SPD was widely suspected of being "too radical," and in which no alternative left wing organization existed, it is evident that any individual expelled from the SPD for "left-wing deviations" could not escape the effects of the anticommunist mentality then predominant in the Federal Republic. Though this extra-party opposition contained a number of capable theorists, publicists and proven leaders, it was never, under these conditions, able to unite on the basis of a common programme, nor, more important, was it able to attract more than a minuscule following.

This was the fate of Gerhard Gleissberg and Rudolf Gottschalk and their *Die Andere Zeitung*. The weekly's contributors were among the most prominent and representative of the independent Left during the 1950's. Gleissberg and Gottschalk, who were well known within the SPD, hoped to mobilize the party Left and individual prominent leftward leaning party members, such as Willi Birkelbach and Peter Blachstein, in their struggle to return socialism to a prominent position among the party's priorities. Viktor Agartz and Theo

Pirker were to arouse critical opinion within the DGB through their many contacts in that organization. On the theoretical level, Kurt Hiller became the spokesman for critical but uncommitted intellectuals and Wolfgang Abendroth carried on a polemic against the SPD ideologists of pragmatic reform, Ulrich Lohmar (editor of *Die Neue Gesellschaft*) and Professor Weisser. Professor Baade's articles were aimed at the pacifist or anti-military wing of the SPD. Thus *Die Andere Zeitung* became simultaneously the spokesman of the so-called homeless Left, a catalyst of critical opinion *within* the SPD and a symbol of critical opinion against the rather conservative political system of West Germany.

But the establishment of a new political party was at first expressly rejected by the periodical's founders. Like the *Sozialistische Politik* and *Funken*, the *Andere Zeitung* regarded itself, initially, as a motor within the party and trade union which would propel the labour organizations to a reflection upon their original aims or compel them to adopt new socialist-orientated policies and tactics. Expressly rejecting the formation of a third socialist party between the KPD and SPD, Gerhard Gleissberg wrote:

> It is not our intention or wish to separate the labour parties from their members — it is rather our desire to see these parties cleansed of their rightist, bureaucratic elements which, through their invective against the 'competition', are becoming increasingly similar and are preparing themselves to go along with the opponent — and by a 'gathering' we understand the opposite of founding groupings and going into isolation: we mean the establishment of contacts and cooperation between all who take seriously the maintenance of peace, efforts toward reunification and the socialist transformation of society, regardless of the parties and groups to which they belong.[1]

Gleissberg and his associates frequently recorded their rejection of attempts to establish a new political party. The foundation of any such new party would come, if at all, much later than the organization of this "gathering"; but that was not their goal. The gathering around the periodical was seen as the first stage toward the establishment of a "permanent cartel" as proposed by Kurt Hiller, or a forum, perhaps even one on a European scale. "This is our goal," Gleissberg wrote, "the inspiration of all socialist and liberal forces with revolutionary ideas for the transformation of the capitalist social order into a socialist order with the ultimate goal of creating prosperity for all."[2]

Despite Gleissberg's undoubtedly sincere intentions, it would seem in retrospect that the establishment of a gathering or grouping or forum on the Left must needs imply the creation of a centrifugal force or spin-off away from the party and toward an independent political organization. This is especially so when such a grouping is constituted of party members or former adherents whose major cohesive force is their opposition to the main lines of the party's policy. As the Bad Godesberg Programme became imminent, it must have grown increasingly obvious that the SPD's policy was more than a temporary aberration that could be rectified by a greater effort on the part of the Left: it was a reflection of the changing balance of social and political power after 1945 and a far-reaching and fundamental — one is tempted to say inevitable — shift in the party's social bases, its electorate and its leadership. Opposition to party policy was thus essentially opposition to the party's substance, even if this fact was not yet fully apparent.

Franz Altmann touched upon this problematic as early as 1956. The establishment of a new political party to the left of the SPD, he wrote, had become a "political necessity". One would prefer, of course, the way of inner reform within the SPD in order to avoid the reproach of "revolutionary impatience," but the time had come in which "impatience has its moral and political justification." With the SPD's abandonment of its socialist principles and the KPD's failure to meet the challenges and new requirements arising from the XXth Party Congress of the CPSU, the Left had become a "no man's land", a vacuum which had to be filled. An independent socialist force organized as a political party would thus, he argued, have a rather more uniting than divisive effect. The way had been shown by the centres like *Funken* and *SoPo*, but these had the twofold disadvantage of failing to operate in party meetings and in actual political events, and of lacking in any kind of co-ordination or co-operation.[3]

The road from the leftist gathering or forum at the extreme perimeter of the SPD to outright anti-party opposition, as events would show, was indeed a short one. Beginning in February 1956, the *Andere Zeitung* sponsored a number of meetings aimed at uniting the Left.[4] The first of these were held in Berlin and Hamburg, followed by Cologne, Dortmund and Lübeck, and were addressed by such prominent members of the Left as Kurt Hiller, Walter Horn, Gleissberg himself, Fritz Kief and Claude Bourdet from France.

Die Andere Zeitung also publicized a number of causes which were extremely unpopular with the leading political parties. For example, on 2 February 1956 it published an appeal by an "Initiative Committee" of jurists, professors and lawyers which was addressed to the federal and regional governments and advocated an amnesty for persons accused in political trials, especially in anticonstitutional cases. The rest of the Federal German press completely ignored this appeal. It was also among the first (and only) to publish the Göttingen Manifesto,[5] and devoted generous space to the anti-nuclear weapons campaign in subsequent years.

For these and other actions, which would have been completely within the party line ten years previously, Gleissberg, Gottschalk and several others were expelled from the SPD. The SPD's attitude toward the *Andere Zeitung* was outlined by Fritz Heine at the Party's 1956 Convention in Munich: "We consider . . . this newspaper in its circulation and content to be insignificant, and we have no doubt that it is not an organ for free discussion but an outright oppositional publication". This statement was greeted with applause.[6]

In one point, at least, Fritz Heine was wrong: precisely in its circulation and content the *Andere Zeitung* was significant. By 1956/57 its circulation reached just under 100,000:[7] more than ten times higher than any other publication of the Left in those years. The unique combination of a weekly edition, a critical socialist interpretation of political, economic and cultural information, and theoretical background articles ensured a broad readership. In addition, *Die Andere Zeitung* had, as Gerhard Gleissberg pointed out in the last political discussion of his life,[8] a certain "sensational" or "shock" value which should not be underrated: its attacks on government policy and its alternaive proposals in a period noted for the sterility and conformity of practically the entire press made it interesting to a variety of nonsocialist groups and individuals as well. For example, in the mid-1950's it was the only publication to call the DDR the DDR (rather than the SBZ or Soviet Zone of Occupation, or the "so-called DDR"); not until the mid-1960's was the German Democratic Republic acknowledged to be the DDR in the Federal German media.

Thus *Die Andere Zeitung* nearly became a rallying-point for the Left. For Wolfgang Abendroth it was the greatest of the leftist publications in this period.[9] Fritz Lamm wrote: "Not voted for, not confirmed and not authorized, but simply because of its existence, it has become a kind of representative — and therefore upon its existence and its appearance depends a part of the fate of the Left in general."[10] For Nikolaus Ryschkowsky, the paper might have been the basis for the development of a "real centre of nonconformist socialist in the Federal Republic . . . "[11]

The "if" that Ryschkowsky attaches to his statement points to the central difficulty which the *Andere Zeitung* had to cope with throughout its existence " . . . if the opinion had not soon arisen that *Die Andere Zeitung* was receiving material assistance from the East".[12] Again, accusations of the paper's having accepted financial aid from a communist regime needed only to be levelled to be effective; certainly they were never proven; and even if they had been, there is no evidence of a communist ideological influence in its articles or actions. According to Pirker, the SPD, fearing the formation of a new political party led by *Die Andere Zeitung*, was in large measure responsible for spreading the rumour that it was communist controlled.[13] And the bourgeois press also appeared to assume that this was the case.

Gleissberg himself was not certain whether communist money ever assisted in the financing of *Die Andere Zeitung*. He was in any case the editor, not the publisher, and was never subjected to constraints or guidelines in the editorial content of the paper.[14] As he conceded, despite its high circulation, *Die Andere Zeitung* nevertheless had a number of financial problems, which necessitated paying low fees to contributors, making constant appeals for donations, giving high commissions to kiosk operators and newsagents (because few readers, fearing reprisals or damaged reputations, would actually sub-scribe), etc., so that additional funds would have been useful.

Why was *Die Andere Zeitung* exposed to a far more extensive slander campaign, why were more of its editors expelled from the SPD and why was it threatened to a greater degree with repressive legal measures than was, say, the *Funken*? Both periodicals had a similar socialist content, raised many of the same issues, spoke openly on the possibilities, of forming a political party to the left of the SPD and organized forums or gatherings for its readers and other independent socialists. Indeed, the *Funken* Congress, held in Frankfurt in February 1958, in some respects was even more "radical" than the meetings held by *Die Andere Zeitung*, attacking as it did the concept of "social partnership", and the SPD's failure to put forward a tactical, ideo-logical and actual alternative to the CDU/CSU.[15]

The answer to this question seems to lie exclusively in the fact of the *Andere Zeitung's* greater size, and therefore threat, to the established power relationships.[16] As a symbol or representative of independent leftist opinion in Federal Germany, the paper was naturally a prime object of clerical anti-communism. After 1959 the campaign against it began to show concrete results in the form of reduced circulation, so that by the early 1960's its circulation had declined to well below 50,000, where it remained until the paper folded in 1969, and its initial ideological impetus was largely diminished.

A careful perusal of the issues of *Die Andere Zeitung* from its founding until 1960 and beyond tends to refute *SoPo*'s criticism that it had a "lack of perspective", or that it failed to propose an "objective socialist critique of Stalinism and communism."[17] The many articles in *Die Andere Zeitung* attacking Stalinist bureaucratism, the blind obedience of the western KPD to policies formulated in the East, the need for more discussion in the socialist countries and, toward the end, a blistering attack on the Soviet invasion of Czechoslovakia[18] give the lie to such criticism. However, it is evident that its main line of attack was overwhelmingly directed at western capitalism, the Federal Republic and the SPD. This approach may have been completely in line with its desire to be precisely "the other newspaper" which, in contrast to the popular press, refused to publish the anitcommunist "horror stories" then so prevalent. But in this very period, in which rumours and imputations of communist sympathy could destroy careers and nullify the effectiveness of political organizations, the *Andere Zeitung*, if it were to increase its influence, would have had to balance its anticapitalist critique with anticommunist polemics. On the other hand, a "balance" of this kind would surely have alienated many of its supporters and contradicted the principles upon which it had been founded.

To be sure, *Die Andere Zeitung* continued to exist until early 1969 with a relatively high circulation but, as Ryschkowsky has pointed out, this may be rather more attributable to the absence of other left wing newspapers than to its own particular appeal.[19] It continued to oppose the SPD's gradual drift to the right and toward the Godesberg Programme. It was to be instrumental in the establishment of the Union of Independent Socialists (VUS) and the Initiative Committee for the Establishment of a Socialist Party.[20] And it was to support the Socialist Centre (SZ), the German Peace Union (DFU) and the Extraparliamentary Opposition of the late 1960's. But it was never again able to achieve the prominence and immediacy which it had during the first years of its existence.

Perhaps the most prominent victim of the Cold War was the economist, Viktor Agartz. Following his controversies with Oswald Nell-Bruening within the DGB, and with Bruno Gleitze for control over the WWI, and his suspension from both organizations in December 1955,[21] Agartz lost almost all his authority within the trade union movement and was, of course, no longer welcome in an SPD increasingly concerned with establishing a "respectable" image for itself. Together with his associates, Walter Horn and Theo Pirker, and with the help of a number of friends and colleagues, such as Werner Hofmann, Oskar Neumann and Wolfgang Abendroth, Agartz founded the *Korrespondenz für Wirtschafts- und Sozialwissenschaften*, or *WISO-Korrespondenz* in March 1956. This fortnightly, which in many respects was a kind of anti-*WWI-Mitteilungen*, was chiefly concerned with economic questions as they affected the working classes and their representatives in the trade unions and political parties.[22] In the new periodical, Agartz further developed his critique of advanced capitalist society, analysed the changing function of the labour movement and its organizations and began to put forward concrete proposals for reversing the Restoration.

For Agartz liberalism was historically obsolete; it had long ago surrendered its central principles of individualism and free competition to the monopoly capitalist order.[23] Similarly, parliamentary democracy was no longer relevant:

"Modern state monopoly capitalism can only develop its expansive dynamic if its political functional partner, which is still called the "state", adapts its central leadership and authoritarian process of decision-making to its economic, monopolistic requirements."[24] The really important decisions were in any case no longer taken in parliament, but were products of extra-parliamentary agreements between the leading elites. In contemporary society, he argued, one could sense a kind of feeling of decline, of inevitable doom.[25]

Starting from his earlier analyses of the labour movement and its problems, Agartz went on to develop his theory of industrial feudalism,[26] which for him was the main support of the advanced capitalist system. Industrial feudalism was basically a combination of three factors: the state-regulated "free"-enterprise economy, Catholic social doctrine and partial codetermination.

Agartz' critique of the entrepreneurial economy remained much as it had been before 1955. It is worth recalling, however, that for him big business had not changed fundamentally from the social function and operational methods it had had before and during the Third Reich, and that the Western occupation powers had greatly favoured the restoration of neo-liberalist capitalism (e.g., forestalling socialist legislation in various *Länder* constitutions, the decreed wage stop until 1950 and taxation of the working classes to support state intervention in the economy). Furthermore, the active involvement of the trade unions and socialist parties in reconstruction and the provision of elementary needs had led to an absorption of the labour movement into, and its close identification with the capitalist order: "The political situation of the Federal Republic was dominated from 1945 to 1955 by a self-disciplining of the trade unions, that is, by a vigorous class struggle from above."[27]

The aspect of Catholic social doctrine acquired an increasingly prominent place in Agartz' thought after 1955. Ultimately, one could conclude that it became the crux of his theory of advanced capitalism. It is difficult to ascertain how much of his critique of Catholicism was motivated by his controversy with Nell-Bruening.

The power of the Catholic Church, he argued, dated in particular from its strength in the immediate postwar period, which in turn was derived from the benefits it had received during the Third Reich. Indeed, the conflict that did eventually occur between it and National Socialism was "the claim to power of two systems of the same nature."[28] After 1945 and the demise of old-style liberalism and the inadequacy of the principles of "free competition" and entrepreneurial initiative, Catholic social doctrine was able to fill the ideological vacuum " . . . because its authoritarian and totalitarian system of social doctrine corresponded to the monopoly capitalist order."[29]

Catholic social doctrine, which had not changed essentially since the Middle Ages when a "natural order" of society prevailed, had now become " . . . in the capitalist countries the one ideology by means of which monopoly capitalism maintains a close connection with, and leads, the working classes.[30] This it accomplished above all by means of a kind of industrial patriarchy, as expressed in the notions of *Betriebsfamilie* (worker and employer as part of a natural, family-like order) and "social partnership." The social function of this ideology was to use such concessions as company housing, increased social welfare benefits, profit-sharing schemes and the like to bind the worker psychologically closer to the firm, thereby destroying his sense of class-consciousness and creating a feeling of identity or solidarity with the firm, and through it the capitalist order.[31]

Closely connected with the Catholic social doctrine and the "free-enterprise" economy was the legislation concerning industrial codetermination, which for Agartz was the "sop" conceded by big business to the then still powerful labour movement. By 1956 it had become evident that codetermination had replaced socialization in the ideology of the trade union leadership, and hence had transformed the latter's subjective role considerably. Whereas the responsibility of the trade unions was exclusively toward the working classes, the inclusion of the trade union representatives in the decision-making process — without, however, according them a controlling share — of individual firms, which were organized according to the profit principle, was bound to deter them from their primary responsibility and increase their identification with the capitalist management.[32] The resultant process was the integration of the trade union bureaucracy into the bureaucracy of big business.[33]

Part and parcel of this industrial feudalism (although not specifically treated as such in Agartz' writings) was anticommunism. Agartz perceived postwar anticommunism as technically far superior to that practised under Hitler, although its content was relatively unchanged: "The conformity of literature, the press and radio achieved by force under fascism has been far superseded today with the simultaneous application of methods which, while preserving the appearance of ostensible freedom, use a huge network of agents to carry on the isolation, defamation and social debasement of all persons or groups who attempt to form an objective opinion." The result of this campaign was the creation of a "psychosis which can normally exist only toward sex criminals."[34]

The effects of industrial feudalism and anticommunism upon the labour movement were profound. The leaders of the SPD and DGB were now almost totally integrated into the monopoly capitalist system. To be sure, this identification with the bourgeois democratic state was not intrinsically a negative phenomenon, provided that this state represented a progressive stage vis-à-vis a former state form. But when this commitment became an absolute one, then there could be no further dynamic, progressive development toward the next higher stage. In this case, "absolute commitment is nothing more than an absolute commitment to the capitalist system without the least desire to change this system."[35] If the workers' organizations supported this order, Agartz implied, they were *ipso facto* supporting the Restoration, renazification, the ascendancy of big business and the perpetuation of monopoly capitalism.

Because of the SPD's adaptation to the existing order, the term "social democracy" had now come to be associated with the capitalist system. For this reason: "A Marxist does not demand democratic socialism, he demands a socialist democracy."[36] Because the SPD no longer had the strength to sustain socialist theory and practice, it resorted to neoliberalist argumentation " . . . because neoliberalism is the only bourgeois remnant of an opposition, but one which is helpless against state monopoly capitalism."[37] Agartz' attacks on the trade union leadership and organization have already been described in Ch. IV.

The way to overcome the passivity of the labour movement, according to Agartz, was a slow and painstaking process. The division between party and trade union — for which of course Catholic social doctrine was in large measure responsible — had to be overcome first of all. For: "The political party and the trade union organization are partial forces in the struggle for the emancipation of the Fourth Estate which, precisely because of the different functions in capitalist society, ought to guarantee the unity of the working class in its dynamism."[38] Secondly, the trade unions themselves must return to their original goals, meaning at first their very basic aims such as wage increases and reduced working hours, until their class consciousness was more developed. They must further withdraw from all capitalist bodies and all national and international institutions, and must eliminate all traces of neoliberal and bourgeois ideology from their programmes (e.g., Keynesian theory, Catholic social doctrine and American planned capitalism). Above all, more direct action and political activity were the order of the day.[39]

Then roughly a year following the outlawing of the Communist Party of Germany, Viktor Agartz was involved in litigation of considerable importance to the German political system and the fate of the Left. In March 1957, a subscription salesman for the *WISO-Korrespondenz* was apprehended returning from the DDR with DM 21,000 in his possession. The salesman was arrested and a search — typical of the treatment of suspected communists — of Agartz' living quarters was carried out, during which copies of the proceedings of the XXth Congress of the CPSU and of speeches by Otto Grotewohl and Walter Ulbricht were found. Agartz himself was charged with accepting group subscriptions from the East German trade union federation, the FDGB, and imprisoned. Somewhat later the charges were reduced to "maintaining contacts pernicious to the state" and he was released against a surety of DM 50,000. The ensuing trial — in which Agartz' defence attorney was Gustav Heinemann, later President of the Federal Republic until 1974 — was inconclusive from a legal point of view. The accused was pronounced not guilty and released unconditionally.

The verdict was in any case only of secondary importance. The real significance of the "Agartz Case" lay in the political realm. Here the instigators of the trial were genuinely successful. By the time proceedings were concluded it was abundantly evident that virtually the entire bourgeois press (in so far as it did not ignore the trial altogether), both the great labour organizations and a large sector within the Left were opposed to Agartz; even among his supporters, opinion was divided.

The *Schwäbische Zeitung*, for example, saw a communist influence in the strikes then taking place in the metal industry and asked " . . . whether apart from Agartz there are still others receiving money who are also interested in creating social unrest." Specifically it named *Die Andere Zeitung* and suggested that publication of it be suspended.[40] The representatives of the "christian" trade union wing within the DGB, as well as a number of individual SPD and DGB members were actively opposed to Agartz,[41] while the SPD and DGB organizations undertook no action which could be interpreted as support for their former leading economic expert. In fact, the SPD capitalized on the next best opportunity to expel him from the party on 13 December 1958.[42]

On the Left, reaction ranged from unqualified support to regret at a political blunder. Calling the Agartz Case "West Germany's Dreyfus Case" and comparing the judges presiding at it with those who sat in judgement at the Dimitrov Trial of 1933 (following the Reichstag fire) and at the trial of the anti-Hitler conspirators of 20 July 1944, Hans-Georg Herrmann declared in defence of Agartz: "If I want to change social relationships, my God, weapons or money, where they come from is of no importance. Did Lenin or Rosa Luxemburg ever ask about that?"[43] For Franz Kief, Viktor Agartz acquired after 1945 a position similar to that of Rosa Luxemburg after 1918. Both, he argued, were concerned to develop the scientific bases of socialism, to avoid opportunism and conformism, and both saw the significance of armaments and militarism to the development of advanced capitalism as well as the growing interdependence of the state machinery and big business.[44]

Even allowing for the correctness of Kief's parallels between the two socialist leaders, his praise of Agartz is probably too generous. For Rosa Luxemburg's greatness lies precisely in her clear analysis and critique of *both* advanced capitalism and the bolshevist dictatorship.[45] Viktor Agartz' works were among the best writings of the Left about the German Federal Republic and the restoration of advanced capitalism there. His insight into the problems and weakness of the labour movement were unsurpassed. But Agartz failed completely to develop a socialist critique of Soviet and East German communism. Concerning the Polish uprising of 1956, for example, he wrote:

> The Polish movement is characterized by the fact that it began with demonstrations by socialist workers imbued with Marxist ideas and ended with the tearing up of the Red Flag, the very symbol which is sacred to the demonstrators . . . Only after the fascist underground movement stepped in and, with shots and charges on public buildings, gave the workers' demonstration a completely different character, did the political organs begin to shoot.[46]

To be sure, this kind of unqualified praise or vindication of Stalinist communist measures is atypical of Agartz' writings. They are rather more characterized by a "blind eye" toward communism, as manifest in undifferentiated praise for partial achievements without reference to other, undesirable aspects,[47] or by scathing attacks on aspects of bourgeois democracy without tempering or countering these with reference to defects in the communist alternatives, or by seemingly innocuous acts such as accepting an honorary doctorate from the Humboldt University of East Berlin in February 1958.[48]

Gerhard Gleissberg was completely correct in pointing out that the bourgeois press had received literally millions of dollars in credits from the USA and that the christian wing of the trade union organization had been given considerable funds by organizations abroad,[49] while the DDR, by whom Agartz was allegedly sponsored, was not even officially considered to be a foreign country. And, as Agartz himself declared, part of the task of socialists in the West was to discuss, debate and exchange ideas and experiences with the working class organizations in the communist countries, notably with the FDGB; refusing to do so while at the same time sending delegations to and carrying on cultural exchanges with the capitalist countries amounted for him to a betrayal of socialism.[50]

All of this notwithstanding, however, Agartz' "blind eye" cost him much of what remained of his prestige within the Left and, more important, provided the Right with one more pretext to carry on its anti-Left campaign under the banner of anticommunism. Although, like the KPD, he was clearly a victim of political justice, the charges to which his actions left consistent socialists open, and their repercussions no doubt ultimately retarded the cause of the Left and contributed in some ways to the ease with which the SPD was able to pass its Godesberg Programme in November 1959.[51]

Though the *WISO-Korrespondenz* carried on until 1961, by early 1959 it had lost virtually all its influence within and outside the Left. As Wolfgang Abendroth wrote, Agartz' fall was a heavy blow to the cause of West German socialism because he " . . . was the best economic expert the West German workers had. It had been a mistake for him to accept funds from the FDGB, but this in no way diminished his importance."[52] In any case it diminished his influence. Like *Die Andere Zeitung*, Agartz later supported the VUS, but withdrew when this organization began to cooperate with the German Peace Union (DFU). The Initiative Committee for the Establishment of a Socialist Party arose partly from out of the groups surrounding the *WISO-Korrespondenz*, it is true, but Agartz soon withdrew from it as well. After then, until his death in 1964, Viktor Agartz, who less than a decade previously had been the SPD's and DGB's economic spokesman and a personal friend of Kurt Schumacher, was "only a memory within non-conformist socialism."[53]

3. Pacifism as Catalyst

In view of the success of the Economic Miracle, the western alliance and clerical anticommunism, such questions as the integration of the labour organizations and the programme discussion became, during the 1950's, largely esoteric subjects outside the mainstream of political discussion. The death of Stalin and the changes in communist theory and praxis resulting from the XXth Party Congress of the CPSU, in this atmosphere, were hardly reflected in the theory and practice of the West German Left at all. No economic crisis, war or even scandal arose to shake the placid, depoliticized consciousness of the working classes or to activate the Left.

The one issue which was still sufficiently volatile to catalyze a popular oppositional movement was that of rearmament and remilitarization. This was so for a number of reasons. Popular opposition to armament rested, firstly, upon immediate and direct historical experience of the war, the four-power occupation and the extensive anti-militarist propaganda contained in the Allied denazification programme. Secondly, it brought together oppositional forces from a number of political persuasions, such as pacifist and anti-conscription groups, neutralists from Left and Right, SPD members still supporting the primacy of reunification, religiously-motivated anti-war groups, independent intellectuals, and those who had suffered directly from the war and its effects. Thirdly, rearmament was a relatively straightforward and tangible issue which could be defined in terms of a single alternative (acceptance or rejection), and which affected the vital interests of most of the population. And fourthly, no political party or labour organization had made the outright rejection of rearmament a central part of its programme, although public opinion polls taken between 1949-1955 consistently showed a large majority opposed to rearmament in any form.[1]

Indeed, as the preceding two sections have demonstrated, the issue of rearmament had invoked much of the intra-SPD and -DGB opposition in the postwar years. For example, Kurt Schumacher's policy of "offensive defence" resulted in a widespread demand by the Left for a popular referendum and a total revision of the party's ambiguous policy.[2] And it was a major factor in the development of extra-party opposition in the early 1950's, as in the case of the *Funken* or *Die Andere Zeitung*.

For these reasons the rejection of rearmament and remilitarization became the central focus and rallying-point for most of the oppositional forces, in particular the Left, in the late 1950's. As essentially a reaction to official government policy, its development can be described in two basic stages: resistance to rearmament and conscription, and opposition to nuclear arms.

The initial opposition to rearmament and conscription originated predominantly from the inner- and extra-party SPD Left, but failed to achieve a broad resonance among a largely passive public concerned with reconstruction and economic progress. Campaigns against the Federal Government's successive steps toward rearmament — from Adenauer's first hint of the possibility of making a West German "military contribution," the pressure created by the Korean War and the rejection of Stalin's Note of 10 March 1952,[3] to the discussions surrounding entry into NATO and national conscription — though supported by a large number of citizens, were not represented by any large political party.

Popular resentment was reflected in the call for a national referendum or general strike by a number of local trade union organizations, in the growing hostility among sectors of the liberal press, and in increasing support for anti-militarist proposals by a number of ecclesiastic and pacifist groups. As such manifestations gradually began marginally to appear as a serious challenge to the hegemony of the ruling parties, the anti-rearmament mood acquired an organizational form, the so-called St. Paul's Church Movement (*Paulskirchen-bewegung*).

On 29 January 1955, Erich Ollenhauer, Walter Freitag, the theologian Helmut Gollwitzer and the sociologist Alfred Weber convened a meeting under the slogan, "Save Unity, Peace and Freedom! Against Communism and Nationalism" in St. Paul's Church in Frankfurt. This occurred shortly after the Treaty of Paris and at the height of the subsequent intra-DGB protest against unilateral western rearmament as the cause of perpetual national division. The meeting attracted about 1,000 speakers and participants, including the instigators, Gustav Heinemann (then leader of the All German Party or GDVP) and representatives of labour, church and pacifist groups. Its "German Manifesto" was a relatively mildly-worded appeal to the government to bring the problem of German reunification and rearmament more force-fully to the attention of the western Allies.[4] Although the "movement" received considerable attention in the media, and subsequently published a number of tracts and leaflets in support of pacifist measures, its influence obviously did not affect the government's policies, since Parliament ratified the Treaties of Paris without difficulty on 27 February.

The contemporary Left rightly reproached the St. Paul's Church Movement with being too institutionally fixed and too narrow in its scope and aims. And indeed the movement was organized and its ends defined by established social institutions (SPD, DGB, some churches) with the intention of influencing parliament by means of moral pressure. But through it, for the first time, many of the heterogeneous groups which supported antimilitarism (anti-conscriptionists, pacifists, neutralists) saw a way to make their views known in the Bundestag. Yet the movement's strength was also its limitation: the representation of oppositional views in this way simultaneously publicized them and precluded any really effective form of bringing about their realization. The alliance of disparate groups did not permit the use of the political or general strike, nor a binding, nation-wide plebiscite, as the Left advocated.[5]

As Theo Pirker has argued, the movement's institutional-parliamentary character meant that:

> Basically the St. Paul's Church Action had the sole purpose of diverting the increasing radicalism among the active party members and trade unionists into legitimate channels. It was conceived as a protest of emotion and word against Adenauer's policies, as a valve to release the pressure in party and trade union, and nothing more. With this action the party was operating at the edge of the constitution, but only at the edge, for it was only too well aware of the anti-plebiscitarian limits of the Basic Law. To regard the St. Paul's Church Action as a popular movement and thus a politically effective action would be a deception and a self-deception . . .[6]

Pirker argued further that Adenauer, at this time, was not concerned with petitions, meetings, resolutions and plebiscites, but did genuinely fear strikes by the trade unions.

But on the other hand, political strikes would have curtailed the supra-class support which the movement briefly enjoyed. For it was significant not as a socialist movement, but as an *oppositional* movement. For the first time it was demonstrated that a variety of disparate groups, acting in concert in opposition to a single issue, could influence the thinking of broad sectors of the population. The real significance of the St. Paul's Church Movement was as a consciousness-provoking phenomenon.

The anti-rearmament campaign failed completely in its goals: armaments expenditures in West Germany increased by almost four times between 1953 and 1964, making her the second largest producer of weapons in NATO. But the campaign against atomic weapons was considerably more successful, not least of all due to the degree of awareness which developed from the anti-rearmament movement. During 1956, the media devoted much attention to the prospect of the Federal Government's acquiring nuclear weapons for the Bundeswehr. On 12 February 1957, Defence Minister Franz-Josef Strauss delivered a well-publicized speech in Bad Böll which stated that West Germany would eventually have to take account of "changed military conditions" in consequence of the existence of atomic weapons. In March it became known that American military units in the Federal Republic were equipped with "tactical" atomic weapons. And in April Konrad Adenauer declared that West Germany must keep abreast of the latest military technology, including the development of nuclear weapons.

It is significant that popular reaction against these developments was triggered not by political parties or labour organizations, nor even by the independent Left, but by a group of "non-political" scholars. On April 12, eighteen prominent scientists, including the Nobel Prize winners Max Born, Otto Hahn and Carl Friedrich von Weizsäcker, presented a public appeal to the press and radio. This appeal, the "Göttingen Manifesto," was by no means a radical document: its signatories regarded themselves as a group concerned with "pure science" who were thus incompetent to make concrete political proposals, and as supporters of freedom " . . . as upheld by the western world today against communism."

But the signatories' influence was, in postwar West Germany, all the greater for its allegedly "non-political" quality, which probably meant that its appeal reached a larger audience than, say, a partisan socialist appeal might have done. The Manifesto called attention to the massive destructive power of nuclear weapons and termed the system of mutual deterrents a "lethal" one. Pointing to science's role in nuclear technology, the authors pledged to aid any efforts at disarmament, and called for an "explicit" and "voluntary" rejection of atomic weapons by the Federal Republic.

Almost overnight a great variety of individuals and organizations took up the issue of atomic weapons: municipal councils, student bodies, women's leagues and church groups pledged their support for the Göttingen scientists as did Albert Schweitzer in an "Appeal to Humanity" from Africa, and Otto Brenner who called for social, rather than military rearmament. The anti-atomic arms movement contained from the outset a greater oppositional potential than had the anti-rearmament movement because it was able to obtain the support of many groups who had been indifferent or even hostile toward the former, because now public opinion against government policy was even higher than it had been against rearmament,[7] and, no doubt, because of the consciousness-inducing role of the preceding campaign against rearmament.

But the most significant difference between the two movements was that the anti-atomic weapons campaign arose more or less spontaneously, without the instigation of institutional or official organizations. Indeed, it often proceeded without reference to them and occasionally over their opposition. The failure of the existing parties and organizations of the labour movement effectively to oppose rearmament and the introduction of atomic arms caused them to lose the initiative in the new popular oppositional movement, at least in the initial stages. The chief centres of resistance largely went over to *ad hoc* and spontaneous oppositional organizations.

The Göttingen Manifesto appeared at a time when the SPD was intensifying its image of "respectability" and "responsibility" in order to win over voters from the bourgeois coalition, in preparation for the 1957 elections in the late autumn. Meanwhile the DGB was chiefly concerned with maintaining its policy of party political neutrality and appeared to be devoting more attention to such issues as higher wages, the effects of automation, etc. Thus both the great labour organizations were more or less taken by surprise[8] when it became evident that the great mass of members and functionaries were primarily concerned with the issue of atomic weapons and shared the general protest mood. In a letter to Alfred Weber, Willy Huhn, for one, argued that the questions of capitalism and the labour movement must now take second place to the problem of nuclear weapons because man now stood " . . . to gamble away or 'tempt' *any* future, regardless of whether one defines it as capitalism or socialism."[9]

It is a lasting indictment of the "official" Left that it failed to assume the initiative in the anti-nuclear arms campaign of the late 1950's. So too did the West German media,[10] who appeared to be either too pro-government or too frightened of anticommunist retaliatory measures to give prominence to the movement which began with the Göttingen Manifesto. In addition to the civic and academic groups already mentioned, the anti-atomic arms wave was largely sustained by a loose association of ecclesiastic organizations, at the centre of which was the Lutheran Church, and by a number of anti-war groups.

Hans-Karl Rupp, author of the standard work on anti-military opposition in the Federal Republic during the 1950's, has written that: "Among all the large organizations in West Germany, the question of rearmament was most intensively — and perhaps most vehemently — discussed in the Lutheran Church (EKD), individual member churches and organizations associated with it."[11] The notion of public responsibility and the Church's duty to intervene in public affairs was founded on the Lutheran Church's Stuttgart Confessional (*Stuttgarter Schuldbekenntniss*) of 1945, which acknowledged the Church's failure to oppose the rise of National Socialism and its complicity during the Third Reich. Now it assumed for itself the right and duty to speak out on public matters involving current politics, even at the risk of alienating certain sectors among its membership.

Another important centre of anti-militarism was a number of extant pacifist and anti-war groups which had hitherto played an insignificant role in political life. The German Peace Society (DFG),[12] whose members included Martin Niemöller and Fritz Wenzel, and among whose honorary members were Albert Schweitzer and Linus Pauling, was a part of the War Resisters' International and the International Peace Bureau. Its traditionally pacifist activities were gradually supplanted by a more activist policy aimed at resisting nuclear armament and achieving national unity. The Union of Persons Persecuted by the Nazi Regime (VVN)[13] was able to enlist the support of both its bourgeois and socialist wings in the anti-atomic arms campaign. The Franconian Circle[14] was particularly active in the preparation of petitions and popular appeals. And the German branch of the War Resisters' International (IdK)[15] aimed at mobilizing and organizing anti-war groups and draft-dodgers through street demonstrations, protest meetings and publicity campaigns.

Gradually the force generated by this extraparliamentary and extra-institutional movement permeated the labour organizations and forced them to take a stand on the issue of atomic arms. Pressure for a more forceful stand was also produced by the CDU/CSU's overwhelming victory in the 1957 elections, in which the SPD's failure to provide a well-profiled alternative may have played a role, despite the fact that the SPD had taken a formal stand against atomic armaments. Goaded by resolutions and demonstrations undertaken by local chapters, the DGB under Walter Freitag began increasingly to voice public criticism of the government, although the issues of higher wages and automation still seemed to predominate in its thinking. A foreign policy debate in the Bundestag on 23 January 1958, the climax of which was the attacks on government policy by two former cabinet ministers, Thomas Dehler and Gustav Heinemann, signalled the start of a long parliamentary struggle concerning national division and atomic armaments. The public attention accorded these debates, including television coverage of parts of them, only served to vindicate what the Left had been asserting since 1948: that every step toward unilateral rearmament by the Federal Republic increased the obstacles to reunification.

The SPD then ultimately — again well behind the main current of public opinion — seized upon these issues as a source of potential popular support, and began to press more vigorously in the Bundestag for a non-atomic weapons policy. Meanwhile, another public appeal by 44 professors and scholars, the so-called "Appeal of the 44," of 26 February, enhanced the anti-nuclear arms mood. It urged support for the principles of the Göttingen Manifesto and called for the creation of an atom-free zone in central Europe. The Appeal complemented an "enlightenment campaign" announced by Erich Ollenhauer and carried on in the SPD party organs and at party meetings. It was intended to create pressure "from below" on the government and the Allied occupation powers to abandon proposals for atomic armament.

This campaign then culminated, in March, in the institutionalization of the antimilitarist movement in the form of the *Kampf dem Atomtod* (Fight Atomic Death or KdA) movement. Its immediate impetus was the Bundestag debate of 25 March 1958 which concluded with the CDU/CSU and DP sponsored resolution to equip the Bundeswehr with atomic weapons. Thus, although the KdA was unquestionably strongly influenced by the British Ban-the-Bomb Movement and the well-publicized pronouncements of Bertrand Russell, it arose from specifically West German conditions. Its founding congress in Frankfurt showed it to derive support from the SPD (Ollenhauer, Paul Löbe, Max Brauer, Carlo Schmid), the FDP (Thomas Dehler), the DGB (Chairman Willi Richter and two deputies), the protestant churches (Niemöller, Kloppenburg), prominent academics from many fields (Gollwitzer, Weber, Max Born, Kogon, Dirks), and literary figures (Heinrich Böll, Stefan Andres).

The Bundestag resolution and the establishment of the KdA signalled the development of a broad and active popular oppositional movement throughout West Germany, with protest meetings and demonstrations occurring frequently. In some universities, students founded "working groups against atomic armament," local DGB and SPD organizations called increasingly for decisive action, and civic and church groups continued with their petitions and leaflets. A high-point was reached on 1 May with large demonstrations and meetings sponsored by the trade unions and attended by thousands of demonstrators and participants in almost all the large cities. Increasingly, the various elements of the KdA began to demand a referendum or national plebiscite on the issue of atomic weapons.

The crucial problem for the success or failure of the KdA was the organizational form and tactics which it adopted in the transition from popular protest to mass movement. By declaring their support of its main goals, the two great organizations of the labour movement, SPD and DGB, *de facto* assumed the movement's leadership. Since its ends contradicted government policy and a specific parliamentary majority decision, however, they could be achieved only by means of *extra-parliamentary action*. Protests, petitions and assemblies were effective means of gaining popular support and arousing mass awareness, but in themselves were inadequate to reverse a parliamentary decision. The realization of the Fight Atomic Death movement's goals necessarily would have meant anti-parliamentary, anti-government and very probably anti-constitutional measures, such as the execution of a national plebiscite or a political or general strike. Certainly such actions would have been legitimated by popular support for them: in March 1958, 83 per cent of respondents to a representative poll, including a majority of CDU/CSU supporters, rejected the government's armaments policy;[16] and 52 per cent of the population as a whole supported the use of a general strike on the issue, while only 31 per cent were expressly against it.[17]

But the official Left again demonstrated its inability to draw the consequences of the radical-sounding policies it had taken over from a popular oppositional movement, and to act decisively in matters not directly affecting its material interests.

In the trade unions there was a widespread desire for direct action in support of the anti-armaments campaign. Many wildcat strikes took place on a local or plant level, usually sponsored by the KPD or other independent socialist movements.[18] The demonstrations jointly sponsored by the SPD and DGB during Easter of 1958 generally met with greater popular support than any other events organized by the labour movement since 1945. Yet the Federal Executive Committee of the DGB, largely in consequence of a government appeal for "responsibility," and with a view to considerations of political party neutrality and the unified trade union, decided to forgo all strike actions. Instead the DGB pledged its formal support of the KdA, agreed to take part in demonstrations, and promised financial backing for the anti-atomic weapons movement. Through this financial support, Theo Pirker has claimed, the trade union leaders ". . . so to speak bought themselves free from their political responsibility. Financial support was for them a kind of indulgence to quiet their democratic and activist souls.[19]

Similarly, when a number of SPD members and functionaries in various SPD-governed *Länder* began to make preparations for a plebiscite or referendum on the issue, this caused considerable consternation in the federal party, as such an action would clearly be unconstitutional; and despite its professed support for the KdA, the SPD still saw itself primarily as a "constitutional" and "responsible" political party. The federal party leadership alternatively proposed to place legislation before the Bundestag calling for a national referendum. Such legislation of course had no possibility of being implemented in a parliament with an absolute CDU/CSU majority. The party's Stuttgart Convention of 1958 showed in any case that it was more concerned with organizational reform and the draft proposals which would be incorporated into the impending Godesberg Programme, than with the issues of disarmament and prevention of atomic armament. Henceforth the SPD's attitude toward armaments was conditioned by a new policy which "affirmed national defence" and even put forward its own defence concept, which was no longer substantially different from that of the CDU/CSU.[20]

By mid-1958 the main impetus of the Fight Atomic Death campaign had spent itself. The chief cause of its demise was surely the withdrawal of the support of the DGB, who had never been wholly behind it, and of the SPD, for whom it had represented rather more an advertising campaign than a vital labour issue. Another contributing factor was the successful counter-campaign promoted by the CDU/CSU. With the elections to the North Rhine-Westphalian *Landtag* in that year, it launched an anticommunist-based campaign under the slogan of "Adenauer or Ulbricht," claiming that the proposed national plebiscite was completely in the interests of the DDR. The christian democrats' subsequent victory in these elections raised anew a question which had presented itself since the 1957 elections: why could the CDU/CSU, despite its pursual of policies enjoying little popular support, consistently gain election victories over the SPD? Here one might well refer to

Rupp's notion of the "secondary importance of non-economic and social motives" in voting behaviour.[21] So long as the Economic Miracle brought tangible and abundant benefits to the great majority, questions of national survival and international peace, according to this theory, had to assume a secondary role in actual voting behaviour.

In fact the christian democrats accused the SPD, in its support for the KdA, of serving the function of "useful idiot" in the communist cause. In a speech to the Bundestag, Gerhard Schroeder, Minister of the Interior, said that among communist tactics ". . . for the achievement of their strategic goals, namely the overthrow of the social order, is to win over broad classes among the people for limited political goals. For this purpose the communist party uses ancillary organizations which fulfil certain tasks in individual fields of interest." Later he accused the SPD of objectively abetting these communist goals:

> For some time one has been able to recognize the communist purpose of spreading mass fear of atomic weapons in order to shake the order of the Federal Republic and to impair our people's desire for freedom. The slogans and mottos thought out by the communists do not become non-dangerous because they are used by legal opponents of the Federal Government . . . Ladies and Gentlemen, whoever, consciously or unconsciously, well-meaning or ill-meaning, becomes involved in this campaign, whether voluntarily or against his will, is playing the game or our common enemy.[22]

The CDU's application to have the proposed plebiscites in three *Länder* rejected as unconstitutional was upheld by the Federal Constitutional Court. Since neither the SPD nor DGB was prepared to pursue the plebiscite idea further the Court's verdict marked the effective end of the *Kampf dem Atomtod* movement. By early 1959, the initiative in the anti-atomic arms campaign had passed, by default, into the hands of minority student groups [23] or back into the safe-keeping of the various pacifist and anti-militarist groups.

But the Fight Atomic Death movement had not been insignificant. It had demonstrated, first of all, that "non-political" groups could mobilize large numbers of people in support of vital single-purpose issues. It had shown anew the traditional labour organizations' decline in socialist theory and practice, and increasing identification with the capitalist order. Further, it had contributed to the development of a critical awareness of the part of large sectors of the population. And finally, it may well have prevented the Federal Republic from actually acquiring atomic weapons. After 1959 the KdA appeared to have run aground. But it was to re-emerge in 1961 as part of the new campaign against nuclear weapons and would figure prominently as an oppositional issue in the mid-'sixties.

REFERENCES

1. Hibernating in the party and trade union

1 See Viktor Agartz, "Sozialismus in Quaräntane" (Speech delivered to the International Society for Socialist Studies in London 20.9.1957) reprinted in: *Die Andere Zeitung*, No.40 1957, p.1f.

2 Here see Gleissberg, "Antikommunistisches Manifest" in: *Die Andere Zeitung*, No.6/1960, p.1.

3 "Für die sozialistische Einheit" in: *Die Andere Zeitung*, No.15/1956, p.4.

4 The "motor theory" was outlined by H. Genschel, "Arbeitsform und Arbeitsziele der Linken in der SPD" in: *Die Andere Zeitung*, No.13 1956, p.5.
5 Here cf. *ibid.*; Peter von Oertzen, "Wohin geht die Partei?" in: *Sozialistische Politik*, Aug./Sept. 1959, p.1; Wolfgang Abendroth in private interview with the author.
6 Agartz, "Sozialismus . . .," p.1.
7 Viktor Agartz, "Was haben wir Marxisten zum Entwurf des Grundsatz-Programms der SPD zu sagen?" Speech delivered on 5.2.1959, issued as a brochure of the Karl-Marx Gesellschaft, Munich 1959.
8 See next chapter.
9 As told to the author in private interview.
10 Willi Birkelbach, *Die grosse Chance. Diskussionsbeitrage zum Thema 'Demokratischer Sozialismus,'* Frankfurt 1956 (circa), p.13.
11 As told to author in private interview.
12 *Ibid.*, p.11.
13 Cf. article by Willi Birkelbach in: *Vorwärts*, 20.11.1959, p.21 and 27. See further his "Was zu tun nötig ist" in: *links* No.13 1953, p.4ff.
14 On this see G.A. "Was nun?" in: *Die Andere Zeitung*, No.42, 1957, p.6.
15 Mimeographed copy of this speech made available to the author from a private collection. Cf. further Blachstein's article in: *Vorwärts*, 20.11.1959.
16 Named of course after the famous opponent of the authoritarian aspects of Martin Luther's teachings, Thomas Münzer who denounced established governments and advocated a "community of goods" and who established a communistic theocracy in Mühlhausen during the Peasant War. In a private interview with the author, Fritz Lamm explained how the original mailing list was prepared on the basis of a list of names of 1200 persons who had sent for books by Paul Fröhlich, how the latter had then made this list available to Fritz Lamm, and how, in order to bypass the Military Government censorship on publications, the periodical was sent quasi-anonymously.
17 According to Peter von Oertzen in a letter to the author dated 13 Sept. 1971.
18 As described by Gerhard Gleissberg in private interview with the author.
19 "Geht es nicht anders? Ein Gespräch der Herausgeber der 'Anderen Zeitung'" in: *Die Andere Zeitung*, No.1/1955, p.2.
20 A really outstanding example of which was Sigfried Einstein's "Wenn sie den Krieg gewonnen hätten . . ." in: *Die Andere Zeitung*, No.19/1960, p.1f.
21 "Geht es nicht anders . . .," p.2.
22 This fact was underlined in private interviews with Frau L. Huhn, Peter von Oertzen, Fritz Lamm and Gerhard Gleissberg.
23 "Die Wahrheit über Korea" in: *pro und contra*, July 1950, p.1f.
24 The text of the SPD's resolution of expulsion is reprinted in: *Die Andere Zeitung*, No.21/1956, p.2.
25 Who had often been former KPD members. Cf. Ch.IV(2) above.
26 For their assistance in pointing out the ideological-political orientation of these individuals, the author is grateful to Professors Abendroth and von Oertzen.
27 For Huhn's version, see "Das Urteil ist gesprochen" in: *Neues Beginnen*, No.12/1951-1/1952, p.16 and 18.
28 Fritz Lamm, "Nachruf auf uns selbst" in: *Funken*, Sept. 1959, p.129.

2. The Left-wing Spin-off

1 G. Gleissberg, "Das Ziel: Sammlung der Linken" in: *Die Andere Zeitung*, No.9/1956, p.4.
2 *Ibid.*, *loc. cit.*
3 Cf. Franz Altmann, "Noch ein wenig Geduld" in: *Die Andere Zeitung*, No.16/1956, p.4f.
4 For a report on these conferences, see Gleissberg, "Das Ziel . . ."
5 See next section for the background and significance of this document.

6 *Protokoll der Verhandlungen des Parteitages der Sozialdemokratischen Partei Deutschlands vom 10. bis 14. Juli 1956 in München*, Bonn 1956, p.281. Of the few party members prepared to defend the *Andere Zeitung*, Hans-Werner Bartsch (himself a frequent contributor to the paper) argued that only free discussion within the party, as promoted by *Die Andere Zeitung*, would prevent a leftist "exfiltration" outside the party. (*Protokoll* . . ., p.277).

7 As told to the author in private interview with Dr. Gleissberg.

8 In private interview with the author.

9 As stated in interview with the author.

10 Thomas Münzer (=Fritz Lamm), "Die Linke — und die Linke der Linken" in: *Funken*, Jan. 1956, p.9ff.

11 *Die linke Linke*, Munich 1968, p.25.

12 *Ibid., loc. cit.*

13 Theo Pirker, *Die SPD nach Hitler*, Munich 1965, p.217.

14 As told to the author in private interview.

15 Cf. Fritz Lamm's report on the Congress, "Die Tagung der linken Sozialdemokraten" in: *Funken*, March 1959, p.33. As Fritz Lamm writes in a letter of 6 February 1972 to the author: "Neither did we have the technical apparatus which could have enabled us to make transcripts, nor did we consider this initial attempt at a somewhat larger-scale meeting of the minuscule Left historically important enough to have any made. The meeting was an experiment, perhaps too late, intended to create a common, somewhat larger unity of the leftist opposition in Germany." Since a number of individuals were present, he continues, who were not interested in establishing an amorphous left wing organization, ". . . there was at first no need to document and transcribe the experiment."

16 A point mentioned by both Gleissberg and Lamm in private interviews with the author.

17 P.v Oe., "Die 'Andere Zeitung' und die SPD" in: *Sozialistische Politik*, No.17/1959, p.3.

18 Concerning the latter, see the issue of 29 August 1968.

19 Ryschkowsky, *op. cit.*, p.25.

20 See Ch.VIII below.

21 See Ch.IV (d) above.

22 Here cf. "Zur Einleitung" in: *WISO-Korrespondenz*, No.1 (15 March) 1956, p.1.

23 Viktor Agartz, "Die Gewerkschaften in der Zeitenwende" in: *WISO-Korrespondenz*, No.17/1959, p.776f.

24 Viktor Agartz, "Die Gewerkschaften zum dritten Mal am Scheideweg" in: *WISO-Korrespondenz*, No.12/1956, p.132.

25 Agartz, "Die ideologischen und soziologischen Wandlungen in der westdeutschen Arbeiterbewegung," reprinted in: Agartz, *Die ideologischen und soziologischen Wandlungen* . . ., p.79.

26 See, e.g. "Industriefeudalismus" in: *WISO-Korrespondenz*, No.17/1957, p.301f.

27 Agartz, "Die enge Arbeitsgemeinschaft von Staat und Gewerkschaft" in: *WISO-Korrespondenz*, No.13/1956, p.158.

28 (". . . es handelt sich um den Führungsanspruch zwei gleichgearteten Systeme"). See Agartz, "Industriefeudalismus" . . ., p.306. See further his "Die Kirche im Spätkapitalismus" in: *WISO-Korrespondenz*, No.16/1958, p.288ff.

29 Agartz, "Die Gewerkschaften in der Zeitenwende . . .," p.785.

30 "Die ideologischen und soziologischen Wandlungen . . .," p.84.

31 *Ibid.*, p.84 and ff; also "Kapital und Arbeit als Sozialpartner" in: *WISO-Korrespondenz*, No.12/1956, p.135ff.

32 Agartz, "Die Gewerkschaften in der Zeitenwende . . .," p.785. A more comprehensive critique of codetermination was presented in: *infra.*, Ch.IV (4).

33 Agartz, "Industriefeudalismus . . .," p.306f.

34 Agartz, "Die ideologischen und soziologischen Wandlungen . . .," p.79.

35 Agartz, "Die Gewerkschaften in der Zeitenwende...," p.784.
36 Viktor Agartz, "Was haben wir Marxisten zum Entwurf des Grundsatzprogramms der SPD zu sagen?" Speech delivered on 5 September 1959 and reprinted as a brochure of the Karl-Marx-Gesellschaft, Munich 1959.
37 Agartz, "Die ideologischen und soziologischen Wandlungen...," p.82.
38 *Ibid.*, p.67.
39 Agartz, "Die Gewerkschaften in der Zeitenwende...," p.794ff.
40 On this see Gerhard Gleissberg, "Die Dschungel-Presse" in: *Die Andere Zeitung*, No.15/1957, p.1f.
41 See, e.g., Fritz Kief, "Enthüllungen zum Fall Agartz" in: *Die Andere Zeitung*, No.33/1957, p.5.
42 See Werner Haak, "Psychologischer Meuchelmord" in: *Die Andere Zeitung*, No.2/1959, p.3.
43 Hans-Georg Herrmann, "Westdeutschlands Fall Dreyfus" in: *Die Andere Zeitung*, No.50/1957, p.1f.
44 Fritz Kief, "Viktor Agartz zum 60. Geburtstag" in: *Die Andere Zeitung*, No.46/1957, p.1f.
45 Concerning the latter, see esp. her three essays in: Rosa Luxemburg, *Selected Political Writings* (ed. R. Looker, trans. W.D. Graf), London 1972, p. 235ff.
46 In *WISO-Korrespondenz*, 15 July 1956.
47 As for example in his article on pension reform in the Soviet Union: "Die Rentenreform in der Sowjetunion" in: *WISO-Korrespondenz*, No.1/1957, p.12ff.
48 Text of his acceptance speech in: *Die Andere Zeitung, No.10/1958, p.8.*
49 Gleissberg, "Die Dschungel-Presse...," p.1.
50 Agartz, "Die Gewerkschaften in der Zeitenwende...," p.790.
51 According to Douglas Chalmers, the Agartz group "... appeared to be so thoroughly compromised by its inclination to think well of the Communist regime in the East that it had no chance of succeeding among the sizable group that was hostile to the line taken at Godesberg but at the same time anti-Communist." See his *The Social Democratic Party of Germany*, New Haven 1964, p.66f.
52 "Das Urteil im Prozess Agartz" in: *Funken*, No.1/1958, p.1f. This view was criticized by Sebastian Frank. "Nur ein Fehler?" in: *Funken*, No.2/1958, p.2.
53 Ryschkowsky, *op. cit.*, p.24.

3. Pacifism as Catalyst

1 A summary of the findings of these polls is presented in Hans-Karl Rupp, *Ausserparlamentarische Opposition in der Ära Adenauer. Der Kampf gegen die Atombewaffnung in den fünfziger Jahren*, Cologne 1970, p.46.
2 Here see F.L. (Fritz Lamm), "Offensive Verteidigung" in: *Funken*, No.5/1950, p.5.
3 Developments which are discussed in detail in Klaus von Schubert, *Wiederbewaffnung und Westintegration. Die innere Auseinandersetzung um die militarische und aussenpolitische Orientierung in der Bundesrepublik 1950-1952*, Stuttgart 1972 (2nd ed.).
4 Cf. *Jahrbuch der SPD 1954/55*, p.354.
5 See, e.g., W. "Die Kundgebung in der Paulskirche. Abschluss oder Auftakt?"; and T.P. (Theo Pirker), "Wirksamste Waffe gegen die Wiederaufrüstung: der politische Streik" both in: *Sozialistische Politik*, No.2/1955.
6 Pirker, *Die SPD nach Hitler*, p.205f.
7 A series of DIVO polls indicated that whereas in the early 1950's barely 50% of the population had opposed rearmament, now between 64 and 72% supported the anti-nuclear arms campaign. Cf. *Rupp, op. cit.*, p.89.
8 This surprise quality is emphasized by Theo Pirker in his *Die blinde Macht. Die Gewerkschaftsbewegung in Westdeutschland*, Vol.II, Munich 1960, p.252f.
9 In a letter of 10 April 1957 (estate of Willy Huhn).
10 A notable exception among the media was *Der Spiegel*. Of course the left wing press

generally supported the movement.

11 Rupp, *op. cit.*, p.56. Emphasis in original.

12 Deutsche Friedensgesellschaft, est. 1892, dissolved in 1933 and re-established in 1945.

13 Vereinigung der Verfolgten des Naziregimes (VVN), est. 1947 in Frankfurt; president Martin Niemöller. Publication *Die Tat*.

14 Fränkischer Kreis, founded in Würzburg in 1953 with the declared objective of hastening reunification; the largest organization of oppositional intellectuals in West Germany in this period.

15 Internationale der Kriegsdienstverweigerer, re-established 1945 in Munich.

16 Quoted in Pirker, *Die SPD . . .*, p.254.

17 Quoted in Rupp, *op. cit.*, p.167.

18 Cf. also Arthur Seehof, "Der Atomtod droht" in: *Die Andere Zeitung*, No.3/1958.

19 Pirker, *Die blinde Macht . . .*, Vol.II, p.260.

20 See the *Protokoll* of the Stuttgart Convention, Resolution: "Entschliessung zur Wehrpolitik," p.485ff.

21 As outlined in *op. cit.*, p.264.

22 *Stenografische Bericht*, session of 13 June 1958, Vol.41, p.1704 and 1712.

23 A development which was to be significant in the growth of the New Left. See Ch's.VIII and IX below.

VII. THE SPD AND THE GODESBERG PROGRAMME

1. The Ascendancy of the Pragmatic Reformers

The programme discussion of the mid-1950's had made abundantly evident the need for a revision and re-definition of the SPD's goals and strategies. Upon this point the various "wings" of the party were in complete agreement; inner-party controversy concerned the substance and purpose of the proposed new programme.

Initially, the formulation of programme proposals was chiefly in the hands of the "traditionalist" group, with the left wing still maintaining some influence. A programme commission of 34 members was first constituted in late 1955 and headed by Willi Eichler. Then the SPD's 1956 Munich Convention agreed that a binding basic programme should be prepared on the basis of three principles: that the developing "second industrial revolution" necessitated a new economic order founded on socialist principles, that automation and atomic energy must be subjected to democratic control and planning, and that important branches of industry and advanced technology must be socialized in order to prevent chaos and injustices which occurred with the first industrial revolution.[1] Most of the proposed fomulations were worked out by such "traditionalist" members as Ollenhauer, Fritz Sanger, Benedikt Kautsky and, of course, Eichler himself.

But after the 1957 elections, as has been discussed above, the reformist-pragmatic wing began to establish its ascendancy within the party. No doubt this group would have preferred to dispense with a binding programme altogether,[2] but some concession to the party's traditional methods of expressing its aims and rallying its members was necessary, particularly in view of the fact that the pragmatic reformers were still by no means fully ascendant.

If the preparation of a new programme was the work of the traditionalist, and to some extent left wing, however, that programme's content and uses were ultimately the work of the pragmatic reformers. The Stuttgart Party Convention of 1958 already omitted all direct reference to socialization, except to warn against the danger of "revolutionary haste" in effecting political change, and to oppose a complete adaptation to the existing system (and even these relatively modest proposals were omitted from the final draft of the Godesberg Programme one year later). The Convention confirmed the need for "national defence" and repeated the old demands for a volunteer army — though it continued to reject atomic arms.[3]

A key section of the 1958 programme draft, entitled "A Liberal Order in the Economy," simply left out the principles of economic planning and socialization of key industries (except for the crisis-ridden coal industry and atomic energy production). These proposals, prepared by the SPD's then economic spokesman, Heinrich Deist, recognized the necessity of large enterprises whose productive power made possible economic improvement and a rapid rise in the standard of living, but at the same time conceded that the economic power which the upper classes had accumulated signified considerable social power as well. But where the SPD had once regarded socialization as the means of controlling such power, it now saw the countervailing forces of "smaller and middle-sized enterprises and a large number of cooperative and public enterprises" as being sufficient to offset the concentration of big business.[4]

If it is recalled that the main objective of the pragmatic reformers was to acquire political power, and that socialization proposals, like the party's espousal of the aims of the anti-atomic arms campaign, had not led to any perceptible increase in the SPD's popular support — indeed may in the short term have detracted substantially from it — then their policy of "embracement" or "rapprochement" toward the CDU/CSU is understandable. For the pragmatic reformers, the imminent basic programme was intended to diminish the party's image as an "outsider," a "negative force" or alternative political policy-maker in order to identify it in the popular mind with the perceived successes of the bourgeois coalition and the CDU State.

In order to make the transition to the acceptance of the Godesberg Programme more palatable to party members and supporters, the party leadership adopted — in 1959, following the SPD's withdrawal of support for the Fight Atomic Death movement — an alternative foreign policy which was expressed in its *Deutschlandplan*. This policy may also have been intended simultaneously to attract support from the large sectors among the population who were opposed to rearmament, atomic weapons and national division. The *Deutschlandplan* called for a reduction of tension in Middle Europe through the creation of a demilitarized zone in both parts of Germany, Poland, Czechoslovakia and Hungary, and for the re-establishment of national unity through a gradual and careful process under the auspices of the four occupation powers and with mutual respect for each side's respective socioeconomic system. In direct opposition to the Adenauer government's policy of non-recognition of the DDR (Hallstein Doctrine), the SPD advocated parity of DDR and BRD in all negotiations, leading ultimately to official recognition of the DDR's existence.[5]

A second factor which helped to allay the Left's apprehensions about the impending basic programme was the emergence of the person of Herbert Wehner as the ostensible spokesman for the inner-party Left. As mentioned Ch. V above, Wehner was elected, with the support of the Left, to the Party Executive Committee in 1957 as an opponent of the party's increasing self-image of a *Volkspartei* or "party of all the people." Against this concept, Wehner had argued for the SPD's remaining a membership and mass democratic party which could attract the subordinate classes to a socialist policy; and this could be accomplished by increased party activity in the plants and firms, and by closer cooperation with the trade unions. In 1958 he was elected Deputy Chairman and was one of the instigators of the *Deutschlandplan*. With Herbert Wehner in the party hierarchy, the Left believed its interests to be represented in the party leadership.[6]

But the strength of the intra-party grouping whose goals were at least partially expressed in the *Deutschlandplan* was undermined by the rapidly shifting inner-party power relationships and by the party's continuing approximation of the bourgeois parties in domestic policy. Serious competition for control of party policy arose between two important factions. On the one hand the parliamentary party, whose spokesman in these matters was Dr Karl Mommer, advocated a firmer delimitation of the SPD as against the "radical Left" or even "communist infiltrators" in the party; and the Berlin party organization, led by Willy Brandt, promoted a "discreet sponsorship of a much firmer line of foreign policy than that advocated by the majority of the party executive."[7]

On the other side were the party Left and the leaders of the party machine. The policies pursued by the parliamentary party and the Berlin SPD were incompatible with the aims of the *Deutschlandplan*, and indeed may have been in some measure conceived and executed in an endeavour to undermine it. During 1959, a fair number of expulsion proceedings were initiated against party members for "deviant behaviour" or for failing to dissociate themselves with sufficient vigour from communist policies;[8] among these were the party's student organization and a number of socialist and antifascist members of long standing.

While Mommer was calling for a return to Kurt Schumacher's policy of uncompromising anticommunism — but neglecting to mention the other aspect of Schumacher's struggle on two fronts, namely against the reaction — and referring to the party's Socialist Student League (SDS) as the "Trojan Asses" of communist infiltration, party spokesmen began to emphasize the SPD's instrumental role as the leader of the working classes' rejection of communism: "To the struggle of the Social Democratic Party — and not to a foolish ban — we owe the fact that the communists shrank into an insignificant sect in the Federal Republic."[9] Willy Brandt warned against an "emotional anti-Americanism" which was said to be diverting members' attentions away from the ominous developments in the East.[10] It only need be mentioned *pro forma* that a "harder line" toward the East and an espousal of uncritical anticommunism — or in Professor Abendroth's words, "the anti-bolshevist hysteria of the class enemy"[11] — were counter to the spirit and ends of the *Deutschlandplan*.

Ollenhauer's declaration of 7 July 1959 that he would not accept any office in a future SPD-led government, and the announcement of the formation of a committee, constituted largely of members of the party's pragmatic-reformist wing (Georg-August Zinn, Max Brauer, Brandt, Deist, Schmid, Erler, but also Wehner), to plan an electoral strategy for 1961[12] signified the decline of the party traditionalists as the determining intra-party tactical and ideological force.

2. The Problem of the Changing Social Bases and Function of Social Democracy

The impending programme, it was now evident, would constitute the basis upon which the SPD's future bid for power would be based. With its formulation and execution now in the hands of the pragmatic reformers, it would have to be orientated primarily toward the acquisition of power within the context of the advanced capitalist system and the CDU State. This orientation, for a mass membership party with a socialist tradition, could be vindicated to the party's traditional sources of support if three central presuppositions of the pragmatic-reformist view could be demonstrated to be true:

a) that, contrary to the Marxist analysis, the nature of the class system and intra-societal power relationships — and hence the objective interests of the subordinate (wage- or salary-earning) classes — were changing radically under advanced capitalism,

b) that the consciousness and values of these subordinate classes were also developing in accordance with these changes, and

c) that the social democratic party's role in the modern capitalist state had therefore evolved from that of educator and consciousness-invoking factor of the working classes and instrument for the historically necessary transition to socialism, to that of conciliator between classes and the representative of the interests of "all the people" within the existing socio-economic context.

On the one hand, the Marxist prognostication that there must be an increase in the numbers of the subordinate classes in capitalist society has certainly been borne out in postwar Germany, as elsewhere in the industrial countries of the West.[1] As Table 1 indicates, the proportion of persons employed in subordinate capacities (civil servants, clerical workers and blue-collar workers), as a percentage of the overall labour force, rose by almost ten per cent during the existence of the CDU State. Wolfgang Abendroth, among others, has seen in this trend a basis for a social democratic strategy aimed at winning the support of these subordinate classes — the "powerless" and "exploited majority" in advanced capitalism — for an anticapitalist and socialist programme. Their objective interests, he argued, coincide with those of social democracy;[2] the problem was basically only one of enlightening the subordinate classes concerning their "true" or objective interests, and showing them that Social Democracy was the representative of those interests.

Table 1
The Labour Force According to Occupational Category[3]
(After 1950 figures given apply only to Federal Republic)

	1882 %	1950 %	1956 %	1961 %	1965 %	1971 %
Self-employed and family assisting	35.6	29.1	24.5	21.9	19.4	16.5
Subordinate (civil servants, clerks, workers)	64.4	70.9	75.5	78.1	80.6	83.5
	100%	100%	100%	100%	100%	100%

Sources: *Statistisches Jahrbuch für die BRD* 1965, p.151; and 1973, p.136; *Statistik der BRD*, Vol.119, p.31; *Wirtschaft und Statistik*, No. 12/1966, p.816.

But on the other hand, the fact of subordinate work had become increasingly less a determining factor in the population's subjective consciousness. The figures presented in Table 2 show that, during the past four decades the percentage of actual workers among the gainfully employed population has remained relatively constant, while the service industries have increased to almost the same size and the numbers of those employed in agriculture have declined stikingly. Table 3, a further breakdown of the subordinate classes' composition, again underlines the growth in the numbers of salaried employees (clerks) and officials (civil servants) within the working force.

Table 2
The Occupational Structure of the Labour Force
(Until 1939 applicable to whole Reich; after 1950 to Federal Republic)

Employed in:	1882	1907	1925	1939	1950	1965	1971
Agriculture	43	35	31	25	22	11	8
Production	34	40	41	41	45	48	48
Service industries	23	25	28	34	33	41	44
	100%	100%	100%	100%	100%	100%	100%

Source: adapted from *Die Zeit*, No.50/1972

The division of labour and the structural changes of advanced capitalist society tend to create a growing class of white collar clerical workers and civil servants, drawn from the classes of industrial and agrarian labour, as well as former self-employed classes. The aggregate of blue-collar and white-collar is, however, by no means a homogeneous one. Among clerical workers, for example, are lumped many women who regard their work as temporary and have little awareness of solidarity with the other subordinate classes, a class of academically trained persons, such as chemists, engineers, economists or lawyers, whose situation is often fundamentally different from that of uneducated clerks with little prospect of advancement or job security, and the class of management or lower management whose identification with owners tends to be very high. Clerical workers, like civil servants, are salary recipients and usually earn (marginally) more than the industrial working classes, but the civil servants enjoy greater security and, usually, guaranteed advancement prospects.[4] In terms of these structural changes:

Table 3
Shifts in Occupational Structure of the Labour Force

	1939	1950	1961	1971
Self-employed (business & professional)	13.5	13.5	10.6⎤	16.5
Farmers	14.9	12.5	8.7⎦	
Farm workers	3.9	5.0	1.6⎤	46.7
Manual workers	46.7	47.1	48.2⎦	
Salaried employees and officials	19.3	21.9	30.4	36.8
Unclassifiable	1.8	—	—	—
	100.1%	100.0%	100.0%	100.0%

Sources: Lewis Edinger, *Politics in Germany*, p.29; *Statistisches Jahrbuch für die BRD 1973* p.138.

. . . the most important event from the point of view of political dynamics appears to be the rise of a quite new middle class consisting of skilled workers and the median levels of clerks and civil servants, all of whom work weith a tolerable guarantee of existence but without economic independence and constitutional powers.[5]

Projecting such trends, a number of sociologists and political scientists in the Federal Republic have purported to see in them a "levelled-off middle-class society" (*nivilierte Mittelstandsgellschaft*), in Helmut Schelsky's words, or a "classless middle-class society," to use Siegfried Landshut's term. Such theories argued that the traditional working classes were becoming more and more "embourgeoised" as a result of increasing wages, more leisure time, enhanced social security, more housing and education and a developing "classless" culture, while on the other hand the old upper classes were becoming increasingly "proletarised" and more like the "rising" working classes. The assumption that this was so seems to underlie the pragmatic reformers' rationale in sponsoring the Godesberg Programme.

It is true that the *Elendsproletariat* described by Marx has, in consequence of the material gains just mentioned, better legal safeguards and greater choices of consumer goods, virtually disappeared in western industrial societies. Marx did not foresee — nor could he have been expected to foresee — that advanced capitalism would be able to unleash such great productive forces and thus afford to concede to the masses an ever growing participation in consumption. In this context, the notion of "social capitalism," as coined by Sombart and MacIver, appears quite applicable. Or, in Professor Flechtheim's words: "The class struggle thus led not so much to the 'revolutionization' of the workers as to the reform of capitalism."[6]

For the material gains and improvements in the economic existence of the subordinate classes, as well an increased rights and leisure time, have corresponded with an increased degree of dependence upon the state and economy. It is a well known fact that outmoded direct forms of rule by men over men have long been replaced by more subtle methods made possible by technology, scientific findings and the mass media: ". . . the problem of (objective) social interest conflicts is by no means *solely* a question of a share in consumption, but primarily of power at the command levels of society."[7] The influence exerted by massive bureaucracies and the technical instruments of communication are relatively "invisible" or not readily comprehensible, but nonetheless powerful.[8]

Moreover, despite all ostensible improvements in the workers' condition, almost three-fourths of West German households saw and see all or most of their current income taken up by day-to-day expenses. This means that, if the proletariat is still defined as Marx defined it, namely in terms of possession or property, then

. . . the mass proletariat still exists in essence and fills greater, ever growing circles with a spirit which counteracts the process of deproletarization. The main root of 'living from hand to mouth' is, however, proletarian existence itself, the separation of work from ownership, the inability to amass property (*Vermögensbildung*) and the neglect of an effort to do so which originates in this inability. Hence even today the central part of the proletarian problem lies in lack of ownership, despite all the changes which have occurred in the meantime.[9]

Even the modest material and legal gains of the working classes have not been voluntary concessions made by the economically powerful classes; they have resulted largely from the struggles of the labour organizations, or have been granted in order to forestall or placate potential labour opposition.

Thus West German society, during the existence of the CDU State — and indeed until the present — was and is still divided into two groups: those who possess or control productive capital, and those who are excluded from its ownership or control. At the conclusion of his empirical investigation of income and income distribution in the Federal Republic, Richard Hamilton found no evidence to support the theory of a "convergence" of the middle and lower classes; on the contrary, income differentials had remained constant over the period covered by his study.[10] Table 4 is ample evidence of the continuing discrepancy in the net incomes of the various classes in West Germany.

Table 4
The Labour Force According to Occupational Group and Net Monthly Income (Apr)

Monthly income (DM)	under 150	150- 300	300- 600	600- 800	800- 1200	1200- 1800	1800 +
Self-employed	1.8	3.7	12.2	16.0	25.7	18.5	22.1/100%
Civil Servants	—	1.0	7.5	19.3	41.7	23.7	6.7/100%
Clerical Employees	5.5	7.2	24.9	23.1	26.2	9.5	3.6/100%
Workers	6.3	9.0	33.7	37.2	13.3	0.5	—/100%
Avg. for population	5.3	7.5	27.6	29.9	20.2	6.3	3.4/100%

Source: *Statistisches Jahrbuch für die BRD 1968*, p.126.

Not only do the working classes have less economic power, and receive incomes lower on average than any other sector of the labour force, they have correspondingly less of the material goods in life: fewer cars, washing machines, refrigerators, savings accounts, shares and stocks, etc., than the other classes.[11]

While the evidence thus indicates that ". . . class differences have *objectively* continued into . . . the present phase of advanced capitalism,"[12] and that the *relative* wealth of the lower classes has, at best, remained constant in relation to that of the upper classes, a crucial factor in the development of the former's awareness is that these differences are *subjectively* being eroded and that the lower classes have enjoyed an *absolute* improvement in their material conditions. If, during the early stages of capitalism, the subordinate classes had an immediate and direct connection, through hunger, cold, inadequate medical care, lack of security, etc., with the socialist cause, then they now have indeed "more than their chains to lose," namely their relative abundance of consumer goods, their legal and social rights and their enhanced security. In other words, the modern working or employed classes have a direct and tangible stake in the advanced capitalist system, although of course some have a greater stake than others. These are trends which can be observed in all highly industrialized countries in modern times.

In the Federal Republic, a number of unique factors further contributed to the decline in working-class consciousness after 1945. The "coordination" and disciplining of labour under the Third Reich has been discussed in ch. VI. This is surely related in some measure to the strong authoritarian tradition in German plants and firms which sees a rigid, hierarchical system of command and execution, complete and conscientious obedience to orders and high individual performance (*Leistung*), rather than labour solidarity, as the prime values in the *Betriebsfamilie* (plant or firm as a large family with common goals). The shortages and deprivations of the postwar years also created an overriding popular desire for security and stability at any price; and this, coupled with the discrediting of many of the former higher ideals (solidarity, the state as organism, the notion of *Gemeinschaft*) through the excesses of the Third Reich, has resulted in a fairly general aversion to political and social commitment, and a retreat into the private sphere of family, personal security and an apolitical attitude. Indeed: "One might almost say that to be unpolitical in those (postwar) years signified an almost extreme degree of political behaviour."[13]

Not surprisingly, therefore, the few empirical investigations made during the 1950's and early 1960's reveal a decline in working-class consciousness coupled with a high degree of resignation.[14] Certainly there is little indication of the collective consciousness which Marx attributed to the proletariat, nor is there a general sense on the part of the workers of being a class formed through the social antagonism of capitalism and bound to solidarity by common class interests and goals. As Hans-Paul Bahrdt has written, many workers have little historical or temporal perspective of themselves or their class, but react largely to immediate experiences:

> They work in large concerns which are connected with the world economy in a thousand ways, live through economic crises, labour struggles, wars, bomb attacks and mass expulsions. But they manage to perceive these events as incomprehensible, as natural catastrophes which one must accept, but the traces of which gradually disappear or which become events within the limited horizon of family and neighbourhood.[15]

But a rudimentary form of class consciousness *has* survived in the form of a dichotomous view of society, in the sense of a fundamental social cleavage between "them" or "those up there" versus "us" or "us workers." This seems to be particularly so when the horizon of everyday experience is exceeded and larger social connections have to be coped with. However, this view of society does not include a belief in a qualitative change in the working man's fate, a concrete utopia or the possibility of revolution and the creation of a classless society. Most workers see no chance of their achieving any kind of social transformation beyond gaining higher wages, shorter hours of work and some social security benefits.

But workers have largely retained a simplified concept of the notion of surplus value in so far as they generally believe that money represents power in economy and society, and are aware of their exclusion from it; they know that a portion of the economic value of their wages is diverted to entrepreneurial profits, but tend to see this as "the natural order of things." The doctrine of imperialist war has also been retained in some measure. Many workers perceive interconnections between technological progress, surplus production, unemployment, armaments production, international markets, war and war profits, and the "little man" as the loser in war and peace.

In summary, as Bahrdt has argued, there is today ". . . at least in the form of criticism, still a working-class consciousness."[16] One can only underline his inference that this elementary awareness could either develop into utter resignation or become the basis of a new political conception or enhanced political activity; the further development of labour's awareness, then as now, depends greatly on the actions or omissions of the leaders and members of the large working-class organizations.

Thus despite all structural and sociological changes in the Federal Republic, it still remained (and remains) a class society; and the consciousness of the subordinate classes had not so much changed as receded — facts which undermined the central arguments of the pragmatic reformist group bent on the SPD's transformation into a *Volkspartei*. The notion of the SPD as *Volkspartei*, it should be recalled, was an old one — Kurt Schumacher had proposed that the party seek to win over all the subordinate classes, but only after having awakened their consciousness and converted them to the principles of socialism and democracy. In other words, the enlightened and informed "new" middle classes would realize that their objective interests were best represented by the SPD, and would come to the party. But the party would not "adapt" to their subjective interests (false consciousness).

But the pragmatic reformers saw the SPD as a "party of all the people in much the same way as did the CDU/CSU: as an organization derived from and owing its strength to the maintenance of the socio-economic status quo. All proposals for the transformation of society or the enlightenment of the subordinate classes were implicitly abandoned, according to this view, and as Herbert Wehner explained later, the party embarked upon a policy of "adaptation to the mood of the West German voters" since "whoever wants to do something here . . . must attempt to win over the people just as they are."[17] This meant that now the SPD was to attempt to attract as many traditionally CDU/CSU voters as it could, simply by becoming as much like that party as possible.

Against this strategy, the Left pleaded for a genuine political alternative and a clearly-defined policy based on the objective interests of the subordinate classes. The SPD did not realize, Wolfgang Abendroth argued, that

> . . .in the state of bourgeois society only the working and employed classes (*Arbeitnehmer*), their trade unions and political parties really embody democracy to the full degree and, through their class struggle against the class rule of finance capital, can control the political powers in a democracy which have become alienated from society, and can fill democratic constitutional norms with vitality."[18]

The intrinsic democratic quality of the subordinate classes was thus seen, on the one hand, to be the guarantee of the protection of hard-won liberal rights, and on the other hand the instrument for the extension of formal political democracy into the social and economic spheres. Only a class-conscious and militant organized labour movement, however, was capable of meeting these tasks. The working classes must be prepared₃ to defend democratic rights both through elections and plebiscites, and extra-parliamentary action when necessary. This was why:

> The only permanent possibility for the rise of the SPD is for it, through tenacious struggle with the other social classes' forms of consciousness, which repeatedly — favoured by the actual power relationships —

dominate broad sectors of the working and employed classes, to lead the subordinate classes to an insight into their real social situation, to an understanding of their permanent interests, to give political expression to this consciousness and to extend it into an awareness of power.[19]

In any case, the alternative between party of all the people and class party was not entirely a clearly delineated choice. For if the objective interests of labour really did represent the true interests of democratic society, then to support the working classes' interests was the implicit task of a genuine *Volkspartei*. And a party which represented the interests of the subordinate classes alone was nevertheless upholding the interests of over eighty per cent of the population. Aspiring to be a *Volkspartei* without representing these objective interests necessarily meant representing the perceived interests of a popular false consciousness.

Peter von Oertzen argued plausibly that the SPD was, and would have to remain, a working-class party which would "stand or fall with the number of working-class votes which it gets."[20] In support of this thesis, he presented figures indicating that almost two-thirds of the SPD's support in the 1957 elections was derived from the working classes (of. Table 5), but that the party was able to gain only about half the working-class vote and barely one-third of the old-age pensioners' vote. Since public opinion polls had shown in 1956 that almost 70 per cent of workers had intended to vote for the SPD, the discrepancy between expressed intention and actual act must lie in a lack of faith in the SPD as the party best representing labour's interests:

> The strengthening of the SPD is primarily dependent upon the trust of the workers in its policies. The working class is the foundation of the socialist movement; but this foundation will not hold forever. Whoever believes that the workers will "in any event" vote for the party, is grossly wrong. The trust of the workers must be earned in the same way as the trust of the other classes[21]

A policy of adapting to the perceived wishes of the middle classes, von Oertzen concluded, would result in a loss of five disappointed workers for every farmer, artisan or intellectual gained.

Not only were a majority of SPD voters derived from the working classes but also a plurality of members and, until 1965, a majority of new members. [22]

Table 5
Class Origin of SPD Voters in 1957 Elections

Occupational Group	No. of SPD voters	No. of voters in overall pop.
Workers	6.1 Mill.	12.9 Mill.
Clerical employees + civil servants	1.0	5.4
Self-employed + independent professional	0.6	3.9
Farmers	0.3	3.0
Old age pensioners	1.5	4.8
	9.5 Mill.	30.0 Mill.

Source: Peter von Oertzen, "Arbeiterpartei oder Volkspartei?" in: *Sozialistische Politik*, No.11/1957, p.1.

The SPD was, it is evident, in its history, tradition, membership and social bases, a working-class party.

3. The Godesberg Programme: A Critique

The SPD's new basic programme, passed at the party's November 1959 Convention in Bad Godesberg, was not, as is sometimes supposed, forced upon a reluctant membership: only 16 of 340 voting delegates opposed its adoption. Significantly, such opposition as existed came primarily from the Left; but this will be discussed in the next chapter. The Godesberg Programme represented one of the few "milestones" in the postwar history of western social democratic parties and a rare documentation of the transition from social democracy to what is usually termed liberal socialism. (In other countries this transition has usually been accomplished *de facto*, without any systematic attempt at ideological justification). This is one reason why an examination of the Godesberg Programme is of interest here. This section will discuss the Programme from two aspects: an immanent critique of the Programme itself and an examination of liberal socialism in West Germany.

The authors of the Godesberg Programme proclaim it to be a "socialist" programme, adapted to changing social and technological conditions of modern industrial society. The problem of defining what socialism is, is one which, despite many attempts, still wants solving, and certainly cannot be attempted here. But, with a view to the various forms of socialism which have arisen in time and place, one can state that, if a movement or party is to be designated as socialist, a number of basic goals must be present. These include at least: social justice and social security measures, socialization of the means of production, redistribution of intra-societal power, and human liberation. These elements should be understood in the light of what has been said in Ch. I and what will be discussed below.

It is logical that modern socialism, born amidst the miseries of the industrial revolution and drawing most of its mass support from the under-privileged and exploited lower classes, should advocate *human welfare, social justice* and *redistribution of the social product*. If there is one single theme in evidence in all western political parties aspiring to be "socialist" — and most of these which do not — it is the call for the amelioration of the worst material conditions suffered by the lower classes. Against this criterion, the SPD remains a socialist party. The Godesberg Programme speaks not only of minimum-wage and standard-of-living guarantees, of subsidies to workers, farmers and the poor, and of the state's responsibility to all its citizens to enable them to live "in freedom without disgraceful dependence and without exploitation," but also of an "incomes and distribution policy" aimed at increasing the lower classes' share of the social product.[1]

A second and crucial tenet of "classical" socialism was the call for the *nationalization or socialization of the means of production* — in order to avoid extreme economic fluctuations and the injustices imposed on the lower classes through them, and most important, to eliminate the concentration of economic power in fewer and fewer hands, the control of man over man through economic exploitation and the exercise of arbitrary power — *coupled with socio-economic planning* aimed at averting the wastage of human and natural resources under capitalism, and at shifting priorities from private gain to the improvement of public services, from the conservation of natural resources to universal education.

The underlying rationale here was the *transferral of socio-economic (and thus political) power* from the ruling classes who had employed it for their own benefit *to the lower or subordinate classes*, i.e., to extend political democracy (if it existed) into the social and economic spheres. It is against this crucial criterion that the Godesberg Programme ceases to be socialist.

To be sure, the Programme does state that:

> Persons in the large organizations of the economy who control millions of marks and tens of thousands of workers do not only carry on big business; they exercise a dominant power over other human beings; the dependence of workers and employees goes well beyond an economic-material dependence.
>
> Wherever large enterprises predominate there is no free competition. Those persons who do not command equal power do not have equal opportunities for development; they are to a greater or lesser extent unfree . . .
>
> Through their power, which is enhanced even more by cartels and associations, the leading men of big business are gaining an influence in the state and politics which is not reconcilable with democratic principles. They are usurping power in the state. Economic power becomes political power.

The logical, socialist conclusion from this analysis would be that, since the capitalist system inherently creates inequalities and permits one class to gain "dominant power over other human beings," this system must be abolished, or at least drastically modified. But the Godesberg Programme is not an anticapitalist programme, and so does not oppose capitalism in principle — only its worst effects. Since "enterprises of the public economy which are orientated toward requirements and not private acquisitiveness have a price-regulating effect and help the consumer," it was evident that the (modified) free-enterprise system was best suited to the needs of society. The "free" economy was, however, in need of regulation which could be accomplished in several ways: "An extensive publicity must provide the public with an insight into power structures of the economy and into the economic conduct of the enterprise in order that public opinion can be mobilized against the abuse of power." But experience has demonstrated that economic power has rarely been very sensitive to public opinion in matters affecting its vital interests; it can itself exercise a not inconsiderable control over "public opinion" if not actually create it.[2]

And ". . . where a healthy ordering of economic power relationships cannot be guaranteed by other means, public ownership is purposeful and necessary." This healthy order was to be assured, according to the SPD's conception, by decentralizing the economy and encouraging the development of small- and medium-sized enterprises:

> Private ownership of the means of production shall have a claim to protection and encouragement, provided this does not hinder the establishment of a just social order. Productive medium and small enterprises must be strengthened so that they are able to survive economic competition against large enterprises.

This policy overlooks several salient features of modern advanced capitalist society. For if a nation is to compete in the world market, if it is to exploit technological developments and evolve a coordinated economic programme, then it must concentrate its resources, not fragment them. This leads inevitably to economic concentration. If a government artificially — through "protection and encouragement" — sustains a large class of small entrepreneurs without simultaneously initiating substantial structural reforms, it cannot help but increase the nation's potential for authoritarianism or fascism, as the experiences of Poujadism in France or the NSDAP and NDP in Germany have demonstrated.

In this one superficial respect, at least, the SPD's policy brought it into rather close proximity to that of the extreme right wing NDP.[3] Instead of formulating a forward-looking policy taking into account and providing broader democratic control over growing economic concentration, the SPD was only able to put forward a series of regressive proposals that ignored historical experience.

Finally, socialism has always believed that the fulfilment of elementary human needs, the nationalization of the means of production and the adoption of a programme of thorough socio-economic planning would bring about a climate in which the individual could develop according to his abilities and inclinations. It aimed at harnessing modern science and technology in order *to improve the quality of human life and to liberate man from his social, economic and ideological shackles.* Freed from material necessity and exploitation, and given increased leisure and access to cultural goods, man would be free to develop his creative and individual talents and in this way to fulfil his own life. Some socialists even foresaw the emergence of a New Man.

The Godesberg Programme still contains some vestigial remnants of this aspect of socialism when it advocates, e.g., a reduction of hours of work against payment of equal wages, increased codetermination (although it fails to make concrete proposals for its implementation and does not show how workers can achieve greater power through it), tuition-free and improved schools and universities, increased adult education programmes and more encouragement of the arts, and its expressed desire to "eliminate the privileges of the ruling classes and bring human beings freedom, justice and prosperity" ("that was and is the meaning of socialism"). But these reforms, effected without making substantial changes in the advanced capitalist system, can only have the effect of making this system more "humane," more flexible, and in this way of perpetuating it. They do not contain concrete measures for the elimination of "power over human beings" or the "control of man over man." There can be no question here of "transcending capitalism" or employing a step-by-step progression toward a new egalitarian sociey. Rather one sees the Godesberg Programme as a comprehensive proposal for the removal of capitalism's worst abuses in order to consolidate the status quo.

Thus the Programme's pre-amble declares that only a new and better social order can lead man to freedom, and that democratic socialism aspires to achieve such an order; but the Programme itself contains proposals which have the effect of stabilizing the existing order.[4] The notion of human liberation permeates the text, but concrete measures to bring about liberation, namely economic measures, are nowhere defined. The "freedom" to which the SPD aspires is connected with human dignity, liberal rights and an absence of authoritarian or totalitarian rule; these are goals which it shares with liberal movements of the nineteenth century. Such goals, presented without reference to the specific means by which they are to be achieved, are little more than

empty formulae which lend themselves readily to the vindication of the
already existing formal democratic (capitalist) order.

With its support for small enterprise as a counterweight to the concentration of big business, and with its notion of a "liberal ordering of the
economy" (*freiheitliche Ordnung der Wirtschaft*), the Godesberg Programme
recognizes and supports private enterprise. But a party committed to such a
programme can no longer place socialization and the elimination of capitalism
at the centre of its social policy. The party's alternative for a "socialist"
economic policy, as outlined by Heinrich Deist at the Stuttgart Convention,
was "a constant expansion of the economy, full employment, increase in the
standard of living." All great tasks in the economic, social and cultural
spheres could be accomplished merely by "increasing productivity," and this
was why the SPD was now "of inner necessity the party of economic
upswing," which it would be by restricting the state's powers and increasing
the scope for the development of free initiative in the form of investment,
prices, sales, etc.[5] Here was the ideological basis for the Godesberg formulation, "as much planning as necessary as much freedom as possible." Again, in
almost every respect, these are economic policies of a "classic" liberal party.

This ambiguous combination of socialist rhetoric and vague formulations
underlies the rest of the Godesberg Programme as well. To illustrate:
"Government and opposition have different tasks of the same order; both
bear responsibility for the state" (and, it must be appended, its socio-
economic system). Although the Programme calls for the renunciation of
atomic weapons by the Federal Republic and a controlled disarmament
policy, it also declares the party's support for "the defence of the liberal-democratic basic order. It affirms national defence." How, the question poses itself,
does a nation create the "requirements for an international easing of tensions"
while simultaneously "affirming national defence," especially in view of the
fact that: "The communists radically suppress freedom. They ravage human
rights and the right of self-determination of personality and of peoples?"

The Godesberg Programme also contains provisions for a rapprochement
between the party and the churches: "The SPD respects the churches and the
religious communities, their special mission and their independence. It is in
favour of their protection (*Schutz*) by public law." This includes, presumably,
continued "protection" of parochial schools and the consequent delay in the
development of *Gemeinschaftschulen* (comprehensive schools), and the system
of *Kirchensteuer* (portion of wages paid to the churches which is neither taxed
nor subject to public scrutiny) to which well over ninety-five per cent of the
West German labour force contributes.

In another context, the SPD's educational policy might be regarded as a
means to ultimate human emancipation:

> All youth must be educated in the schools and universities in the spirit
> of mutual respect for freedom, independence, an awareness of social
> responsibility and the ideals of democracy and understanding among
> peoples in order that they might attain, within our society with its
> manifold convictions of *Weltanschauung* and value systems, a disposi-
> tion toward an understanding, tolerant and helpful attitude.

However, in view of the foregoing discussion of the Godesberg Programme, it
seems probable that this "social responsibility" would be developed in the
service of a (more humane) capitalism, that the "manifold value systems"

would not include those hostile to this system.

This brief discussion of the Godesberg Programme shows that the development from social democracy to liberal socialism signified a shift in both the party's strategy and goals: where it once aspired to influence society directly, by enlightening the lower classes, it now concentrated on gaining political power within the liberal-capitalist state; and where it once sought a mandate to change state and society, it now accepted the social and political institutions as they existed.

The theory of liberal socialism is closely connected with the idea of freedom. The German etymology of the term reveals this connection even more clearly: *freiheitlicher Sozialismus.* Willy Brandt has written: "The question which after my experiences of the last decade occupies me most is: how can individual freedom be protected from the political, economic and spiritual powers? How can it be defended against totalitarian threats and bureaucratic tutelage?"[6] As has been discussed at length in Ch. V above, this emphasis on the liberal right of freedom had a real basis in Germany's experience of the *Obrigkeitsstaat* of the past one and one-half centuries, the Third Reich and the communist dictatorship in the DDR.

But the Cold War, West German identification with the capitalist West, the the actual constellation of powers arising from the Western Alliance and the SPD's desire to gain power within this context led to an excessive concern with the "threat to freedom" posed by "undemocratic" communist socialism, so that the SPD tended increasingly to define "liberal socialism" merely as the opposite of communist dictatorship. The fact that the authoritarian tradition still existed in large sectors of society and economy, and that a form of liberal capitalism had produced the Third Reich was largely forgotten. The struggle against the "antidemocratic" forces was thus essentially a struggle against the Left.

This may account for the tendency of the Godesberg programme and of many German liberal socialists to present a dichotomous, undifferentiated view of socialism as either a Marxist-communist-dictatorial or liberal-humanist-democratic grouping.[7] Once this distinction is made, the former can be regarded negatively and derogatorily, using many of the clichés and stereotypes already made available by the bourgeois parties, press and professional anticommunist organizations. The communist theory of democratic centralism was rejected as being an integral part of communism, and not seen as a tactic originating in a specific time and place, namely in Russia in 1917. The aberrations of the DDR and the Soviet Union were held to be inevitably inherent in all communist movements at all times and in all places. This was a progression beyond even Kurt Schumacher's anticommunism, for Schumacher did not oppose the radical-socialist programme or socialist goals of the SED; his quarrel was solely with the undemocratic organization of the SED and its dependence on Moscow. Similarly, the SPD was unable to account for the changes in Soviet Communism after Stalin's death: the SPD Yearbook of 1958/59 argued that only the forms of "sovietization" had changed, but that the terror remained as it always had.[8]

And the SPD rejected the idea of a class struggle in capitalist society because, as the leadership argued, it must lead to the "dictatorship of the proletariat." For the SPD this meant the dictatorship of the Communist Party, as had occurred in the Soviet Union, rather than rule by the majority, as Marx had intended it. Bolshevism was equated with communism, bolshevist methods with communist methods, and these were contrasted with the paliamentary road to power, the only road which the SPD would take. Completely lacking were socialist critiques of communism, the CPSU, the SED or the DDR.

It is abundantly evident that for liberal socialists, freedom was at least freedom from: communist dictatorship, democratic centralism, bolshevist terror and leftist totalitarianism. To repeat: an awareness of these very real dangers to democratic rights was of the utmost importance in postwar Germany. But the alternative values of liberal socialism, namely freedom, justice, peace and social conscience,[9] were never concretized, except as a series of reforms within the existing power structure. These amounted to, basically: control over excessive economic power by creating or promoting small enterprise, "planning where necessary" (or in Professor Ortlieb's words, "separation of powers in the economic sector"[10]), extension of social security measures and labour rights, reform of the educational system to allow greater access to higher education, and increased economic planning to reduce economic crises and create more prosperity and higher living standards.

Schumacher's concept of the inseparability of democracy and socialism became, in the Godesberg Programme: "Socialism will be realized only through democracy, democracy fulfilled only through socialism." This represents an important diversion from the old principle that democracy can only exist in the form of socialism and that political leadership must be held by socialists. Democracy as the realization of socialism signified a renunciation of the postwar SPD view — which had been anchored in the party's last basic programme, the Heidelberg Programme of 1925 — that democracy, or the democratic state was ultimately only a preliminary stage toward socialism.

In this way the Godesberg Programme made a theoretical distinction between socialism and socialization. Willy Eichler asked: "Does general socialization of the means of production promote freedom and equality?" If not, he continued, " . . . then we must not give up socialism, but socialization."[11] On this crucial point, Eichler, like so many liberal socialists, omitted the essential corollaries: why has socialization become unnecessary or even undesirable? Without nationalization or some alternative form of ownership and control transferral, how is social and economic power to be transferred to the majority? Or how can liberal socialism change the existing power relationships in order to achieve a concrete form of "freedom," "social justice" and "human dignity," or "guarantee peace?"

The answer to such questions must be sought in the Godesberg Programme's greatest single omission: a thorough analysis of contemporary society and economy in the Federal Republic, from which specific political guidelines can be derived. This is no accident for, in Wolfgang Abendroth's words, " . . . only the party that aspires to *change* reality needs real programmes."[12] The Godesberg Programme is, in the light of the above considerations, a confirmation, affirmation, vindication and apology for the advanced capitalist system. When liberal socialists reject the possibility of ultimate socialist goals and "other forms of utopia," saying that socialism is an ongoing and constant task, a series of "ethical principles"[13] and a refutation of the communist-opportunistic belief in progress,[14] far from arguing for a more "flexible" and "undogmatic" approach to politics, they are implying that the ideal basic system has been attained with liberal (-capitalist) democracy and needs only constant reform and improvement to sustain it. When Ralf Dahrendorf, as quoted in Ch. I, argues that political problems have become problems of detail, or when Professor Hodges sees socialism as less and less a "doctrine" and more a "political temper," they are underlining further the lack of alternatives which liberal socialism presents vis-à-vis the advanced capitalist order.

The fundamentally regressive quality of liberal socialism is again symbolized by another omission in the Godesberg Programme. Discussing the ideological persuasions from which "socialists" may derive their beliefs, it mentions only the pre-Marxist sources of christian ethics, humanism and classical philosophy. These are also among the acknowledged sources of liberal and conservative philosophy. The post-Godesberg SPD, with its commitment to this programme, is necessarily also a liberal party, but it is no longer socialist.

Yet the term liberal socialism, in postwar Germany, may have been useful — though not accurate — to distinguish the SPD in the popular consciousness from the clerical-conservative CDU/CSU and the (at least until 1969) partially right-wing, partly pro-big business FDP. Heinz-Dietrich Ortlieb was one of the few liberal socialists who recognized that, despite the similarity of socialism's and liberalism's ends, the difference between the two theories was that socialists emphasized more firmly "that man is a social being, that therefore part of man's 'happiness' (apart from exceptional asocial natures) is his place in the *Gemeinschaft* and his work on behalf of the *Gemeinschaft*."[15] Problems of "detail" or differences of "political temper" can, after all, involve the fates of many people, the shifting of priorities or a great variety of economic and social policies *within* the framework of the advanced capitalist system. And liberal socialism, as perhaps the most humane, most socially orientated point of the political spectrum in West Germany is one of the best guarantees for the correction and perpetuation of this system.

4. Tendencies in the Political System After Godesberg

What has been said above tends to refute H. K. Schellinger Jr.'s argument that the Godesberg Programme " . . . adheres to and confirms the trends apparent since Kurt Schumacher's first postwar statements."[1] For Schumacher's struggle against the undemocratic communist dictatorship and the authoritarian reaction was reduced after Godesberg to anticommunism alone; of his tenet of the indivisibility of democracy and socialism, only democracy, defined as an abstract "freedom," remained. Perhaps Schellinger's argument applies only in an unintended sense: the Godesberg Programme did restore some measure of unity between theory and practice, since the SPD had been tending toward a *de facto* form of liberal socialism since Schumacher's death, and the Programme was largely a formal confirmation of that trend.

As Edinger and Chalmers have written, the Bad Godesberg Convention " . . . was a necessary transition stage in the attempt to transform the SPD from a *Weltanschauungspartei* into a multi-interest party. The past could not simply be forgotten, it had to be formally disposed of — for the benefit of the party members as well as the voters."[2] The Programme itself, as Chalmers has pointed out elsewhere, is formulated in general and unbinding terms, and contains goals which, in his words, "pertain to no particular group, are for all practical purposes unrealizable and are purposely vague about the steps the party might take to achieve them."[3] For Theo Pirker, the Programme passed

at Bad Godesberg was an attempt by the SPD to forget its entire history and
all its programmes and policies since 1945.[4] And Ossip Flechtheim wrote that
the renunciation of ideology " . . . signified primarily an adaptation to the
ruling ideas, usages and prejudices of today and yesterday — not to the
opportunities, expectations and demands of tomorrow."[5]

This process of disposing of the past, de-emphasizing ideology and defining
programmatical principles in terms of "values" rather than goals had the
twofold purpose of facilitating the SPD leaders' bid for power within the
framework of existing state and society, and of integrating the party, its
membership and its supporters into this changed social perspective. The
absence of binding principles, it is evident, gave the leaders a greater scope
or freedom of movement and the ability to alter policies as circumstances
changed. The use of the Godesberg Programme as integrating factor is
equally obvious:

> Making absolute the parliamentary road to power, as the programme
> of democratic socialism has done, is however not only a concession to
> the forces of Restoration, it has at the same time the function of
> providing protection against the democratic forces in the party's own
> lines. Once in political power, it sought to avoid giving these democratic
> forces the possibility of invoking legally fixed positions against the lack
> of socialist practice by the leadership. That making absolute the
> parliamentary road had, in addition, the function of losing sight of the
> actual goals for which one wanted to obtain political power is
> demonstrated by the lack of a substantial definition of goals in [the
> party's] constitution (absence of social basic rights).[6]

Anticommunism was, of course, likewise intended as an integrating factor
in much the same way as the SPD had used it during the Weimar Republic:
the party could set itself up as a collection of anticommunist, socialist and
leftist elements, claiming that any party or movement to the left of it was
bound to become communist, or at least a "communist tool." This principle
could then be applied to "left-wing deviations" within the party, as it indeed
was, increasingly so after the Godesberg Programme.[7] The further removed
the SPD's praxis became from its former socialist goals, the more prominent
became the role of anticommunism as a method of discipline and integration.

These — real — functions of the Godesberg Programme were abundantly
illustrated in Herbert Wehner's *volte-face* renunciation of the SPD's *Deutschlandplan* in a speech delivered to the Bundestag on 30 June 1960. Wehner
argued for a "maximum degree of agreement" (*ein Höchstmass an Gemein-
samkeit*) between the government and opposition in the issues of foreign
policy and, in order to achieve this, agreed to meet a series of preconditions
set by then Defence Minister Franz-Josef Strauss, which included recognition
of the Atlantic Alliance and the European Defence Community as the
"foundation and framework for all efforts of German foreign and reunification
policy," a commitment to remain in a European security system following
reunification, and affirmation of national defence.[8] For Herbert Wehner, the
Deutschlandplan, which was said to have originated "because of concern for
Berlin and as an attempt to relieve the pressure on Berlin," now "belonged to
the past," and, in response to a question from the CDU, he added: "in all its
elements." Henceforth the SPD would completely espouse the government's
foreign and defence policies because:

In reality all the controversies (between government and opposition) have been about the way in which we can mobilize the West, upon whom both of us, the majority and minority, are dependent, for the German questions. When I say 'are dependent' I mean that both of us, despite all our differences, belong spiritually to the West.[9]

This complete and unannounced abandonment of the SPD's last alternative to the government's foreign policy — domestic policy alternatives had been largely abandoned with the Godesberg Programme — the way in which it was effected without reference to members' opinions, and the fact that it was done by Herbert Wehner, who less than a year previously had been considered the intra-party spokesman for the SPD Left, confirmed the ascendancy of the reformist-pragmatic group in the SPD, and was a highpoint of the party's policy of "embracement" or rapprochement vis-à-vis the Federal Government, a policy of which the Godesberg Programme was the ideological justification.

Significantly, there was very little "visible" opposition to Wehner's speech. In the parliamentary party, Franz Neumann (who, as a delegate from Berlin, had no voting rights in any event) and Professor Baade found little enthusiasm for their pleas for a return to an independent foreign policy. More opposition, focussing on the significance of the speech to the decline in inner-party democracy and its failure to provide alternative policies, came from the grass-roots, in particular the Munich and Frankfurt party organizations.[11] When the Frankfurt district organization attempted to formulate its opposition, it was opposed by Willy Birkelbach, who argued that the new line must be maintained at all costs until the next elections; members who disagreed were free to resign from the party. He was overridden at a delegates' conference.[12]

Similar trends were evident in the SPD's Hanover Convention of the same year. For the first time in the party's history the vital questions of defence, foreign, social and cultural policy were not first discussed in a plenary session of the party convention, but were prepared and "pre-packaged" by a series of specialist committees — an obvious method of enhancing the leadership's power over policy content and formulation. And where the SPD had previously opposed any form of "emergency legislation" as irreconcilable with the Basic Law, it now declared itself prepared " . . . to discuss without prejudice the dangers which threaten freedom, and to cooperate in such measures as are compatible with the principles of freedom and the *Rechtsstaat*."[13] The Convention's "Appeal of Hanover" declared that: "With the efficiency (*Tüchtigkeit*) of our people and the strength of our economy, we can make an aspiration of today into a reality of tomorrow: the doubling of our standard of living, in this generation! In this way everyone will finally gain the freedom to arrange his life in dignity."[14]

The SPD's conscious de-emphasizing of ideology thus facilitated a more flexible — the standard phrase henceforth used on the Left was "opportunistic" — scope for manoeuvre on the part of the leadership, as well as a greater degree of integration of the party into advanced capitalism. But downplaying ideology is by no means synonymous with "the end of ideology;" it merely reflects a high degree of consensus among the ruling political parties — and presumably among the population — concerning the ground rules and possibilities of the existing system. To declare the extant socio-economic order as the best attainable is itself a highly ideological act, although it may not generally be perceived as such.

Since the Godesberg Programme, the SPD's official self-image has been that of a "party of all the people," a *Volkspartei* concerned not with "particular" or single-class issues, but with the *Gemeinwohl* (common weal).[15] Willy Brandt has said that: "But we are no longer a party struggling only for the 'working class,' we are fighting for the whole people. This extension is decisive for the mission of the SPD."[16]

The adoption of a *Volkspartei-Gemeinwohl* ideology both reflects the fundamental ideological transformation of the SPD and is indicative of the changing strategy the party must adopt. The problem is one of retaining and mobilizing the party's traditional supporters while simultaneously gaining new converts. The appeal to new adherents usually takes the form of promises to certain well-defined socio-economic groups — say farmers or self-employed professionals — in terms of their own interests, while old supporters are kept by an appeal to generalized, "inoffensive" and non-specific ideological clichés "transcending" individual class interests. And the SPD has invoked the German Question, anticommunism, preservation of the economy and the need for security against threats from outside and inside the nation, in order to attract "above-class" support.

The ideology of an all-embracing party "above" individual classes has played and plays an important role in the political life of western democracies. Because it tends to adhere to well-accepted concepts and generalized slogans, it can serve the twin function of attracting voters from all social classes while insulating the party leadership from having to make specific or binding commitments, and therefore rendering it relatively independent of the demands of its supporters both within the party itself and among the electorate. Moreover, actions or policies carried out on behalf of certain interest groups or lobbies can then be publicly justified as pertaining to the common weal. Yet sooner or later the *Volkspartei*, especially when in power, must come down in favour of this or that competing or conflicting group. Higher subsidies for agriculture at the expense of the consumer? Increased minimum wages at the risk of reducing corporate profits? Genuine codetermination (i.e., a shift in intra-plant power relationships) which would detract from owners's rights?

Reflected in post-1959 election campaigns, this common-weal ideology has helped to effect a perceptible decline in the general level of West German political debate. A general overview of the campaigns from 1961 to 1969 demonstrates a syndrome of general characteristics already associated with such countries as the United States, Canada and Great Britain: a high degree of personalization of leading party candidates, appeal to emotions, frequent use of generalized formulations, unsubstantiated and unwarranted claims, defamation of opposition parties or (more commonly) their leaders, and an absence of concrete proposals for change or improvement in virtually all areas of traditional political concern. (The 1972 campaign, for reasons which cannot be entered into here, was the first in over a decade which involved substantial political controversy and a choice of relatively well-defined political alternatives.)

The SPD, in the CDU State, adapted to this policy of personal appeal even to the extent of its well-known concern with the colour of Willy Brandt's car (it was changed to cream because public opinion polls had "proven" that the electorate were more sympathetic toward this colour), or the replacement of the traditional red colouring of campaign literature and posters with blue for the same reason.

A party attempting to appease all social groups displays two trends: a decline in intra-party democracy due to the need to settle a great variety of conflicting interests or claims, and an increase in patronage aimed at winning over the support of these disparate groups (a factor which then further increases the power of the executive). The outcome of an uncoordinated policy aimed at appeasing the shrillest or electorally most important groups *of the moment* is basically the strengthening of the status quo and the surrender of the party's long-term or system-transforming goals.

It is sometimes claimed that when all political parties embrace the "common good" and extend their appeal to all classes, each party then becomes a microcosm of the social system, and social conflicts are carried out within each party, so that a higher degree of consensus and thus efficiency are manifest in the political system. But such inner-party conflicts are relatively invisible — because they are enacted in party conventions, local meetings, etc., rather than in election campaigns — and hence contribute little to political awareness. Such *Volksparteien* also do not represent political alternatives but rather the general "consensus" within the respective party, and between the various parties. Their existence, furthermore, is the most certain guarantee for the perpetuation of the capitalist system. By means of merging the state bureaucracies with political party leaderships and the top levels of business, they have succeeded in down-playing and removing from public view the contradictions which have arisen in the process of production in advanced capitalism. Global tax measures, state intervention in the economy, selective subsidies, the "socialization" of deficits, etc. have decreased the probability of economic crisis. And the parties themselves have become the agencies for the integration of the subordinate classes into a system which operates in conflict with their (real) interests.

In a speech just prior to the 1961 elections, Willy Brandt suggested an important aspect of the changing role of the SPD as political opposition:

> In a healthy and self-developing democracy, it is not uncustomary but rather quite normal that the parties represent similar or identical demands in a number of areas. The questions of priorities, the order of precedence of the tasks to be discharged, the methods and accents — these will always be part of the substance of political opinion.[17]

Commenting on this statement, Otto Kirchheimer asked what meaning opposition had if only priorities, not basic goals, were at stake.

Part of the answer to Professor Kirchheimer's question seems to lie in the ethos of the *Volkspartei*. Where the SPD at least until 1952 — and after that at least nominally — had carried on a policy of system-altering, fundamental or principle opposition aimed at a qualitative — socialist — transformation of economy and society, its policy after that has been to attain and maintain power within the given political system. The former type of opposition may be referred to, as Kirchheimer has written elsewhere: as "opposition on principle," which aims at "(snatching) political power from the government of the moment *and* (clearing) away once and for all the present social and political institutions of which the government of the moment is only the form of expression."[18] Instead of continuing this (unrewarding) form of "disloyal" opposition, the SPD chose to become what Kirchheimer described as a "classical parliamentary opposition," of which the British political parties were said to be the prototype.

It is argued here, however, that while the Godesberg Programme presented a suitable ideological foundation for a policy of classical parliamentary opposition, the use of that programme — abandonment of foreign policy alternatives, failure to develop an individual platform — contributed to the development, in the last years of the CDU State, to a form of "authoritarian democracy" or a "one and one-half party system," in which government was "no longer, as in liberal democracy, 'rule for a limited period', but 'permanent rule.' Within the framework of authoritarian democracy there is neither the possibility of radical or revolutionary minorities gaining political influence.'"[19] In this view the parliamentary opposition sees its tasks less in controlling government and administration and preparing alternative policies than in preparing for elections and downplaying all points of conflict or antagonism. The social democratic opposition succumbs to the temptation of working "constructively" in collaborating with the ruling parties, in return for which it receives a number of perquisites such as offices, secure posts for party members, etc., and thus overlooks the substantial questions of political life — both those which do and do not go beyond the capitalist order. Hence the determination of the direction of political life goes over increasingly to the ruling parties who are able to make binding, long-term decisions and commitments with regard to supra national economic agreements, military policy, socio-economic problems, etc.[20]

Authoritarian democracy or a one and one-half party system thus represent a qualitative stage beyond the CDU State in its original form. For the latter was at least subject to some degree of control by a fundamental and alternative opposition, however weak that opposition may have been. In authoritarian democracy, parliamentary opposition tended to become rule by consensus or even rule by political cartel.

It has already been suggested that the SPD's disproportionate emphasis on increasing its share of the popular vote and its attendant ideological veil of "the party of all the people" have led to extensive changes in intra-party structure and democracy. If the party's policy is aimed at preserving and maintaining the general (existing) interest, then those groups or individuals within it who make specific proposals for changing the status quo or demand qualitative social changes must be rejected as "particularist" or "radical." This explains in some measure the exclusion of many old party members, the SDS and the "radical professors" who had supported it, in the year following the Godesberg Programme.

The SPD's attempt to transform itself into a system-immanent *Volkspartei* created an internal contradiction within the party. Unlike the CDU/CSU, which in its long postwar development as a multi-interest party, had permitted factions to develop and continue within the party organization, corresponding with the various interests represented in it, the SPD had traditionally been a class party exacting solidarity and unanimity from its members in its struggle against the social, economic and political order. Inner-party discipline was needed in the struggle of a working-class movement against the ruling classes and their system; and this discipline was produced almost automatically from the mutuality of interest of the working classes whose interests were represented in the SPD. A *Volkspartei* aspiring to incorporate supra-class support, however, cannot demand from its members the same degree of unanimity and discipline because the representation of all interests is implicit in the concept of the "party of all the people."

The metamorphosis into a *Volkspartei* is, however, only one of several factors which have conspired, as it were, to reduce the SPD leadership's dependence upon intra-party democracy. Despite high court precedent and popular debate, West German political parties until 1968 did not need to reveal their sources of financial contributions. State financing of political parties, alloted according to the parties' share of the popular vote — and not granted at all to parties achieving less than 2.5 per cent (until recently 5%) or a plurality in at least three constituencies (until 1957 one constituency) — combined with large financial contributions from outside the parties, renders their leaders less and less dependent upon financial support from party members and thus on those members' expressed will. The "Five Per Cent Clause" (which bars from parliamentary representation any party obtaining less than 5% of the popular vote) effectively eliminates new and protest parties from representation. This regulation also gives the lie to Article 21 of the Basic Law which provides for the unimpeded right to establish political parties.

Professor Flechtheim had such developments in mind in referring to the "institutionalization" and "constitutionalization" of the large political parties and their evolution into "quasi-state" parties.[21] The decline in the number of alternative political parties and the development toward a two-party system is illustrated in Table 6.

Table 6
Combined Share of SPD and CDU/CSU in Federal Elections Since 1949

Year	1949	1953	1957	1961	1965	1969	1972
%	60.2	74.0	82.0	81.5	86.9	88.8	90.7

Source: H. Jäckel, *Wahlführer 1969*, Munich 1969, p.96; *Die Zeit*, No.40/1969, p.3; and *Statistisches Jahrbuch für die BRD 1973*, p.126.

Moreover, this process of concentration of political parties and their transformation into patronage-geared "state parties" fortifies their leaders' interest in preserving the existing system. A series of interlocking party oligopolies is created which tend to become more autocratic, centralistic and monolithic. Entrenched leadership tends to stagnate: as Ulrich Lohmar has pointed out, a turnover of 10 per cent in the SPD party elite following an election would be "very high."[22] As a consequence, intra-party democracy has further declined. Party conventions, instead of being forums where diverse views are aired and discussed and resolutions based on majority decisions and binding on the leadership are reached, have degenerated into displays of teamwork, into gatherings whose principal function is to affirm and acclaim a predetermined policy presented intact to the "tribune" by the leadership oligopoly.[23] And this policy is frequently the outcome of direct consultations between the party leaders and various "experts" — frequently appointed by powerful lobbies — or captains of industry and other sectors of the economy or society not subject to democratic control or public scrutiny.

Increasingly too, leaders are not recruited from party ranks. They may be appointed *ex-officio*, for example by virtue of their position in government or the parliamentary party, or through co-optation from outside or "above" the party. (Until recently, to take an extreme example, only about ten per cent of the Federal Directorate of the CDU were elected by the party convention, the remainder being chosen ex-officio or thorough co-optation, chiefly from industry. Since 1967, two-thirds of this body have been elected at the party convention.)

When party democracy becomes party discipline, when elections become a question of personnel rather than programme, then the qualitatively better members of that political party tend to lose interest in it. The rank and file is thus not replenished by the critical and committed but instead by "drones and opportunists . . . who regard the party primarily as an employment office."[24]

After Godesberg, corresponding with the growing ideological similarity of the major political parties and their increasing tendency to merge with the state and big business, the social bases of the SPD and CDU/CSU have become more similar. Prior to 1961, roughly 49 per cent of all skilled workers and 43 per cent of semi- and unskilled workers cast their votes for the SPD.[25] Or considered another way, in 1953, 70% of the SPD's support came from the working classes; in 1961 the comparable percentage, at 69, had hardly changed. But between 1961 and 1969 this percentage had dropped from 69 to 58 (see Table 7), while labour votes became a larger part of the CDU/CSU vote.

These similarities are particularly important if one agrees with Hans See that inner-party life cannot be separated from social life.[26] He has argued plausibly that the real relationship between the political parties and their voters became after 1959 essentially that of industrial concerns vis-à-vis consumers: "The constantly growing capital concentration in the economy corresponds with the formation of two monopolistic party concerns which, with a huge expenditure of material and psychological means, struggle for the currently largest market share of democratic legitimation."[27]

Table 7
Growing Similarities Between Class Support of CDU and SPD

		1961	1969
Percentage of clerical workers (Angestellte) among the supporters of the:	CDU	19	23
	SPD	15	24
Percentage of leading clerical workers among these	CDU	5	6
	SPD	3	6
Percentage of upper social classes	CDU	25	24
	SPD	12	19
Percentage of workers	CDU	36	42
	SPD	69	58

Source: *Der Spiegel*, No.32/1969, p.39.

The thesis of voter as consumer and political parties as competitors in the political marketplace brings with it a number of corollaries. The depoliticization of voters through the mass media and the personalization of politics cause the parties to adapt to the voters' perceived "degree of awareness," to the attitudes and prejudices which they hold, in order to attract more votes. Or, if expedient, the party may attempt to divert or modify such views. But the fears, beliefs and prejudices of the lowest common denominator are largely a form of false consciousness in the sense of pre-formulated opinion or confirmation of existing resentments and prejudices and as such completely within the ideological framework set by the advanced capitalist system. The nature of the "freedom of choice" offered by such a system in which " . . . political competition is more and more like competition for similarly-constituted, homogeneous consumer goods,"[28] does not include the right to vote for a party whose aims point beyond liberal capitalism, for no such party is allowed to exist. This is particularly so in view of the fact that the public opinion polls, upon whose results party policies are presumably based, seem never to involve questions touching upon the existence of the basic socio-economic order.

For the Left, the SPD's pursual of such methods represented both an ideological and tactical error: "A party which runs after the questionnaire findings of the opinion research institutes, instead of seeing them for what they are, the mere *starting point* of a conscious opinion formation has, precisely among voters who do not decide rationally and are socially unaware, no chance whatever."[29] A too-pronounced policy of embracement, as the SPD carried on between 1959 and at least 1967, violated even the laws of good marketing: " . . . a market article must never be offered in a similar package and with the same content as another. A market article must set itself off from the others, must have its own, unmistakable image. Copying the opponent only works to the benefit of the opposition."[30] Or, in Gerhard Gleissberg's words: "Would a Catholic, if the Protestants decided to recognize the Pope, convert for this reason to Protestantism?"[31]

Although it is evident that the SPD came increasingly to resemble the CDU/CSU during the 1960's, it is also true that the two parties still exhibited a number of differences, not least of all in their intra-party democracy. For example, the SPD still enjoyed a greater mass membership than the CDU; the former's stood, at the end of the 'sixties, at about 750,000, the latter's at 280,000 (the CSU had an additional 100,000). While three per cent of the enfranchised West German population were party members, 6.5% of all SPD voters were members of their party and only 2.2% of those voting for the CDU belonged to it. Consequently the SPD remained more dependent upon its members' contributions. In 1968, members' donations constituted a mere 6.9 million DM of the CDU's total revenues, one-fifth of that total. But SPD members contributed 18.9 million DM to the party's coffers, a full 40% of its total finances.[32]

And the degree of co-optation and *ex-officio* acquisition of offices, of the number of intermediate stages in the party hierarchy between local and national level, of the accumulation of offices by individual members and of the representation of non-elected groups (e.g. the "Exile-CDU") was still less within the SPD than the CDU/CSU. With some qualifications, these factors were reflected in the respective parties' internal democracy, with the SPD still having to take greater account of members' opinions and to pay more attention to maintaining the channels of communication.

Though the period between the Bad Godesberg Basic Programme and the formation of the Grand Coalition in December 1966 delimited the SPD's greatest degree of adaptation or accommodation to the ruling political parties and the capitalist system in that party's approximately one hundred year history, its still largely working-class mass basis, the vestigial remnants of its socialist tradition, and not least of all, growing competition from the Left, maintained an oppositional potential within the SPD into the years when alternative political policies were to promise some prospect of success.

REFERENCES

1. The Ascendancy of the Pragmatic Reformers
1 Corresponding resolution reproduced in: Ossip K. Flechtheim, ed., *Dokumente zur parteipolitischen Entwicklung in Deutschland*, W. Berlin 1962-1970, Vol.III, p.103.
2 A view shared by, among others, Peter von Oertzen, ''Wohin geht die Partei?'' in: *Sozialistische Politik*, No.8-9/1959, p.2.
3 *Protokoll der Verhandlungen des Parteitages der SPD vom 18.-23.5.1958 in Stuttgart*, Bonn 1958, p.488.
4 *Ibid.*, p.489.
5 SPD, ed., *Deutschlandplan der SPD. Kommentäre, Argumente, Begründungen*, Bonn 1959 (brochure). Even the brief summary presented here tends to refute Douglas Chalmers' assertion that the *Deutschlandplan* was part of a process of ''marginal differentiation'' in advertising and marketing, and that: ''Although on a different scale, the party was comparable to a toothpaste manufacturer adding a ''secret ingredient'' to his product to provide the slightest differentiation that will lead the consumer to his rather than his competitor's toothpaste.'' (*The Social Democratic Party of Germany. From Working-Class Movement to Modern Political Party*, New Haven 1964, p.94). Though these statements certainly apply to the SPD's foreign policy after 30 June 1960, the *Deutschlandplan* was, during its brief existence, a genuine foreign policy alternative.
6 On Wehner's role in the SPD Left, see Theo Pirker, *Die SPD nach Hitler*, Munich 1965, p.247ff; and Hans Brakemeier, ''SPD — The Spirit of Routine'' in: *International Socialist Journal*, No.19 (Feb.) 1967, p.34.
7 *The Manchester Guardian*, 1 June 1959.
8 Here see Gunther Gillesen, ''Kampf um die Linke'' in *Frankfurter Allgemeine Zeitung*, 4 June 1959.
9 *Ostspiegel* (*Sozialdemokratische Pressedienst*), 4 July 1959, p.2. This onesided critique of communism was at least partially contradicted by Herbert Wehner, who argued that the preservation of democracy was best served by a clear distancing from both the SED and the reactionary forces in the Federal Republic. See, e.g., ''Der Streit über Mommers Äusserungen geht weiter'' in: *Frankfurter Allgemeine Zeitung*, 4 July 1959; and the report of Wehner's speech in Nurnberg in: *Stuttgarter Zeitung*, 6 July 1959.
10 See Fritz Rene Allemann, ''Wo steht die SPD'' in: *Die Zeit*, 5 June 1959.
11 In ''Der Kongress fur Demokratie — gegen Restauration und Militarismus'' in: *Sozialistische Politik*, No.6-7/1959, p.3.
12 See *parlamentarisch-politische pressedienst* (ppp) of 7 July 1959, p.1.

2. The Problem of the Changing Social Bases and Functions of Social Democracy
1 Comparative statistics given in Wilbur E. Moore, ''Changes in Occupational Structure'' in: S.M. Lipset and N. Smelser, eds., *Social Structure and Mobility in Development*, New York 1966.

2 Cf. Wolfgang Abendroth, "Aufgaben einer deutschen Linken" in: Horst Krueger, ed., *Was ist heute links? Thesen und Theorien zu einer politischen Position*, Munich 1963, p.144f; and his *Antagonistische Gesellschaft und politische Demokratie. Aufsätze zur politischen Soziologie*, W. Berlin 1967, p.68ff.

3 *Ibid.* ("Aufgaben . . .") cites slightly deviating — but tendentially similar — statistics, but without citing a source (p.145); see also special ed. of *Frankfurter Hefte*, May 1969, for a further discussion of this problem.

4 Cf. C. Wright Mills, *White Collar. The American Middle Classes*, New York 1954.

5 Otto Kirchheimer, "Vom Wandel der politischen Opposition" in: *Archiv fur Rechts- und Sozialphilosophie*, Vol.43(1957), p.78.

6 *Eine Welt oder Keine? Beiträge zur Politik, Politologie und Philosophie*, Frankfurt 1964, p.169.

7 Abendroth, *Antagonistische Gesellschaft . . .*, p.71 (emphasis in original).

8 Here see Burkhart Lutz, "Technischer Fortschritt und Gesellschaft" in: Marianne Feuersenger, ed., *Gibt es noch ein Proletariat?* Frankfurt 1962, p.54.

9 Paul Jostock, "Gibt es noch ein Proletariat?" in: *ibid.*, p.13.

10 "Affluence and the Worker. The West German Case" in: *American Journal of Sociology* 71 (1965), p.144ff.

11 See Kurt Gehrmann, "Gehören die Arbeiter zum Mittelstand?" in *Gewerkschaftliche Monatshefte*, Nov. 1958, p.788ff.

12 Wolfgang Abendroth, discussing a speech by Herbert Marcuse, in: *Das Argument*, No.5-6(Dec.) 1967, p.409, italics in original.

13 Klaus Eberlein, *Was die Deutschen möchten. Politische Meinungsumfragen in der Bundesrepublik*, Hamburg 1968, p.81f.

14 See above all the trail-breaking study of 600 workers in the iron industries of the Ruhr, carried out between 1953-1954: H. Popitz, H.P. Bahrdt, *et al.*, *Das Gesellschaftsbild des Arbeiters*, Tübingen 1957, p.173.

15 Hans-Paul Bahrdt, "Marxistisches Denken in der deutschen Arbeiterschaft?" in: *Die Neue Gesellschaft*, No.6/1956, p.403ff.

16 Bahrdt, *op. cit.*, p.411.

17 Quoted in: *Der Spiegel*, No.40/1969, p.27.

18 "Arbeiterklasse, Staat und Verfassung" in: *Die Neue Gesellschaft*, No.6/1959, p.42.

19 Abendroth, "Analyse des sozialdemokratischen Wahlkampfes" in: *Frankfurter Hefte*, No.11/1961, p.726.

20 "Arbeiterpartei oder Volkspartei?" in: *Sozialistische Politik*, No.11/1957, p.1.

21 *Ibid.*, Part 2 in: No.12/1957, p.3.

22 See the table in: Heino Kaack, *Geschichte und Struktur des deutschen Parteiensystems*, Opladen 1971, p.484; and *Der Spiegel*, No.20/1970, p.54.

3. The Godesberg Programme: A Critique

1 These, and all subsequent quotations from the Godesberg Programme, based on SPD, ed., *Das Godesberger Programm*, Bonn 1959. Although an English-language version is available (Bonn 1961), I have preferred to use my own translations here.

2 See Ralph Miliband, *The State in Capitalist Society*, London 1969, p.211ff; and P.A. Baran and P.M. Sweezy, *Monopoly Capital*, Penguin 1968, p.117ff.

3 Chapter V of the NPD Programme (Hanover 1967) reads: "The middle-class economy is a vital part of our national economy. Since it is less susceptible to crises [!] it secures the stability of the overall economy. A large number of independent and self-sufficient units guarantee simultaneously the democratic social order." But even the NPD considered a "large industrial sector in the national economy" as indispensable and proposed therefore a combination of all industries producing the same products because "only in this way can the competitive capacity of German industry be ensured in relation to larger foreign concerns."

4 On this see Gerhard Gleissberg, *SPD und Gesellschaftsystem. Aktualität der Programmdiskussion 1934 bis 1946*, Frankfurt 1973, p.74f.

5 Deist's speech, delivered to the Convention, mimeographed abridged version, complete with author's comments and amendments: *Freiheitliche Ordnung der Wirtschaft*, published by SPD, n.p., n.d. (Bonn 1958?), esp. p.7ff.

6 *My Road to Berlin*, p.269.

7 A typical statement of this view is Klaus-Peter Schulz, *Opposition als politisches Schicksal*, Cologne 1958, esp. p.43ff.

8 *Jahrbuch der SPD 1958/1959*, Bonn 1959, p.363.

9 Cf. one statement among many of this view: Willy Brandt, "Vordringliche Aufgaben sozialdemokratischer Politik" in: *Die Neue Gesellschaft*, No.3/1956, p.194 and ff.

10 Ortlieb, "Krise des Sozialismus" in: *Gewerkschaftliche Monatshefte*, No.1/1950, p.543.

11 Willy Eichler, *Grundwerke und Grundförderungen im Godesberger Programm der SPD*, Bonn 1962, p.15.

12 *Wirtschaft, Gesellschaft und Demokratie in der Bundesrepublik*, Frankfurt 1965, p.90. The original reads: "Denn wirklicher Programme bedarf nur diejenige Partei, die die Wirklichkeit *verandern* will."

13 Eichler, "Sozialismus als ethischer Realismus" in: *Geist und Tat*, August 1952, p.225.

14 Ulrich Lohmar, "Zum Godesberger Programm der Sozialdemokratie" in: *Die Neue Gesellschaft*, Nov./Dec. 1959, p.417.

15 Ortlieb, *op. cit.*, p.545.

4. Tendencies in the Political System After Godesberg

1 "The Social Democratic Party after World War II. The Conservatism of Power" in: *Western Political Quarterly*, No.19 (June) 1966, p.255. Later he calls the programme "a progressive, even radical step," requiring "active, daring leadership" in order to "overcome intraparty resistance to the development of the new programme." (p.264)

2 Lewis Edinger and Douglas Chalmers. "Overture or Swan Song. German Social Democracy Prepares for a New Decade" in: *Antioch Review*, XX (1960), p.169.

3 Chalmers, *op. cit.*, p.85.

4 Pirker, *op. cit.*, p.8ff.

5 "Die Institutionalisierung der Parteien" in: *Zeitschrift für Politik*, Vol.9, 1962, p.103.

6 Gerhard Stuby, "Bürgerliche Demokratietheorien in der Bundesrepublik" in: Reinhard Kühnl, ed., *Der bürgerliche Staat der Gegenwart. Formen bürgerlicher Herrschaft II*, Reinbek 1972, p.103.

7 Cf. Ch.VIII below.

8 Wehner's speech reprinted in: *Vorwärts*, 8 July 1960, p.5ff.

9 *Ibid.*, p.7.

10 "SPD sucht 'schwatzhafte Trottel'" in: *Deutsche Zeitung*, 4 July 1960.

11 See "SPD-Kritik am neuen Kurs der Partei" in: *Süddeutsche Zeitung*, 11 July 1960; and "Wir schlucken Wehners Politik nicht" in: *Neues Deutschland*, 12 July 1960.

12 Cf. *ibid.*

13 *Jahrbuch der SPD 1960/61*, Bonn 1961, p.431.

14 *Ibid.*, p.419f.

15 This is essentially the view represented in Willy Eichler, *Grundwerte und Grundforderungen . . .*; and in Carlo Schmid, *Hundert Jahre Sozialdemokratische Partei*, Hanover 1963.

16 "Die Lage der Nation" in: K.D. Arndt, ed., *Mündige Gesellschaft. Die SPD zur Lage der Nation*, Munich 1964, p.12.

17 Quoted in Otto Kirchheimer, "Deutschland oder der Verfall der Opposition in: *Politische Herrschaft*, Frankfurt 1967, p.71.

18 Kirchheimer, "Vom Wandel . . .," p.69.

19 Pirker, *loc. cit.*, *Die SPD nach Hitler*, p.12.

20 Here see variously: Waldemar Besson, "Regierung und Opposition in der deutschen Politik" in: *Politische Vierteljahresschrift*, No.3/1962, p.225ff and esp. 239; Ralf Dahrendorf, *Society and Democracy in Germany*, Garden City 1967, p.194f; and

Otto Kirchheimer, "Germany: The Vanishing Opposition" in: R. Dahl, ed., *Political Oppositions in Western Democracies*, New Haven 1966, esp. p.243f.

21 "Die Institutionalisierung...," p.97.

22 *Innerparteiliche Demokratie. Eine Untersuchung der Verfassungswirklichkeit politischer Parteien in der BRD*, Stuttgart 1963, p.86.

23 This discussion of inner-party democracy is based largely on: Ute Müller, *Die demokratische Willensbildung in den politischen Parteien*, Mainz 1967; and Bodo Zeuner, *Innerparteiliche Demokratie*, W. Berlin 1969.

24 Abendroth, *Wirtschaft, Gesellschaft...*, p.100.

25 Arnold Heidenheimer, *The Governments of Germany*, New York 1961, p.77.

26 *Volkspartei im Klassenstaat oder das Dilemma der innerparteilichen Demokratie*, Reinbek 1972, p.48.

27 *Ibid.*, p.56.

28 Manfred Friedrich, *Opposition ohne Alternative*, Cologne 1962, p.98.

29 Abendroth, *Antagonistische Gesellschaft...*, p.74f, italics in original.

30 Eberlein, *op. cit.*, p.75; cf. further: Jürgen Schaltenberg on the 1961 elections: "Die SPD in der gesellschaftlichen Entwicklung nach dem 2. Weltkrieg" in: *Neue Kritik*, 10 May 1962, p.14ff.

31 "Die sichere Niederlage der rechten SPD" in: *Die Andere Zeitung*, No.30/1960, p.1.

32 *Der Spiegel*, No.42/1969, p.30.

PART C

OPPOSITION FROM BELOW
1960-1967

VIII. THE GREAT SCHISM: THE TRANSITION TO EXTRA-PARTY OPPOSITION

1. Reaction on the Left to the Godesberg Programme

> If it were only a question of personal disputes, of trifling matters, of some kind of minor disputatiousness, of an oversight or of so-called 'speaking out of turn' on the part of a few individuals, then every serious person must call it an outrage, indeed a crime, if such petty matters were to cause a split in the opposition.
>
> But this is not so, Comrades! What has caused this division is fundamental questions of policy, the whole conception of the ways and means that are supposed to lead us from out of the party's present desperate situation into more worthy circumstances . . .
>
> Suddenly, as though by evil magic, the party of the proletarian international class struggle has become a national liberal party. Our organizational strength, of which we were so proud, has proved to be completely impotent, and where we were once respected and feared mortal enemies of bourgeois society, we have now become the irresolute and justly despised tools of our mortal enemy, the imperialist bourgeoisie . . .[1]

This quotation from Rosa Luxemburg points to what is perhaps the greatest fundamental difference between the pre-World War II and the postwar German Left: then as now the Social Democratic Party was repeatedly rent and split by "fundamental questions of policy," by differences concerning its relation to the (capitalist) state and society and by the conflicting claims of the party's Left and Right. But before 1933 any significant shift to the right on the part of the party leadership,[2] such as the parliamentary party's approval of war credits in 1914, its truck under Ebert in the Weimar Republic with the conservative-reactionary forces, its periodic lapses into "parliamentary opportunism," or the right wing's acceptance of Hitler's Enabling Law in 1933, would be countered and challenged by the Left on every occasion. The success of the USPD, the rise of the Spartakus movement and the periodic increases in mass electoral support for the KPD throughout the Weimar era were all concrete and positive reactions to the SPD's failures to represent the labour movement in the way that the socialist Left believed it ought to be represented.

After 1949, as the preceding chapters have demonstrated, the situation changed considerably. Each successive move by the SPD away from a socialist, anticapitalist position invoked at most isolated, but largely ineffectual protest from the Left, but never resulted in the establishment of an independent political force. The causes of this, it has also been argued, must be sought in the changing nature of modern capitalism and its political and social representatives, in the effectiveness of clerical anticommunism fostered by the Cold War, and in the ostensibly apolitical nature of postwar German society.

And indeed, in the years immediately following the SPD's final and formal transformation into a "liberal socialist" party, i.e., after the Godesberg Programme and Herbert Wehner's foreign policy speech of 30 June 1960, the Left, so it seemed, had reached its nadir. The process had begun, termed by Helga Grebing "the disintegration of the Left, which set in with the exclusion of Marxist ideas from the Godesberg Programme."[3] The CDU State, sustained by the Economic Miracle, the mass party "of a new type", the bourgeois coalition and the social and economic Restoration with its manifold international obligations and commitments, was at the crest of its power. All attempts to put forward a left wing alternative were drastically inhibited, not by lack of theory or an objective *raison d'être*, but because of an almost total absence of mass popular support. The trade unions had also passed their own programme of integration in 1959. The few leftist stirrings of the late 1950's no longer found any popular resonance: the intra-party "adapters" or "hibernaters" had (reluctantly, of course) endorsed the Godesberg Programme; the *Funken* had folded in early 1959; the *Sozialistische Politik* group had split, and the periodical was now published by the Trotskyists and Wolfgang Abendroth; *Die Andere Zeitung* was so suspect of being "communist-influenced" as to have become largely ignored; Viktor Agartz and his *WISO-Korrespondenz* were practically only a memory; and finally, the peace movement, for the time being, had foundered after the SPD's precipitate withdrawal from it.

But this disintegrating process simultaneously contained a regenerative potential. Even now there remained a number of dormant factors which, if recognized and acted upon, offered some prospect of preserving the Left from utter extinction. These were: the fairly widespread (though by no means majority) resentment at the grass-roots level of the SPD's new course, the relatively large number of intellectuals disillusioned by developments in the Federal Republic but unwilling to commit themselves to a co-ordinated political programme, and a minority of the increasingly politically minded student body who had been to some extent influenced by the anti-atomic arms campaign, the SPD's opportunistic withdrawal of its support for both it and the *Deutschlandplan*, and the larger issues which all this raised.

The Left's resistance to the SPD's post-Godesberg course was embodied by Wolfgang Abendroth, who had been one of the most consistent opponents within the party of its relentless accommodation to the CDU State after Schumacher's death.[4] By 1958 and the SPD's first draft of what was to become the Godesberg Programme, most of the "programme debate" of the mid-'fifties had receded as the ascendancy of the pragmatic reformist group in the party became increasingly evident. Criticism of the Stuttgart draft programme was largely confined to peripheral changes and minor insertions, but the basic direction that the new programme would take was already determined in principle. The Left and the traditionalists were for the most part resigned to this fact.

In this context, Wolfgang Abendroth put forward an alternative programme for Social Democracy which, by its existence, was an indictment of what the Godesberg Programme was not: a consistent socialist programme containing a thorough analysis of the existing social and economic relationships, incorporating the latest findings of the social sciences, specifying the changes necessary to bring about a socialist society, and outlining in concrete terms the role of the labour movement and its political arm, the SPD, in this process of transformation.

Abendroth's opposition to the Godesberg Programme dated back to the Stuttgart draft programme of 1958 (although, of course, his opposition to the SPD's changing course throughout the 1950's has already been documented). In an article which anticipated his alternative programme, he laid down his fundamental objections to the Godesberg Programme. They were: (1) that it represented a break with the intellectual and moral tradition of the party and the labour movement, (2) that it was "a-historical" and acted "as though the real history of the last 40 years had never taken place," (3) that it lacked socialist goals and means of attaining them, (4) that it failed to analyse concretely the contemporary historical situation, and (5) that it was a facile adaptation to the existing order, a "programme of conformity and resignation." [5]

Abendroth's anti-Godesberg Programme, in an analysis of "the social situation in the capitalist parts of the world," demonstrated that growing concentration in advanced capitalism had increased the numbers of the subordinate classes, who were forced to live by the sale or alienation (*Verausserung*) of their labour, while economic power was increasingly concentrated in fewer and fewer hands. [6] The development of monopoly capitalism, uniting as it did industrial, commercial and bank capital into great "blocks of finance capital," enabled small oligarchical groups to control all sectors of society. The huge costs of developing technology and the productive forces ensured that initiatives toward progress would be under the aegis of finance capital. Particularly in consequence of wartime technology, the large concerns had been excessively encouraged and assisted by the state. The "internationalization" of capital had drawn the whole world into a global productive process, but the method of assimilation had remained private-capitalist, so that the old social contradictions were still extant, only now on an international level.

The economic crisis inherent in this system had to be overcome by means of armaments production, and in order to facilitate this unproductive economic process, the state must be further subordinated to the interests of finance capital and the people trained to fear and resentment through public opinion manipulation and anticommunism. The one alternative to these developments was a socialist society, economy and government.

The development toward monopoly capitalism caused the state to acquire an ever growing role in economy and society: a monopoly of legislation and of use of weapons, the organization of culture, social security and legal rights. The state's function was to guarantee that the inevitable crises and conflicts would be carried off with as little difficulty as possible and to ensure the masses' loyalty in such times. Thus where the upper capitalist social classes in the last century had aimed at reducing the state's powers as far as possible, they now desired the extension of its power into almost all spheres of life, but in their own interests.

The influence of the capitalist classes in the state had been achieved by, e.g., reducing parliament's power in favour of an extension of the higher bureaucracy's legislative authority. The bureaucracy then controlled further the application of the laws — the administration through its decrees and the judiciary through its verdicts and precedents. The bureaucratic and managerial classes — often interchangeable — had thus mutually enhanced one another's power. The growth of the military and armaments technology had further concentrated vital decisions in fewer hands. Society had come to resemble a "latent siege condition" in the interests of the ruling classes. The latter retained power, in times of prosperity, with a "conformism of public opinion produced by social pressure," and in times of crisis "with the methods of open and brutal fascist terror." Hence:

> The advanced capitalist social structure repeatedly produced the tendency toward fascist dictatorship which — regardless of the ideology it may be concealed by — in periods of economic crisis or of immediate war preparation throws off the democratic-liberal legal order, which has long been devoid of any content, as a mere guise of the power of the bourgeois state machinery and of finance capital, in order to be able to lead the masses of the middle classes and sectors of the intellectually backward classes among the workers, in the interests of the ruling classes, to an attack on the democratic class organizations of the workers.

The danger of a reversion to anti-democratic methods was particularly great in Germany, whose military, bureaucracy and judiciary had already helped to undermine the Weimar Republic and had supported the Third Reich.

These factors could be overcome if political power were in the hands of the working classes and their party, the SPD, who had always advocated a democratic organization of the state, and who had no particular profit interests to represent. This was why political democracy was the precondition for the struggle for socialism, for, in the workers' hands, the principle of democratic equality could be transferred by means of legislation into the economic and social spheres. The first concrete steps in this direction would be the enhancing of the power of communal organizations, the enlargement of parliament's powers vis-à-vis the government, and the parties' powers over the parliamentary party, the sponsoring and development of inner-party discussion, and the extension of the liberal rights of freedom of information, freedom of speech, etc. The most important step, however, would be the strengthening of the powers of the large democratic organizations: the trade unions, cooperatives, consumers' associations, small producers and the socially disadvantaged.

The success of all such measures depended above all upon the readiness of the workers to support democracy "not only in elections and plebiscites, but also through extra-parliamentary actions." The mission of the Social Democratic Party was to awaken this readiness and to inspire the workers to realize that socialist democracy depended upon the acts of the individual citizen in participating in decision-making.

Abendroth went on to discuss the need for socialization of the important industries and the introduction of economic planning in order to remove the excessive power of finance capital and to provide greater social and cultural benefits for the subordinate classes. The trend toward bureaucratization and socialization could be overcome by a broad democratic organization of all the classes. A central tenet of this proposal was the workers' unlimited right to strike which, in bourgeois society, would inevitably increase the subordinate classes' share of the overall social product, and which, in the coming socialist society, would be a counterweight to all bureaucratic tendencies.

To this end, trade unions must be organized into a single democratic unit with complete independence, so that they might better develop the workers' day-to-day interests into a long-term and general interest of all the working classes. Similarly, small producers and small industrialists would be organized into cooperatives and enabled to make a rational contribution to socialist society. Agriculture too, would be modernized and organized cooperatively, while consumer cooperatives could be the beginning of a modern socialist system of distribution which would "replace the profit motive by the idea of democratic cooperation."

Wolfgang Abendroth's programme draft went on to close the further gaps left by the Godesberg Programme: a socialist critique of communism, the CPSU and the East-West conflict, proposals for large-scale reforms in the fields of education, culture, social security and the general quality of life, an analysis of the significance of the Third World, and an assessment of the possibilities for socialism. On the basis of this searching inquiry, he concluded that the SPD's role ought to be quite different from that which the party had set for itself:

> For social democracy, therefore, foreign policy and domestic policy, economic policy, social policy and cultural policy are an indivisible unit. Through its struggles it educates the workers (*Arbeitnehmer*) whose political party it is, to a recognition of their interests. By bringing these interests into awareness, it represents the vital claims (*Lebensansprüche*) of all other classes of the people who suffer under the continuation of capitalist exploitation. By struggling for a socialist society, for the abolition of the classes, it shows a world threatened by atomic war the only alternative to the threatening decline of civilized humanity into barbarism: international solidarity of the working people in a cooperative construction of a peaceful world of prosperity for all peoples.

These alternative proposals, which the *Sozialistische Politik* called "the first attempt at an overall socialist conception in the Social Democratic Party,"[7] were first taken up by the Young Socialists in the SPD, who published them in a brochure. Shortly thereafter the same version appeared in *Der Sozialdemokrat*, which was by far the more important one, since here it was more accessible to a larger readership. And, at the Godesberg Convention itself, Marburg City sponsored Abendroth's programme in the form of a series of demands. Since this version only appeared in the party organ, *Vorwärts*,[8] a short time before the convention, it obviously did not play as great a role as the first draft.

A comparison between the Godesberg Programme and Abendroth's anti-Godesberg Programme is instructive in several respects. It brings to light many of the fundamental cleavages which by then had developed between the mainstream SPD policy — formulated and executed largely by the pragmatic reformers — and the party Left. A further comparison between these two documents and the resolutions of the Wenningsen/Hanover Convention of 1946 or Kurt Schumacher's "Political Guidelines" indicates that the aims and proposals of Abendroth's draft had far more in common with the latter two documents than did the Godesberg Programme.

By 1960, then, the SPD's political theory and practice could no longer be the theoretical or practical basis for a genuinely socialist movement. This faced the party Left with a relatively clear-cut choice: either continue even further the policy of "hibernation" in hopes that profound external factors — an internal socialist regeneration of the party was now beyond question — would alter the socio-economic context sufficiently drastically as to force the party to re-assess its course of "accommodation"; or abandon the party and its working-class mass following and attempt to win over the politicized sectors among the subordinate classes by forming a genuine socialist movement, centre or party. And herein lay the importance of Abendroth's alternative programme: it represented the uncompromising articulation of the minority SPD Left's views and was the symbol of leftist opposition to the Godesberg Programme.

As so frequently in the years before and after the Godesberg Programme, the SPD leadership met this "challenge" from the Left by the simple expedient of ignoring it. The one "case" it presented against Abendroth was an anonymous[9] mimeographed document, *Professor Abendroth und das Godesberger Programm*,[10] a selective conglomeration of excerpts from Abendroth's writings, some of them dating back to the pre-Hitler era.

The alternative programme itself never came to a vote; the overwhelming support given by the party convention to the Godesberg Programme — only 16 delegates voted against its adoption — made a vote superfluous. Why did Abendroth's draft fail to find greater support among the party Left? Nikolaus Ryschkowsky believes that it was "too fixed on economic questions" to appeal to all oppositional forces within the party.[11] Yet this thesis is not entirely tenable after a closer examination of the voting on the separate sections of the Godesberg Programme: 42 delegates voted against the section "Property and Power" and 21 against "The Economic and Social Order"; an amendment declaring that socialist measures were necessary in order "to protect freedom against the great power of large economic concentration" was supported by 99 of 340 voting delegates.[12] Most of the intra-party opposition it is obvious, was precisely against the economic sections. Moreover, the only other two drafts which could be considered leftist-oppositional, namely those submitted by Peter von Oertzen[13] and by the Frankfurt-Neiderrad constituency organization,[14] were also "fixed on economic questions," the latter exclusively so.

It seems more likely that the absence of an organized left-wing opposition to the SPD's Godesberg course could be traced to two basic factors. The "adapters" and "hibernaters" were simply and logically continuing their by now well-established tradition of waiting for an "opening to the left" which, at the height of the CDU State, was extremely unlikely. And some sectors among the intra-party Left still advocating the primacy of foreign policy still remained within the party in hopes — at least until Herbert Wehner's speech the following year — of ultimately being able to realize some of the aims of the *Deutschlandplan*.

The other two important alternative proposals to the Godesberg Programme raised no substantial issues not already accounted for in Abendroth's counter-programme, but were also interesting in so far as they indicated the existence of further intra-party opposition. The Frankfurt-

Niederrad draft demanded the immediate socialization of key industries, together with public control of private industry, as the initial stage toward the implementation of socialism. It further proposed the creation of a democratic economic order by means of extending the right of codetermination and planning according to social needs.

Peter von Oertzen's programme draft was far more comprehensive, and paralleled the Godesberg Programme point-by-point, at the same time tightening or revising it as necessary. Indeed, one of its more positive features was that it eliminated many of the nebulous formulations and even grammatical errors of the original. But the document was, and was intended to be, a compromise. In a covering letter sent with his programme to a number of party colleagues, Professor von Oertzen wrote: ". . . my draft is a compromise. It is modelled upon the Party Executive Committee's draft and attempts to iron out only the worst creases. In preparing it, I have used the existing proposals and amendments so far as possible . . . Nevertheless I would of course prefer by far the Marburg draft, i.e., Abendroth's taut draft." Arguing that Abendroth's programme could not hope to gain a sufficiently substantial amount of support within the party, von Oertzen attempted to outline a minimal programme, not too unlike the Godesberg Programme, but one which "even determined socialists" could support "without strong moral and political reservations."[15]

Von Oertzen's draft did add some dimensions to the Stuttgart-Godesberg formulations. the need for solidarity with the developing countries, emphasis on the fact that "internal and external security" (rather than "national defence") was "not only" a military question, the need for extensive control over the free economy and for the socialization of vital interests. But on the other hand, he also accepted a number of the controversial formulae of the SPD platform, notably the principle of "competition so far as possible, planning so far as necessary." Where his programme did deviate from the Godesberg Programme was in the sections on "The Economic and Social Order," "Property and Power" and "The Trade Unions in the Economy" (the latter renamed "Democratization of the Economy"). Here he discussed at length the notion of the "democratization of the entire sphere of economic life" by means of full codetermination for the workers at all levels: "Men cannot be free citizens on the one hand, and on the other subordinated to an economic order which denies them any responsibility and thus deprives them of the opportunity to develop any initiative and to develop their abilities completely." This must not, however, lead to a blind centralism; here "organizational decentralization" and "responsible participation" by all the working or employed classes were called for. Such reforms would mean a far stronger social and economic position for the trade unions as the body to organize and educate the masses.

A great deal can be understood about the nature of the Godesberg Programme and its significance to the changing quality of labour representation in Federal Germany by a close examination of Abendroth's and von Oertzen's alternative programmes. More than any other contemporary writings on the Left, they make it definitively clear that, after 1959, the prospects of the intra-party Left's gaining a share in the formulation of the SPD's programmes and policies were almost non-existent, especially since the Left lacked a coherent organization, a minimal consensus-producing programme (as Abendroth's draft might have been), capable leaders — and above all a mass basis.

2. The SPD-SDS Split as the Genesis of a New Left

In view of the extensive integration of the traditional representative organizations of the labour movement, the SPD and DGB, into the capitalist system after 1959, and the low level of militant working-class consciousness, the necessary organization, programme and leadership for a revival of the Left had to originate elsewhere. And when the first impulses finally came, they were precipitated by the student Left, but in an almost fortuitous manner, as a reaction against the decline of intra-party democracy within the SPD, against its failure to support consistently the anti-atomic weapons campaign and against its increasing unwillingness or inability to present an effective alternative to the CDU State.

The German Socialist Student League (*Sozialistischer Deutscher Studentenbund* or SDS) was founded in the first postwar years as the youth organization of the SPD in the universities and colleges, and as such had always been an adherent of the party line. Under such chairmen as Helmut Schmidt and Ulrich Lohmar, it had become an established school for future party functionaries and leaders. Its general line was reflected in its organ, *Standpunkt* (initially *Unser Standpunkt*), which took up the SPD's uncritical anticommunism, contained few articles of any substance and concentrated on extraneous student problems. Such criticisms of the SPD as the periodical made were limited largely to changes in personnel, party image or organization.

Still, there had always been a left-wing minority within the SDS. During the late 1950's there was a notable increase in the frequency with which terms like "class-consciousness," "exploitation," etc. were employed. And such names as Horkheimer, Lukacs, Marcuse and Adorno began to appear in *Standpunkt* or were heard in SDS debates. As the anti-atomic arms campaign neared its climax in late 1958, various embryonic "factions" began to develop within the SDS organizations in the larger cities, e.g., in West Berlin (critique of Marxism-Leninism), Frankfurt (the interconnections between psychology, philosophy and Marxism as developed by the "Frankfurt School"), Hamburg (extreme antimilitarism) and Marburg (neo-Marxism under Abendroth's influence)[1] The Left, which may have represented as much as half of the total SDS membership, finally gained temporary ascendancy — together with a "radical" group — over the Right at the Mannheim Delegates' Conference of 1958, when a Left-Radical Executive Committee was elected, including Oswald Hüller as Chairman, Günther Kallauch as Deputy Chairman and Monika Mitscherlich, Jürgen Seifert and Horst Steckel as members.[2]

Hüller and his supporters subsequently became known as the "*konkret-group*" because of their direct and indirect support of the periodical, *konkret*. The first of a new kind of magazine in postwar Germany, *konkret* was a well laid out, glossy journal aimed at a young, anti-authoritarian audience. It was characterized by a strong (almost "militant") pacifism, concern for the Third World and the oppressed classes everywhere, a desire for an immediate *modus vivendi* between the two Germanies and an overriding emphasis on sex: liberation from sexual taboos, the joys of sex and the absurdness of sexual-moral legislation. On the other hand, it was hardly theoretically oriented or consistent. One searches in vain for an overall socio-economic interpretation of existing society, for a coordinated programme of strategy and tactics leading to definite goals.[3] The important aspect of *konkret* was its style, its image, its direct appeal to rebellious youth. It was edited and published by Klaus Rainer Röhl and the leading articles written by his then wife, Ulrike Meinhof.[*]

The SDS first entered on its collision course with the SPD with the participation of a number of its members — albeit as individuals — in the two anti-atomic weapons congresses organized by various peace movements in the early part of 1959.

The Berlin Student Congress, held on 3 and 4 January 1959, was organized primarily by the leading members of the Fight Atomic Death movement at about the same time as the SPD withdrew its support of the latter. Among the scheduled speakers were a number of prominent people, including Helmut Schmidt, Otto Stammer and Erich Müller-Gangloff. Willy Brandt, then mayor of Berlin, decided not to appear and sent instead his representative, Kurt Mattick, a right-wing SPD deputy in the Berlin parliament. Müller-Gangloff's speech, quoting Clemenceau, summed up the spirit of the Congress: "Politics is too serious an affair to be left to the politicians."[5] But it was the resolution, formulated by the *konkret* editors Reinhard Opitz and Hans Stern,[6] and passed by the Congress, which led to a strong reaction from the Right. After hastily cancelling his scheduled speech, Helmut Schmidt later declared: "That was not only an indirect, but also a completely and obviously direct cooperation with the infiltration bureaux which are today on the other side of the Wall. There can be no doubt about it."[7] Professor Stammer and other SPD members also dissociated themselves from the resolution, which subsequently became the target of widespread attacks by the bourgeois press.[8]

In retrospect, the resolution itself appears very mild. That the SPD should have opposed it so vehemently was yet another indication of its impending abandonment of all efforts toward the conceptualization of an independent foreign policy. The resolution read:

> The world political situation will soon force both parts of Germany to negotiate with each other. In order to make such negotiations possible, it is necessary that such formulae as 'no negotiations with Pankow' disappear from political argumentation. The aim of the necessary negotiations, which until now have always been rejected by the Federal Government, must be:
> 1. to develop the outlines for a peace treaty
> 2. to examine the possible forms of an interim confederation.[9]

Moreover, the Congress' leaders — but not the SDS members among them— had been at pains to prevent hundreds of members of the SED youth organization, the FDJ, from attending. The sole participant from East Germany was the *Rektor* of the Humboldt University. The SPD's accusations of excessive communist influence were thus unfounded, and appeared to be a method of enforcing intra-party discipline.

The Berlin Congress was followed in May by the similar Frankfurt Congress "For Democracy — Against Restoration and Militarism," with Wolfgang Abendroth, Ossip Flechtheim and Arno Behrisch among the main speakers.

Once again the "Hüller Group" or *konkret* group, acting on its own responsibility (i.e., not representing the SDS), together with individual members of the Young Socialists, *Falken* and *Naturfreudejugend*, drafted a controversial resolution attacking the Federal Government's economic, military and propagandistic contribution to international tension, and calling for disarmament, the banning of all weapons of mass destruction, the abolition of conscription and military traditions, and efforts of reunification of the basis of the acceptance of the Oder-Neisse Line as Germany's eastern frontier.[10]

These foreign policy proposals, in particular the recognition of the Oder-Neisse Line, went well beyond even the then still current *Deutschlandplan* — indeed Abendroth argued against the adoption of the resolution for this very reason — and hence aroused a considerable reaction of the Right. Herbert Wehner forcefully attacked the resolution at a session of the Party Presidium. And Karl Mommer delivered his famous "Trojan Ass" speech as an answer to the Congress' goals. Mommer's speech, which also included attacks on SPD journalists who had allegedly addressed Nikita Khrushhev as "Comrade" and had failed to defend the latter's defamation of Willy Brandt,[11] was given a great deal of attention in the bourgeois press and found a fairly wide resonance within the SPD. The CDU said of the Frankfurt Congress: "That is class struggle, that is Third International, that is — so oddly antiquated — the old humbug of a stale Marxism of the former kind, with which (to use Lenin's words) 'the cadaver of social democracy is to be galvanized!' "[12]

Developments showed clearly that the resolutions of the two Congresses were neither instigated nor supported by the SDS qua SDS, but by individual members within it belonging to the *konkret* group. The SDS formally dissociated itself from the Berlin Congress' resolution[13] and rejected the Frankfurt demands with the counter-proposal that the question of reunification be settled within the framework of the *Deutschlandplan* and that of the final eastern borders be deferred to a peace treaty.[14] In view of the fact that West German renunciations of nuclear weapons, official recognition of the Oder-Neisse Line and negotiations on equal terms with the DDR were to become an integral part of the party's *Ostpolitik* less than a decade later, the SPD's official reaction to the two student congresses was another indication of how monolithic and lacking in alternatives political life was becoming.

By mid-1959, then, three main factions had taken form within the SDS: the *konkret* group already mentioned, a left-wing group critical of, but basically loyal to the SPD, and a right wing completely in line with party policy and owing its primary loyalty to the SPD rather than the SDS. The scene of the impending power struggle was the SDS' Göttingen Conference of July 1959, and the central issue, as described by a supporter of the left wing, was this:

> Should a small, uncontrolled force scarcely visible to the outside incite as large a number of supporters as possible with the use of simplistic, emotion-laden slogans urging them to demonstrative 'actions,' or should young intellectuals train themselves to be members of the socialist labour movement in a necessarily considerably less spectacular educational process, and in basic theoretical and practical schooling? The former is Stalinist 'popular front tactics,' the latter responsible socialist politics under the conditions of a non-revolutionary situation.[15]

The tone of the conference was foreshadowed by the preceding expulsion of

Opitz and Stern, the authors of the Frankfurt resolution, and of Runge, another member of the *konkret* group.

The outcome of the conference's debates was crucial for the future of the SDS. The main issues revolved around three central topics: (1) the strategy and tactics to be employed by the SDS, as suggested in the quotation above, (2) the role and influence of *konkret* in the SDS, and in particular, (3) the SDS' future relationship with the SPD.

For Hüller the SPD was no longer capable or qualified to lead the struggle for socialism, and any impetus toward fundamental social change now had to come from outside the party, viz. from a radical youth movement. The time had come, therefore, to *"Geh' mit der Zeit, geh' aus der SPD!"* (roughly: "Get up to date, get out of the SPD" —a parody on a current SPD "new image" slogan). Both the Right and Left, however, still saw the future of the SDS within the SPD. A right-wing delegate from Wilhelmshaven, one Hasselbung, brought with him a draft resolution for the formation of a "League of Democratic Socialist Students" whose aim would be to increase the SPD students' organizational and ideological dependence upon the party and to confine its activities to student academic affairs.[16]

The SDS Left rejected all attempts to bind the movement organizationally to the SPD and argued that student socialist groups must go beyond the university sphere. It further rejected the SPD's current form of uncritical anticommunism as being fundamentally identical with that of the bourgeois parties. On the other hand, there could be no alliance with the *konkret* group in "isolated student politics." Jürgen Seifert argued that ". . . blind and unconsidered action does not just fail, but runs aground — which has an even greater crippling effect — and hence spreads despair and a feeling of impotence." For him "blind activism" and a "retreat into pure socialist theory" were only different forms of "political self-satisfaction."[17]

Though, for opportunistic reasons, the right wing had occasionally supported Hüller against the left wing,[18] it could not go so far as to condone any policy of an open break with the SPD. The combined vote of the right and left wings was sufficient to depose Hüller and his deputy, Werner Bessau. Günther Kallauch, a member of the Left, was elected chairman in his place. This was followed by the expulsion or resignation of a further thirteen members of the *konkret* group, and with this the SDS' first "purge" was complete. The conference concluded by affirming the principles of political democracy and its basic agreement with the SPD's policies, but at the same time expressly declared the SDS' organizational independence from the sponsoring party. It conceded further that the foreign policy disagreements arising from the Frankfurt Congress were questions of detail, not principle.[19]

Meanwhile, another compaign had begun within the SDS, which aimed at exposing the Nazi records of prominent people in the judiciary, administration and civil service. The "Action for Unatoned Nazi Justice" (*Aktion Ungesühnte Nazijustiz*) originated in the Free University of Berlin as a one-man effort by Reinhard Strecker, who began publicizing the records of many leading judges who had served under the Third Reich. Much of his material, although amply documented, was derived from East German and Czech sources. In the spring of 1959, he was able to enlist the support of the Marburg VUS (Association German Student Bodies), and subsequently a large number of photocopied documents attesting to the "brown" past of many German judges was exhibited at the Frankfurt Congress. At its Göttingen Conference, the SDS then placed its support behind the movement, and indeed even coined the term "Action for Unatoned Nazi Justice." The SDS' position was to use concrete examples to expose the larger issues of renazification and restoration. In a circular sent to all local groups, the Executive Committee declared that the SDS should oppose the "Nazi judges" as a threat to the working of democracy,

> ... but the argumentation must not stop at individual cases; the action must be used as an impetus to point out the tendencies toward restoration in the Federal Republic's judicial system, in particular the questions of political justice, the crime of being a danger to the state, and the government's efforts at reintroducing the death penalty and at passing emergency legislation. [20]

Shortly after the Göttingen Conference, the Hüller group entered into the movement against Nazi justice as a kind of compensation for its loss of power in the federal SDS organization. Another power struggle, involving the group's attempt to take over the movement by way of the Karlsruhe SDS organization, ended with the expulsion of the initiators, Bessau and Höch, from the SPD, and with the SDS' public denunciation of the entire group. In an open letter of 9 February 1960, Bessau and Höch attacked the SPD as an authoritarian party run by a small clique which did not permit intra-party democracy and used "opinion terror" to enforce its views. "This party," they wrote, "will go the way of Saragat and Mollet. We will support it from now on, on this road, to the best of our abilities, in order to clear the way for an effective oppositional party."[21] When the Karlsruhe chapter refused to follow the Executive Committee's demand for the expulsion of Bessau and Höch for this violation of the Göttingen resolution, the whole Karlsruhe organization was expelled from the SDS.

The exhibition "Unatoned Nazi Justice" was later shown successfully in a number of German cities as well as in Holland and England, and received extensive publicity throughout western Germany.

All these developments appeared, by late 1959, to have brought about a truce between the SPD and SDS, and within the SDS itself, between the left and right wings. The party established an SDS secretariat in Bonn and paid the debts left by the Hüller-*konkret* group, and a number of prominent SPD leaders (Erler, Deist, Mommer, von Puttkamer) spoke at SDS meetings. But in early 1960, a faction in the SPD Executive Committee, which was antagonistic toward the SDS and emboldened by the mandate which it felt the Godesberg Programme had given the pragmatic reformist group, gradually gained ascendancy. Its attacks on the SDS were based on the pretext of the "aberrations" of the Hüller group (though the group itself had of course long been expelled from the SDS) and on articles in *Standpunkt* by Abendroth (attacking the Godesberg Programme) and Jürgen Kraft (arguing that the SPD has become estranged from the masses). In a resolution of 5 February 1960, the SPD Executive Committee distanced itself from *Standpunkt* and declared its readiness to support other student organizations which recognized the Godesberg Programme.[22]

In May, a considerable proportion of the SDS' right wing, encouraged by the Party Executive Committee, with whom it had been preparing secretly for some months, broke away from the SDS and constituted itself as the Social

Democratic University League (*Sozialdemokratischer Hochschulbund* or SHB). The latter's initial membership may have been between 100 and 150, cf. a total SDS membership of roughly 1,000 — clearly a minority.[23] In a press statement of 9 May 1960, the SHB stated its position: "We do not want to be wanderers between two worlds, but want to work for the cause of the free West . . . We deplore expensive congresses by uninfluential people about great political issues." It agreed completely with the SPD's policy of "reunification in guaranteed freedom," supported "national defence," and declared itself to be a group of "responsible democratic socialists" who would not be used for "communist infiltration."[24]

The SPD Executive Committee then — without consulting the party membership — almost immediately recognized the SHB, while simultaneously omitting all references to the SDS. In an official statement, the SPD Executive Committee acknowledged the SHB's Declaration of Principles and ". . . welcome(d) the unambiguous attitude of the SHB toward the Godesberg Programme and its strong rejection of totalitarianism and its most dangerous form at present, communism." It further urged all SPD members at institutions of higher learning to support the SHB.[25] Waldemar von Knoeringen, who had been at the centre of the party's efforts to keep the SDS within the SPD, complained of the growing radicalization of the SDS during 1959, its "one-sidedness" on the issue of totalitarianism and its failure to see the communist "threat." The Party Executive Committee, he wrote,

> . . . is of the view that the Social Democratic Movement neither can nor should avert a conflict with communism. This conflict is unavoidable, it will be a hard one, and it can be conducted by the SPD only with a student union which is prepared to take the same road as the SPD in this question.[26]

In an interview with the Marburg student newspaper, the *Marburger Blätter*, Herbert Wehner took these accusations a step further when he alleged that the SDS was receiving "support from the East" and was thus no longer able to act independently.[27]

In July, the SPD finally severed its connections with the SDS. Urging members of the SPD who were still associated with the SDS to join the SHB, the Party Executive Committee decided to (1) withdraw all financial assistance from the SDS, (2) break off formally all relations with it, and (3) lend financial and moral support to the SHB.[28]

This unilateral action by the SPD was a logical manifestation of the party leadership's overriding desire to reinforce its popular image of "respectability" and free itself from any "red" associations in the public's mind. It represented an intensification of its hard-line policy, which was becoming increasingly evident after the Godesberg Programme, and was sometimes referred to as *Spaltung von rechts*, or dividing the party from the Right. Characteristic of this policy was that drastic measures (censure, expulsion, etc.) were initiated by the party leadership without (undue or unwarranted) provocation from the Left. For, once the *konkret* group had been removed from its ranks, the SDS was hardly an extreme left-wing organization, much less "communist infiltrated." Its foreign policy conception, as has been discussed, was much like what would become the SPD's *Ostpolitik* in subsequent years, and only marginally exceeded the provisions of the *Deutschlandplan*. And its social and economic policies were, at that stage, not nearly as "radical" as the party-sponsored Young Socialists (Jusos) of today, the successor organization (though with a broader membership basis) to the SHB after the latter itself ultimately grew "too extreme" for the SPD leadership.

Despite the Party Executive Committee's attacks, the SDS had always pronounced itself, and had felt itself to be, an integral part of the SPD. A declaration to this effect was made by the Frankfurt Delegates' Conference as late as October 1960.[29] But "this expressly declared solidarity with the SPD and the trade unions never meant organizational dependence."[20] In fact, Günther Kallauch came out specifically against "isolated student politics," affirming that a close association between the working classes, the SPD and its youth organization was the only guarantee for the continuation of democracy.[31] Monika Seifert's attitude was typical of many. Although opposed to some sections of the Godesberg Programme, "as a member of the SPD it is self-evident to support this programme in public and to work for its realization." She claimed only the right to work *within* the party in order to bring about the desired socialist policies.[32] Kallauch elsewhere defined the source of the SPD's implacable attitude toward the SDS:

> The SDS has not been forgiven for being a heretic toward the new Federal German state religion, blind anticommunism, although the SDS has at the same time, in binding constitutional resolutions and in its political practice, unequivocally rejected any joint action with the KPD-SED and their supporters.[33]

The withdrawal of the SPD's financial support meant that the SDS was forced to rely upon the resources of the government-sponsored *Bundesjugendplan* (Federal Youth Plan),[34] which funds were dependent upon government approval and inadequate to meet the maintenance costs of the SDS' various conferences and publications, especially its periodical *Neue Kritik* (first published in June 1960), which was to play a crucial role in the development of the New Left. In order to guarantee the SDS' financial independence, Professor Abendroth and Heinz Brakemeier began taking steps during 1960 which culminated in the establishment of the Society for the Promotion of the SDS (*Sozialistische Förder-Gesellschaft* or SFG) in October 1960. Among its founding members — who still saw themselves as a critical leftist force within the SPD — were professors Abendroth, Heydorn, Dücker, Flechtheim, Langerhaus, von Oertzen and Mitscherlich, as well as Brakemeier, Fritz Lamm, Michael Schumann (the new SDS Chairman) and the writer Gerhard Zwerenz. According to its charter, the SFG's objectives were quite straightforward: to aid the members of the SDS, to provide them with social and scholarly assistance and to support their educational and theoretical tasks.[35]

Then the SPD Executive Committee made a tactically very unwise move: it declared membership in the SFG and/or SDS incompatible with membership in the SPD.[36] This decision necessarily meant a hardening of the fronts, the driving of an irreversible wedge between the SPD and the consistent student Left. Initially six, then most of the professors and other members of the SFG declared that they would not submit to the party directive. As a result of their stand, the professors were roundly applauded as they entered their lecture-rooms, but were increasingly isolated from party activities and offices. Most stood by the SDS and subsequently resigned or were expelled from the SPD. A few, such as Peter von Oertzen, chose to remain within the party. The line was drawn, but very unevenly: the great mass of the party plus much of the left wing and the "adapters" vis-à-vis the minuscule SFG-SDS. Willy Birkelbach, for one, confirmed once again where the "adapters'" primary loyalties lay when a positive choice had to be made. Concerning the SFG, he said: "For myself, I must admit openly that in this area . . . there is a group of persons who are attempting to conceptualize and coordinate factional work within the SPD."[37]

Both SFG and SDS were aware that the SPD resolution had brought about a qualitative change in the roles they had to, or could, play. Professor Abendroth demonstrated that a number of unpopular SPD decisions in history — support for the Kaiser in the first world war, the granting of war credits, failure to oppose the Brüning-Hindenburg "emergency cabinet" — were, like the SDS-SPD controversy, followed by the expulsion of dissident party members.[38] Eberhard Dähne declared:

> The resolution places us in a situation which requires us to recognize our position clearly and to find in it starting points for our future political praxis . . . For, despite all our scepticism toward the policy of the SPD leadership, which in our opinion by its almost complete identification with the present political and social relationships, has lost its chance to conduct an effective opposition policy, we never forgot who the real opponent was.[39]

This was basically the quandary in which the SDS was now placed. It could not possibly support the "real opponent," namely the CDU/CSU and the bourgeois coalition. But on the other hand, if the SPD had itself become an integral part of the CDU State, a product among many offered in the political "market" and incapable of presenting an alternative, then: "To expect of such an apparatus a progressive policy going beyond the existing order, a socialist democratic transformation of society, is absurd. Too strong is the compulsion upon it to adapt to the existing order."[40] In order to promote socialism, it was clear, the SDS would have to operate as an independent organization. But this in turn involved a considerable risk of becoming isolated from the rank-and-file working class membership, which was still overwhelmingly attached to the SPD and DGB. The solution was to bring pressure to bear upon the SPD from outside the party structure in order to compel it to renew its socialist purpose, while at the same time to work directly at the lower party levels in order to develop members' socialist consciousness and perhaps persuade them to support the Left.

This position was outlined in the SDS' Action Programme of October 1961:

> The SDS opposes the depoliticization and the simulation of partnership in this society which is determined by the contradiction between capital and labour . . . An important task of the SDS is to awaken a critical political consciousness. By means of social analysis and information it is attempting to reveal the roots of authoritarian tendencies and the possibility of a democratic and socialist alternative.

Thomas von der Vring advocated the revival of an ossified organization such as the SPD, not by forming a rival party, but by working at the party base, organizing members and functionaries in order to prepare them for an independent commitment initially outside the party, but one which they would then carry into the party itself.[42] A similar concept was developed at the

Berlin Federal Delegates' Conference of the SDS in October 1961. A resolution prepared by Erich Nohara, but not voted upon, proposed to avoid the formation of a new party because it was impossible at that stage to free the "genuine democratic and socialist potential" from the SPD; such an action would in any case leave the SDS open to the charge of dividing the labour movement. Since the SPD had not yet "deteriorated" as far as, say, the SFIO in France, it was still advisable to keep the working classes together in the SPD and DGB in order either to transform these organizations through grass-roots pressure, or to detach them for a new mass movement when the times were more propitious.[43]

Here were the premises of the concept of a "New Left" which began to take root in the SDS at this time. Thomas von der Vring concluded that

> . . . it will by no means be the NEW LEFT'S task to fight the SPD. We do know how to judge what it would mean if, e.g., in Hesse the government were to go over to a CDU coalition, and we would prefer *any* Willy Brandt to Adenauer, Schroeder, Strauss, Jäger or Mende. Disappointment and bitterness must not play a role here.[44]

The *Neue Linke*, which SDS Chairman Michael Schumann compared with the New Left in Britain and the French *Nouvelle Gauche*,[45] would thus actively maintain its connections with the labour movement while still developing the theory and strategy to be employed in the proper historical situation. Or, as Nohara argued:

> The task of a New Left (this concept must be understood as differentiating it from the traditional leftist groups in the party whose impotence is obvious) is thus to use the discussions following the elections, to gather the dissatisfied and to lead them into a new organization when their futher work in the party is made impossible by administrative terror.[46]

At this stage, it must be recalled, the SDS' political weight was slightly more than negligible. By the beginning of 1962 it had a membership of around 1,000, organized at 26 universities and colleges. What it had achieved as a result of the split with the SPD was the formation of a nucleus for the development of the New Left and through it the Extra-parliamentary Opposition (Apo) of the later 1960's. Now it was the symbol ". . . of how a working-class youth organization (and by implication a determined socialist organization) was able to hold its own against the massive pressure of the Party Executive Committee of the SPD."[47] *Neue Kritik*, already the most widely read student periodical at West German universities, would become the most important forum for the New Left. And *Das Argument*, begun by a number of students after the Berlin Congress, was to become a centre of the most radical student movement of all, the Berlin SDS.

By the end of 1960, then, the SDS had defined the issues which would dominate discussion on the Left for the next decade: criticism of the internal organization, strict parliamentarism and absence of alternative foreign and domestic policies on the part of the SPD, merciless exposition of the symptoms and causes of the Restoration, advocacy of demonstrations and extra-parliamentary actions, rejection and refutation of anticommunism and the basic premises of the Cold War, and the fact of youth as an independent political force. It had also developed the organization, the theoretical basis, the organs and the will to become an independent socialist oppositional force.

3. Attempts at an Alternative Grouping on the Left of the SPD

As has already been suggested above, the SPD's attitude toward the SDS must be seen as a part of the overall "hard-line" adopted toward the Left after the Godesberg Programme in an endeavour to rationalize the party's adaptation of its policies and image to voter expectations and the preconditions of the CDU State. Dr. Mommer's "Trojan Ass" speech was not only the signal for a campaign against the SDS, but also for increased repressive measures against the party's Left! Shortly after the speech, for example, ten SPD members from Kassel were expelled for participating in a peace conference in Leipzig, Harry Ristock was censured in Berlin for advocating foreign policy measures like those of the SDS, Heinz Brakemeier in Frankfurt was threatened with expulsion for opposing the uncritical anticommunism of the SPD's *Ostbüro*, and Albert Berg, a member of the Hamburg Parliament, had his membership revoked for "left-wing deviations." As the ascendancy of the pragmatic reformists became institutionalized in the form of the new triumvirate at the party summit, consisting of Brandt, Wehner and Fritz Erler, party discipline was intensified even further, and frequently exceeded even that achieved within the CDU.[2]

Most of the SPD members expelled in this period — from the founders of the SFG to those removed for other reasons, such as Gleissberg and Agartz — left the party only reluctantly. Many could look back on strong ties with the SPD dating back thirty and forty years, through the Weimar Republic, concentration camp, exile and postwar re-construction. Expulsion or resignation almost inevitably meant isolation and the end of effective political work. One very prominent member of the intra-party Left, shortly before his expulsion from the SPD in connection with the SFG-SDS events, told Gerhard Gleissberg that, in order to stay within the party, he would "crawl on his knees from (the city where he lived) to Bonn," if the party made his doing so conditional on his remaining a member.[3] But after the SDS affair and the campaign against the Left, most left-wing party members saw the choice presented to them as: either fidelity toward the party or fidelity toward the socialist cause. Although most opted for the latter alternative (when the choice was theirs to make), for the most part they had serious reservations and were aware of the limited possibilities now open to them.

The difficulties of reconciling a socialist commitment with membership in a "liberal socialist" SPD were summarized by Fritz Tewes, in his discussion of the party's "adaptions" to foreign policy exigencies:

> We must set ourselves off from those Social Democrats who have allied themselves to the bitter end with capitalism — because we must not and will not make ourselves guilty by association! . . . We regret this development, but for political, historical and moral reasons, we must take this step.[4]

As Arno Behrisch, in a letter to Erich Ollenhauer written shortly before his resignation from the party, explained: "I am sometimes not exactly on the party line. But where is the new line? When I recall what was said about the *Deutschlandplan*, then it cannot be a sin if one does not necessarily believe in the eternal value of day-to-day political statements and explanations."[5]

In a telegramme sent to the SPD Chairman, Professor Flechtheim, Wolfgang Haug (editor of *Das Argument*), Carola Stern (biographer of Walter

Ulbricht) and others announced their resignation from the SPD. Though they could not identify themselves with all the SDS' actions, they stated: "The expulsions of SDS members and sponsors represent in themselves a false understanding of the principles of academic freedom and a violation of intra-party democracy as required by the Basic Law." It was, they continued, very difficult to separate themselves from a party which contained "many good democrats and socialists," but they "could not answer to (their) conscience" if they failed to "turn away from every form of authoritarian manipulation in precisely the democratic parties."[6]

Lorenz Knorr, the former Federal Secretary of the *Falken*, wrote an open letter to Herbert Wehner. Objecting to the "complete militarization of all life" and the SPD's cooperation with the bourgeois coalition in preparing the "emergency laws," Knorr levelled a devastating attack on Wehner and the SPD leadership:

> Unfortunately I have deceived myself — or better, you have deceived me! Your 180-degree turn from consistent opponent of, to capitulant before, Adenauer I shall never forgive you! The fact that you, together with Willy Brandt, have managed to force your accursed will upon the majority of the party convention compels me to resign from the party.[7]

One of the most interesting documents which survives from this period is Fritz Lamm's self-published brochure, *Briefwechsel mit der SPD* ("Correspondence with the SPD") which, in a series of letters, none of them intended for publication when written, reveals the growing differences between one left-wing member and the party organization, leading to that member's expulsion in 1963 in consequence of his support for the SFG-SDS.[9] In it, one can see how a speech by Fritz Lamm for the 1962 May Day celebrations sponsored by the SDS cast him, in the SPD leaders' eyes, into a certain "guilt-by-association" defensive position. For the speech itself was relatively harmless. It discussed the errors of the Weimar SPD in integrating itself into the capitalist system, went on to oppose atomic weapons and advocated a socialism which would be "much more than a question of a full stomach." Another flurry of letters from the SPD inquired ominously into Lamm's membership in the SFG and later Socialist League, and requested him to renounce these. When Lamm refused to do so, outlining at length his reasons, but declaring that he would prefer to remain an SPD member, he was abruptly expelled. None of his questions or arguments were answered.

In mid-1960, after the expulsion or resignation of many members of the intra-party Left, the SDS-SPD split and the transferral of inner-party power to the pragmatic reformist group, the situation of the Left, to an observer on the Right, appeared as follows:

> The SPD leadership has eliminated both errors (having fought the 1953 and 1957 elections with foreign policy slogans and alternative plans, and failing to impress voters with the competence of individual party personalities) so radically that a few members and functionaries, who still cling to the old concepts, stand apart bitterly. The sand which they are throwing into the gears only grinds — it does not hinder the party machine. There is, for example, the small group around the Berlin people's tribune, Franz Neumann, who was defeated by Willy Brandt, a group which goes peddling the demand that Brandt should not remain Lord Mayor after accepting the Chancellor candidacy; then there are the Fighters Against Atomic Death who give vent to their

dissatisfaction because the party no longer takes them seriously. Then there are still the sects of those for whom Adenauer is Beelzebub, Krupp the banker of the fascists and NATO a pact with the Devil. The sowing of dissension, against which the SPD defended itself when Adenauer was doing the sowing, has now grown in the party's own ranks.

The brightly chequered group of the dissatisfied — prisoners of their own slogans of the past or the propaganda assaults of the communists — now constitute a diminishing minority. The men at the rudder, in the navigation room and at the machine of the party ship have other concerns . . .[10]

Now that persons like Lamm, Knorr, Flechtheim, Behrisch, Abendroth, Berg and many SDS members had become politically "homeless," the question of the form of their continued political activity became compelling. For the most part they were persons who would not or could not retreat into the apolitical sphere. Professor Heydorn, in a mimeographed letter of August 1962 to a number of colleagues and SPD members, wrote: "Unfortunately, one can no longer expect any socialist perspective from the SPD. We need people who are resolved to make an effective, new and absolutely independent socialist force . . ."[11] Since there was as yet no mass following to take into consideration, the scope of possibilities for an independent Left was relatively broad, but prospects for success very limited. What was important at this point was that these former SPD members and supporters were now, for the first time, compelled to conceptualize a left-wing strategy and policy outside or "beyond" the SPD.

This situation raised anew the problems of socialist organization in advanced capitalism. As Willy Huhn wrote, the structure and form of the socialist Left had been conditioned by the pre-existing and predominant structure and form of the status quo. The masses had tended to transfer the responsibility for their own obligations and actions to paid officials of the labour organizations, and this act had relieved them of the necessity of planning, reflecting and acting according to the changing situation, ". . . until one day they realized that their servants had become their masters, their representatives their oppressors" (*aus ihren Vertretern ihre Zertreter*).[12] In considering the forms of a new party or movement could take, the independent Left thus had to reject, on the basis of previous experience, the idea of a "general staff" to plan an active strategy without reference to members' views, and the concept of mere parliamentary representation of the subordinate classes.

Out of this situation, the Left more or less spontaneously evolved three basic forms of opposition; and these forms determined the profile of the independent leftist opposition to the end of the CDU State. They were briefly: (1) a forum to develop further socialist theory and a critique of the SPD's praxis, working from outside the party in much the fashion of the SDS-SFG, (2) a loose, undogmatic nuclear organization for the formation of a future new party, which would preformulate the coming socialist organization's theory, programme and tactics while waiting for more favourable conditions for the transition to socialism, and (3) a broadly conceived political party with a minimal, consensus-producing platform aimed at enlisting the support of whatever oppositional groups were at hand, including non-socialist elements, in order to gain a share, however limited, of political power; and to achieve parliamentary representation of unrepresented vital views. (A possible fourth alternative, namely a conspirative, tightly-organized party drawing its ideological inspiration and tactical methods from an outside power or party, was of course both illegal and unpopular.) These three alternatives found their expression in, respectively, the Socialist League, the Union of Independent Socialists and the German Peace Union.

In October 1962, the Socialist League (*Sozialistischer Bund* or SB) was established in Frankfurt upon the organizational framework of the SFG. Its membership was essentially derived from the former's, but also included a number of other expelled SPD members, participants of the 1958 *Funken* Congress in Frankfurt and supporters of Abendroth's anti-Godesberg Programme. Among the main speakers at the organizational meeting in late 1961 were Abendroth, Heydorn, Lamm and Flechtheim. The Socialist League's aims, according to its Charter, were "to create the theoretical and practical pre-conditions for the movement of the 'New Left' in the Federal Republic," to support the SDS and to maintain contact with international socialist movements.[13] The Charter expressed aims and means not fundamentally different from Abendroth's counter-programme. It presented an analysis of the growing power of monopoly capital and its control over the state, the increase in the numbers of the subordinate classes and the problems of overcoming their "false consciousness." It advocated contact with the independent Left throughout Europe and firm personal commitment in decisive political questions. Its proposals for action were based on the failure of the traditional working-class parties in the Federal Republic, namely the SPD which it saw as incapable of going beyond "parliamentarism," and the KPD which had succumbed to Stalinism. The traditional Left's failure had brought about a strengthening of the latent tendencies toward an authoritarian state and the danger of war. Now, the Charter continued, the trade unions represented the main hopes for a revival of working-class consciousness. SB members must exert every effort to strengthen the anti-war movement and its influence on the trade unions, and to make three central demands for social change the core of trade union action: nationalization of key industries, extension of codetermination at all levels and coordinated social and economic planning.[14]

The importance of the Socialist League lay above all in its role as a link between the Old and the New Left. It had room and tolerance for a whole gamut of socialist theories ranging from semi-orthodox Marxism to emergent attempts to combine psychology, philosophy and Marxism. It represented, indeed was largely founded upon the basis of, the Old Left lending a helping hand to the New. As Professor Abendroth said:

> The special task of the Socialist League appears to me to be that of mediator between critical democratic currents in the 'free intelligensia' and critical — simply born of the situation — efforts to revive the store of ideas of the labour movement within the movement itself . . . Theory and practice cannot be radically separated. Voluntaristic praxis without a theoretical concept is blind and achieves nothing; but continuous theorizing is just as great a danger if it is not directed toward praxis. Both accents will always exist in the leftist movement, both dangers will always be present. To contribute to their mediation is one of the tasks of the Socialist League.[15]

A "Central Committee of Former and Expelled Social Democrats," led by

Gleissberg, Agartz and Berg, was successful in creating the Union of Independent Socialists (*Vereinigung Unabhängiger Sozialisten* or VUS) in November 1960 in Düsseldorf. In many respects less "exclusive" than the Socialist League, its membership of several hundred came to include, among others, Oswald Hüller and Gerhard Bessau who had been expelled from the SDS at the 1959 Göttingen Conference, as well as many who had been excluded from the SPD due to alleged contacts with the DDR regime or trade union representatives from East Germany.

The VUS' self-image, as described by Gerhard Gleissberg at the founding conference, in many respects paralleled the movement which had gathered around *Die Andere Zeitung* in the mid- and late 1950's. It was not the VUS' intention to split the SPD; the party Right had already precipitated this split by its expulsion of the SDS and the old Social Democrats. The VUS as a "collective movement" was not seen as an end (i.e. party) as such, but a "refuge for Social Democrats become homeless." It would demonstrate the way to a clear socialist alternative but not (yet) as a party because it sought to avoid dividing the labour movement, because sufficient funds and adequate organization were non-existent, and because there was still no mass socialist consciousness among the working population.[16]

The programmes of the Socialist League and the VUS had a great deal in common, e.g. willingness to negotiate with the DDR on the basis of the status quo, disengagement from supra-national defence organizations, rejection of the proposed "emergency laws" and all other forms of domestic authoritarianism, social reforms, especially in education and social security; and extension of worker codetermination at all levels.[17] But there were also important differences between the two organizations which precluded any real chance of their close cooperation.

Firstly, the SB was quite free from suspicion of any communist influence. Its connections were almost exclusively with western European socialist movements and the Socialist International. But the VUS could be accused of affiliations with the East German trade union organization, the FDGB (through Agartz), with the SED regime (Gleissberg) or with the "beat generation" (Hüller). Whether or not such charges could be proven, or were even remotely true, was, as chapter IV has demonstrated, not so important in postwar Germany as whether they could be plausibly levelled.

Secondly, and probably more important, the SB and VUS often operated at different levels. The VUS tended largely to take up and reiterate the ideas of the intra-SPD Left during the mid-'fifties, while the SB also incorporated the theories of the New Left, the "Frankfurt School," and other new currents in the European Left into its discussions. This important difference was manifest in the VUS' organs: *Die Andere Zeitung* and the *VUS-Organ* (later re-titled *Sozialistische Hefte*). There is very little in these two publications which one has not already encountered in the writings of the independent Left after Schumacher's death.

Yet the fact that the VUS had these organs while the Socialist League had none (although its members frequently contributed to *Neue Kritik*), points to the superior organizational capacity of the VUS. Indeed, the two socialist organizations might have had a great deal to offer each other, but even now many of the same divisions still existed within the independent Left as had hampered it throughout the 1950's: "The differences in basic attitudes toward the formation of a popular (leftist) front, as represented in this country, have shifted into the realm of ideological hair-splitting."[18] That there were indeed a number of points which could have served as a common platform for the Left was suggested by the VUS Central Committee when it laid down what would become the central issues of oppositional politics for the next few years. They were: uncompromising rejection of all emergency legislation and of "mutuality" with militarism, opposition to atomic weapons, cut-back on armaments, abolition of conscription, end to armaments monopolies, elimination of former Nazis from the judicial system, police, government and administration, and creation of a left-wing alternative to the SPD.[19]

For the SPD, the VUS was predictably a "communist front" organization. Despite the fact that Hermann Matern, a SED Central Committee member, had expressly rejected the establishment of a left-wing party in the Federal Republic and had urged all communists to support the SPD and DGB,[20] the SPD Executive Committee, in a press release, called the appeal for the founding of the VUS "a creation of the SED" which was "communist-inspired." Such considerations no doubt prompted the SPD later to declare membership in the VUS incompatible with SPD membership.

The Left, it must be remembered, was by no means the only opposition to the existing political system; nor was the extreme Right. There still remained the postwar tradition of the "apolitical" single-purpose movement — as had developed in the Saint Paul's Church Movement, the Göttingen Manifesto Campaign or the Fight Atomic Death Movement — which aimed at gathering as much support as possible from as many sources as possible in order to bring pressure to bear upon the government and other political parties. This strategy had been particularly successful in mobilizing large numbers of people in foreign-policy and armament issues, and now formed the basis for the establishment of a new political party, the German Peace Union (*Deutsche Friedens-Union* or DFU).

The impulse for the formation of the DFU came from the circle around the *Blätter für deutsche und internationale Politik*, founded in 1958 by Professor Renate Riemeck and others associated with the anti-atomic weapons campaign, and initially concentrating almost exclusively on foreign policy issues with a pacifist-antimilitarist accent. The party was constituted in the autumn of 1960 on the initiative of fifty prominent people, almost all academics, and their call for the establishment of an independent political force.[22]

The DFU's platform has been referred to as a political "minimal programme" or an "emergency programme." These terms suggest that the DFU may well never have come into being without the preliminary work of the anti-armaments campaign or the SPD's abandonment of its *Deutschlandplan*. The DFU incorporated both these currents, as well as many of the groups whose interests were no longer represented in a popular movement or large political party. Hence the focus of the DFU's demands was on foreign policy: German military neutrality, peaceful reunification, disarmament, abolition of conscription and the proposed emergency laws, and the elimination of former Nazis from public office.[23] None of these demands was specifically socialist because they omitted the preconditions for the establishment and maintenance of peace, disarmament and reunification; but all coincided in some measure with the goals of existing socialist movements.

However, to state that the DFU was not socialist is in itself by no means a criticism of the party, for the DFU's founders did not intend to create a socialist party. They felt that a left-wing party, at the peak of the CDU State, was bound to fall into isolation or sectarianism. The DFU aimed at enlisting support wherever oppositional groups could be found, and at uniting them on the basis of the common denominator of an oppositional foreign policy. Indeed, the term "Union" was intended to express the idea of a party of a new type, in a manner analogous to that of the CDU. Karl Graf von Westphalen, one of the party's founders, declared that: "The DFU did not and does not want to be a party in the usual sense, but a genuine union, an association, a gathering of different groups and forces united in the pursuit of a superior, common interest."[24] The DFU's long-term aim was to place the issues relating to peace and disarmament before the tribune of parliament, where they would receive extensive publicity, force the other parties to re-assess their policies, gain public support and eventually find their way into legislation; the party never developed a plan or strategy for the event that it would be called upon to form a government, because it never sought to achieve political power.

The DFU was thus essentially a protest movement and collection of various national, neutralist, pacifist and some socialist oppositional groups. From the extreme right came, e.g., the League for German Unity Inc. (*Bünd für deutsche Einheit, e.V.*) which in 1955 had evolved from the crypto-Nazi "Working Group for National Military Questions" and whose Chairman was former SS Lieutenant-General Georg Ebrecht; and the Hamburg group of the German Saar League under Dr. Heydt. But the influence of the extreme Right was minimal from the outset and declined as the party grew.[25]

Among the most prominent members of the Independent Left to support the DFU were Lorenz Knorr and Arno Behrisch. More left-wing individuals and SPD members joined after the three SPD deputies participating at a NATO conference of 27 November 1960 consented to the atomic armament of NATO forces (and hence the Bundeswehr).[26] From the Left also came the support of a number of ex-KPD members and the VUS — which action caused Viktor Agartz to leave the organization and which also appeared to detract from the VUS' political importance.[27] Other DFU members and supporters came from the independent intelligentsia, the Union of Victims of the Nazi Regime, the War Resisters' International, the German League for Human Rights, the German Peace Society, former members of the League of Germans Party (BdD), former Zentrum party voters, some previously non-voters and a number of "progressive" members of the Protestant clergy.[28]

This great proliferation of individual, and to some extent antagonistic groups was bound to create internal problems. One of these was that, in time, many of the key positions in the party came to be held by persons associated with the KPD, while the party's spokesmen and public representatives were the independent pacifists, well-known scientists and academics, and "unpolitical" neutralists. This is why, according to Professor Flechtheim, ". . . the history of the DFU is above all a history of constant struggles between these two groups, struggles which always ended with the defeat, resignation or expulsion of the independent personalities."[29]

A second problem which arose was that the party was not representative of the population as a whole, nor even of a broad class of persons within it. The language it used, the appeals it made, the problems and issues it raised, appealed largely to the intellectual classes. One symptom of this problem was that the DFU went into the 1961 and 1965 elections with more professors and parsons as candidates than did any other party.[30] It was unable to attract support from the broad middle classes who were frightened off by the "communist influence" ascribed to the DFU by the ruling political parties, and it spoke a language and raised issues which were not perceived by the working classes as being in their immediate interests.

From the point of view of the independent Left, the most serious problem in supporting the DFU was its inability to formulate a thorough and coherent programme. The one common denominator uniting all its various component groups and factions was opposition to the Federal Government's foreign policy and resentment at the SPD for accommodating itself to it. Its cohesive force was its negative goals, not positive proposals anchored in a clear political programme. The DFU failed to understand, as Artur Seehof argued, that peace and socialism were part of an indivisible unity: "One reads its programme and one sees that the DFU supports the private economy, i.e. the capitalist order . . ."[31] Arno Behrisch, who resigned his SPD membership and seat in the Bundestag to campaign on behalf of the DFU, was aware of this short-coming but argued nevertheless that the SPD's approximation of the CDU forced socialists to search for other political representation of their interests. A foreign policy of disarmament and reduction of tensions was at least a step toward an overall socialist policy.[32]

The attitude of a large sector among the independent Left was expressed by Professor Abendroth: "One cannot found a political party on the sole basis of foreign policy problems . . ."[33] But here the Left overlooked the mobilizing potential of protest based on issues of principle. Most of the DFU's support seems to have been protest-motivated, and this protest, rather than coordinated political programmes, was most nearly successful in creating an alternative political force to the ruling political parties. As Franz-Paul Schneider, chairman of the Franconian Circle, stated: "Only when the SPD finally went over to the government's course did we — with heavy heart — decide to support the newly established and not yet determined DFU."[34]

Many such groups who had previously supported SPD or FDP now simply saw no other alternative but the DFU. With its extensive publicity and contact with the people, Arno Behrisch explained, the DFU had a far more profound influence on public awareness than did, e.g., the anti-Godesberg movement around Abendroth or the SPD-SDS conflict.[35] The fact that the DFU was able to present candidates in almost every constituency, that it would lay its proposals before a large number of people in all classes, and that it was the object of attack by all the ruling political parties is evidence that in the Federal Republic in 1960-1961, one *could* found a political party on the sole basis of foreign policy issues.

Socialists in the DFU were largely represented as individual members, because very few socialist organizations — e.g., the SDS or Socialist League — could agree to a total commitment to the DFU. In the one case mentioned above, when a left-wing association, viz. the VUS, placed its support behind the DFU, the latter, with its superior organization and political exposure, nearly eclipsed the socialist group. Although the VUS' alliance with the DFU was made subject to certain points being included in the latter's platform (mostly centred around the issues of "political justice" and a more precise definition of political neutrality), and although the VUS attempted to present its own proposals alongside those of the DFU (socialization of basic industry and large property holdings, increased social services), its membership and activities began to stagnate. After the 1961 elections, the VUS then hastily returned to socialist theory formulation and its former function as left-wing forum, and concentrated on publishing its *Sozialistische Hefte*.[36]

The SPD leadership certainly took the new party seriously. From the outset it called the DFU an "agency of communist infiltration," a collection of "useful idiots" for the CPSU and SED, and the "vanguard of communist take-over" tactics.[37] The Party Executive Committee then declared membership in the DFU incompatible with membership in the SPD,[38] basing its decision on these unfounded arguments. The SPD's irrational and vehement campaign against the DFU caused a number of members to ask where the source of this hostility lay. Pointing out that in 1956 the SPD had opposed the banning of the KPD because "it was then of the opinion that political controversies ought to be conducted with political arguments and not with police measures," Arno Klönne declared that the SPD leadership's call for the banning of the DFU, which would have been inconceivable a few years beforehand, was "a step away from democracy."[39]

It is significant that the SPD's campaign against the DFU by far exceeded in extent and intensity those against the SDS, Socialist League and VUS. For as a party of political protest against the abandonment of policies that the SPD had espoused until recently, the DFU had become a direct competitor for some of the SPD's votes. Any increase in popular support for the DFU would presumably be at the SPD's expense. Moreover, the SPD, as one of the "pillars" of advanced capitalism, now had an interest in the elimination of the DFU for many of the same reasons that the CDU/CSU had had in banning the KPD in 1956. The realization of the DFU's foreign policy proposals — though the party seems not to have comprehended this at the time — would have necessitated huge social and structural changes in domestic policy. Disarmament alone would have meant the re-tooling or re-functioning of a large sector of the economy, and the effects would have been felt at all levels of society. The aggressive foreign policy of the Federal Republic, as discussed in ch. IV, was one of the ideological supports of the CDU State and the private capitalist economy. Deténte and relaxation of tension would certainly have caused the raison d'être of this system to be called into question. Now that the SPD saw itself as an integral part of the CDU State, it was bound to oppose any movement which challenged the latter's existence.

Hence the SPD's accusations of communist infiltration and the like represented a reversion to the methods of the CDU's anticommunism, in defence of much the same interests. It is true, however, that the DFU had within its ranks a number of ex-communists, and that the party never supported an anticommunist line. The DFU's attitude toward its communist members was described by Professor Riemeck:

> It is not a question of distancing oneself or of making common cause. It is here, very simply, about the question: Do you, like me, want peace? If one receives a clear 'yes' to this question, without ifs and buts, then one must extend one's hand. This applies to the DFU. We

will not reject someone who espouses the DFU's goals.[40]

Wilhelm Elfes declared that: "We are citizens of the Federal Republic and for us it is above all a question of creating order in our own house. And we would not want to conceal our own defects and inadequacies by an unkind criticism of others." [41]

Both the organizational principles upon which it was founded and the goals which it espoused prevented the DFU from subscribing to an anticommunist policy or refusing to accept communists as members. The "collection" or "protest-movement" quality of the party compelled it to accept communists who supported its minimal programme. The party also saw the prevalent anticommunism as a means of reinforcing the government's "policy of strength" toward the East, and therefore rejected it as contributing to the heightened tension and Cold War which the DFU aimed at overcoming. In any event, the persecution and defamation of communists in the West, and of "bourgeois elements" in the East, was not suited to bringing about an understanding between the communist and capitalist governments of Germany.

However, the fact of the DFU's unwillingness to take part in the defamation of the KPD and SED also made it more susceptible to attacks based on irrational anticommunism, which reduced its mass appeal. Thus when, during the summer of 1961, the USSR resumed nuclear tests and the SED regime erected the "Berlin Wall" in August, the party failed to take a credible stand on these developments, which certainly cost it a great deal of support.[42] Yet had the DFU actually subscribed to the temptation to join in the prevalent anticommunist attacks, it would have been operating against the purposes for which it had been founded: international understanding and peace. The building of the "Wall" was indeed the symbol and logical culmination of the utter failure of the CDU/CSU government's hard-line foreign policy — and implicitly a confirmation of the DFU's alternative policy — but of course was not perceived as such by the general population. Instead, the DFU, which had appeared to many observers to have had a good prospect of breaking through the "Five Per Cent Hurdle" and gaining Bundestag representation (and thus public financing),[43] obtained only 1.9 per cent of the popular vote in the 1961 elections.

After the elections, a number of party members and groupings began to look for, and believed to have found the reasons for defeat in the "excessive communist influence" in the DFU.[44] But without the communists, much of the day-to-day work, the campaigns in firms and plants, and party organization might well not have been accomplished. And the DFU's platform, implying as it did the rejection of an essential part of the ideological and strategic foundations of the CDU State, would certainly have invoked anticommunist defamations in any case: "With rational arguments the politics of the Cold War, which was menacingly turning toward a Hot War, could not be substantiated. For this reason, defamation had to take place, with or without the communists' participation."[45]

The story of the anti-Godesberg movement, the SDS, the Socialist League, the VUS and DFU is by no means concluded with the end of this chapter. On the contrary, their influence was, directly and indirectly, to continue into the era of the New Left and Extra-parliamentary Opposition. The forms of opposition which they developed have not fundamentally changed since. But here we have been concerned to demonstrate that their establishment in every case coincided with, and was directly related to the SPD's final transformation into a "liberal socialist" party and its abandonment of substantial foreign and domestic policy alternatives. By late 1961, the basic types of organization and the fundamental issues were already present which would make the German Left a considerable oppositional force in the late 1960's.

Lack of mass support and serious economic crisis, as well as uncertainty as to the methods and course to be followed, of course, precluded the development of a massive or effective opposition at this time. But what was significant about the left-wing opposition originating between 1959-1961 was that, for the first time, the independent Left began — indeed was compelled by the actions of the SPD leadership to begin — to search for solutions to its problems of strategy, tactics and theory *outside* the SPD.

REFERENCES

1. Reaction on the Left to the Godesberg Programme

1 Rosa Luxemburg, *Selected Political Writings* (ed. R. Looker, trans. W.D. Graf), London 1972, p.211f.

2 On this see Ossip K. Flechtheim, "Die Anpassung der SPD: 1914, 1933 und 1959" in: *Kölner Zeitschrift für Soziologie und Sozialpsychologie*, Vol.17 (1965), p.584ff.

3 Helga Grebing, *History of the German Labour Movement*, London 1968.

4 In fact, there is probably no more important figure in the West German Left during the period of CDU ascendancy than Professor Abendroth. Born in 1906 in Wuppertal-Elberfeld, Wolfgang Abendroth was closely associated with the labour movement during the Weimar Republic. Dismissed by the Nazis from his civil service post (in the Justice Department) in 1933, he completed his doctorate in law at the University of Bern, Switzerland. In 1937 he was arrested and imprisoned for 'illegal activities' against the Third Reich, then spent the war years in the so-called Penal Battalion 999 (hard labour). After 1945 he was briefly active in the Ministry of Justice in the *Land* of Brandenburg and in the German administration of the Soviet Zone, and later was appointed professor at the universities of Leipzig and Jena. In 1949 he left the Soviet Zone to take up a professorship at the School of Social Sciences in Wilhelmshaven. He was then appointed to the chair of political science at the University of Marburg in 1951, where he remained until his retirement in 1972. Throughout the period of "hibernation" in the SPD and DGB, it was Professor Abendroth who worked for a coordination, for the settlement of factional disputes within the fragmented Left, and who attempted in articles, speeches and in organizations and demonstrations, to provoke discussion and action on the Left in those years.

   Now, in the period of the virtual disappearance of the West German Left, he was at the centre of most socialist endeavours and was to aid in the initial attempts to form an independent Left in the early 1960's. Once the New Left had taken on the force of a mass movement, he was also a connecting link between it and the Old Left. A man with roots in the traditional labour movement, the mediator between the multiplicity of left-wing factions and a theorist whose attempts to adapt Marxism to the situation of contemporary advanced capitalist Germany are still widely influential within the independent Left, combining in his person the union of theory and practice too rare in the postwar Left, Wolfgang Abendroth has perhaps become a symbol of the German Left after 1945.

5 "Der Entwurf eines Grundsatzprogrammes der SPD" in: *Sozialistische Politik*, No. 6/1958, p.6f.

6 This, and all subsequent references to Abendroth's anti-Godesberg Programme,

taken from 'Aufgaben und Ziele der deutschen Sozialdemokratie. Programm-entwurf 1959" in: *Der Sozialdemokrat* (Frankfurt), No. 5/1959, p.10ff; and No. 6/1959, p.10ff.

7 B. Sch. 'Zur Programmdiskussion" in: *Sozialistische Politik*, No. 5/1959, p.7.

8 *Vorwärts*, 23 October 1959, p.17; the convention was held from 13-15 November 1959.

9 The author was probably Bruno Friedrich (author's personal information).

10 Bonn, n.d. (mimeographed). Copy available in the SPD Archives (Friedrich-Ebert-Stiftung), Bonn.

11 N.J. Ryschkowsky, *Die linke Linke*, Munich 1968, p.26.

12 *Protokoll der Verhandlungen des Parteitages der SPD vom 13.-15.11.1959 in Bad Godesberg*, p.322. The only other section opposed by a significant number of delegates was "national defence" with 23.

13 "Neufassung des Entwurfes für ein Grundsatzprogramm" (mimeographed), n.d., reprinted in Flechtheim, *Dokumente*, . . . , vol. VII, p.119ff.

14 "Antrag 155, Distrikt Frankfurt/M-Niederrad. Entwurf für ein wirtschaftliches Grundprogramm" in: *Vorwärts*, 23 October 1959, p.20.

15 Peter von Oertzen, "Brief an einige Delegierte zum ausserordentlichen Parteitag in Bad Godesberg" (mimeograph), n.d.; also reproduced in: Flechtheim *Dokumente* . . . , vol. VIII, p.1181.

2. The SPD - SDS Split as the Genesis of a New Left

1 See Ernst Richert, *Die radikale Linke*, Munich 1968, p.86.

2 N.J. Ryschkowsky, "Zur Geschichte des Sozialistischen Deutschen Studenten-bundes," mimeo. Paper made available to the author by Herr Ryschkowsky, p.51.

3 Peter von Oertzen has called the *konkret* group in the SDS "a group of pacifist, emotionally radical, instinctively oppositional students" and argued against the "blind opposition" it advocated. See his "Ein politisches Lehrstück" in: *Sozialistische Politik*, No. 8-9/1959, p.6.

4 Who of course subsequently gained some notoriety as a leader of the "Bader-Meinhof" (BM) Group.

5 Quoted in Helmut Jaesrich, "Studenten und Atombomben. Ein Kongress stolpert über den Vulkan" in: *Der Monat* 125 (Feb. 1959), p.22ff.

6 According to Hans-Karl Rupp, *Ausserparlamentarische Opposition in der Ära Adenauer. Der Kampf gegen die Atombewaffnung in den fünfziger Jahren*, Cologne 1970, p.255.

7 SPD(PV), ed., "SPD und SDS. Die Vorgänge um den Unvereinbarkeitsbeschluss" in: *Tatsachen-Argumente*, No. 30 (Jan.) 1962, p.4. The "Wall," it should be recalled, was built in August 1961.

8 SDS, "Die Spaltung des SDS" in: *Sozialistische Politik*, No. 5/1960, p.4f.

9 SDS Executive Commiteee, ed., *Dokumentation. Unveröffentliche Dokumente aus der Arbeit des Sozialistischen Deutschen Studentenbundes* (mimeograph) Frankfurt, n.d. (1961), p.3.

10 SDS, *Dokumentation* . . . , p.6.

11 "Selbstkritik in der SPD" in: *Süddeutsche Zeitung*, 29 May 1959.

12 From the *Deutschland-Union-Dienst* (= CDU press service) of 29 May 1959, p.3.

13 See the press statement of 4 January 1959 in: SDS, *Dokumentation* . . . , p.3.

14 See "Erklärung des Bundesvorstandes vom 3.6.1959" in: *ibid.*, p.7.

15 von Oertzen, "Ein politisches Lehrstück . . . ," p.6.

16 Cf. Ryschkowsky, "Zur Geschichte . . . ," p.14.

17 Quoted in *ibid.*, p.14.

18 Oertzen, "Ein politisches Lehrstück . . . ," p.7.

19 SDS, *Dokumentation* . . . , p.16.

20 Dated 30 October 1959 in: *ibid.*, p.9f.

21 Quoted in Ryschkowsky, "Zur Geschichte . . . ," p.22; Cf. further "SPD antwortet Ausgeschlossenen" in: *Deutsche Zeitung*, 18 February 1960.

22 *Ibid.* (Ryschkowsky), p.25.
23 SDS, "Die Spaltung des SDS . . . ," estimates the number at "at most" 150 (p.4); Kallauch, "Der unbequeme SDS . . . ," puts it at 111 (p.6).
24 Mimeographed copy of statement in SPD Archives, Bonn. Not only the facts refuted the implicit accusation that the SDS was "communist infiltrated," but also the backgrounds of its members. E.g. Günther Kallauch had been sentenced in Thuringia in 1946 to eight years' imprisonment for illegal activities on behalf of the SPD (Ryschkowsky, "Zur Geschichte . . . ," p.29).
25 "Zur Gründung des Sozialdemokratischen Hochschulbundes," statement of SPD Party Executive Committee of 23 May 1960 in: *Jahrbuch der SPD 1960/61* p.45.
26 "SPD und politischer Studentenverband" in: *Vorwärts,* 16 June 1960, p.5.
27 Second June issue 1960. Wehner was forced to promise not to repeat such accusations after a court injunction brought by Günther Kallauch.
28 "Abbruch der Beziehungen zwischen SPD und SDS," Party Executive Committee Resolution of 19 July 1960 in: *Jahrbuch der SPD 1960/61,* P.452.
29 SDS, *Dokumentation . . . ,* p.2.
30 "Sozialistische Studentenarbeit heute" in: *Neue Kritik,* No.2 (July) 1960, p.29.
31 In "Der unbequeme Verband" in: *Neue Kritik,* No.2 (July) 1960, p.3.
32 Monika Seifert, "Keine unlauteren Bekenntnisse," letter to the editor in: *Vorwärts,* 19 August 1960, p.6.
33 "Der unbequeme SDS" in: *Vorwärts,* 15 July 1960, p.6.
34 These were funds set aside by the Federal Government for the assistance of youth organizations "deserving of support," and were withdrawn from the SDS in 1966. See Richert, *op.cit.,* p.88 footnote.
35 Here see Kurt Kusch, "Förderung des SDS" in: *Sozialistische Politik.* 10 October 1961, p.5.
36 See "Gegen 'Sozialistische Fördergemeinschaften'" Party Executive Committee resolution of 6.11.1961 in: *Jahrbuch der SPD 1960/61,* p.477; and the Party Council's confirmation of this decision: "SDS und Fördergemeinschaften" in *ibid.,* p.477. The SPD's case is presented comprehensively in "SPD und SDS . . ."
37 Quoted in "SPD und SDS . . . ," p.14.
38 Wolfgang Abendroth, *Aufsteig und Krise der deutschen Sozialdemokratie,* Frankfurt 1964, p.75.
39 Eberhard Dähne, "Die grundsätzliche Entscheidung des SDS" in: *Neue Kritik* No.8 (Nov.) 1961, p.2.
40 Thomas von der Vring, "Neue Linke-Partei-Staat" in: *Neue Kritik,* No.9 (Jan.) 1962, p.22.
41 Reproduced in Flechtheim, *Dokumente . . . ,* vol.VII, p.184.
42 Von der Vring, *op.cit.,* p.22.
43 "SPD und SDS . . . ," p.9.
44 Von der Vring, *op.cit.,* p.23, emphasis in original.
45 Quoted in Jürgen Seifert, "15 Jahre Sozialistischer Deutscher Studentenbund" in: *Sozialistische Politik,* No. 10/1961, p.5.
46 "SPD und SDS . . . ," p.9.
47 Seifert, *op.cit.,* p.4.

3. Attempts at an Alternative Grouping on the Left of the SPD

1 "Die SPD will 'trojanische Esel' ausstossen" in: *Die Welt,* 30 May 1959.
2 E.g., SPD party workers were forbidden to travel in or through communist countries, while CDU workers needed only to inform the party of their intentions. See Karl-Hermann Flach, "Deutsches Armutzeugnis" in: *Frankfurter Rundschau,* 27 July 1963.
3 As told to the author by Gerhard Gleissberg in private interview. In not giving the name of the person concerned, I am respecting Dr Gleissberg's expressed wish.
4 "Absage an der SPD-Führung" in: *Die Andere Zeitung,* No.30/1960, p.2.

5 Reproduced in Hans Frederik, *Die Kandidaten*, Munich, n.d. (ca.1961), p.244.

6 Reprinted in Flechtheim, *Dokumente* . . . , vol.VII, p.190.

7 Lorenz Knorr, "Offener Brief an Herbert Wehner und Erklärung zur politischen Situation und zum Austritt aus der SPD" in: *Blätter für deutsche und internationale Politik*, No.1/1961, p.81ff.

8 Stuttgart, n.d. (1963).

9 That the expulsion took place almost 1 1/2 years after the Party Executive Committee resolution is due to the fact that all such proceedings were executed by the *Land* or district party organizations, and the Baden-Württemberg SPD was somewhat more hesitant. Cf. letter to the author from Fritz Lamm, dated 6 February 1972.

10 Dieter Schröder, "Die SPD rüstet zu grosser Fahrt" in: *Süddeutsche Zeitung*, 22 July 1960.

11 Quoted in Ryschkowsky, *Die linke Linke*, p.34 footnote.

12 (Writing anonymously), "Brauchen wir eine neue Arbeiterpartei?" in: *Der Sozialist* (Stuttgart), June 1960, p.8.

13 "Satzung des Sozialistischen Bundes," reprinted in: Ryschkowsky, *Die linke Linke*, p.131.

14 Cf.*ibid.*, p.141ff.

15 Quoted in *ibid.*, p.34f.

16 "Was will die Vereinigung unäbhangiger Sozialisten?" in: *Die Andere Zeitung* No. 46/1960, p.5f.

17 "VUS-Erklärung" in: *Blätter für deutsche und internationale Politik*, No. 11-12/1960, p.1189ff.

18 Günther Bröhl, "Einheit — aber wie?" in: *Organ der VUS*, No. 2 (April) 1962, p.10.

19 VUS Zentralausschuss, "Erklärung zum Kölner Parteitag der SPD" in: *Organ der VUS*, No. 3 (May) 1962, p.4.

20 According to *Neue Züricher Zeitung* ("Die kommunistische Infiltration in der SPD"), 13 March 1960.

21 ppp, 7 March 1960.

22 "Aufruf zur Sammlung" in: *Blätter für deutsche und internationale Politik* No. 10/1961, p.1050ff.

23 DFU, "Programm der DFU" and "Anträge der DFU im nächsten Bundestag," both mimeographed, n.p., n.d. (1961?).

24 Quoted in: Kai Hermann, "Verkannt, verleumdet, diffamiert" in: *Die Zeit*, 30 July 1965.

25 Cf. Heinz-Dieter Zutz, *Die DFU und die politische Opposition in der Bundesrepublik zu Beginn der 60er Jahre*, mimeographed Staatsprüfung thesis, Pedagogical University Westfalen-Lippe (Bielefeld), n.d. (ca.1971), p.155.

26 "Mit Brandt ist Adenauer nicht zu schlagen" in: *Die Andere Zeitung*, 2.12.60

27 According to Ryschkowsky, *Die linke Linke*, p.56.

28 Here we have Ernst Richert, *op.cit.*, p.92f; *Der Spiegel* internal memorandum from Wolfgang Becker to Dr Wild, 9 August 1961.

29 Flechtheim, *Dokumente* . . . , introduction to vol. VII, p.xvi.f.

30 *Der Spiegel*, 8 September 1965, p.51.

31 "Notwendige Einheit" in: *Die Andere Zeitung*, No.5/1961, p.15.

32 "Offener Brief an alle Sozialdemokraten" in: *Die Andere Zeitung*, No.18/1961.

33 "Der ausgebliebener Sieg" in: *Sozialistische Politik*, No. 9/1961.

34 "Die unheilige Allianz" in: *bulletin*, no.76 (July 1965), p.3.

35 As described in private interview with the author.

36 Behrisch, in private interview with the author: Zutz, *op.cit.*, p.45.

37 See, among others, SPD, ed., Über das Wesen und die Absichten der 'Deutschen Friedens-Union'. Informationsmaterial," Bonn, n.d. (1961); *Die Freunde Ulbrichts*, SPD "Dokumentation" series, Bonn 1961.

38 "Abgrenzung zur 'Deutschen Friedens-Union'" Party Executive Committee resolution of 9-10 January 1961, in: *Jahrbuch der SPD 1960/61*, p.463.

39 In an interview, published as "Wirklich das Letze" in: *Die Andere Zeitung* No. 32/1961, p.2.
40 "Die Gretchen-Frage. Gespräch mit Prof. Dr Renate Riemeck" in: *konkret*, No. 17/1961, p.4.
41 *Rede auf dem Bundeswahlkongress der DFU in Wiesbaden* (mimeo.), n.p., n.d. (1961), p.4.
42 Johannes Bahr, "Die DFU kann man nicht wählen" in: *Vorwärts*, 6 September 1961, p.6.
43 Zutz, *op.cit.*, p.41.
44 As explained by Behrisch in private interview with the author. Cf. further "Reinigung" in: ppp, 23 October 1961.
45 Zutz, *op.cit.*, p.60.

IX. Factors in the Development Toward Extra-parliamentary Opposition

The evolution of the SPD into a liberal *Volkspartei* following the promulgation of the Bad Godesberg Programme coincided with developments in domestic and international politics which might well have tended to favour socialist party advocating an alternative political programme. The years after 1960 marked the end of the "Adenauer Era" and brought substantial changes in the quality and composition of the CDU State, precisely at a time when the SPD was concerned with achieving power solely within and through this state. This situation of course was bound to enhance the subjective and objective prospects for an independent Left.

1. Authoritarian Trends in Politics and Society

Previous chapters have argued that the integration of the SPD into the CDU State was a logical part of the development which began with the postwar decisions for the re-establishment of a liberal-bourgeois-capitalist state and western integration, and which involved the Restoration, clerical anticommunism and the absorption of the labour organizations into the capitalist system. But by the early 1960's, as economic development began to stabilize after the era of reconstruction, and as coexistence and East-West trade began to replace the tensions of the Cold War, the central ideological and economic supports of the CDU State increasingly lost their postwar relevance. At the same time, broader sectors of the population were becoming more and more aware of the high degree of economic concentration, the advanced stage of bureaucracy and administration, the entrenchment of the "one and one-half party system," and the reduction in the powers of the labour organizations to the extent that the latter ". . . no longer represent(ed) the interests of their members to the state, but the interests of the state to their members."[1]

This awareness of the concentration of economic, social and political power implied an understanding of the need to develop the consciousness of the subordinate classes and to increase and extend democratic rights and codetermination into broader social sectors.

But at this juncture — after Godesberg — there was not, in Reinhard Kühnl's words, "even one larger party which would be prepared decisively to defend only the existing degree of political democracy, that is to say there (were) basically only right-wing parties."[2] The CDU State had established what Ralf Dahrendorf has termed "a cartel of elites at the expense of

society," Karl Jaspers a "party oligarchy" or Peter von Oertzen a "constitutional oligarchy"; and a growing awareness that this was so became a crucial
factor in political developments during the 1960's. However, there was still no
large-scale party movement or grouping to articulate this changing
consciousness. In particular the integration of the SPD meant that groups and
movements aiming at a fundamental transformation of socio-economic
relations were not represented in the political system at all, and were forced
out onto the perimeter of political events.

Under these conditions the VUS (Union of Independent Socialists) evolved
an "Initiative Committee for the Establishment of a New Political Party,"
arguing that the working class no longer had a political organ to represent its
views and interests, and that ". . . only for propaganda reasons, as its name
implies, can the Social Democratic Party claim to represent the working
classes," while ". . . the trade unions have developed into bureaucratic
enterprises." Both institutions were seen to be part and parcel of the state
machinery.[3] The Initiative Committee, as a logical development from the old
VUS, now began to advocate the formation of an independent socialist party
which would maintain a direct connection with the working classes and would
be organized "from bottom to top."[4] But the central difficulty which plagued
the VUS, like all aspiring independent political organizations after 1949, was
its inability to win over large sectors of the working classes, a development
which was still unlikely in the absence of some compelling economic force or
series of consciousness inducing events.

Economically, the major tendency of the early and mid-'sixties seemed to be
the retardation of the prosperity and expansion induced by the Marshall Plan,
the Korean export boom, rearmament and the inequitable system of tax
incentives and investment subsidies. Now there was a light economic recession
common to all EEC countries, and the DDR was beginning to reduce the
economic gap between it and the Federal Republic. Such developments
tended to increase pressure by big business and the ruling political parties for
greater government intervention in the economy and for enhanced measures
to stabilize economy and society.[5]

The problem of the government's attempts at instituting authoritarian
measures aimed at achieving stability crystallized around the issue of the
proposed new "emergency" laws. Initial draft legislation containing severe
internal controls in potential domestic "emergency" situations had first been
formulated and submitted by government ministers Gerhard Schröder and
Hermann Höcherl — both former NSDAP members, like the leading
bureaucrats in their ministries[6] — after 1958. These first proposals had
foundered on the resistance of the SPD, since any legislation affecting the
provisions of the Basic Law required a two-thirds majority in the Bundestag.
But by the early 1960's, the SPD had abandoned its opposition in principle to
such measures and now formulated 7 further points designed marginally to
prevent excessive abuse of emergency powers.

The proposed laws, which in their conception and formulation in many
ways paralleled the former Article 48 of the Weimar Constitution — press
censorship, banning of the opposition, suspension of the right to strike, vague
definition of the "state of emergency," etc.[7] — were transparently directed at
potential domestic opposition, particularly trade union demands, anti-nuclear
arms groups and left-wing anti-system opposition, for:

The laws legalize the establishment of a complicated bureaucratic machine whose finely meshed gears can only function if the verbally invoked 'external emergency' and the atomic catastrophe do *not* occur. They can — patently conceived for 'times of peace' — only be directed at securing the social status quo against social crises.[8]

Moreover, as Professor Abendroth pointed out, sufficient legislation already existed to enable the government to act "decisively" in times of national crisis, minority government, criminal conspiracy or natural disaster.[9] The laws now proposed were obviously aimed at enhancing the powers and security of the upper social classes and government bureaucracy in the event of a profound economic or social upheaval.

Opposition to the emergency laws, not surprisingly, originated among the groups against whom they were directed: the trade unions, left-wing SPD members, the left-liberal press, the academic community and, to some extent, individual liberal clergymen. This was essentially the same constellation which had sustained the anti-nuclear arms campaign and the peace movement of the late 1950's.

The issue in fact led to the first fundamental difference between the trade unions and the SPD in some years, and this dispute mirrored the changing roles of SPD and DGB following the Godesberg Programme. Where, in the first years of the existence of the Federal Republic, the Trade Union Federation had frequently regarded the SPD as "radical", e.g., in the question of European integration, now it was the Social Democratic Party who was attempting to draw the unions into an even closer collaboration with the capitalist state. The DGB had remained the representative and advocate of the workers' interests as against this system; indeed this was of necessity its *raison d'être*. But after 1959 the SPD's objective function had become that of agency for the integration of the labour movement into the state system. Although both organizations were system-immanent, the SPD was bent on the full integration of labour into the CDU State, while the DGB was vitally concerned with preserving the workers' rights and increasing their share of this system's social product. Hence social class antagonisms were produced on several levels: within the SPD itself, as a contradiction between the interests of the party leadership and the working classes which supported it, and as a conflict between the political party SPD seeking to acquire power within and through the CDU State and the unions as the pressure group of organized labour.

In any event, it was now objectively necessary for the DGB to operate more independently of the SPD, much in the fashion of a single-issue movement or even oppositional political party. As party political differences declined, in other words, the potential political importance of the trade unions increased. In this situation, a fair number of members of the Left began to see the trade unions as the future organizational centre of a new development toward socialism. They argued that economic dynamics would compel the trade unions to oppose the emergency laws, labour's integration into advanced capitalism, etc., and in this way eventually create a system-opposed socialist force apart from the established parties. Such hopes failed to take into account the already-accomplished integration of the trade unions into state and society, the interlocking elites between the SPD and DGB on the one hand, and the DGB and the state bureaucracy on the other, and the trade unions' direct material stake in the continuation of the CDU State.

Nevertheless the proposed emergency laws concerned the immediate and vital interests of the workers, and were widely perceived as an infringement upon labour rights, so that the trade unions were bound to resist them in the form in which they were proposed. The DGB's 1962 convention rejected out of hand all forms of emergency legislation and all attempts to delimit trade unions' rights, and set the promulgation of a new basic programme on the agenda of the 1963 Convention. The events of the latter demonstrated convincingly that labour had not been as integrated into the post-Godesberg political system as had been commonly supposed. Thus while the Convention affirmed DGB support of "the state" and "the market economy," it defeated the SPD- or "right"- wing under Georg Leber in rejecting the emergency laws, excessive integration of labour and all unequal forms of social partnership.[10] Indeed, the 1963 Convention may be regarded as a limited victory for the Trade Union Left, though by no means the genesis of a resurgence of socialism for:

> The Bad Godesberg Party Convention had brought the pendulum of the labour movement far over to the right; . . . But meanwhile the pendulum has swung back. Among Social Democrats voices are becoming audible expressing doubts as to whether the road after Godesberg was the right one.[11]

The DGB's opposition was not part of a larger overall strategy aimed at bringing about a fundamental change in social relationships. At best it represented an attempt to preserve labour's basic rights in a system increasingly tending toward the right. The trade unions' forms of protest consisted of meetings, demonstrations and propaganda brochures, but these hardly reached the mass membership. After 1966, in fact, the DGB as organization ceased to support the anti-emergency laws campaign, leaving further action to individual members or industrial unions.[12]

The attempts to impose more stringent emergency laws coincided with another government attempt to curtail the liberal press, viz. the much-publicized "Spiegel Affair" of October 1962. A very important part of the post-Godesberg oppositional forces against the CDU-led government was represented by the liberal and left-wing press, a small number of writers and artists and by individual radio and television stations. Although this group was very small, it frequently raised issues which, in another parliamentary democracy, might have been espoused by the parliamentary opposition. Indeed, *Der Spiegel* itself, with its circulation of one-half million and estimated readership of five million, was frequently referred to as the Federal Republic's real "loyal opposition" because of its exposure of corruption in government, its criticism of the ruling political parties and its repeated revelations of facts unpleasant to the government: "In the years 1961 to 1966, all facts and situations which really gave cause for alarm were uncovered by the journalistic Left or by academic circles."[13] The government's action of 26 October in occupying the periodical's offices and arresting its leading editors under circumstances which represented a flagrant abuse of elementary civil rights,[14] and the infringement upon the right of freedom of speech and free expression which it constituted, invoked considerable protest from student bodies, leading writers and intellectuals, most of the press, some clergymen and a number of academics. Significantly, the SPD failed to take an unequivocal stand, as did the DGB: "The party had devoted too much attention to cultivating an image of 'responsibility' and 'moderation' to embrace uncritically the charges being laid against the government and Strauss by the newspapers. Especially it did not want to provide ammunition for the old charge that the SPD was not patriotic."[15] And the DGB, despite some feeble protests, again demonstrated its inability to go beyond issues not immediately and directly affecting its material interests.

Popular opposition to these growing authoritarian tendencies originated increasingly outside, or at the fringe of the established parties and trade unions: in the academic world, some sectors of the press, the nascent student movement and among disillusioned liberals. These groups organized a movement which became known as "Democracy in Distress" (*Notstand der Demokratie*) which reached a high point in a congress held in Bonn on 30 May 1965. The Congress condemned the ruling political parties for their failure to inform the public on the significance of the emergency legislation. For Werner Maihofer, a leading spokesman of liberal opinion, the latter was the "logical consequence of the process of dismantling of our Basic Law since 1956," and the factor uniting the oppositional forces was an "unqualified *No* to the infringement upon the most elementary rules of the hitherto course of the legal process."[16] For, as Karl-Dietrich Bracher pointed out, the transition from a constitutional to a permanent dictatorship was an extremely brief one, as the lessons of the Weimar Constitution had shown.[17]

On the Left, the entire socio-economic development after 1948/49 — the Restoration, Western European integration, the Cold War, renazification, the predominance of big business, clerical anticommunism, etc. — was now interpreted in the light of emergency legislation, the question of political justice and the decline of the Left, as evidence that the Federal Republic had become "neo-fascist," "crypto-fascist," "clerical fascist" or a "fascism of the centre."[18]

> Just as in the social situation of the Federal Republic after the currency reform, the old power relationships were restored which had once brought about the decline of Weimar democracy and then, in the economic crisis after 1930, had carried National Socialist barbarism to victory, so again, in political life, in the judiciary, in the administration, the economy and even in the political parties, parliaments and the governments of the Federal Republic and the *Länder*, forces have come to the fore which not only served the presidial dictatorship after 1930 and National Socialist barbarism after 1933, but which also were captivated by them or played leading roles in them.[19]

The re-emergence of these forces was seen as the result of the failure to achieve a wide social restructuring after 1945, so that essentially the social and economic order of the Federal Republic was substantially similar to that of the pre-fascist Weimar Republic. In an essay which at the time gave rise to considerable controversy, Ekkehardt Krippendorff argued that West Germany could be "designated as an order which does not regard itself as a contradiction to National Socialism and its principles," and that "the Right is not a threat to the Federal Republic and its establishment because the Federal Republic and its establishment are already on the right."[20] These theses were said to be borne out by the success of the extreme right-wing NPD which

... above all succeeded because this Right — in comparison with the

Left — is a legitimate child of the order and the ideology of the
Federal Republic. Basically it — unlike the Left — would like to do
the same, only better, more thoroughly, more honestly, less
ambiguously and even more severely than it trusts the Federal
Government and the big parties supporting it to do — parties whose
leaderships have become uncertain in view of the objective crisis which
they themselves have induced.[21]

And further, the extreme Right was a genuine product of the West German
social order because:

> . . . virtually all of its demands, virtually all of its programmatical
> points can be supported with similar statements by prominent
> politicians from the CDU/CSU and FDP, and to some extent from the
> SPD — whether it is a question of the Oder-Neisse Line, the DDR, our
> relation to German history, criticism of the decline of morals and
> values, or disciplining the 'seditious intellectuals' of the 'homeless
> Left.'[22]

In any case, as Professor Kühnl has argued, two important preconditions
for a further development of some form of fascism or authoritarianism were,
in the mid-'sixties, extant in the Federal Republic. They were: a people who
were characterized by authoritarian and to some extent antidemocratic
attitudes, and a ruling class who still regarded democracy as a threat to its
own pre-eminent position and who might mobilize this fascist potential in the
event of an "emergency."[23] The difference was now that the Left, instead of
representing a serious oppositional potential to be terrorized and confined to
concentration camps, had become seemingly irrelevant.

2. Changes in the Front Lines of the Cold War

The last years of the 1950's have frequently been termed the end of the
postwar era. Global developments during the 'sixties tended toward an
international detente and a relaxation of tensions: the nuclear arms stalemate,
the exhaustion of markets in the West with the resultant need to find new
ones in the East, the realization that the status quo could only be changed by
force, and the nascent Sino-Soviet conflict which seemed to compel the Soviet
Union to seek guarantees of peace with the West.

Within the Federal Republic the factors promoting a coming to terms with
postwar realities and leading to deténte were even more compelling. The
CDU-led government's "policy of strength" had made prospects for reunification — the avowed principal objective of West German foreign policy — more
and more remote. Then the erection of the "Wall" in August 1961, by
preventing large-scale immigration from the DDR as well as ruinous currency
speculation, led rapidly to economic consolidation and prosperity in the
former Soviet Zone. Moreover, the "Wall" demonstrated anew what had long
been implicit in the Federal German foreign policy of reunification on the
basis of the absorption of the DDR: that the only means of achieving it was
force. And force, in the nuclear arms era, was increasingly inconceivable.

In other words, the "policy of strength", of "confrontation", of undifferentiated anticommunism and the "Hallstein Doctrine," which had been
at the core of the foreign policy (and, ideologically, of domestic policy as well)
of the bourgeois coalition and which, after June 1960, was no longer even the

subject of political party debate, was manifestly inadequate for the changed circumstances of the 1960's. And as the "Economic Miracle" began to slow down in consequence of the end of the postwar reconstruction phase and the saturation of western markets, German business began considering the tangible advantages of an "opening to the East."

But the ruling political parties in the Federal Republic still had a vital interest in the perpetuation of the Cold War, for: "With every step toward relaxation in Europe, political and military interest in the BRD declines, while every aggravation of the situation increases the BRD's significance as the exponent and vanguard against the communist peril and for the preservation of the capitalist social order." [1] For the CDU/CSU, of course, anti-communism and the policy of strength represented two of its central tenets of domestic and foreign policy respectively. For the party to repeal the ban on the KPD or to recognize the DDR would have amounted to weakening its political-ideological sources of strength (e.g., abandonment of the all-pervasive external and internal enemy, decline in the urgency of emergency laws, broadening of political debate to include socialist alternatives, etc.) upon which its success had been established — though persisting in these policies continued to provide evidence of their inapplicability in the changing socio-economic situation (e.g., outright rejection by the Federal Government of the Rapacki Plan of 1963 which would have instituted progressive mutual disarmament).

Having espoused the fundamental policies of the CDU State as a means of achieving political power, the SPD was also compelled to adhere to them, precisely at a time when a need for alternatives was broadly perceived among the population. At the SPD's Karlsruhe Convention of 1965, for example, the party displayed a huge map of Germany, in its 1937 frontiers, behind the speaker's rostrum with the slogan, *Erbe und Auftrag!* ("Heritage and Mission!").

As the actual "threat" from the external "enemy" declined, as the real possibility of a "hot" war in the nuclear age receded, and as the status quo became more irreversible, the persistence of the major political parties in irrelevant doctrines made their — virtually unchallenged — ruling ideology less rational, less credible. And this tended to increase the already extant comprehensive collaboration among the parties in an ideological coalition or cartel aimed at preserving these "orthodox" presuppositions and suppressing new ones.

Criticism from the SPD's left wing developed only slowly, in particular following the 1965 elections, and came from individual local party organizations, e.g., West Berlin, Schleswig-Holstein, South Hesse, Swabia and parts of Bavaria. Significantly, almost all the Left's proposals advocated a return to, or limited extensions of the *Deutschlandplan* of 1959/60, the party's last attempt at formulating an independent foreign policy.[2] In a series of memoranda, supplemented by published interviews, Harry Ristock, a leader of the West Berlin intra-party Left, argued for a reunification policy based on the realities of 1965, not 1937: acceptance of German war guilt and of the Oder-Neisse Line, renunciation of the Hallstein Doctrine and payment of reparations to the East European countries who had suffered at the hands of National Socialism. Further attempts to isolate the DDR, he argued, could only "cement" the Ulbricht Regime's position and increase the possibility of military hostilities.[3]

That most of these proposals, vehemently rejected by the SPD leadership at the time and largely responsible for Ristock's subsequent expulsion from the party somewhat later, were a few years later incorporated into the SPD-led government's *Ostpolitik*, is indicative of the contemporary SPD's tenacious adherence to an obsolete policy.

Once again, as during the 1950's, popular opposition to the conservative trends in politics and society was supported and articulated not by a resurgent, organized Left, but instead crystallized in a single-purpose, extra-party protest movement. The Campaign for Disarmament/Easter March Movement, a direct derivation from the old St Paul's Church and Fight Atomic Death Movements, began with a modest protest march campaign in North Germany at Easter of 1960. The March's organizers and supporters were largely pacifists and independent intellectuals operating outside the parties and labour movement. But the 1961 March, which was also supported by the remnants of the KdA movement as well as many local organizations of the *Falken* and *Naturfreunde-Jugend*, and prominent individual members of the SPD and DGB, achieved an impressive nation-wide support and made the peace movement, almost instantaneously, the first important political factor outside the established political parties for half a decade.[4]

Though the Easter March was concerned to remain "above" political party affiliation — an official declaration of 8 October 1964 reaffirmed that it would operate in the "pre-parliamentary sphere" where it would attempt to influence all parties and organizations to work toward peace through detente and disarmament[5] — its espousal of the important issues of armament and diplomatic relations necessarily made it a political movement. Its aims in themselves were a tacit condemnation of the SPD's abandoned alternative foreign policy, and the party's reaction was predictably to accuse the March of contributing to communist ends. In a statement of January 1962, the Party Presidium declared: "In the conception of these marches . . . it is inevitable that (the movement's) activities will be exploited — even though against the organizers' will — by persons who, for their part, are carrying on or supporting a policy of atomic blackmail."[6]

To be sure, as the movement gained support, it became increasingly attractive to former KPD members, who seem to have joined in large numbers. But there is no evidence of any considerable communist influence on the March's policies or actions. Similarly, the DFU, who for its part had taken over the principal policy goals of the *Deutschlandplan*, found a close correspondence between its aims and those of the Easter March Campaign. And organizationally the DFU had temporarily abandoned its political party structure after the 1961 elections in order to become an organization of several component parts united by their opposition to the official foreign and armaments policies. Thus, not surprisingly, a number of DFU members or sympathizers also came to play important roles in the Easter March Movement.

But the latter was by no means merely an extension of the DFU. From its original nucleus of pacifist and anti-war groups, the March incorporated, firstly, religious circles and nationalist-neutralist groups, the non-organized youth and intellectual classes, denominational associations and younger SPD and DGB members, so that gradually it began to take on the character of a youth-orientated protest movement. At the same time its forms of protest and action began to evolve:

> While during the years after 1960 the Easter March originally had the bearing of an accusing protest of conscience, since about 1963 it has developed, on the one hand, political enlightenment and information going into detailed argumentation, and on the other, spectacular action forms which do not disdain a joke and are aimed at getting attention . . .[7]

From signature-gathering for petitions and marches on behalf of a vaguely-defined "peace," the movement came to pressure directly against all forms of emergency legislation — indeed supporters and organizers of the anti-emergency laws campaign and of the Easter March had a great deal in common, including personnel — to specify issues and alternatives (e.g., creation of a European Security Force), to oppose the American involvement in Vietnam and to investigate the social, economic and political preconditions of armament and international tension.

In undertaking social and economic analyses and defining concrete remedies, the Easter March movement went beyond the former KdA and, far from alienating the multifarious groups which supported it, increased its nationwide support from, perhaps, 1,000 participants in 1960 to about 100,000 in 1964, to over 150,000 in 1967.[8]

Of course a substantial part of the March's success was no doubt attributable to the growth of the student movement in the mid-1960's and the formation of the Grand Coalition in late 1966, developments which will be discussed in the following two sections.

3. The Central Role of the Student Movement

Together with the "embourgeoisement" of the SPD and the integration of the labour organizations into the CDU State, the increase in student political involvement must be considered the most important factor in the development of a socialist opposition in the Federal Republic in the early and mid-'sixties. The West German student body, in these years, became politicized to a degree which it had not achieved since the Third Reich, and this politicization was aided by — indeed itself helped to cause — a rapidly growing mass youth oppositional movement rooted in the realities of the social situation.

Here it is difficult to underestimate the role of the SDS, whose expulsion from the SPD has been described in the previous chapter. By the end of 1962, the SDS had about 1,000 members organized in twenty-six university groups, with particularly strong concentrations in West Berlin (200 members) and Frankfurt (120). At the SDS' Delegates' Conference of 1962, and subsequently, the youth organization reaffirmed its extra-party quality, continuing to regard itself as a coordinator and catalysator of the various leftist groups and movements. To fulfil adequately such a role, the SDS correctly saw, it would have to extend its mass basis and develop a socialist body of theory.

As an organization of and for students, the SDS also saw that its primary source of support would have to derive from the universities and technical colleges. Hence education and higher education were among its main areas of concern, and it sought discussion and cooperation among other student

groups in matters affecting students as a whole. In a later draft for a new
basic programme, the Federal Executive Committee defined the SDS as: ". . .
the most aware and most consistent representative of those working
productively and reproductively at universities and colleges . . .," whose task
was to show the "intellectual workers" where their true interests lay and to
expose the undemocratic educational system.[1] Chairman Helmut Schauer, in
his speech to the Conference, defined the SDS as a kind of vanguard of the
revolutionary student movement:

> It is not only a matter of making student parliaments into tribunes of
> political discussion. We must, above all, establish positions in the stu-
> dents' actual workplace, in the seminars and institutes; we must create
> a counterweight to the authoritarian structure of the university. But
> this means that we must be good students. The conscious cadres of the
> labour movement and their trade unions are always recruited from the
> most qualified workers. Comrades, among many groups politics in the
> universities and colleges has been irresponsibly neglected. But when
> our activities outside the university lead to this situation, we are
> imperiling our substance. In everything we do, we are only as strong as
> we are in the universities.[2]

Within the university, the SDS gradually came to play a determining role in
student affairs, as will be discussed below. It was successful in co-ordinating
joint actions on single issues by several student organizations, in politicizing
large sectors of the student body and repeatedly came into conflict with the
official student representative organ, the VDS (*Verband deutscher
Studentenschaften* or Union of German Student Bodies).

But collaboration with other sectors of the working classes, dissident
political groups and the like — also the SDS' declared goal — was more
problematic. The differences in age and educational backgrounds between the
students and members of the labour movement were in themselves bound to
create difficulties. And the SDS' willingness to cooperate with former
communists (though as organization it clearly distanced itself from the KPD-
SED) or with socialist members of the DFU made it suspect in the eyes of
many SPD and DGB left-wing members who still supported the Schumacher
line of uncompromising opposition to both capitalism and communism. The
few experiments in achieving direct cooperation with the working classes
which the SDS undertook — on-the-job agitation and work in Frankfurt,
attempts in Munich to establish a "circle for worker education" — could not
be evaluated as great successes.

The relationship between the SPD and SDS was now seen as only "of
historical value," although the SDS did not abandon until much later its
hopes of winning over still-socialist groups and individuals within the party.
But in a negative way, the SDS tended frequently to define its own position in
terms of the alternatives it presented to the SPD's policies. For the SDS, like
virtually all left-wing and single-purpose movements of the 'fifties and 'sixties,
derived much of its *raison d'être* from perceived errors or omissions of the
SPD. Indeed it may be hypothesized that a more oppositionally oriented SPD
could have effectively eclipsed the entire left-wing opposition until at least the
mid-1960's.

Thus the SDS' policy toward the DDR — detente, mutual recognition and
peaceful co-existence based on the status quo — was, like the DFU's foreign
policy, basically a reiteration and logical development from the SPD's

abandoned *Deutschlandplan*. To this end the SDS advocated the readmission of the KPD, attempted to obtain and disseminate more information on the DDR (because the SDS, ". . . as a socialist students' association, must be concerned with a system which claims to be socialist") and initiated a series of discussions and seminars with the FDJ, the youth organ of the SED, to consider ways in which to achieve détente and normalization of relations between the two Germanies.[3]

One sphere in which the SDS was relatively successful was its work in the Easter March Movement and the anti-emergency laws campaign. In some larger centres, SDS members constituted the leadership and nucleus of these groups, and practically everywhere were an important force in them. Although the SDS' self-image was that of mediator between academic and labour circles,[4] its real contribution lay rather more in coordinating and activating the various academic and independent-intellectual groups (who made up by far the greater part of popular support for these oppositional movements), and in bringing these issues into the student body. In any case, there can be no doubt that the SDS here supplied many of the activists and initiated many of the actions against nuclear weapons and emergency legislation. In particular the SDS was instrumental in organizing and executing the 1965 Congress "Democracy in Distress" in Bonn, which has been discussed above.

Throughout the first half of the 1960's, the SDS laid the theoretical foundations for the student movement and Extra-parliamentary Opposition of subsequent years, and this represents one of its most significant accomplishments. The system of "working groups", which had begun in 1959 on Jürgen Seifert's proposal, was enlarged, in 1964, into a "scientific council" (*Wissenschaftsrat*) to coordinate research projects within the organization, maintain an archive, attend to liaison with former SDS members, arrange conferences and seminars,[5] and provide an information service.[6] The council was intended to provide a theoretical framework for the SDS' work on university policy, problems of disarmament and relations with the communist countries, to account for the changes in world communism after the XXth conference of the CPSU and in particular to reveal the larger social and political inter-connections between the emergency laws, nuclear armament, the American war in Vietnam, etc. Through the council, and through the work of a number of individual SDS members, new ideas and theories were gradually brought into West German socialism, as associated with names such as Marcuse, Adorno, Horkheimer, Habermas, Fromm, Ernst Fischer, Garaudy, Mandel, Gorz, Gramsci, Castro, Fanon and Guevara.

In this context the SDS took up the old question of the extension of the basic political rights anchored in the Basic Law into the social and economic spheres, and made it the starting point of a theory of socialist action. The resultant notion of "double strategy" not only played an important part in contemporary political debate, but was later incorporated into the vocabulary of the Young Socialists (Jusos) and today still represents a focal point of leftist theory in the Federal Republic.

The concept of double strategy — in contrast with less differentiated theories — starts with the assumption that the liberal constitution, the Basic Law, represents a positive historical achievement on the road to socialism, inasmuch as it guarantees liberal rights which are a precondition of socialism; the logical extension of these rights, under propitious conditions, must bring about the realization of socialism. Liberal rights are not static, however; they must be actively defended and actively extended, for:

> The SDS' double strategy is a defensive strategy which aspires to pre-serve liberal-democratic structures; and it is an offensive strategy which under the protection of these structures and through the broad commitment of the population, introduces elements of economic democracy which alone can safeguard the continuation, in the long term, of political democracy.[7]

In terms of double strategy, then, the Basic Law is regarded firstly as a last line of defence from which to protect existing rights against intrusions by the Right (e.g., the emergency laws, nuclear arms production), and secondly, an offensive position from which assaults on the Right can be launched (protests, demonstrations, provocations, etc.), with the aim of effecting changes in the status quo. Using the "socialization articles" of the Basic Law, socialist measures can be introduced over the long term ("system-overcoming reforms") whose cumulative effect may be the abolition or drastic modifi-cation of capitalism.

The rapid growth of the student movement was not, however, solely a result of the politicization process as promoted by the SDS and other student organizations and deriving its impetus from the perceived failures of the traditional labour movement. Student protest of the 1960's was rooted firmly in the actual socio-economic situation of the students. The need for substantial reforms in the educational system, a system which, Ralf Dahrendorf wrote "offers little to all and everything to a few,"[8] had been apparent since 1945. The proposed reforms of the postwar era, like other pressing changes in the social structure, had been simply abandoned in the wake of the Restoration, the Economic Miracle and the Cold War, leaving intact the old authoritarian administrative structures, the notorious *Ordinarienherrschaft*, and above all the inegalitarian system of access to higher education. (Until very recently, children of the rural and working classes, who constituted about two-thirds of the population, made up only slightly less than ten per cent of the student body.)

Academics and student representatives, after 1948, had tended to advocate limited individual reforms within the university, a strategy which assumed that the university system could be treated as an institution in isolation from the overall social context, and that the desired reforms could be achieved within the liberal-democratic state which the Basic Law proclaimed the Federal Republic to be. But these reformers, as Wolfgang Lefèvre has argued pointedly,

> . . . derived the importance and correctness of their demands from the *concept* of a democratic society. But at the same time, by failing — the SDS less than the VDS — to work out the specific historical difference between their concept of democracy and the real "democracy" in the Federal Republic, in order thus to determine with whom and against whom in the Federal Republic their ideas could be realized, they failed basically to bring about the realization of the demands themselves.[9]

The first attempts at regarding the universities and university reform within and as part of their actual socio-economic conditions were first made only in 1961, in the form of an SDS mimeographed report, *Hochschule in der*

Demokratie,[10] and in 1962 as the VDS internal study, *Studenten und die neue Universität.* Neither of these works, however, found a broad readership, and their influence seems to have been minimal at the outset, except within the SDS and VDS respectively.

A general awareness of the inadequacies of the educational system only came about as a response to concrete economic developments. By the beginning of the 1960's, the technology gap between the USA and the Federal Republic had grown so wide as to give rise to fears for the future of German export markets. During the 1950's an undervalued currency and a seemingly inexhaustible reservoir of cheap labour deriving from the influx of DDR refugees had promoted and fuelled the Economic Miracle. But during the last years of the 'fifties, full employment was attained, and the erection of the "Wall" on 13 August 1961 ended the source of cheaper labour. The long-term solution to these difficulties was evident: intensification of production.

And it is equally evident that the first step in streamlining the process of production must be the training of experts and specialists, together with a rapid increase in the output of university and college graduates. The 1964 Conference of German Ministers of Culture proposed, among other things, a reduction in the time allotted for certain courses of study and compulsory expulsion (*Zwangsexmatrikulation*) of students who could not meet the new norms. Admittedly a reduced period of study was compatible with most previous proposals for university reform, including those of the SDS and VDS. But these proposals, by leaving the outmoded regulations and structures of existing programmes of study intact, rather than coupling the reduced period of study with corresponding substantial course content changes — as the reformers had proposed — were merely modifying the symptom of the problem without altering the situation which gave rise to it. In effect, students would be compelled, under the proposed changes, to complete the same course of studies in less time.

In mid-1963 the deficiencies of the West German educational system came suddenly before a broader public. Following the publication of Georg Picht's pioneering work, *Die deutsche Bildungskatastrophe* ("The German Educational Catastrophe"), the topic was taken up by the press and other media, and even became an issue in the 1965 election campaign. A brief period of cooperation began between liberal academics and university administrators, more funds were made available for study, new institutes established and greater efforts made to increase the size of the student body.

But such forms found their limitations the moment they began to affect the power structure of the higher education system. As the students began to press for the realization of the begun reforms, they encountered resistance which demonstrated clearly "with whom and against whom" these reforms could be realized. At the same time, political developments increasingly underlined the growing authoritarian elements in society as a whole.

These developments tended to vindicate the SDS' contention, as presented in its 1961 memorandum, that the repressive tendencies in society found their corresponding tendencies in the universities and colleges, who were after all its organs. Not only did the university supply society with research and technology, but it also contributed to the stabilization and justification of existing power relationships. The holders of professorial chairs (*Ordinarien*) were, in the vast powers they held, not unlike the power holders of big business or big government. They determined the direction, purpose, and ideological rationale of the work carried out in their departments, thereby reducing their assistants and students to mere executors of policy. The chairholders, moreover, as appointees of the state whose careers depended on the good will of that state, were extremely unlikely to undertake scholarly work which would not find official approval.

The SDS Federal Executive Committee later defined more precisely the role of students and younger academics in this process: the rationality of scholarly endeavour was increasingly conflicting with the ruling ideology of the CDU State, hence causing many intellectuals to oppose, or at least question that ideology. Changing methods of production and the growth of a great army of specialists were, at the same time, transforming the academics' role from members of the bourgeoisie to members of the working class, albeit privileged members.[11]

These insights implied several things which would be crucial to the SDS' theory and praxis in subsequent years: that the university, as an integral part of society, could only be transformed in connection with an overall social transformation; that students' and intellectuals' interests were identical with those of the working classes and that they must be made aware of this identity; and that, using the university as a power base, changes in the university system could be translated into social change.

Then in December 1964 the SDS' and other student groups' protests against the official visit of the Congo leader, Tshombe, who ostensibly was responsible for the murder of Lumumba, the socialist leader, were countered by police actions and attacks by the West German press; virtually no mention was made anywhere of the "rightness" or "wrongness" of the students' case.

The May 1965 Congress "Democracy in Distress" demonstrated that the manifold student organizations could achieve a positive collaboration on common issues. It brought together the SDS, SHB, Liberal Student Union (LSD), Humanist Student Union (HSU) and the German-Israeli Student Group, together with a number of trade union leaders, prominent academics, independent socialists and dissident SPD members, in protest against the pending emergency legislation, against nuclear armament and in favour of a less aggressive policy toward communism. This was the last large joint political demonstration during the 1960's which was carried out along the same lines as the St Paul's Church Movement, the KdA and the Easter March, namely as an ostensibly non-partisan political protest demonstration. The "Democracy in Distress" participants still regarded their role as one of exerting influence on the parties in the so-called pre-parliamentary sphere.

This cooperation among student groups was further enhanced during the "Kuby-Krippendorff semester," as it became known, in Berlin in 1967.[12] Erich Kuby, a prominent oppositional journalist, had been refused permission to speak at the Free University, allegedly because of his 1958 assertion that the notion of a "free" university whose establishment and continued *raison d'être*, as the antithesis of the "unfree" Humboldt University in East Berlin, was a false one, that in fact it represented only a negative freedom, as positive freedom could not have an antithesis. Krippendorff, a junior lecturer in political science, had alleged that the administration had refused the philosopher Karl Jaspers permission to speak at the Free University. When he discovered that this had been an error, Krippendorff retracted his allegation and apologized to the rector. Nevertheless his contract was not renewed. Both incidents invoked extensive student opposition and further increased cooperation among the various student groups, who began to see that their aims could be better achieved not in direct confrontation with an ossified and authoritarian bureaucracy, but by publicizing their case both to the student body and the general public. The negative press reaction also demonstrated anew that the students ought not look to the media for support in their efforts at reform.

Perhaps the most significant motivation of student protest in the mid-'sixties was the Vietnam war. This can, of course, be said of virtually every western student movement. What to a large sector among the student body was the brutal suppression of a genuine movement of national liberation and an international crime on the scale of those committed by the National Socialist Regime, appeared to be supported, or at least passively accepted, by the government, the political parties, the labour organizations and the press. The students' views had to be brought before a broader audience by means of separate, all-student initiatives: student publications, demonstrations, literature, etc., and for the first time in June 1966, the sit-in. The existing institutions of communication and information were seemingly incapable of taking account of views and interests diverging from the ruling orthodoxy.

One of the initiatives undertaken by the SDS against the Vietnam war was an illegal placard-posting action in Berlin in February 1966. The Free University's Rektor, Lieber, subsequently wrote a letter to the U.S. Commander, Franklin, expressing his "deepest regret" at the "irresponsible" actions of "a few" students. He wrote: "It is incomprehensible that these students cannot or will not understand that it is primarily due to the presence of the United States and its Allies in Berlin that they can study here in freedom and can freely express their opinion at any time." Later discussing the Rektor's letter, Rudi Dutschke wrote:

> The implication contained in this statement is that in West Berlin Vietnam is being defended, as though precisely the Americans, with their immoderate war in Vietnam, had not lost all moral justification to be able to talk about the defence of freedom in any place in the world. The cynical recognition of the American position by the Rektor and the Lord Mayor had to shake those students who had been convinced of the integrity and sincerity of the university authorities and the Senate authorities.[13]

Faced with uncomprehending bureaucracies, as typified by the Rektor's letter, and with a uniformly hostile press, the oppositional students tended to resort more and more to direct action. On one occasion a few eggs and tomatoes were thrown at the America House in Berlin. This action was immediately attacked and denounced, by the media and official institutions, with a vehemence far out of proportion to the act itself. They invoked calls for forcible suppression of the perpetrators and denounced them as "violent left-wing fanatics" and the like. Far from containing student protest, such incidents suggested a means of obtaining a wider publicity:

> The measure of irrationality inherent in throwing eggs and tomatoes is not an irrationalism of fascists urging violence as an end in itself; it is the surrealistic and provocative symbolization of the irrationalism of a society which documents the insignificance of political reason and the

language of humanity by placing a Hyde Park Corner at its disposal. If it should happen, moreover, that a caricature of violence, as an expression of our own impotence in the form of eggs and tomatoes, can provoke the machinery of violence, which passes itself off as tolerant, to abandon the democratic and constitutional forms and undisguisedly to "get down to business" namely to do violence to people, then this provocative irrationalism contributes more to political enlightenment than most political podium discussions.[14]

Thus, by 1966, the anti-emergency laws campaign, the Easter March Movement, the SDS' groundwork in theory and practice, and the growing collaboration of the student groups had helped to politicize thousands of students. Their actual social situation, the obstacles placed in the way of any attempt to improve it, and bureaucratic reaction to what to them were reasonable and necessary proposed reforms, helped further to activate the young.

For example, the SHB which, it will be recalled, had been founded as an "anti-SDS" and an organ for the recruitment of students to the SPD, also became rapidly alienated from its sponsor. The SHB's 1964 Delegates' Conference unequivocally advocated recogintion of the Oder-Neisse Line,[15] and the next year's conference demanded renunciation of the Hallstein Doctrine and the goal of full national reunification. The 1965 executive in fact resigned in protest against the party's treatment of the SHB. By 1966 the SHB's critique shifted from foreign to domestic policy in its criticism of the pending emergency legislation and German reactions to Vietnam. Within a few years, the SHB, like the SDS before it, was to become an extra-party opposition.

By 1966 it was also evident that the politicization of youth, in particular the student body, was an accomplished fact. Where in 1956 two-thirds of the 14-21 age group had not been politically interested, now every second youth was "interested in politics." Fifteen per cent were actually politically active (cf. four per cent in the general population).[16] And the great majority of these newly politicized young people were, for reasons of social situation or intellectual conviction, on the left.

4. The Grand Coalition

During 1966 the Federal German economy was overtaken by its inherent structural defects. As unemployment rose and industry slowed dramatically, Chancellor Ludwig Erhard, finance minister during the Economic Miracle and leading advocate of German neo-liberalism, was replaced by Kurt Georg Kiesinger, a former member of the NSDAP. An internal dispute with the Free Democratic coalition partner led to the breakup of the CDU/CSU-FDP coalition. In December the SPD and CDU/CSU formally agreed to form a Grand Coalition.

The coalition partners' joint Declaration of Government, delivered by Kiesinger on 13 December 1966, presented a series of policies and proposals frequently paralleling Erhard's notions of the *formierte Gesellschaft* (which had been an attempt to establish a form of "social peace" based on the perceived "common good" of society as a whole and on making the status quo as efficient as possible[1]). The joint programme included: the introduction of the constituency or majority electoral system which would of course effectively bar minor parties from parliamentary representation; agreement on the necessity for some form of "emergency legislation"; finance reforms restricting the autonomous fiscal powers of the *Länder* and communities; curtailment of social welfare benefits; greater controls on, but also greater incentives for, capital investment; wage directives as part of an incomes policy to restrict general income; non-recognition of the DDR and persistence in the Hallstein Doctrine and an increase in federal spending powers generally.[2]

The political, social and economic ramifications of the Grand Coalition, which held together until September 1969, are manifold, and cannot be incorporated adequately into a work on the German Left. Our concern here is with the Grand Coalition's role in stimulating intra-party, extra-party and extra-parliamentary opposition. To anticipate, what the SPD later wrote of its role in that coalition is perfectly true: "We are again on firm ground; the economy is again running at full steam. Our coffers are full again . . ."[3] The SPD, in the Grand Coalition, did help to stabilize the economy, did contribute to "social peace", did help to avert a crisis of confidence in the government.

But the "three-way alliance" of the state, the entrepreneurs and the workers of which SPD Finance Minister Karl Schiller spoke,[4] was manifestly an alliance to the disadvantage of the classes from which the SPD drew the majority of its supporters: the subordinate classes. The economic crisis was overcome by the implementation of state guarantees of big business' profits in the form of capital accumulation, tax-free investment and of a reduction in mass purchasing power. This was not the first time in history, as Hans See has pointed out, when the SPD

> . . . chained its workers and members to the interest of capital in a moment in which capital, for reasons of its own inner contradicting laws, created firstly an economic and then — not least of all for reasons of the mass media's one-sided criticism of the parties' economic policies and their diversion away from the real cause of the recession — a political crisis.[5]

The *Frankfurter Rundschau* asked whether, at Godesberg, the SPD had cast overboard not only its Marxist ballast but also its entire profile. The SPD had consciously striven to emulate the CDU, A.A. Guha argued there, but where as the Union had a firm conservative ideological and social base, the SPD did not; and consequently the SPD leaders' actions in entering into a Grand Coalition and helping to promote anti-labour policies ". . . ironically had to be implemented, with almost masochistic severity, against a large part of the membership and the trade unions, against the intelligentsia and against scholars, in short against all real friends of democracy, whose democratic predisposition is beyond doubt."[6]

And although no doubt the SPD did make a distinct contribution to the coalition government's policies — notably in the fields of foreign policy, economic recovery and social welfare benefits — the CDU/CSU, as the "senior" partner, received by far the greatest public accord for the Grand Coalition's accomplishments. In a speech to a Juso gathering in Cologne, Joachim Steffen declared: "'For us the Republic comes first,' Herbert Wehner said. And with the Grand Coalition he is *perhaps* saving the Republic, but with certainty the CDU!"[7] The real function of the *Grosse Koalition*, it is evident, was to preserve West German capitalism from the extreme consequences of its own structural defects. A socialist, or even loyal oppositionalist SPD would have had an unprecedented opportunity, perhaps within a left-liberal coalition, to effect a series of basic economic and social reforms. The crisis was the potential starting point for a new political awareness. However:

> Social conflicts were not revealed. Faithful to the 8-Point Programme of the Grand Coalition, the SPD strove for 'a cooperative relationship between the social partners.' The policy of mutuality, which had been in preparation for years — and conceived as an anticommunist cooperation between the social classes — has primarily filled the coffers of the entrepreneurs and suppressed the budding awareness of the necessity for basic social reforms.[8]

The SPD's role in rescuing the CDU/CSU and the CDU State from potential political bankruptcy was recognized negatively in the *Länder* elections following the formation of the Grand Coalition, as Table 1 indicates. Elections held prior to December 1966 — as the economic crisis worsened — demonstrated positive gains for the SPD, while those held subsequently revealed — occasionally drastic — declines in the SPD's share of the vote. In the case of the one exception, Schleswig-Holstein, the presence there of Joachim Steffen, an outspoken left-wing opponent of the Grand Coalition, may have helped to avert an SPD loss.

Table 1
Länder Elections Before and After the Formation of the Grand Coalition

A. Before 1.12.66			B. After 1.12.66		
Land	Date	Result	Land	Date	Result
Saarland	27.6.65	+10.7%	W. Berlin	12.3.67	—5.0%
Hamburg	27.3.66	+ 1.6	Rhineland-Palat.	23.4.67	—3.9
N. Rhine-Westphal.	10.7.66	+ 6.2	Schleswig-Holst.	23.4.67	+0.2
Hesse	6.11.66	+ 0.2	Lower Saxony	4.6.67	—1.8
Bavaria	20.11.66	+ 0.5	Bremen	1.10.67	—8.7
			Baden-Württemberg	28.4.68	—8.2

Source: "Wahlen" in: *Der Spiegel*, No.19/1968, p.27ff.

Protest from the Left against the SPD's entry into the Grand Coalition seemed to originate almost exclusively from within the party itself, the trade unions and the youth organizations. The extra-party Left, from the Union of Independent Socialists and the Socialist League to the SDS, saw it merely as a continuation of the Godesberg and post-Godesberg course of the SPD. For the Left the Grand Coalition was nothing more than a logical development from the surrender of an alternative domestic policy to the abandonment of an independent foreign policy, the adoption of uncritical anticommunism and the use of intra-party discipline to contain the Left. But the extra-party Left also saw that the formation of the Grand Coalition had caused a fairly widespread disillusionment among SPD supporters, and had alarmed many who had hitherto professed no political allegiance. Popular resentment against the coalition accordingly became an important propagandistic and strategic factor in the growth of popular support for an opposition "transcending" the existing parties.

Within the SPD, what the *Grosse Koalition* did effect was undoubtedly a heightening of members' and voters' consciousness. Members now began to consider ways of obtaining a better hearing for their views within the party — through, e.g., group petitions, protest letters, attendance at congresses, etc. — or of organizing groups parallel to, or even outside the party, in order to bring new ideas into it.

One of the latter was a "Working Group of Progressive SPD Supporters" established in Munich in 1968 by Dr. Theodor Lin and Werner Mitkin. Its goals were relatively simple: to contradict and expose the SPD leaders' policies and to promote an ideological and practical discussion at the grass-roots level.[11] Intra-party oppositional centres began also to coalesce around Joachim Steffen in Schleswig Holstein, who argued that the SPD's lack of priorities — especially socialist priorities — had caused the party to lose its direction and revert to political opportunism; and around Harry Ristock in West Berlin, who continued his appeal for an alternative foreign policy based on recognition of the DDR.

In particular the programme of the Grand Coalition conflicted directly with the interests of labour. Continuation of the policy of strength and the Hallstein Doctrine ensured further huge expenditures for armaments. The promulgation in 1968 of the long-pending emergency laws, as was argued in section (1) of this chapter, was a measure aimed directly at securing the privileges of the upper social classes. The introduction of value-added tax on various consumer-goods purchases, the tax reductions accorded to big business and cutbacks made in federal public projects and spending for social welfare measures were also in conflict with labour's material interests.

Where traditionally economic crises, such as after 1945, had led to greater collaboration between SPD and DGB in preparing and proposing protective measures for the working classes, the 1966 crisis only heightened the antagonism between organized labour and what had been "its" party. For the first time in the SPD's 100-year existence, observers within and outside the party, on the Left and on the Right, began to refer to the party's "labour wing" (*Arbeitnehmerflügel*) in much the same manner as the CSU's "labour wing" which was considered one interest group among many within Christian Democracy.[12]

And within the SPD, the fact that the coalition was opposed by several industrial trade unions, in particular the powerful *IG-Metall* (Metalworkers' Union), which represented over one-third of the total DGB membership, made labour a still-powerful "lobby" within the party. Some SPD members were aware of labour's strength and dissatisfaction, and attempted to convince the workers that the Grand Coalition also represented their interests. SPD deputy Wilhelm Druscher, for example, declared that economic reform was imminent once stability had been achieved: "The entrepreneurs for their part have now been aided immensely by tax concessions and write-offs. Therefore they must later honour what Social Democracy had already made in the way of an advance commitment, and what especially the great mass of workers has already done."[13]

The trade unions were, however, still far removed from political party commitment, or indeed from independent political activity which would change the shifting balance of domestic power. On the contrary, the DGB held tenaciously to its policy of extracting specific concessions, where possible, from the existing system. But now the unions tended even more to see their opportunities for success through the other political parties as well as the SPD. When Egon Lutz, an Executive Committee member of the IG Printing and Paper, in early 1965 made the following statement, he summarized what was to be a growing trend within the DGB after December 1966:

> We are trade unionists and must decide according to our own interests. We know that until now there was a party who supported our essential demands. Times are changing. We must in future struggle for influence in both *Volksparteien*. And that if possible before the election, in the nomination of the candidates. That is perhaps a bit arduous for us all . . .
>
> For the trade unions have the weight of large numbers behind them. They must only learn to politicize their members. Not for this or that party, but for the trade unions' interests. We must learn to inspire our members in the two *Volksparteien* to a competition between the competing interest groups. We must learn to impress the parties with the fact that the vote of a trade unionist has at least the same weight as that of a landowner, handworker or a refugee. We must now learn to think and act in terms of *Volksparteien*.[14]

Hence after 1966, the SPD leadership's abandonment of social reformism and its transition to active and direct participation in the CDU/CSU's conservative foreign and domestic policies conflicted increasingly with the expressly reformist course of the majority of the trade union leaders. Initially labour pressure was unable to affect the SPD's course — there was still no alternative left-wing force — but the potential antagonism inherent in this situation was diffused by the trade unions' shifting political loyalties; that they did not opt for independent political action or for a direct challenge to the essentially bourgeois Grand Coalition, ensured a continuation of "social peace" and, in fact, vindicated the political and economic order.

The already existing conflicts between the SPD and its youth organizations, the SHB and Jusos, was certainly exacerbated by the SPD's participation in the Grand Coalition. Younger Social Democrats had of course been particularly involved in the anti-nuclear weapons and anti-emergency laws campaigns, and had perceived the CDU-led regime as chiefly responsible for the Restoration and the "educational catastrophe." The party youth was especially concerned with altering the status quo which the SPD leadership now seemed intent upon preserving.

The SHB, like the SDS some years before, saw itself a rapidly isolated minority in a party which no longer represented its beliefs and interests. At the same time it realized that organizational separation from the party would, as in the case of the SDS, isolate it from the subordinate classes, on behalf of whom it aspired to effect reform, and from the political structure which provided it with greater possibilities for articulating its views. A first solution presented itself with the notion of working with extra-party socialist groups (SDS, KPD, SB, etc.) on the basis of common socialist goals which could be developed outside the party in hopes eventually of bringing them into the SPD.[15]

The SPD's response had its precedent: the party resolved temporarily to discontinue funding the SHB, and to establish a special commission to re-examine its relations with the student organization.[16] A Delegates' Conference of the SHB in March 1968 then proposed to sever relations completely with the SPD. A vote subsequently taken at an extraordinary convention in July in Saarbrücken, however, produced a majority of three in favour of continuing institutional affilition with the party. But at the same time the SHB stressed its inability to cooperate fully with the SPD, declaring that the party leadership had aided the progress of the Restoration and betrayed the subordinate classes. It advanced the idea of a limited participation in party organs and policies, and decided to concentrate instead on local initiatives. It would no longer support the party as a whole, but only individual left-wing candidates who expressly declared their opposition to official party policy.[17]   Shortly thereafter the SHB was expelled from the SPD.

Even the party's Young Socialists (Jusos), the organization of all SPD members between 18-35 years, underwent a rapid politicization in connection with all these developments. Juso opposition was more significant than that of the SDS or SHB (each with somewhat more than 1,000 members), moreover, as its membership was about 170,000, of whom about 153,000 were simultaneously SPD members — that is, about one-fourth of the overall party membership. The Jusos could not simply be ignored or expelled.

The Young Socialists' Federal Congress in Mainz on 10 December 1967 revealed how widespread opposition to the party's policies had become among its youth membership: more than 170 written proposals were submitted which could be said to reflect left-wing opposition to the dominant political and economic development of the Federal Republic. Of these only three were direct criticisms of the Grand Coalition, it is true, but many of the remainder could be interpreted, and indeed were largely intended, as such. Protest was voiced against: the pre-eminence of business and the decline in social services (8 proposals), Vietnam (14), the Greek military dictatorship and Bonn's failure to condemn it (10), the growth of neo-Nazism (4), lack of intra-party democracy (6), the emergency laws (11), the Hallstein Doctrine (6), the proposed constituency electoral system (4), excessive press concentration (6). And further, 8 demanded more worker codetermination, 8 wanted to lower the voting age and 4 proposed to recognize the Oder-Neisse Line.[18]

A further congress held in May 1968 in Frankfurt envisioned the Juso's role as one of bringing the issues raised and the problems posed in the extra-parliamentary sphere into the mainstream of party debate. Such measures were now called for, as the Bavarian Jusos argued in their Haushamer Manifesto of 1968, as the SPD had abandoned itself entirely to opportunism and pragmatism, and now sought merely to administer existing society, rather than changing or even reforming it. After the Grand Coalition, the SPD had become only "the tenant in the cellar dwelling of a building which it once wanted to tear down and, upon its foundation, to build anew the democratic basic order."[19]

If the post-Godesberg course of the SPD had eliminated substantial political choices and alternatives, the Grand Coalition temporarily removed even choices of detail, of minor reform. Heinrich Hannover has written: "Political opposition is not exhausted . . . in discussions of reform of the health system and civil service salaries. Only subjects, the discussion of which touches the nerve of the government's policies, such as withdrawal from NATO, atomic armaments or reunification through negotiations with the DDR, show whether or not we have freedom of opposition."[20] But the Grand Coalition seemed to remove even civil service salaries and health system reforms from political debate. The CDU/CSU's former coalition partner, the FDP, was not a real alternative, as it had been instrumental in the establishment and continuation of the CDU State, and its programmes — in so far as these were formulated at all — amounted to minor variations of the Programme of the Grand Coalition. It is no coincidence that the pseudo-fascist NPD began to register its greatest gains in *Länder* elections following December 1966.[21]

This "renunciation by the SPD of the general rules of parliamentary democracy" represented for Theo Pirker "an uncontrolled pragmatism which raises the arbitrary rule of the few in the party and state to a political virtue and declares it to be policital reason *per se.*"[22] For Ekkehard Krippendorff, the *Grosse Koalition* was "fundamentally nothing but a preliminary form of the one-party state in which various factions balance out one another in the struggle for political leadership."[23]

This is largely the way in which the Grand Coalition was — correctly — perceived by the Left immediately after its formation. But in time the SPD leadership was forced to yield to the great popular pressure exerted upon it by the mobilization of the lower and middle party levels, and quite possibly by the large Extra-parliamentary Opposition movement which gained its mass following essentially as a protest against the Grand Coalition. By the time of the SPD's 1968 Nuremberg Convention, more than 1,000 proposals for changes — "normal" conventions had to deal with from 200-300 proposals, not more — ranging from condemnation of the *Grosse Koalition* to recognition of the DDR and the Oder-Neisse Line, were submitted to the party headquarters.[24]

The SPD leadership had carried too far the policy of "embracement" of the CDU/CSU, and this fact was generally perceived by the electorate, as the *Land* elections of 1967 and 1968 repeatedly underlined. To prevent further defections and drastic voter losses like those incurred after December 1966, the SPD was gradually compelled to search for image-altering policies. This it found in the protest movement, the ideas of social reform (pensions, education, limited codetermination) and above all an alternative foreign policy, which later became the SPD's *Ostpolitik*. Indeed, it can plausibly be argued — but not here, as this chapter is already anticipating somewhat — that the entire complex of *Ostpolitik* initially represented an opportunistic attempt by the SPD leaders to regain some of the mass support which the party had lost through its entry into the Grand Coalition.

For our purposes, however, the central importance of the Grand Coalition was that it marked the end of formal political opposition in the Federal Republic. As such it was an important catalyst of inner- and especially extra-party opposition. And hence it was perhaps the most significant motivating force of the Extra-Parliamentary Opposition of the late 1960's.

REFERENCES

1. Authoritarian Trends in Politics and Society

1 Arno Klönne, "The Concept of an Integrated Society" in: *International Socialist Journal*, special issue on Germany 1967, p.40.
2 *Deutschland zwischen Demokratie und Faschismus*, Munich 1969, p.23.

3 VUS, *Programmatische Erklärung*, mimeographed brochure, Cologne, n.d. (1962) 4th unpaginated page.

4 Cf. Gerhard Bessau, *Über die Organisationsprinzipien einer linkssozialistischen Partei I*, mimeographed circular, n.p., n.d.

5 On this see a speech delivered by Peter Gäng at a SDS-FDJ seminar on 9 Dec. 1966 in Frankfurt, reprinted in *Studien von Zeitfragen*, 8 Feb. 1967, p.15f.

6 As pointed out by Wolfgang Abendroth, "The Resistable Ascent of the German Reaction" in: *International Socialist Journal*, special issue, *op,cit.*, p.13.

7 The 26 May 1965 version is published, in mimeographed form, as: Entwurf eines Gesetzes zur Änderung des Grundgesetzes (Notstandsgesetz)," special publication of the Presse- und Funknachrichten, n.p., 1965.

8 H. J. Blank/J. Hirsch, "Parlament und Verwaltung im Gesetzgebungsprozess" in: G. Schäffer/C. Nedelmann, eds., *Der CDU-Staat*, Munich 1967, p.96, italics in original.

9 "Zusätzliche Notstandsermächtigungen," reproduced in his *Antagonistische Gesellschaft und politische Demokratie*, W. Berlin & Neuwied 1967, esp. p.179.

10 Here see variously: "Georg Lebers fragwürdige Grundsätze" in: *Die Tat* (Frankfurt), 6 July 1963; "Die Präambel als Basis künftiger Arbeit" in: *Die Andere Zeitung*, 4 July 1963; G. Gaus, "Der DGB und sein neues Programm in: *Süddeutsche Zeitung*, 23 Nov. 1963; and Raimund Klinkhammer, radio programme for the Hessischer Rundfunk, 22 Nov. 1963, typewritten M/S available in DGB Archives, Düsseldorf.

11 Commentary by Fritz Richert in: *Stuttgarter Zeitung*, 23 Nov. 1963.

12 Here see Eberhard Schmidt, *Ordnungsfaktor oder politische Gegenmacht? Die politische Rolle der Gewerkschaften*, Frankfurt 1971, p.64f.

13 Ernst Richert, *Die radikale Linke*, W. Berlin 1968, p.95.

14 Full descriptions and chronology of the government's actions are presented in: Otto Kirchheimer, "A Free Press in a Democratic State? The Spiegel Case in: G. M. Carter and A. F. Westen, eds., *Politics in Europe*, New York 1965; R. Bunn, "The Spiegel Affair" in: Bunn and Andres, eds., *Politics and Civil Liberties in Europe*, Princeton 1967; and A. Grosser/J. Seifert, *Die Spiegel-Affäre I*, Olten & Freiburg 1966.

15 Bunn, *op.cit.*, p.96.

16 From a mimeographed copy of a summary of Maihofer's address to the Congress n.p., n.d. (Bonn? 1965).

17 Mimeographed press release, "Zusammenfassung des Referats," 1st unpaginated page.

18 For a discussion of the application of such terms to the Federal Republic, see Heinrich Hannover, *Diffamierung der politischen Opposition im freiheitlichen Rechtsstaat*, Dortmund-Barop 1962, p.65f.

19 Wolfgang Abendroth, "Obrigkëitsstaat oder Soziale Demokratie?" in: *Gewerkschaftliche Monatshefte*, No. 10/1959, p.343ff.

20 Ekkehardt Krippendorff. "Die Rechte in der Bundesrepublik — Zehn Thesen" in: F. Duve, ed., *Die Restauration entlässt ihre Kinder oder der Erfolg der Rechten in der Bundesrepublik*, Reinbek 1968, p.163 and 165.

21 *Ibid.*

22 *Ibid.*

23 Kühnl, *op.cit.*, p.271.

2. Changes in the Front Lines of the Cold War

1 Ursula Schmiederer, "Eine neue Aussenpolitik?" in: Fritz Lamm. *et al.*, *Die Grosse Koalition und die nächsten Aufgaben der Linken*, Frankfurt 1967, p.28.

2 See here Arno Nasse, "Der Traum von einer 'Grossen Linken'" in: *Die Zeit*, 4 March 1966.

3 See esp. the interview with Ristock in *radikal*: "Eine sozialdemokratische Alternative" reprinted in: *Studien von Zeitfragen*, No.9/1965, p.7ff.

4 Cf. K. A. Winken, "Ostermarsch der Atomwaffengegner in der Bundesrepublik" in *Studien von Zeitfragen*, No. 2/1963.

5 *Erklärung des Zentralausschuss*, mimeographed copy, n.p. 1964, p.2

6 "Zur Ostermarschbewegung" Party Presidium Statement of 23 January 1962, reprinted in: *Jahrbuch der SPD 1962/63*, Bonn 1963, p.503.

7 K. A. Winken, "Strukturprobleme der Kampagne für Abrüstung in der BRD," supplement to *Studien von Zeitfragen*, No. 6-7/1966, p.8.

8 See, respectively, "Erfolgreicher westdeutscher Ostermarsch 1965" and "Deutscher Ostermarsch" in: *Studien von Zeitfragen* (respectively), No.14/1965 and No.5/1967.

3. The Central Role of the Student Movement

1 From the summary of the Conference, reproduced as: "Jahrestagung 1965 des SDS" in: *Studien von Zeitfragen*, No. 10/1965.

2 *Ibid.*, p.8.

3 These conferences were, however, singularly unsuccessful, as the FDJ was far too bound to the East German state and state party to be able to go beyond the official "hard-line" policy. Cf. "Chronologie und Dokumentation eines versuchten Brückenschlages zwischen sozialistischen Organisationen aus 'West' und 'Ost'" in: *Studien von Zeitfragen*, No. 2/1965, p.5 and ff.5 Cf. "Jahrestagung . . . ," p.4.

5 The proceedings of an SDS-sponsored conference on modern capitalism, including speakers such as Abendroth, Behrisch, Gleissberg, Flechtheim, Eduard März, Hans-Heinz Holz, Ernest Mandel and Norman Birnbaum, survives as: *Neokapitalismus, Rüstungswirtschaft, Westeuropäische Arbeiterbewegung*, Frankfurt 1965.

6 As described by Manfried Liebel, "Zur politischen Konzeption des SDS in einigen Fragen" in: *Neue Kritik*, No. 25-26, October 1964, p.6.

7 Michael Vester, "Zur Dialektik von Reform und Revolution. Die Arbeitnehmer in der sozialistischen Strategie" in: *Neue Kritik*, No. 34/1966, p.20.

8 *Society and Democracy in Germany*, Garden City 1967, p.75; Cf; also Rainer Elsfeld, "Studentische Politisierung — eine Antwort auf die Hochschulkrise" in: *Zeitschrift für Politik*, No. 2/1969, p.171ff.

9 "Reichtum und Knappheit. Studienreform als Zerstörung gesellschaftlichen Reichtums" in: Bergmann, Dutschke, *et al.*, *Rebellion der Studenten oder die neue Opposition*, Reinbek 1968, p.99, italics in original.

10 Reprinted in 1965, in book form, as: Nitsch, Gerhard, Offe und Preuss, *Hochschule in der Demokratie*, Neuwied.

11 See the Executive Committee's draft of a new basic programme, reprinted in: "Materiellen zur SDS-Tagung 1965" in: *Studien von Zeitfragen*, No. 10/1965, p.9.

12 Events at the Berlin Free University are described in Uwe Bergmann's untitled essay in: Bergmann, Dutschke, *et al.*, *op.cit.*, p.7ff.

13 "Die Widersprüche des Spätkapitalismus, die antiautoritären Studenten und ihr Verhältnis zur Dritten Welt" in: *ibid.*, p.67.

14 From a pamphlet issued by various student groups at the Free University, entitled "Von der Freien zur Kritischen Universität", quoted after Dutschke *op.cit.*, p.70.

15 As reported in: *Beschlüsse und Stellungnahme des SHB*, Bonn 1966, p.18.

16 Elisabeth Noelle-Neumann, ed., *Jahrbuch der öffentlichen Meinung 1965-1967* Allensbach 1967, p.249.

4. The Grand Coalition

1 For a critical analysis of the *formierte Gesellschaft*, see Klönne, *op.cit.* p.38ff.

2 "Regierungserklärung (Das Programm der Grossen Koalition)" in: *Das Parlament*, No. 51-52/1966, p.1ff; see further Heinz Laufer, "Institutionelle Leistungen und Versuche. Zur Innenpolitik der Grossen Koalition" in: *Zeitschrift für Politik*, No. 4/1967, p.405ff.

3 SPD, ed., *Soll und Haben* (brochure) Bonn 1968, p.15.

4 In a speech. "Rede des Bundeswirtschaftsministers Schiller" in: *Bundesanzeiger*, 8 September 1967.

5 *Volkspartei im Klassenstaat oder das Dilemma der innerparteilichen Demokratie* Reinbek 1972, p.117.

6 "Offene Diskussion" in: *Frankfurter Rundschau*, 13 Nov. 1967.

7 Quoted in: Rolf Seeliger, ed., *SPD — Grosser Kompromiss ohne Ende?*, Munich 1972, p.16, italics in original.

8 Walter Möller, writing in *Der Sozialdemokrat* (1969), quoted in: *ibid.*, p.28.

11 As described in Seeliger, *op.cit.*, p.98ff.

12 On the subject of the SPD labour wing, see esp. mimeographed transcript of the television programme "Panorama" of 6 Nov. 1967 which brought together a series of SPD members, representing the party Left, Right and Centre, for a lively panel discussion.

13 *Ibid.*, p.2.

14 "Gewerkschaften manöverfähig machen," reprinted in: *Studien von Zeitfragen* No. 5-6/1965, p.16.

15 On this see SHB (PV), ed., *Informationen und Dokumente des SHB*, No. 2/1967.

16 See "SPD dreht ihrem Hochschulbund den Geldhahn ab" in: *Frankfurter Rundschau*, 4 March 1967; and "SPD denkt an Trennung vom SHB" in: *Frankfurter Rundschau*, 17 November 1967.

17 The relevant resolutions are reproduced in Seeliger, *op.cit.*, p.121ff.

18 Richard Kumpf, *Tendenzen der Formierung einer klässenmässigen Opposition in der Sozialdemokratie unter den Bedingungen der Grossen Koalition*, unpublished doctoral thesis, Humboldt University (E. Berlin) 1970, p.222 and 225.

20 The Manifesto is reproduced in part in Seeliger, *op.cit.*, p.113.

20 Hannover, *op.cit.*, p.98.

21 For an excellent analysis of the social and political factors contributing to the NPD's "successes" see Reinhard Kühnl, *Die NPD*, Berlin 1969.

22 Theo Pirker, *Die SPD nach Hitler*, Munich 1965, p.339.

23 "Das Ende des Parteienstaates" in: *Der Monat*, No. 160, Jan. 1968, p.70.

24 "Starke Strömung in der SPD für Ende der Grossen Koalition" in: *Der Tagesspiegel*, 22 February 1968.

X. Conclusions:
From Extra-party to
Extra-parliamentary Opposition

Prior to the establishment of the German Federal Republic in 1949, one cannot speak of a strictly socialist opposition in Germany. For virtually all political parties and movements originating in this period, as chapters II and III have demonstrated, espoused socialist goals. The Military Governments installed by the western occupying powers decreed in effect the restoration of a liberal capitalist system and, through firstly passive, then active interventions, prevented indigenous socialist tendencies from developing. The Left in these years may therefore be seen as the German political parties, and the Right as the western occupation powers.

In recapitulating the postwar development of the West German Left, one must reiterate the crucial importance of the years 1945-1949. The popular antifascist mood, the realization of the complicity of capitalism and fascism, the desire for social justice and the elimination of arbitrary class rule, and the almost total discrediting of the Right were all sufficient preconditions for a qualitative socio-economic transformation of German society.

The prevention of such an historical development was immensely facilitated by the East-West division and Germany's inevitable position as the "front line" of the Cold War. And without a divided country, the CDU State in the West and the SED State in the East also could not have been sustained. An intact Germany, in all probability, would have been Social Democratic. The Cold War was the precondition for the success of Adenauer's reactionary policies of the Western Alliance, NATO, economic integration (EEC), the socio-economic Restoration, neo-liberalism and clerical anticommunism. These policies, inflated by spectacular economic accomplishments, ensured the decline of the Left throughout the 1950's.

In this situation, the achievement of both socialism and democracy, or democracy through socialism, as Kurt Schumacher correctly perceived, depended upon the restoration of national unity and the withdrawal of all four occupation powers. But this policy of "with equal severity against communist dictatorship and capitalist reaction," when unmodified in the light of shifting power constellations, assumed a socialist opposition directed in equal measure against both opponents. The Cold War and the hardening of zonal frontiers, however, made the "capitalist reaction" by far the most formidable of the two antagonistic forces. Persisting in virulent anti-communism after 1946 indirectly strengthened the reaction, since anticommunist resentment, for a variety of reasons, largely benefitted the bourgeois coalition. Social Democracy's real "enemy" in the western partial state was the Right.

Here perhaps the SPD leaders overestimated the force and extent of the anticapitalist mood and underestimated the degree to which the occupation powers were prepared to intervene in political developments. Nevertheless, as the party most consistently advocating the achievement of democracy through socialism, the SPD became the party of the system-opposed Left until at least the early 'fifties.

The story of the socialist opposition from 1949-1967 is essentially an examination of the reasons for its lack of success. The continuing Cold War, the Economic Miracle and the effectiveness of clerical anticommunism combined to prevent the development of a West German communist party as well as any traditional political movement "to the left of the SPD." Hence the Left was essentially an intra-SPD force during the period covered by this work.

But, as we have been concerned to demonstrate, each stage in the progression of the SPD's opposition to the CDU State, from fundamental opposition to outright adaptation, corresponded with a qualitatively different form of socialist opposition. Serious extra-party opposition became objectively necessary — if a socialist opposition was to exist at all — following the Godesberg Programme and the SPD's renunciation of an independent foreign policy. By 1961, that is, the SPD completed the transformation from democratic socialism to liberal socialism. But only the actual conditions of the early and mid-'sixties created a subjective need — a larger mass basis — for a leftist opposition.

The formation of the Grand Coalition in December 1966 may be regarded as the cumulation of a series of socio-economic factors. The most salient of these were probably: (a) the end of economic boom and prosperity, with an attendant loss of the ruling political parties' central *raison d'être* and sense of purpose; (b) connected with this, a series of structural problems in many social and economic spheres, which made abundantly evident the absence of long-overdue reforms and the class nature of society. In particular the fields of education and higher education, social welfare measures, social planning and redistribution of the social product were affected; (c) a substantial shift in the front lines of the Cold War. Detente and relaxation of tensions, partly due to the erection of the "Wall," reduced the credibility of the spectre of a one-dimensional, threatening communist enemy, and hence called into question the central ideological support of the CDU State; (d) increasing tendencies by the upper social classes and their political parties in the bourgeois coalition to revert to authoritarian methods (emergency legislation, censorship, "criminalization" on nonconformist political groups) to enforce social discipline; and (e) a general sense of disillusion with politics and political parties regarded increasingly as monolithic, as part of an all-embracing "system" against which the individual was increasingly impotent and the object of powerful forces or groups.

And these factors in turn prompted a search for a new form of political opposition during the late 1960's. This search eventually became known as the Extra-parliamentary Opposition, or Apo.

Implicit in the notion of the Extra-parliamentary Opposition was that the goals of the manifold groups supporting it could not be realized through the existing political parties in the parliamentary system. Extra-parliamentary politics had of course been carried on for years by many groups whose interests were represented within the existing system. Powerful lobbies, in the CDU State, had consistently obtained large tax write-offs for investment capital, subsidies for agriculture and special concessions for industry by means of direct and largely "invisible" influence in ministerial bureaucracies and cabinet ministries. And extra-parliamentary opposition had been exerted by various single-purpose groups and organizations in the form of limited actions to call attention to specific proposals.

The post-Grand Coalition Extra-parliamentary Opposition, however, espoused goals which pointed beyond the existing system, of which all the established political parties were now an integral part. The SPD's entry into the Grand Coalition effectively ended any possibility of the parliamentary articulation and representation of the interests of such groups as those concerned with the prevention of emergency legislation, with the anti-nuclear arms campaign, university reform, political justice, renazification, women's rights and an outmoded foreign policy whose continued existence was a threat to peace.

Hence the Extra-parliamentary Opposition represented an attempt to overcome the "closed" political system of the Federal Republic, to demonstrate that the great *"Volksparteien"* did not represent the interests of "all the people." As essentially a movement of protest — against: emergency laws, blind anticommunism, anti-abortion legislation, Vietnam, armaments, lack of political alternatives, etc. — the Apo was by no means simply a reaction, as has often been claimed. For a positive commitment was implicit in the negation — for: constitutional freedoms, East-West deténte, women's rights, peace, political debate, liberal rights, etc.

These goals, if realized, would have revolutionized, if not transformed the CDU State. As such they were potentially system-opposed or system-transcending goals.

And, unlike most single-purpose movements, the Apo could not represent particular interests. Substantial university reform, for example, would have meant equally substantial changes in society, of which the university was an integral part. Or the abolition of armaments production would have brought with it profound changes in economic policy, and very likely in the ruling ideology as well. The realization of such *universal* goals obviously required a broad publicity to enlighten all groups and classes affected by them, namely all of society.

But it would be inaccurate to regard the Extra-parliamentary Opposition as a consistent system-opposed, or even class movement. Many of the groups sustaining it no doubt were, but the movement as such was basically a continuation of the type of radical-democratic organization such as had coalesced in the Fight Atomic Death Movement, the anti-emergency laws campaign or the Easter March, as an examination of the various groups supporting it clearly shows. At the same time, however, the Apo represented a qualitative step beyond past single-purpose movements, since its declared purpose was opposition to the entire political "system" of the Federal Republic.

Spontaneity was the really striking feature about the Apo's development. As though as on a signal — after the formation of the Grand Coalition — a large number of groups and movements came together in demonstrations, petitions, actions, etc. opposing selected aspects of political life. Though it would be futile to distinguish each of these individually, four occasionally overlapping main directions stand out as important:

(a) A pacifist-neutralist group consisting of persons, many of them former DFU members, who had supported the Easter March, ban-the-bomb movement and the various congresses and actions against re-armament and the Western Military Alliance.

(b) A radical-democratic group, including organized and unorganized humanists, semi-anarchist organizations and supporters of the anti-emergency laws campaign.

(c) A more of less tiaditional Marxist-socialist group, including supporters of the anti-Godesberg movement, members of the VUS, Socialist League and the circles around *Die Andere Zeitung*. These groups collectively might be termed the Old Left. In an attempt to bring together the disparate socialist groups within the Apo, the Old Left established a Socialist Centre (subsequently Socialist Opposition) as a kind of gathering or meeting-place of these groups, a Socialist Office to provide for information and coordination of socialist activities, and a periodical, *Information der sozialistischen Opposition*. All these efforts were largely unsuccessful, except when supported by the SDS, or as part of larger demonstrations or campaigns. The Old Left, with its by now traditional emphasis on bringing socialism into the large labour organizations, its primacy of theory and its use of outmoded means of articulation, was simply eclipsed by the New Left and its mass youth basis and practice of direct, spontaneous action. By 1969, even *Die Andere Zeitung*, once at the centre of socialist opposition, was forced to cease publication.[1]

(d) The New Left which developed from the student movement and the SDS after 1960. As the largest socialist organization — though divided increasingly into several factions — as the source for the real mass basis of the Extra-parliamentary Opposition (as even a cursory examination of the participants of virtually any Apo demonstration or action revealed), and as the theorist and innovator of socialism after the Grand Coalition, the New Left was by far the most important element in the new opposition. And within the New Left, the SDS was, in terms of organization, planning and initiative, undoubtedly the "practical avant-garde of the new anti-authoritarian and anti-capitalist movement."[2]

The New Left's main contributions to the socialist opposition were in the areas of organization, ideology and action.

Organizationally, the New Left emphasised spontaneity and decentralization, with a multiplicity of groups and movements operating at various levels and spheres. Such organizational forms were conceived as the opposite pole to the centralized, authoritarian and bureaucratic state. When Rudi Dutschke argued that any possible party would only reproduce the contradictions and confinements of existing political parties, he was in one sense advocating a form of blind "actionism"[3] which found limited resonance on the Left. Against this, Johannes Agnoli stressed the need for some form of organization in order to attain a "concrete emancipation" which would "attack and break the political structure of oppression." He continued: "Only an *organized* No can break through the bounds of bourgeois-parliamentary coordination (*Gleichschaltung*) and can enlarge the leadership conflict for ruling power."[4]

In a genuine revolutionary situation with a large mass basis, of course, an adequate organization would have been indispensable. But, even at its peak, the Extra-parliamentary Opposition, with all its supporting groups, probably never had the support of more than a few hundred thousand persons. This was not a revolutionary situation.

In times when a movement for revolutionary emancipation is carried on by a minority in isolation from the masses, any strategy of revolution can be no more than the strategy for the creation of a revolutionary situation. This involves enlightening the masses as to the injustices of the existing system of power and privilege, and transforming this awareness into a desire for revolutionary change. Emphasizing spontaneity, solidarity and direct action, in this situation, was more important than establishing an organization. Indeed, such a strategy coincided with the SDS' idea that not merely the goals aimed at, but the methods by which they were achieved — provocation, sit-ins, confrontation — were revolutionary and could revolutionize the revolutionary subject.[5]

Ideologically, secondly, the New Left introduced a great number of socialist and emancipatory theories into political life, including the application of findings from sociology, psychology, anthropology, literature and economics to the idea of a "total" revolution of all spheres of life. It further promoted theories of communal enterprise and participatory democracy.

And thirdly, the SDS developed revolutionary forms of action, including the sit-in and the notion of direct action as a consciousness-producing factor. In particular it evolved the idea of the strategic legitimation of the use of force, with praxis seen as its own justification. This amounted to a kind of revolutionary pragmatism.[6]

The subject of the Extra-parliamentary Opposition, the New Left, the many groups and goals they incorporated, the reasons for their successes and ultimate demise, and their permanent effects on political life in the Federal Republic must be examined in a separate volume. For purposes of this study, however, the Apo must be interpreted primarily as a response to (a) the SPD's evolution into a liberal socialist *Volkspartei* and (b) the party's further development into a "state party" and partner in a reactionary Grand Coalition. By 1968, the once intimate connection between the SPD and the socialist Left — the subject of this study — was virtually severed. An analysis of the socialist opposition in the subsequent period would be far more concerned with phenomena of the international youth movement, the revival of Marxism and neo-Marxism, the proliferation of single-purpose movements and civil disobedience groups, etc. than with the SPD.

REFERENCES

1 In a private interview with the author, Gerhard Gleissberg stated that *Die Andere Zeitung* was simply "overtaken" by current issues which included emphasis on moral, psychological and sexual liberation.

2 "22. ordentliche Delegiertenkonferenz des SDS" in: *Neue Kritik*, No. 44, November 1967, p.12.

3 For a critical refutation of this theory, see Frank Deppe, "Parlamentarismus — Parlamentarische Aktion — Sozialistische Politik" in: *Neue Kritik*, No. 44. November 1967, p.48ff.

4 *Transformation der Demokratie* (with Peter Brückner), Frankfurt 1968, p.74.

5 Here see Rolf Düspohl, *Das Verhältnis von Theorie und Praxis in der Revolutionären Opposition der Bundesrepublik*, unpublished doctoral thesis, Free University of Berlin, Faculty of Political Science, 1971, p.111.
6 *Ibid.*, p.113.

XI. EPILOGUE

by Ossip K. Flechtheim

Professor of Political Science
at the Free University of Berlin

William D. Graf's work is a successful analysis of the development of the German Left since 1945. This important monograph presents an original and well-founded contribution to the theory and practice of what, from 1945 to the present, has repeatedly been proclaimed the Third Way. It was and remains a question of the possibility of a genuine overcoming of the dualism between western capitalism and eastern communism, of a dialectical — in the best sense of this very ambiguous word — synthesis of democracy and autonomy, of liberalism, socialism and pacifism.

With this statement, we have already touched upon a problem which Dr. Graf rightly sees, but his solution to it differs somewhat from ours. The author starts from the assumption that liberalism and socialism are essentially contradictions, that liberalism is inseparably bound up with capitalism, and that a liberal socialism, such as that which the S.P.D. opted for at the latest by 1961, can at best effect an insignificant modification of capitalism, but cannot realise a breakthrough to socialism. For the implementation of socialism would require the temporary suspension of liberal rights, while in any form of liberalism the maintenance of capitalist private property is indispensable. In contrast to this view, we should like to enter the consideration that, in our opinion, the essence of liberalism is not the safeguarding of capitalist private property, but rather the preservation of the dignity of the individual by means of inalienable basic and human rights. In this sense liberalism is more comprehensive and older than the industrial capitalism of the 19th century. Thus Jefferson, unlike say Locke, intentionally spoke not of liberty and property, but of life, liberty and the pursuit of happiness. Numerous modern constitutions, which are based upon the rule of law and are in this sense liberal, provide not by chance for the expropriation of capitalist private property and the transition to new forms of ownership — to be sure (and here lies the crux of the synthesis of liberalism and socialism) subject to the maintenance of the individual's right to protection from arbitrary discrimination or even "liquidation." Admittedly, the Universal Declaration of Human Rights contains, in Article 17, a guarantee of private property. However, it does not establish the limits of private property; moreover, this guarantee expressly refers to the property of any person "alone or in community with others." The possibility of establishing collective socialist property of the most varied kinds is thus unambiguously postulated. In principle and in theory, this seems to us to preserve/abolish/raise to a higher level [*aufheben*] (in the Hegelian sense) a more modern and more humane liberalism within a genuine socialism.

Whether and how, in terms of practical politics, a humane and democratic movement might be able to overcome the capitalist principle in such a way as to avoid serious and relatively permanent infringements on the remaining more fundamental human rights (life, freedom, personal safety, and so on) is still the question, a question whose difficulties we would not wish to play down, and which we shall therefore consider more precisely and concretely later. The answer to this question, for Germany in particular, depends not least upon an evaluation of the character of the German Left, i.e., both the S.P.D. and K.P.D., as well as other left-wing tendencies and groupings.

Concerning the K.P.D., the author emphasises with reason its static-dogmatic nature. But is he aware of the entire fateful significance of the problem of the Bolshevisation and Stalinisation of the Communist International and the K.P.D.? The author speaks of a left-right continuum; so long as one thinks in this categorical system, the K.P.D. or C.P.S.U. appear to be decidedly left-wing parties — "located" further to the left than, say, the S.P.D. or other left-wing socialist movements.

It seems to us, on the other hand, that the evolution of communism after 1917 is less a straight line than a circle. Communism — the extreme Left — approximates the extreme Right and exhibits important similarities to it. The Bolshevisation, Leninisation and Stalinisation of communism began in the early 1920's and was perfected in Stalin's totalitarian terror system in the 1930s. It coincided with the strengthening of ideological-regressive and authoritarian-totalitarian features, and with the recession of the utopian-revolutionary-radical aspects — precisely as in the case of the K.P.D. in the Weimar Republic. Paul Sering, whom Dr Graf quotes, pointed out this contradiction in orthodox communism as early as 1946: "As an organisation of the revolutionary antifascist struggle, the communists are a component part of the labour movement, and indeed a militant and hence often extremely valuable part. As an organisation of training for contempt of democracy, belief in authority, using various demagogic means to effect the permanent goals of the Russian state, they are a foreign body in the labour movement, and indeed, in many critical situations, a destructive and lethal foreign body."

That is also one of the reasons why we, in opposition to a number of recent apologists, believe we must support the characterisation of both orthodox communism and fascism as totalitarian. Communism and fascism are like streams whose sources were very disparate, but which, during the period of Hitler and Stalin, increasingly converged. The climax of this development can be found in the purges of the 1930s, as well as in the conclusion of the German-Soviet Non-Agression Pact of 1939. Fascism, which itself originated as a counter-movement and reaction to communism, acquired a number of communistic points of view, as conversely Stalin incorporated a great deal from Hitler. Seen thus, those who have attempted to interpret fascism as "brown Bolshevism" or communism as "red fascism" were not entirely wrong, though of course the adjectives brown and red point to significant differences. With reason, therefore, one can also state that communism and fascism may be compared with one another in one single, but important aspect: they are both totalitarian.

Like fascism, communism represents what has been characterised as a secular or social religion. The moving toward religion or "clericalisation" of established communism, incidentally, has been outstandingly depicted by none other than Thomas Mann. More than a quarter-century ago, the same author who coined the adage, which has with some justification been frequently quoted, that communism is the greatest folly of our century, also defined communism in this way: "The holy terror, the new church, the faith which offers a new universal bond, which among all its other promises, promises liberation from freedom, has been found: Byzantine Russia, where there has never been a bourgeois democracy, and where despotism is an accustomed way of life, created it. Upon the foundation of a pan-economic global declaration and doctrine of salvation of limited validity, which is by no means eastern, but originates in the evolution of western industrialism, it has erected its orthodox church, ostensibly possessing the sole power of salvation, with its holy books, a sacrosanct robe of dogmas and all the trappings pertaining thereto."

Admittedly, there is one other component of communism, however much it may have been mutilated and perverted to the point of non-recognition. Even a Stalin was not able to destroy the last remnants of humanism. Only in this way can one explain the very modest destalinisation following the tyrant's death, and above all the Prague Spring. National Socialism, however, was never a fallen angel; it always embodied only evil *per se*, and signified a definitive break with the history of humanity.

Precisely in the period of late Stalinism, covered by the author, the counter revolutionary, reactionary and aggressively imperialist nature of established communism achieved its most drastic results, not least of all in East Europe and Germany. If what Dr Graf here calls clerical anticommunism could become so strong and successful, then there were several reasons for this. One factor, which should not be overlooked, may have been the fact that Stalin's communism all too soon acted and operated not only as the liberator from fascism, but as the basis of a new terroristic, totalitarian rule. So-called anticommunism was thus hardly less complex and contradictory than communism itself. Animosity toward the remnants of the October Revolution and the progressive elements in communism was one side — and opposition to Stalin's reactionary policies was the other side of the coin. Right into the S.P.D., surely in the case of Kurt Schumacher, and definitely in the case of left-wing socialists and heretical communists, the anticommunism described by Dr Graf was above all anti-Stalinism. It did not by any means preclude the struggle for a genuine humanist socialism or even a democratic communism (as is today undergoing a revival in Italy, Spain, and elsewhere). We still see, as before, an anticommunism, or better anti-Stalinism of this kind as legitimate and progressive; the socialist humanist cannot dispense with this critique for two reasons: in consideration of the reactionary and authoritarian elements in communism itself, and because of the impossibility of any criticism of the holders of power and their system in countries ruled by the communists. If the humanist or liberal socialist must never slip into a position which, as political or psychological war-preparation, could increase the danger of war, so too he must not capitulate to those in power, whether in the West or East, North or South. With complete independence, with objectivity and due consideration, he must criticise communists everywhere where, despite all left-wing phraseology, they carry on right-wing politics and infringe upon human rights.

This variant of anticommunism can even, sooner or later, benefit communists themselves. Advocating tolerance and lawfulness, human and basic rights may well make it more difficult for communists to seize power. But taking power and establishing a dictatorship can prove to be a Greek gift for precisely the best communists, just as conversely the maintenance of an even so inadequate and formal or bourgeois democracy also guarantees the communists a minimum safeguard against persecution and liquidation. Would not Slansky, Rajk and many others still be alive if Czechoslovakia and Hungary had not been communist? Ernst Fischer once declared that "a revolution in whose name torture is carried out will in the end itself be the victim of this torture." What would have been Ernst Fischer's fate if, after 1945, he had succeeded in bringing the communists to power in Austria?

To take a position such as this, of course, implies a maximal degree of flexibility and differentiation on the part of the opponent of established communism. And this, as Dr Graf very well demonstrates, was sometimes absent in Kurt Schumacher. However, if communism to us must never be a red cloth, to be charged in blind rage like a bull, then too no one ought to expect us always and everywhere to see in it an immaculate red flag before which we must always bow.

In view of our critical attitude toward Stalinist, as well as Leninist, communism, the reader will not be surprised to learn that we must evaluate the role of the Soviet Union (the citadel and fortress of Stalinism in the 'forties) less positively than does Dr Graf. Anyone who, like us, has himself spent the years 1945 and after in the U.S.A. and West Berlin, knows how unambiguous the policies of both the Soviet Union and the western powers then were. Neither of the two sides can simply be classified as reactionary, aggressive or imperialist, nor by the same token as progressive, defensive, pacifist. It would be too simplistic to interpret Stalin's policies as, say only a reaction to the aggressive imperialism of the western powers, and to attribute to the latter sole responsibility for beginning the Cold War. The relationship between East and West after 1945 was more one of action and reaction, here and there: truly a dialectical and tragic interplay of error and confusion.

If totalitarian terror had eased in the Soviet Union during the war, it was rapidly re-kindled after war's end, in the Soviet Union as in the countries it occupied. Let us not forget that, together with the Red Army, the G.P.U. always entered into the occupied country and immediately began to "purge" it. This was particularly so in Germany, where the Soviet Union even maintained the same concentration camps (Sachsenhausen, Buchenwald, etc.) as the National Socialists. To this extent Stalin violated his agreements with the western powers immediately after the conclusion of the war. The western powers, of course, had never given the Soviet Union a free hand in the sense that the latter was permitted to establish authoritarian communist regimes in eastern Europe. Governments friendly toward the Soviet Union had been envisioned which, however, would uphold the rules of democracy, which naturally meant democracy as understood in the West, not by Stalin. Stalin's violation of this rule contributed to the re-awakening of a distrust toward him which had receded during the war, not only in the U.S.A. but also in Labour England and within the Left. This does not change the fact that the Soviet

Union, in these years, surely did not desire a new war; but neither did the
U.S.A., who immediately began to disarm, nor Labour England, nor De
Gaulle's France. What all these powers aimed at was the securing of as broad
a forefield as possible for the "defence" of their power. The conquest of this
forefield between 1945 and 1953, however, where the Soviet Union was
concerned, was achieved under Stalin with thoroughly Stalinist methods.

Since the sudden change-over by the Social Democratic majority to the
"defence of the fatherland" in 1914, and since the persecution by the ruling
Bolsheviki of social democrats, social revolutionaries, and others, which began
all too quickly after the October Revolution, there has existed a bitter
Bruderkampf between the two workers' parties which reached its climax in
Germany. Even during the era of the United Front and Popular Front of the
1930s, mistrust did not disappear, especially since this policy coincided with
the establishment of an increasingly closed and totalitarian party of a new
type. Distrust found new reinforcement in the period of the German-
Soviet Pact from 1939 to 1941, and again all too soon after 1945.

One of the last opportunities for the unity desired by many communists and
social democrats in the concentration camps of the Third Reich was destroyed
by the 1946 fusing of the S.P.D. and K.P.D. The author's description of these
epochal events is quite terse. Although, as he emphasises, many Social
Democrats in the East Zone surely were in favour of the unified party, there
was also a strong opposition — above all against the manner in which the
Social Democratic Party leadership was forced into the union. There is
unambiguous evidence demonstrating the massive pressure which the
occupying power brought to bear on contrary Social Democrats. The extent of
terror and deception, in any event, was a factor which for the first time led to
a situation in which, in all centres of the labour movement, as in Leipzig, the
socialists did not gain a majority in the elections, and many old-time Social
Democrat voters now even voted for the L.P.D. rather than S.E.D.

The impression of the forced unification upon Schumacher and the bulk of
the socialists in the western zones was unequivocal: it was now proved to
them, once and for all, that the communists' new democratic line was only a
sham, and would be abandoned in favour of Stalinist monopoly rule wherever
and whenever the communists achieved power. Perhaps the founding of the
S.E.D. guaranteed the triumph of Stalinism in the Soviet Zone; but now the
division of the German labour movement into a communist wing in the East
Zone and a Social Democratic wing in the West Zones was a virtual certainty.
And also from now on there was a particularly heavy obstacle in the way of
prospects for maintaining or restoring German unity. With the now rapidly
progressing polarisation of the wings of the labour movement, the two parts of
Germany, the western and eastern powers, prospects for a Third Way of
course became increasingly remote. In the East, instead of socialist
democracy, there developed a Stalinised "People's Democracy"; at the same
time the traditional bourgeois-capitalist forces grew stronger in the western
zones. In the collision zone between eastern "anti-imperialism" and western
"anti-Bolshevism" the scope for a democratic (and for a genuinely Christian)
socialism grew smaller. A unique opportunity thus seemed lost; it was perhaps
only a question of time until the S.P.D. would opt for the western democratic
capitalist road.

This development the author analyses minutely. Let us here append only this: perhaps this development was not quite as straightforward as it might appear at first glance. In the 'fifties it seemed initially that the party would orientate itself according to new forward-looking methods and findings of critical modern science. Beyond Marx, but not behind him, a third way presented itself between adhering to an empty vulgar Marxism and the acceptance of mundane neo-liberal dogmas. In 1956 the S.P.D.'s Munich convention seriously came to grips with the new problems of the "second industrial revolution," automation and the atomic age. The Programme Commission convened by the Party Executive Committee submitted a number of significant analyses which admittedly then largely remained submerged; even the draft of a basic programme submitted to the 1958 Stuttgart convention only reflected inadequately its plethora of investigations and ideas. Nevertheless, the last section, entitled "The Only Way," represented a last attempt to delimit the labour movement on two sides: not only against the revolutionary skipping of stages, as was attempted in Russia with disastrous results, but also against the policy of merely improving the situation of the worker and of adapting to existing conditions. This version was already omitted in the final draft of the 1959 Godesberg Programme — which also failed to mention the class struggle or Karl Marx. In the basic question of the structuring of the economic system, therefore, the differences between the S.P.D. and the bourgeois parties paled into a question of degree. More prominent were still the differences in the spheres of social and fiscal policy.

All these greater or lesser differences, however, receded increasingly behind the more fundamental contradictions in the complex of reunification, which also governed defence policy and foreign policy. Here the parties clashed with particular vehemence, for it was ultimately a question of the existence of the Federal Republic today and tomorrow. Purposefully and undeviatingly, the CDU/CSU pursued its policy of increasingly greater integration of the Federal Republic into the western European-North Atlantic systems (N.A.T.O., E.C.M., and the rest). The maximal strengthening of the Federal Republic, attainable only in this way, could later compel the Soviet Union to surrender the "Soviet Zone" and to accept reunification in freedom and peace. On the other hand, the S.P.D.'s reservations grew against this policy of definitively consolidating and subordinating West Germany within the western system, since this would never overcome national division, but only cement it. The F.D.P. too, who initially had backed Adenauer's foreign and defence policies, grew more sceptical. Following its departure from the coalition in 1956, its arguments were closer to those of the S.P.D. Since the Federal Republic was now strengthened and had realised its equal status vis-à-vis the West, it was now time to achieve reunification in negotiations with the Soviet Union, at the cost of arms limitations, tension-free zones, disengagement, special status for a reunified Germany, and so on. This phase of the controversy reached its dramatic climax in 1958 in the great Bundestag debates over atomic arms and reunification; its conclusion was the S.P.D.'s *Deutschlandplan* of 1959, which was submitted perhaps five, if not ten years too late.

As already mentioned, Dr Graf suggests that the transition to socialism presupposes the suspension of certain liberal rights. This means, no doubt, that he regards as limited the possibility of a transformation of the capitalist system by means of system-changing reforms. Indeed, the question of reform or revolution has moved socialists ever since the controversy between Bernstein and Rosa Luxemburg, and it has split the socialist movement into reformers and revolutionaries, moderates and radicals, into a Right, a Left, and so-called centrists who repeatedly try dialectically to remove this contradiction. Decades of experience, at first glance, seem to make it evident that "reformist" politics has never and nowhere overcome capitalism and realised socialism, while conversely "revolutionary" politics, though it has overthrown the old private capitalist system, has never replaced it with a democratic-humanist socialism, but instead has established an order whose substance has been described by such concepts as state capitalism, bureaucratic étatism or even neo-Caesarist technocracy. On closer consideration, of course, one sees that, in a country such as Sweden, for example, reformist policies have already "socialised" capitalism to a not inconsiderable degree, while in Yugoslavia or in particular in Czechoslovakia in 1968, the established system was to a large extent democratised and liberalised, which is to say genuinely socialised. Largely forgotten, however, is the fact that, between 1945-1948, Czechoslovakia, on the reformist road, came very close to the goal of a socialist democracy. We refer here to R. Künstlinger's illuminating study, *Parteidiktatur oder demokratischer Sozialismus: der tschechoslowakische Weg nach 1945*. Perhaps these examples will allow us to conclude that the question of the transition from capitalism to socialism cannot be answered abstractly and globally, but rather more historically and specifically according to the country concerned or respective region.

And this brings us back to Germany and the Federal Republic. With reference to the latter, Peter von Oertzen believes today that the S.P.D. here will be able to effect the transition to socialism by means of reforms, not overnight but likely in the course of the next few decades. With its Godesberg Programme, he says, the S.P.D. has opted to be a democratic socialist reform party. Admittedly, this programme means by democratic socialism not consistent Marxian socialism "which is characterised by its socialisation of all the means of production, a democratic planned economy and workers' self-administration, and whose goal is the non-governed classless society." By contrast, the S.P.D.'s basic programme strove "by reconciling planning and competition, by public control of economic power (if necessary with the aid of socialisation), by employee codetermination, and by systematic social and education policies, to achieve a many-sided, liberal social democracy." This goal alone could be realised in the coming years; only thereafter, say after 1985, a date also envisioned by the S.P.D.'s *Orientierungsrahmen* [General Guidelines], can one begin to talk about a full socialism.

The question remains, however, as to whether a large *Volkspartei*, such as the S.P.D., is able to carry out such a difficult task. One of the major factors against it is the strength of the conservative forces which Dr Graf describes. The sheer force of their number would induce any party to adapt to the average, to the so-called objective requirements of power and "responsibility." In particular, this applies to any party which forms the government, or even which is in a governing coalition. After all, any governmental soup is boiled with much water, regardless of whose stove it is on. And the larger the party is, the more difficult will it be for it to avoid placing patronage before its programme, tactics before strategy. Hence, short-term particular interests prevail again and again, and this gives rise over and over to a vacuum of global policies and long-term planning. The politicians' selfish interest in the organisation, the machine, the "operation" works rather more to the advantage of the preservation of "privatist" modes of behaviour and rigid structures than to the realisation of global and dynamic concepts of the future. However democratic or socialist a party may make itself out to be, its typical day-to-day politics are conditioned by the past; indeed what not coincidentally in the U.S.A. is rather more deprecatingly called "politics", that is, personality politics and patronage, narrow-mindedness and duplicity, yes even horse-trading and corruption; and this will not disappear overnight.

All this must be taken all the more seriously, since those in the Social Democratic Party who would like to go further, mostly do not dare openly to concede the existence of such forces and tendencies. Similarly, the right wing or even the centre of the S.P.D. do not dare openly to bare the difficulties which must confront any policy which affects the direct and special interests of significant capitalist groups. Though there is much talk of the objective problems involved in investment control, the fact is largely ignored that this is not merely an objective question, and that any form of investment control, even if it were established by factual circumstances, would meet with decisive resistance by capitalist interests. And indeed, beyond this, it must not be glossed over that in our society, as it is now structured, these ideas of the leading classes are more or less shared by the so-called underprivileged; at the very least the latter will not develop or accept counter-concepts spontaneously and automatically.

It is, however, not only a question of the reforming power and socialist potential of the S.P.D.; it is also a question of how capable of reform capitalism is. Can it be reformed at all? And are these reforms, which may have to be forced, steps and stages in the transformation into socialism, or do they ultimately serve only to prolong capitalism's life-span? Now since the 19th century capitalism has demonstrated its unforeseen absorptive capacity; no reform has caused its demise; on the contrary, it has strengthened and rejuvenated itself by draining these reforms. It has become more social, but at the cost of new dependencies and conflicts. It has largely overcome its acute crises, but a latent crisis still appears inevitable. Even where capitalism has become more social, certain regressive and repressive features remain, or are even stronger. Investments are still made according to the profit motive. When profits are too threatened, the spectres of recession and unemployment appear on the horizon. Downward pressure on wages, despite the trade unions' countervailing force, has by no means disappeared; wage rises are increasingly threatened by inflation, precisely in periods of prosperity and full employment. Marginal groups such as old-age pensioners, invalids or immigrant workers are still largely forgotten. Private wealth is increasing immensely, but public poverty, despite all taxation measures, remains. Old privileges, such as the right of inheritance or property monopoly, have not been challenged or are being increasingly restored. The control of markets by the monopolies, oligopolies or multi-national corporations facilitates a neo-feudal concentration and tribute raising. Reforms such as those made by the British Labour Government come to nothing, or are undermined. Though social democracy might gain some ground here and there, it is still threatened by an increasingly powerful plutocracy and bureaucracy.

Which reform strategy, then, is at all possible and necessary? In recent years, the Young Socialists have spoken a great deal about a "double strategy"; they seek, as members of the S.P.D., to achieve positions within this party, while simultaneously to win over the masses outside the party for their socialist aims. Peter von Oertzen formulates it similarly: "The realisation of democratic socialism, i.e., a comprehensive democratisation of society, cannot be accomplished by the party alone; it requires a broad movement rooted in society as a whole. A socialist policy confined to parliament, government and administration would become lodged in the existing power structure and would not really change society. Democratic socialist politics thus requires a double 'strategy', i.e., work inside and outside the state machinery (in society, at the 'basis')."

Similarly, Fritz Vilmar speaks of a "comprehensive, multi-frontal reform strategy." We ourselves have proposed a "circumventing strategy" which would initially concentrate on the so-called superstructure. In any event, sectors among youth, the intelligentsia, and other groups, have here and there been successful in "re-functioning" schools and colleges, theatres and publishing houses, indeed churches and hospitals. Can this process not be carried on further? Cannot, say, liberation in the "marginal spheres" (such as the family, education, leisure or judiciary) help to create a new human type, who would more or less consciously oppose exploitation and oppression in politics and the economy? The core institutions in the economy and politics which represent the rulers' power centres would admittedly be left out initially, but at the same time would be isolated and eventually made vulnerable. Of course this strategy would no doubt have good chances of success if the actions of the Social Democratic Party were co-ordinated, prudently and over the long term, with those of the masses at the grass roots, as well as with those of other forces, such as single purpose movements, interest groups and other progressive forces in the parties and parliaments.

In all this, the use of force, particularly against persons, should be very consciously avoided. Peter von Oertzen emphasises that the scope of existing laws is great enough to allow for peaceful and legal demonstrations, enlightening campaigns and citizens' initiatives, which are legitimate and indispensible means of politicising and mobilising people. "Direct actions which touch upon the limits of the effective legal order, or even infringe upon them, can be humanly, socially and politically understandable, especially if they express vital and simultaneously unfulfilled human needs, or if they are used demonstratively to call attention to serious adverse social conditions. It also cannot and should not be denied that, in the history of social and political reform movements up to the present, violation of the effective legal order, under certain circumstances, has helped to pave the way for necessary reforms. Nonetheless, illegal actions cannot be the legitimate substance of the S.P.D.'s policies, sub-organisations or working groups. It also cannot and must not be demanded of Social Democratic office holders that they ignore or abuse the law in force."

On the other hand, one might consider whether precisely a limited breaking of the rules, civil disobedience and mass non-violent resistance, indeed, in exceptional cases, a well-considered use of violence against objects, for which the actors would assume full responsibility, does not present a solution to the dilemma: bloody revolution or timid patchwork. Gandhi and Luthuli, Martin Luther King and Danilo Dolci have shown that non-violent mass actions can be thoroughly successful. Martin Luther King even went so far as to characterise non-violent action as a kind of Third Way: "The supporter of non-violent resistance is in agreement with the person who surrenders to his fate in that one should not attack his foe violently. But conversely, he agrees with the person who advocates violence in that one must resist evil. He avoids the former's lack of resistance and the latter's violent resistance."

Let us then assume that in the Federal Republic system-changing reforms, non-violent mass actions, double strategy, and other methods were to meet with success. They would lead not only to a democratisation in the so-called superstructure, but also to democratisation and socialisation in politics and the economy. Then no doubt a further question would immediately arise: how far could the Federal Republic progress alone on the road to democratisation and socialisation? Has the international capital nexus already grown so strong that the individual state's struggle against multi-national concerns and other giant capital conglomerations is ineffectual? Has the Federal Republic already been so far integrated into the European Community, N.A.T.O., and other organisations that the question of capitalism or socialism can only be decided within this broader framework? Would the Europe of the large concerns prove to be stronger than the Federal Republic, however progressive it might be? And what about West Germany's dependence upon a world market still primarily determined by capitalism?

In any case, there seems to be much in favour of seeing the answer to these questions as being not purely economic, but always political as well. And in the political balance of forces, the ideological, organisational, psychological and, not least of all, military elements also count substantially. Today more than ever, domestic and foreign policy, "defence" of the state and of the status quo, are intimately interconnected. We cannot overlook the fact that even Eisenhower warned of the "military-industrial complex." In the United States, one rightly speaks of the welfare and warfare state. Hence the growing number of plans have a Janus head: to the extent that the tone is set by profit-orientated private enterprise, state planning will repeatedly be tempted to orient itself primarily according to the interest of profit and to the needs of the privileged and the powerful, and the military state itself, whereas planning for full employment, mass consumption, and social infrastructure will often take a back seat. Militarisation represents not only a great risk to the maintenance of peace, it also places a heavy burden on all attempts at democratisation. Less than ever before, in the age of mass weapons of destruction, is an army in a position to operate really democratically and humanely.

Surely it would be illusory to expect a total disarmament or a radical re-adjustment from military to non-violent civil defence in the next few years. Under the aegis of *détente*, however, there must be a start to the dismantling of arms, even if this inevitably means an initially limited military weakening of the one side. In a highly armed world, a total power vacuum could well entail serious perils. But the risk of an armaments reduction should be largely offset by rationally calculated moral, political and economic advantages, especially since Europe of course cannot be "defended" in a serious "emergency." Shall we not sooner or later see this, and perhaps turn to the neutrality and disengagement conceptions of the 1950s, such as the Rapacki Plan and *Deutschlandplan*? According to W. Möller and F. Vilmar (in *A*

Socialist Peace Policy for Europe), this would mean for Europe a "freeing of western European and particularly West German defence policy from the (long obsolete) tutelage of the U.S.A. and its armaments interests. This task must be approached from two sides: through reciprocal arms reductions in Europe within the framework of the European Security Conference, and through a new sovereign definition of the defence mandate of the Bundeswehr within N.A.T.O."

Thus the question of a Third Way beyond capitalism and communism applies not only to Germany but to western Europe. Let us quote once more from Möller's and Vilmar's book: "No one but a confidently European labour movement can help West Europe achieve a reasonable place between East Europe and the U.S.A., a geo-political, peace-stabilising position and self-determination . . . Only in a climate of long-lasting peace and guaranteed *détente* will the voting masses be prepared to affirm the necessary social policy "experiments", to turn to domestic conflicts, and to solve them through radical social reform. In short: peace and socialism are interdependent; everywhere, but here in particular, they are the two sides of the same coin."

The challenges of the next years and decades have a truly global scope. Therefore they demand the collaboration of all progressive forces far beyond the frontiers of any one state, and possibly any one continent. In this way the fusion of socialist and democratic organisations and parties will become a positive key to a long-term global strategy. Admittedly, one cannot put together from nothing a new International to plan the strategy for the transition to socialist democracy. Nonetheless, we should keep on demanding and promoting the further development of parties delimited by the national state in the direction of continental and global parties. Party federations of this kind will likely be able to survive once we are well on the way toward "world domestic politics", which for its own part would be an important instrument for the dismantling of world-threatening state sovereignties and power blocs.

Here the question of closer European ties cannot be averted. In 1971, the Dutch *Partij van de Arbeid*, at its party convention, went so far as to demand the formation of a progressive European party which was to be constituted of more than only social democratic forces. Unfortunately, the reaction of the parties concerned, including the S.P.D., was predominantly negative. Only the Schleswig-Holstein Social Democrats, at their state convention in November 1973, resolved "to strive for the formation of European parties." It is perhaps also no coincidence that a Dutchman like Sicco Mansholt has again come out in favour of strengthening the "League of Social Democratic Parties of the E.C.M." He is concerned about the tendencies of capitalist development in western Europe and the socialists' lack of influence: "Europe is a Europe of business, which socialists desire to change very much." Similarly, Wilhelm Dröscher hopes that the social democratic parties, "as the strongest pro-gressive political force in this community" will play "a great and significant, a transnational and conciliating rôle."

Indeed, a western European federal state under decisive socialist leader-ship, prepared to take disarmament seriously, would already be a significant step forward on the road toward a democratic socialist world federation. A union of this kind naturally must never become a brake on the already overdue unification of the world. It would therefore be very much a matter of how much a European federation would behave toward the Third World. Ultimately, one can also hope that one day this development in western Europe, with its weakening of private capitalism here, might contribute to the breaking up of state capitalism or state bureaucracies in the East.

A party such as the S.P.D. can never tackle this task alone. Not only is it forced to rely on the cooperation of progressive forces in other parties, but at least as important would be its ties with extra-party groups and personalities. One thinks here of various ecclesiastical movements of opposition and renewal, as well as youth and student organisations or certain cultural organisations and not least of all the trade unions. No less significant would be a re-orientation toward those communist parties and trade unions in western and southern Europe attempting to free themselves from the totalitarian burden of their past. Many of these parties, like those in Italy or Spain, are also searching for a new way beyond western capitalism, eastern Stalinism and world-wide conservatism.

One final consideration. The S.P.D. until now has been too little aware that the most disparate disciplines have begun systematically to analyse problems of cleaning up the environment, development policies and safeguards of peace. Future research and planning, including environmental and developmental research, can also aid parties wanting to go beyond the status quo to understand the opportunities and hazards of the future. Is it not time for a party like the S.P.D. to promote more intensively than hitherto efforts outside its own ranks aimed at this problem? A global and futurological dimension which thus entered into party policy, and which of course is all too weakly hinted at in the S.P.D.'s Long-term Programme, could ultimately build bridges to all progress-minded forces among the young intelligentsia and scientists. If Marx, in the first half of last century, envisaged the emancipation of man from his connection with philosophy, and philosophy as the head of this emancipation, the proletariat as its heart, then perhaps in the last quarter of this century a new alliance between labour and science will be able to preserve mankind from the very worst catastrophes.

Translated by W. D. Graf

Selected Bibliography

A. PRIVATE INTERVIEWS

1. Professor Wolfgang Abendroth, 5 January 1972 in Marburg
2. Herr Arno Behrisch, 26 February 1973 in Cologne
3. Herr Peter Blachstein, 7 February 1973 in Hamburg
4. Professor Ossip K. Flechtheim, 30 and 23 January 1973 in Berlin
5. Dr. Gerhard Gleissberg, 5 February 1973 in Hamburg
6. Frau Lisa Huhn, 2 February 1973 in Berlin
7. Herr Fritz Lamm, 28 February 1973 in Stuttgart
8. Professor Peter von Oertzen, 2 December 1971 in Hanover
9. Herr Nikolaus Ryschkowsky, 22 February 1973 in Wächtersbach nr. Frankfurt
10. Herr Reinhold Walz, 7 March 1973 in Berlin

B. ARTICLES, PAMPHLETS, ETC.

Note : Due to the relatively large scope of this book, not all the articles and pamphlets used can be listed here; this compilation includes only the most salient works, or items used but not contained in the footnotes.

1. Abendroth, Wolfgang, "Die akklamierte Stagnation. Die Parlamentswahlen in der Bundesrepublik" in: *Internationale Politik* (Belgrade), Vol. 16 (1965), No. 374, p.13ff
2. ———, "Analyse des sozialdemokratischen Wahlkampfes" in *Frankfurter Hefte*, No. 11/1961, p. 723ff
3. ———, "Entkrampfung oder Entspannung? Illusion der 'Alleinvertretung' oder Annährung der deutschen Staaten." in: Leonard Froese, ed., *Was soll aus Deutschland werden*? Munich, Wilhelm Goldmann Verlag 1968
4. ———, "Das KPD-Verbotsurteil des Bundesverfassungsgerichts. Ein Beitrag zum Problem der richterlichen Interpretation von Rechtsgrundsätzen der Verfassung im demokratischen Staat" in: *Zeitschrift für Politik*, vol. 3 (1956), p. 305ff
5. ———, "Soziale Sicherheit in Westeuropa nach dem zweiten Weltkrieg" in: *Festschrift zum 80. Geburtstag von Georg Lukacs*, Frank Benseler, ed., Neuwied & W. Berlin, Luchterhand, 1965, p. 151ff
6. ———, "Über die Notwendigkeit sozialistischer Opposition. Rede anlässlich der Arbeitskonferenz der Sozialistischen Opposition am 17.6.1967 in Frankfurt" in: *Information der Sozialistischen Opposition*, No. 1 (Aug.) 1967
7. ———, "Zu den Problemen des Sozialistischen Zentrums und sozialistischer Strategie in der BRD" in: *Information der sozialistischen Opposition*, Extra No. 3/1967
8. Ackermann, Anton, "Gibt es einen besonderen deutschen Weg zum Sozialismus?" in: *Einheit. Monatschrift zur Vorbereitung der Sozialistischen Einheitspartei*, No. 1 (Feb.) 1946
9. ADF (Aktion Demokratischer Fortschritt), "ADF zum Fall Kiesinger" (leaflet) Bonn, n.d. (ca. 1968)
10. Adorno, Theodor, "Sociology and Psychology" in: *New Left Review*, No. 46-47, 1969
11. Agartz, Viktor, "Die Bedeutung der Angestellten und geistig Schaffenden in Wirtschaft und Staat" speech at the first convention of the DAG held 25-27 April (leaflet), n.p., n.d.

12. ———, "Entwicklung und Struktur der europäischen Gewerkschaften" in: A.Pass and R. Darius, eds., *Europa, Erbe und Auftrag*, Cologne, Universitätsverlag, 1951, p. 180ff
13. ———, "Expansive Lohnpolitik" in: *Mitteilungen des Wirtschaftswissenschaftliches Institut der Gewerkschaften (WWI-Mitteilungen)*, No. 12/1953, p. 245
14. ———, "Zur Situation der Gewerkschaften im liberal-kapitalistischen Staat" in: *Gewerkschaftliche Monatshefte*, No. 3/1952, p.220ff
15. Agnoli, G., "Le regime parlamentaire en Allemagne de l'Ouest" in: *Revue Internationale du Socialisme*, No. 15/1966, p. 287ff
16. Agnoli, Johannes, "Thesen zur Transformation der Demokratie und zur ausserparlamentarischen Opposition" in: *Neue Kritik*, No. 47, 1968, p. 33ff
17. Ahlberg, Rene, "Der Neomarxismus" in: *Osteuropa*, No. 20, May 1970, p.301
18. ———, "Die politische Konzeption des SDS" in: *Aus Politik und Zeitgeschichte* supplement to *Das Parlament*, No. 20/15 May 1968
19. "Aktionsgemeinschaft SPD/KPD München 1945" in: *Kürbiskern*, June 1970, p. 430ff
20. Allemann, Fritz Rene, "Das deutsche Parteiensystem" in: *Der Monat*, January 1953, p. 365ff
21. Almond, Gabriel A. and Wolfgang Kraus, "The Social Composition of the German Resistance" in: G. Almond, ed., *The Struggle for Democracy in Germany*, Chapel Hill, University of North Carolina Press, 1949
22. Altmann, Rüdiger, "Die formierte Gesellschaft beschwört keinen Mythos. Der überentwickelte Pluralismus — Interpretation einer Formel" in: *Handelsblatt*, No. 122, 30 June 1966, p. 2ff
23. Arendt, Hannah, "Aftermath of Nazi Rule. Report from Germany" in: *Commentary*. No. 10/1950, p. 342ff
24. "Ausserparlamentarische Opposition durch die Parteien provoziert?" in: *Der Gemeinsame Weg. Informationen des Ringes politischer Jugend* (Stuttgart) 12 December 1967
25. Bahrdt, Hans Paul, "Marxistisches Denken in der deutschen Arbeiterschaft" in: *Die Neue Gesellschaft*, No.6/1956, p. 403ff
26. Baier, H. "Soziologie und Geschichte. Überlegungen zur Kontroverse zwischen dialektischer und neupositivistischen Soziologie" in: *Archiv für Rechts- und Sozialphilosophie*, 1966, vol. III/I
27. Barnes, Samuel *et al.*, "The German Party System and the 1961 Federal Elections" in: *APSR*, vol. 56 (1962), p. 899ff
28. Bergmann, Joachim E., "Konsensus und Konflikt. Zum Verhältnis von Demokratie und industrieller Gesellschaft" in: *Das Argument*, No. 1/1967, p. 42ff
29. Besson, Waldemar, "Regierung und Opposition in der deutschen Politik" in: *Politische Vierteljahresschrift*, No. 3/1962, p. 225ff
30. Beyme, Klaus von, "Parlamentarismus und Rätesystem — eine Scheinalternative" in: *Zeitschrift für Politik*, No. 17 (April) 1970, p. 27ff
31. Borosnjak, Alexander, "Der Kampf um Artikel 41 der Verfassung Hessens in den Jahren 1946/47" in: *Beiträge zur Geschichte der deutschen Arbeiterbewegung*, E. Berlin, Dietz, 1962, vol. 3, p. 711ff
32. Böttcher, Karl W., "Die neuen Reichen und die Neureichen in Deutschland" in: *Frankfurter Hefte*, No. 6/1951, p. 331ff
33. Brandt, Willy, "Eigentum verpflichtet" in: *Die Neue Gesellschaft*, No. 18 (May) 1971, p. 301ff
34. ———, "Vordringliche Aufgaben sozialdemokratischer Politik" in: *Die Neue Gesellschaft*, No. 3/1956, p. 194ff
35. Breitling, R., "Das Geld in der deutschen Parteipolitik" in: *Politische Vierteljahresschrift*, No. 4/1961
36. Broecker, Bruno, "Wirtschaftliche Mitbestimmung der Betriebsräte? Eine Frage aus dem Bereich der Wirtschaftsdemokratie" in: *Die Neue Gesellschaft*, No. 2/1948, p. 34ff
37. Bunn, Ronald F., "The Federation of German Employers' Associations. A Political Interest Group" in: *Western Political Quarterly*, vol. XIII, September 1960, p. 652ff

38. ———, "The Spiegel Affair" in: R. Bunn and S. Andres, eds., *Politics and Civil Liberties in Europe. Four Case Studies*, Princeton, van Nostrand, 1967
39. Childs, David, "The SPD at Dortmund, Ulbricht sets the Pace" in: *World Today*, vol. 22, July 1966, p. 285ff
40. ———, "The New Germanies: Restoration, Revolution, Reconstruction" in: *Encounter* XXII (1964), p. 50ff
41. ———, "Conflict and Liberty. Some Remarks on the Social Structure of German Politics," in: *British Journal of Sociology*, No. 14/1963, p. 197ff
42. ———, "Wie ist Freiheit in der modernen Welt möglich?" in: *Junge Generation und Macht*, Hanover 1960, p. 33ff
43. Deist, Heinrich, "Wirtschaftsdemokratie" in: *Die Neue Gesellschaft*, No. 2 (Mar.-Apr.) 1957
44. ———, "Die demokratische Aktion gegen Neonazismus und Restauration" in: *gestern und heute*, No. 34 (1968), whole issue
45. Deutscher, Isaac, "Germany and Marxism" in: *New Left Review*, No. 47 (Jan.-Feb.) 1968, p. 61ff
46. Dirks, Walter, "Das Abendland und der Sozialismus" in: *Frankfurter Hefte*, No. 3 (June) 1946, p. 67ff
47. ———, "Sozialisten ausserhalb der Parteien" in: *Das Sozialistische Jahrhundert* II (1949), p. 5ff
48. ———, "Rechts und Links" in: *Frankfurter Hefte*, No. 6 (Sept.) 1946, p. 24ff
49. ———, "Das Wort Sozialismus" in: *Frankfurter Hefte*, No. 9/1946-47, p. 628ff
50. Dulles, Allen W., "Alternatives for Germany" in: *Foreign Affairs*, No. 6/1947, p. 421ff
51. Dutschke, Rudi, "Brief für die Herren der anderen Seite" in: *Der Spiegel*, No. 50/1968, p. 185f
52. ———, "Liberalisierung oder Demokratisierung. Ein Interview" in: *konkret*, No. 5/1968, p. 19ff
53. Eberlin, Klaus, "Die Wahlentscheidung vom 17. September 1961. Ihre Ursachen und Wirkung" in: *Zeitschrift für Politik*, vol 9, 1962, p. 255ff
54. Edinger, Lewis J., "Kurt Schumacher's politische Perspektive. Ein Beitrag zur Deutung seines Handelns" in: *Politische Vierteljahresschrift*, No. 3/1962, p. 331ff
55. ———, "Post Totalitarian Leadership. Elites in the German Federal Republic" in: *APSR*, No. 1 (March) 1960, p. 58ff
56. ——— and Douglas Chalmers, "Overture or Swan Song? German Social Democracy Prepares for a New Decade" in: *Antioch Review* vol. XX (1960), p. 163ff
57. Elsner, Wolfram, "Westeuropäische Integration und Arbeiterbewegung" in: *Blätter für deutsche und internationale Politik*, No. 12/1971, p. 1233ff
58. Fisher, J.M. and S. Groennings, "German Electoral Politics in 1969" in: *Government and Opposition* 5 (2), Spring 1970, p. 218ff
59. Flechtheim, Ossip K., "Die Anpassung der SPD: 1914, 1933 und 1959" in: *Kölner Zeitschrift für Soziologie und Sozialpsychologie*, No. 17/1965, p. 584 ff
60. ———, "Die Institutionalisierung der Parteien" in: *Zeitschrift für Politik*, vol. 9 (1962), p. 101ff
61. ———, "Die KPD nach 1945" in: *Der Politolog*, vol. 7 (1966), No. 21, p. 3ff
62. ———, "Staatsparteien und freie politische Gruppen" in: *Werkhefte*, vol. 16 (1962), p. 228ff
63. ———, "Widerstände gegen Abrüstüng" in: *Frankfurter Hefte*, No. 6/1966, p. 463ff
64. Franz, Alfred, "Heimatlose Linke?" in: *Die Neue Gesellschaft*, No.3/1956, p. 207ff
65. Greiffenhagen, Martin, "Der Totalitarismusbegriff in der Regimenlehre" in: *Politische Vierteljahresschrift*, No. 3/1968, p. 101ff
66. ———, "Totalitarismus rechts und links. Ein Vergleich von Nationalsozialismus und Kommunismus" in: *Gesellschaft—Staat—Erziehung*, No. 12/1967, p. 287ff
67. Grosser, Alfred, "La structure du parti social-democrat d'Allemagne" in: *Occident*, No. 1/1955, p. 58ff
68. Habermas, Jürgen, "Thesen gegen die Koalition der Mutlosen mit den Machthabern" in: *Diskus* (Frankfurter Studentenzeitung), No. 8/1966, p. 2

69. Hamann, Andreas, "Das Recht auf Opposition und seine Geltung im ausserparlamentarischen Bereich" in: *Politische Vierteljahresschrift*, No. 3/1962, p. 242ff

70. Hanke, Irma, "Zur Identität des neuen Programmentwurfs der KPD in: *Zeitschrift für Politik*, Vol. 4, December 1968

71. Hannover, Heinrich, "Die Verteidigung des Staates als Gewissensfrage" in: Martin Niemoller, ed., *Tempelreinigung*, Frankfurt, Stimme-Verlag, 1962

72. Heidenheimer, Arnold J., "German Party Finance. The CDU" in: *APSR* LI (June 1957), p. 369ff

73. Hennis, Wilhelm, "Verfassungsordnung und Verbandseinfluss" in: *Politische Vierteljahresschrift*, No. 1/1961, p. 25ff

74. ———, "Parlamentarische Opposition und Industriegesellschaft" in: *Gesellschaft —Staat—Erziehung*, No. 5/1964, p. 205ff

75. ———, "Verfassung und Verfassungswirklichkeit. Ein deutsches Problem" in: *Recht und Staat*, No. 373-74 1968

76. Hermann, Kai, "Germany's Young Left" in: *Encounter*, April 1968, p. 67ff

77. Hillmann, Günther, "Neue Linke und kommunistische Selbstkritik" in: *Atomzeitalter*, No. 1-2/1967, p. 36ff

78. Hirsche, Kurt, "Gewerkschafter im Bundestag" in: *Gewerkschaftliche Monatshefte*, December 1957, p. 705ff

79. Hodges, D.C., "Liberal Socialism. On the Horns of a Dilemma" in: *American Journal of Economics*, vol. 22 (Oct. 1963), p. 449ff

80. Jaesrich, Helmut, "Studenten und Atombomben. Ein Kongress stolpert über den Vulkan" in: *Der Monat*, No. 125 (February) 1959, p. 22ff

81. Jung, Heinz, "Zur Diskussion um den Begriff Arbeiterklasse" in: *Das Argument*, No. 4/1961, p. 681ff

82. Kirchheimer, Otto and C. Menges, "A Free Press in a Democratic State? The Spiegel Case" in: G.M. Carter and A.F. Westin, *Politics in Europe. Five Cases in European Government*, New York, Harcourt, 1965.

83. ———, "German democracy in the 1950's" in: *World Politics*, January 1961, p. 254ff

84. ———, "Majoritäten und Minoritäten in westeuropäischen Regierungen" in: *Die Neue Gesellschaft*, vol. 6 (1959), p. 256ff

85. ———, "Notes on the Political Scene in Western Germany" in: *World Politics*, April 1954, p. 306ff

86. ———, "Vom Wandel der politischen Opposition" in: *Archiv für Rechts- und Sozialphilosophie*, vol. 43, 1957, p. 59ff

87. ———, "West German Trade Unions. Their Domestic and Foreign Policies" in: H. Speier and W.P. Davidson, eds., *West German Leadership and Foreign Policy*, Evanston, Row, 1957

88. Krippendorff, Ekkehard, "Das Ende des Parteienstaates" in: *Der Monat*, No. 160, January 1962, p. 64ff

89. ———, "Die Rechte in der Bundesrepublik — Zehn Thesen" in: Freimut Duve, ed., *Die Restauration entlässt ihre Kinder oder der Erfolg der Rechten in der Bundesrepublik*, Reinbek, ro-ro-ro, 1968

90. Kühnl, Reinhard, "Konstituierung und Regierungssystem der Bundesrepublik — übersicht über die Gesamtdarstellungen" in: *Politische Vierteljahresschrift*, No. 2 (June) 1967, p. 323ff

91. "Die Landtagswahlen in den Ländern der Bundesrepublik Deutschland in den Jahren 1949-52 nach Bundeswahlkreisen 1953" in *Statistische Berichte*, No. VIII/5/6, 12 August 1953

92. Lehmann, Lutz, "Die Mörder sind unter uns" in: *Gewerkschaftliche Umschau*, vol. 13, 1969, p. 36ff

93. Lens, Sidney, "Social Democracy and Labour in Germany" in: *Foreign Policy Reports* XXVI (1950), p. 142ff

94. Lenz, Helmut and Christoph Sassel, "Parteiausschluss und Demokratiegebot" in: *Neue Juristische Wochenzeitschrift*, No. 8 (19 Apr.) 1962, p. 233ff

95. Linz, Juan, "Cleavage and Consensus in West German Politics: the early 1950's" in: S.M. Lipset and S. Rokkan, eds., *Party Systems and Voter Alignments*, New York 1967

96. Lipset, Seymour M., "The Changing Class Structure and Contemporary European Politics" in: *Daedalus*, vol. XCIII of the Proceedings of the American Academy of Arts and Science, Winter 1964, p. 280ff

97. Lorwin, Val, "Working Class Politics and Economic Development in Western Europe" in: *American Historical Review*, LXIII, January 1958, p. 338ff

98. Löwenthal, Richard, Lewis Coser, Irving Howe, "The Worldwide Revolt of the Young. A Discussion" in: *Dissent*, vol. XVI, 1969, No. 3, p. 214ff

99. Marcuse, Ludwig, "German Intellectuals Five Years after the War" in: *Books Abroad* 24, No. 4/1950, p. 346ff

100. Matthöfer, Hans, "Internationale Kapitalkonzentration und Gewerkschaftsbewegung" in: *Gewerkschaftliche Monatshefte*, No. 8/1971, p. 470ff

101. Mayer, Carl, "The Crisis of German Protestantism" in: *Social Research*, November 1945, p. 397ff

102. Merkl, Peter, "Comparative Study and Campaign Management. The Brandt Campaign in West Germany" in: *Western Political Quarterly*, vol. 15, December 1952, p. 681ff

103. Mey, Harald, "Marktwirtschaft und Demokratie. Betrachtungen zur Grundlegung der Bundesrepublik" in: *Vierteljahresschrift für Zeitgeschichte*, vol. 19, No. 2/1971, p. 160ff

104. Meyer, Heinz, "Zur Struktur der deutschen Sozialdemokratie" in: *Zeitschrift für Politik*, No. 3/1955, p. 348ff

105. Molt, Peter, "Wertvorstellungen in der Politik" in: *Politische Vierteljahresschrift*, No. 4/1963, p. 350ff

106. Moscowitz, Moses, "The Political Re-education of the Germans" in: *Political Science Quarterly*, No. 12/1946, p. 535ff

107. Nell-Bruening, Oswald von, "Mitbestimmung und Partnerschaft auf der Ebene von Betrieb und Unternehmen" in: *Wege zum sozialen Frieden*, Stuttgart & Düsseldorf, Akademie für Gemeinwirtschaft (Hamburg), 1954

108. ———, "Oswald von Nell-Bruening contra Viktor Agartz" in: Special issue of *Gesellschaftspolitische Kommentare*, vol. 2, Feb. 1955

109. Nettl, Peter, "Economic Checks on German Unity" in: *Foreign Affairs*, vol. XXX, No. 4 (July) 1952, p. 554ff

110. Oertzen, Peter von, "Betrieb und Gesellschaft. Demokratisierung der Wirtschaft als Bedingung der politischen Demokratie" in: *Werkhefte* vol. 17, No. 11/1963, p. 375ff

111. Ortlieb, H.-D., "Krise des Sozialismus?" in: *Gewerkschaftliche Monatshefte*, No. 1/1950, p. 539ff

112. Panter-Brick, S. Keith, "Adenauer's Victory in Munich" in: *Political Studies*, Vol. 7, No. 3, October 1959, p. 262ff

113. Paterson, W., "The German Social Democratic Party and European Integration 1949-1952. A Study of "Opposition' in Foreign Affairs" in: *Res Publica. Revue de l'Institut belge de science politique*, No. 3/1969, p. 539ff

114. Petry, Hans (=Peter von Oertzen), "Die SPD und der Sozialismus" in: *Frankfurter Hefte*, No. 10/1954, p. 663ff

115. Pirker, Theo, "Warum sind wir gegen die Remilitarisierung?" (pamphlet) Munich, DGB Kreisausschuss Munich, 1952

116. "Porträt des SDS" in: *Der Spiegel*, No. 26/1968, p. 38ff

117. Rappaport, Anatol, "Neue Linke und Machtelite" in: *Atomzeitalter*, No. 1-2/1967, p. 27ff

118. Riemeck, Renate, "Macht und Ohnemacht der öffentlichen Meinung" in: *Blätter für deutsche und internationale Politik*, No. 1/1958, p. 1ff

119. Risse, Heinz Theo, "Die Situation der christlich-sozialen Arbeitnehmerschaft in der Bundesrepublik" in: *Frankfurter Hefte*, No. 5/1960, p. 321ff

120. Roskamp, Karl W., "Distribution of Tax Burden in a Rapidly Growing Economy. West Germany in 1950" in: *National Tax Journal* XVI (1963), p. 20ff

121. Schellinger, H.K. Jr., "The Social Democratic Party after World War II. The Conservatism of Power" in: *Western Political Quarterly*, No. 19/June 1966, p. 251ff

122. Schottlander, Rudolf, "Die Wandlung im Kommunismus" in: *Blätter für deutsche und internationale Politik*, No. 8/1959, p. 671ff
123. Schram, Glenn, "Ideology and Politics. The Rechtsstaat Idea in West Germany" in: *Journal of Politics*, vol. 33, Feb. 1971, p. 133ff
124. Schub, A., "Can Germany ever go Left?" in: *Encounter*, February 1967, p. 27ff
125. Seifert, Jürgen, "Innerparteiliche Opposition" in: *Frankfurter Hefte*, No. 11/1960, p. 765ff
126. Smith, Gordon, "The New German Politics" in: *The Political Quarterly*, vol. 44, No. 3/1973, p. 283ff
127. Sontheimer, Kurt, "Student Opposition in Western Germany" in: *Government and Opposition* 3 (1), Winter 1968, p. 49ff
128. Speier, Hans, "German Rearmament and the Old Military Elite" in: *World Politics*, vol. VI, No. 2 (Jan.) 1954, p. 147ff
129. Stern, Leo, "Die klerikal-imperialistische Abendlandideologie im Dienste des deutschen Imperialismus" in: *Zeitschrift für Geschichtswissenschaft*, No. 2/1962, p. 303ff
130. Vardys, V.S., "German's Postwar Socialism. Nationalism and Kurt Schumacher" in: *Review of Politics*, vol. 27, April 1965, p. 220ff
131. Vincent, Jean Marie, "West Germany. The Reactionary Democracy" in: *The Socialist Register 1964*, London, Merlin Press, 1964, p. 68ff
132. Wellmann, Thomas, "Die soziologische Lage der Bundesrepublik" in: *Deutsche Rundschau*, vol. LXXIX (1953), p. 591ff

C. BOOKS, DISSERTATIONS, ETC.

1. Abendroth, Wolfgang, *Antagonistische Gesellschaft und politische Demokratie. Aufsätze zur politischen Soziologie*, W. Berlin & Neuwied, Luchterhand, 1967
2. ———, *Aufstieg und Krise der deutschen Sozialdemokratie*, Frankfurt, Stimme-Verlag, 1964
3. ———, *Das Grundgesetz, Eine Einführung in seine politischen Probleme*, Pfüllingen, Gunter Neske, 1966
4. ———, *Sozialgeschichte der europäischen Arbeiterbewegung*, Frankfurt Suhrkamp, 1965
5. ———, *Wirtschaft, Gesellschaft und Demokratie in der Bundesrepublik*, Frankfurt, Stimme-Verlag, 1965
6. ———, Kurt Lenk, eds., *Einführung in die politische Wissenschaft*, Bern & Munich, Francke Verlag, 1968
7. ———, Helmut Gollwitzer, et al., *Bedingungen und Organisation des Widerstandes. Der Kongress in Hannover*, Frankfurt, Voltaire, 1970 (2nd ed.)
8. ———, et al., *KP-Verbot oder mit den Kommunisten leben?*, Reinbek, ro-ro-ro, 1968
9. ———, Heinz Brakemeier, et al., "West Germany: The Authoritarian Syndrome", special issue of *International Socialist Journal*, No. 19, Feb. 1967
10. Adorno, Theodor W., et al., *Der Positivismusstreit in der deutschen Soziologie*, Neuwied, Luchterhand, 1967
11. ———, *Jargon der Eigentlichkeit. Zur deutschen Ideologie*, Frankfurt, Suhrkamp, 1965
12. ———, *Minima Moralia. Reflexionen aus dem beschädigten Leben*, Frankfurt, Suhrkamp, 1964
13. ———, E. Bloch, L. Goldmann, et al., *Diskussion der Schriften von Georg Lukacs*, Frankfurt, Suhrkamp, 1972
14. Agartz, Viktor, *Gewerkschaft und Arbeiterklasse. Die ideologischen und soziologischen Wandlungen in der westdeutschen Arbeiterbewegung*, Munich, Trikont Verlag, 1971
15. ———, *Die Gewerkschaften in der Bundesrepublik* (brochure), Düsseldorf, DGB, n.d. (1950).
16. ———, *Sozialistische Wirtschaftspolitik* (brochure), Schwenningen, Neckar-Verlag, 1971

17. ——, *Wirtschaftspolitische Aktivität*, special publication of Rhein-Echo, 6 November 1946, vol. 1, no. 70
18. ——, *Wirtschafts- und Steuerpolitik. Grundsätze und Programm des DGB*, speech delivered to Third Regular Congress of the DGB in Frankfurt from 4-9 October 1954 (brochure), Cologne, DGB, 1954
19. Agnoli, Johannes and Peter Brückner, *Transformation der Demokratie*, Frankfurt, Europäische Verlagsanstalt, 1968
20. ——, Solveig Ehrler, *et al.*, *Journalismus in der ausserparlamentarischen Opposition*, W. Berlin, ad-hoc-Gruppe Extra-Dienst im Republikanischen Club e.V., n.d. (1969)
21. Ahlberg, Rene, *Die politische Konzeption des Sozialistischen Deutschen Studentenbundes*, Bonn, Bundeszentrale fur politische Bildung, 1968
22. ——, *Ursachen der Revolte. Analyse des studentischen Protestes*, Stuttgart-W. Berlin-Cologne-Mainz, Kohlhammer, 1972
23. Albers, Johannes, *et al.*, *Grundgedanken zum Thema: Christlicher Sozialismus*, Cologne (no publisher given) 1946
24. Allemann, Fritz Rene, *Bonn ist nicht Weimar*, Cologne, Kiepenheuer & Witsch, 1956
25. Allensbach-Institut (Deutsches Institut für Demoskopie), *Das Dritte Reich. Eine Studie über Nachwirkungen des Nationalsozialismus*, 2nd ed. 1949
26. ——, *The Germans. Public Opinion Polls 1947-1966* (trans. Gerhard Finian), Allensbach am Bodensee, 1967
27. Almond, Gabriel, *The Politics of German Business*, Santa Monica, Rand Corp. Research Memoranda 1506, 1955
28. ——, and Wolfgang Kraus, eds., *The Struggle for Democracy in Germany*, Chapel Hill, University of Carolina Press, 1949
29. Altmann, Rüdiger, *Das Erbe Adenauers*, Stuttgart-Degerloch, Seewald-Verlag, 1960 (3rd ed.)
30. ——, *et al.*, *Zensuren nach 20 Jahren Bundesrepublik*, Cologne, Verlag für Wissenschaft und Politik, 1969
31. Arndt, Adolf, *Das nicht erfüllte Grundgesetz. Ein Vortrag*, Tübingen, Mohr, 1960
32. Augstein, Rudolf, *Konrad Adenauer* (trans. W.Wallich), London, Secker & Warburg, 1964
33. ——, *Meinungen zu Deutschland*, Frankfurt, Suhrkamp, 1967
34. ——, *Opposition heute*, speech delivered to the Rhein-Ruhr-Klub in Düsseldorf on 9 April 1964, mimeograph
35. Authors' Collective, *Der Imperialismus in der BRD*, Frankfurt 1971
36. ——, *Ideologie des Sozialdemokratismus in der Gegenwart*, Frankfurt, Verlag Marxistische Blätter, 1972
37. Badstübner, Rolf, *Restauration in Westdeutschland 1945-49*, E. Berlin, Dietz-Verlag 1965
38. Balfour, Michael, *West Germany*, London, Benn, 1968
39. ——, *Four-Power Control in Germany and Austria 1945-46. I. Germany*, London, Oxford University Press, 1956
40. Bandholz, Emil, *Zwischen Godesberg und Grossindustrie oder wo steht die SPD?*, Reinbek, ro-ro-ro, 1972
41. Bartel, Walter, *Die Linken in der deutschen Sozialdemokratie im Kampf gegen Militarismus und Krieg*, E. Berlin, Dietz, 1958
42. Barthel, Eckhardt, *Hat die Grosse Koalition in der BRD zu einer Korrosion des Parlamentarismus geführt?*, unpublished Diplom thesis, Otto-Suhr-Institut (Free University of Berlin) 1971
43. Bärwald, Helmut, *Deutsche Kommunistische Partei. Die kommunistische Bündnispolitik in Deutschland*, Cologne, Verlag Wissenschaft und Politik, 1970
44. ——, *Die DKP—Ursprung, Weg, Ziel*, Bonn, Bundeszentrale für politische Bildung, 1969 (2nd ed.)
45. Behr, Hermann, *Vom Chaos zum Staat. Männer, die für uns begannen 1945-1946* Frankfurt, Verlag Frankfurter Bücher, 1961
46. Behrendt, Wolfgang, *Die innerparteiliche Auseinandersetzung um die Ost-*

politik in der SPD 1960 bis 1969, unpublished Diplom thesis, Otto-Suhr-Institut (Free University of Berlin), 1972

47. Berg, Albert, *Die Entwicklung der Vereinigung Unabhängiger Sozialisten (VUS) 1960-1967*, (mimeograph), n.p., n.d., (Hamburg, 1967)
48. Bergmann, Uwe, Rudi Dutschke, *et al.*, *Rebellion der Studenten oder die neue Opposition*, Reinbek, ro-ro-ro, 1968
49. Bergsträsser, Ludwig, *Geschichte der politischen Parteien in Deutschland*, Munich, Olzog, 1960 (10th ed.)
50. *Bericht des Parteivorstandes der SED an den 2. Parteitag* (mimeograph), Berlin, SED, 1947
51. Bethusy-Huc, Viola Gräfin von, *Das politische Kraftspiel in der Bundesrepublik*, Wiesbaden, Steiner, 1965
52. ———, *Sozialpolitische Alternativen*, Pfüllingen, Neske, 1968
53. ———, *Das Sozialleistungssystem der Bundesrepublik Deutschland*, Tübingen, Mohr, 1965
54. ———, *Die Soziologie wirtschaftspolitischer Entscheidungen*, Wiesbaden, Steiner, 1962
55. Berthold. L. and E. Diehl, eds., *Revolutionäre deutsche Parteiprogramme vom Kommunistischen Manifest zum Programm des Sozialismus*, E. Berlin, Dietz, 1967
56. Bienko, Gertrud, Karl-Jakob Jockers, *et al.*, *Schulbücher auf dem Prüfstand Antikommunismus, Antisowjetismus und Revanchismus in Lehrbüchern der Bundesrepublik*, published by DFU Landesverband Rhineland-Palatinate, Frankfurt, Röderberg Verlag, 1972
57. Birkelbach, Willi, *Die grosse Chance. Diskussionsbeiträge zum Thema "Demokratischer Sozialismus"*, Frankfurt, Union Verlagsanstalt, ca.1956
58. Birnbaum, Norman, *The Crisis of Industrial Society*, Oxford, University Press, 1970
59. Bleyer, Wolfgang, *et al.*, *Deutschland 1939-1945*, E. Berlin, VEB Deutsche Verlag der Wissenschaften, 1969
60. Borst, Manfred, *Der wirtschaftliche Aspekt amerikanischer Deutschlandpolitik während des zweiten Weltkrieges und nachher*, unpublished doctoral thesis, University of Tübingen, Faculty of Law, 1951
61. Börnsen, Gerd, *Innerparteiliche Opposition*, Hamburg, W. Runge Verlag, 1969
62. Bracher, Karl D., ed., *Nach 25 Jahren. Eine Deutschland-Bilanz*, Munich, Kindler, 1970 (2nd ed.)
63. Brandt, Gerhard, *Rüstung und Wirtschaft in der BRD*, vol. 3 of Georg Picht, ed., *Studien zur politischen und gesellschaftlichen Situation der Bundeswehr*, Witten and W. Berlin, 1967
64. Brandt, Willy, *Friedrich Engels und die soziale Demokratie*, Bonn-Bad Godesberg, Verlag Neue Gesellschaft, 1970
65. ———, *In Exile. Essays, Reflections and Letters 1933-1947* (trans. R.W. Last), London, Wolff, 1971
66. ———, *My Road to Berlin* (as told to Leo Lania), London, Peter Davies, 1960
67. Brant, Stefan, *Der Aufstand, Vorgeschichte, Geschichte und Deutung des 17. Juni 1953*, Stuttgart, 1954
68. Braunthal, Gerhard, *The Federation of German Industry in Politics*, Ithaca, Cornell University Press, 1965
69. Brill, Hermann L., *Gegen den Strom. Berichte und Entschliessung des Buchenwald-Kongresses*, Offenbach/Main, Bollwerk Verlag, 1946
70. Brückner, Peter, *Zur Sozialpsychologie des Kapitalismus*, Amsterdam, Verlag Van Huiten, 1972
71. ———, *Kritik an den Linken. Zur Situation der Linken in der BRD*, Cologne, Rosa Luxemburg Verlag, 1973
72. Bundesministerium für Gesamtdeutsche Fragen, ed., *Das Verbot der KPD. Urteil des Bundesverfassungsgerichts——Erster Senat——vom 17. August 1956*, Karlsruhe, Verlag C.F. Müller, 1956

300   The German Left Since 1945

73. Bunn, Ronald, *German Politics and the Spiegel Affair. A Case Study of the Bonn System*, Baton Rouge, Louisiana State University Press, 1968
74. Burgbacher, F., *et al.*, *Einkommensverteilung und Vermögensbildung in der BRD*, Opladen, Leske, 1964
75. Chalmers, Douglas, *The Social Democratic Party of Germany. From Working-Class Movement to Modern Political Party*, New Haven, Yale University Press, 1964
76. Childs, David H., *The Development of Socialist Thought within the SPD 1945-1958*, doctoral thesis, University of London (L.S.E.), 1962
77. ———, *From Schumacher to Brandt. The Story of German Socialism 1945-1965*, Oxford, Pergamon Press, 1966
78. ———, *Germany Since 1918*, London, Batsford, 1971
79. Claessens, Detlev and Regine Dermitzel, eds., *Universität und Widerstand* Frankfurt, Europäische Verlagsanstalt, 1968
80. Claessens, Dieter, Arno Klönne, Armin Tschoepe, *Sozialkunde der BRD*, Düsseldorf, Diedrichs, 1968 (2nd ed.)
81. Clay, Lucius D., *Germany and the Fight for Freedom* (Harvard University Godkin Lectures 1949), Cambridge, Mass., Harvard University Press, 1950
82. ———, *Decision in Germany*, London, Heinemann, 1950
83. Conway, John S., *The Nazi Persecution of the Churches 1933-1945*, London, Weidenfeld & Nicolson 1968
84. Conze, Werner, *Jakob Kaiser. Politiker zwischen Ost und West 1945-1949*, Stuttgart-Berlin-Cologne-Mainz, W. Kohlhammer, 1969
85. Czichon, Eberhard, *Der Bankier und die Macht. Hermann Josef Abs in der deutschen Politik*, Cologne, Pahl-Rugenstein, 1970
86. Dahl, Robert, *Political Oppositions in Western Democracies*, New Haven, Yale University Press, 1966
86a Dahrendorf, Gustav, *Der Mensch, das Mass aller Dinge. Reden und Schriften zur deutschen Politik 1945-1954*, (ed. by Ralf Dahrendorf), Hamburg, Verlag Ges. Deutscher Konsumgenossenschaften, 1955
87. Dahrendorf, Ralf, *Für eine Erneuerung der Demokratie in der Bundesrepublik. Sieben Reden und andere Beiträge zur deutschen Politik 1967-8*, Munich, Piper, 1968
88. ———, *Society and Democracy in Germany*, Garden City, Doubleday, 1967
89. Davidson, Eugene, *The Death and Life of Germany. An Account of the American Occupation*, New York, Knopf, 1959
90. Deppe, Frank, *Das Bewusstsein der Arbeiter. Studien zur politischen Soziologie des Arbeiterbewusstseins*, Cologne, Pahl-Rugenstein, 1972
91. ———, Jutta von Freiberg, *et al.*, *Kritik der Mitbestimmung. Partnerschaft oder Klassenkampf?*, Frankfurt, Suhrkamp, 1970 (2nd ed.)
92. Deutsch, Karl and Lewis Edinger, *Germany Rejoins the Powers*, Stanford, University Press, 1959
93. Deutscher Gewerkschaftsbund, *Protokoll des ordentlichen Bundeskongresses des DGB, 1949-1974*, Düsseldorf
94. Dietze, Lutz, *Über Grundlagen und Entwicklungs-Tendenzen der Linken. Eine Inside-Analyse*, ed. by Landesverband der Deutschen Jungdemokraten, Rhineland-Palatinate chapter, Mainz, mimeograph, 1971
95. Dirks, Walter, *Die zweite Republik*, Frankfurt, Verlag Josef Knecht, 1947
96. *Dokumente der Kommunistischen Partei Deutschlands 1945 bis 1956*, E. Berlin, Dietz, 1965
97. *Dokumente der Sozialistischen Einheitspartei Deutschlands*, E. Berlin, Dietz, 1951
98. *Dokumente und Materialien zur Geschichte der deutschen Arbeiterbewegung*, E. Berlin, Dietz, 1959
99. Droz, Jacques, *Histoire des doctrines politiques en Allemagne*, Paris, "Que sais-je?" No. 1301, 1968
100. Düspohl, Rolf, *Das Verhältnis von Theorie und Praxis in der revolutionären Opposition der Bundesrepublik*, unpublished doctoral thesis, Free University of Berlin, Faculty of Political Science, 1971

101. Duverger, Maurice, *Political Parties. Their Organization and Activity in the Modern State*, London, Methuen, 1964
102. Eberlein, Klaus, *Was die Deutschen möchten. Politische Meinungsumfragen in der Bundesrepublik*, Hamburg, Wegner, 1968
103. Edinger, Lewis J., *German Exile Politics. The Social Democratic Executive in the Nazi Era*, Berkeley, University of California Press, 1956
104. ———, *Kurt Schumacher. A Study in Personality and Political Behaviour*, Stanford, University Press, 1965
105. ———, *Politics in Germany*, Boston, Little, Brown & Co., 1968
106. Ehmke, Horst, ed., *Perspektiven Sozialdemokratischer Politik im Übergang zu den siebziger Jahren*, Reinbek, ro-ro-ro, 1969
107. Ehrler, Solveig, Hartmut Häussermann, et al., *Sozialdemokratie und Sozialismus heute. Beiträge zur Analyse und Veränderung sozialdemokratische Politik*, Cologne, Pahl-Rugenstein, 1968
108. Eichler, Willi, *Grundwerte und Grundforderungen im Godesberger Programm der SPD*, Bonn, Neuer Vorwärts, 1962
109. Enderle, August (with the assistance of Bernt Heise), *Die Einheits-gewerkschaften*, Düsseldorf, mimeographed MS of DGB Bundesvorstand, 4 vols., 1959
110. Epstein, Leon, *Political Parties in Western Democracies*, London, Pall Mall, 1967
111. Eschenberg, Theodor, *Staat und Gesellschaft in Deutschland*, Munich, Piper, 1965 (3rd ed.)
112. Evaluation Staff, Office of Public Affairs, Office of the U.S. High Commissioner for Germany, *A Survey Analysis of the Factors Underlying the Outcome of the 1953 German Federal Elections, December 11, 1953*, n.p., n.d. (1954)
113. Feuersenger, Marianne, *Gibt es noch ein Proletariat?*, Frankfurt, Europäische Verlagsanstalt, 1962
114. Flechtheim, Ossip K., ed., *Dokumente zur parteipolitischen Entwicklung in der BRD*, 8 vols., Berlin, Wendler, 1962-1974
115. ———, *Eine Welt oder keine? Beiträge zur Politik, Politologie und Philosophie*, Frankfurt, Europäische Verlagsanstalt, 1964
116. ———, *Westdeutschland am Wendepunkt?*, Berlin, Voltaire, 1967
117. Folmert, Charlotte, *Ideologie und Politik der 'Werkhefte'. Ein Beitrag zum Studium der demokratischen Opposition in Westdeutschland*, unpublished doctoral thesis, Humboldt University, E. Berlin, 1967
118. Friedmann, Wolfgang, *The Allied Military Governments of Germany*, London, Stevens, 1947
119. Friedrich, Carl J. and associates, *The Soviet Zone of Germany*, MS mimeographed by Human Relations Area Files, Yale University, 1956
120. Friedrich, Manfried, *Opposition ohne Alternative. Über die Lage der parlamentarischen Opposition im Wohlfahrtsstaat*, Cologne, Verlag Wissenschaft und Politik, 1962
121. Froese, Leonard, ed., *Was soll aus Deutschland werden?*, Munich, Fischer, 1968
122. Gablentz, Otto H. von der, *Über Marx hinaus*, W. Berlin, Wedding Verlag, 1946
123. ———, *Die versäumte Reform. Zur Kritik der westdeutschen Politik*, Cologne and Opladen, Kiepenhauer, 1960
124. Gaus, Günter, *Staatserhaltende Opposition oder hat die SPD kapituliert? Gespräche mit Herbert Wehner*, Reinbek, ro-ro-ro, 1966
125. Gimbel, John, *The American Occupation of Germany. Politics and the Military 1945-1949*, Stanford, University Press, 1968
126. ———, *A German Community Under American Occupation. Marburg 1945-1952*, Stanford, University Press, 1961
127. Gleissberg, Gerhard, *SPD und Gesellschaftssystem. Aktualität der Programmdiskussion 1934 bis 1946. Dokumente und Kommentar*, Frankfurt, Verlag Marxistische Blätter, 1973
128. Gollancz, Victor, *In Darkest Germany*, London, Gollancz, 1947
129. Görlich, Ina, *Zum ethischen Problem der Atomdiskussion. Verlauf der Atomdiskussion in der BRD und Versuch einer Darstellung der durch sie aufbrechenden ethischen Probleme*, unpublished doctoral thesis, Albert-Ludwig-Universität, Freiburg, 1965

130. Gotthardt, Horst, *Ursachen und Wirkungen des Niederganges der KPD in Westdeutschland*, unpublished Diplom thesis, Otto-Suhr-Institut (Free University of Berlin) 1962
131. Grebing, Helga, *The History of the German Labour Movement. A Survey* (trans. E. Körner), London, Wolff, 1969
132. Grosser, Alfred, *Die Bonner Demokratie*, Düsseldorf, Rauch, 1960
133. ———, *Germany in Our Time. A Political History of the Postwar Years*, London, Pall Mall, 1971
134. ———, and Jürgen Seifert, *Die Spiegel-Affäre I. Staatsmacht und ihre Kontrolle*, Olten and Freiburg, Walter-Verlag, 1966
135. Habermas, Jürgen, *Protestbewegung und Hochschulreform*, Frankfurt, Suhrkamp, 1969
136. ———, *Theorie und Praxis. Sozialphilosophische Studien*, Neuwied, Luchterhand, 1963
137. Hack, Lothar, Oskar Negt, *et al.*, *Protest und Politik*, Frankfurt, Verlag Neue Kritik, 1968
138. Hannover, Heinrich, *Politische Diffamierung der Opposition im freiheitlich-demokratischen Rechtsstaat*, Dortmund-Barop, Pläne, 1962
139. Heidenheimer, Arnold, *Adenauer and the CDU. The Rise of the Leader and the Integration of the Party*, The Hague, Nijhoff, 1960
140. Hemberger, Horst, *et al.*, *Imperialismus heute. Der Staatsmonopolistisch(e) Kapitalismus in Westdeutschland*, E. Berlin, Dietz, 1966
141. Hennis, Wilhelm, *Grosse Koalition ohne Ende?*, Munich, Piper, 1968
142. Herrmann, Hans-Georg, *Verraten und verkauft*, Fulda, Fuldaer Verlagsanstalt, 1959 (2nd ed.)
143. Hess, Gerhard, ed., *BRD-DDR. Vergleich der Gesellschaftssysteme*, Cologne, Pahl-Rugenstein Verlag, 1971
144. Hirsch-Weber, Wolfgang, *Gewerkschaften in der Politik*, Cologne and Opladen, Westdeutscher Verlag, 1959
145. Hiscocks, Richard, *Democracy in Western Germany*, London, Oxford University Press, 1957
146. ———, *Germany Revived. An Appraisal of the Adenauer Era*, London, Gollancz, 1966
147. Hitzer, Friedrich and Reinhard Opitz, eds., *Alternativen der Opposition*, Cologne, Pahl-Rugenstein, 1969
148. Hofmann, Werner and Heinz Maus, *Notstandsordnung und Gesellschaft in der Bundesrepublik*, Reinbek, ro-ro-ro, 1967
149. ———, *Stalinismus und Kommunismus. Zur Soziologie des Ost-West Konflikts*, Frankfurt, Suhrkamp, 1967
150. Hondrich, Karl Otto, *Die Ideologien von Interessenverbänden*, W. Berlin, Duncker & Humbolt, 1963
151. Horkheimer, Max, *Kritische Theorie. Eine Dokumentation*, ed. by Alfred Schmidt, Frankfurt, Fischer, 2 vols., 1968
152. Horowitz, David, *Kalter Krieg. Hintergründe der US-Aussenpolitik von Jalta bis Vietnam*, W. Berlin, Wagenbach, 2 vols., 1969
153. Huffschmid, Jörg, *Die Politik des Kapitals. Konzentration und Wirtschaftspolitik in der Bundesrepublik*, Frankfurt, Suhrkamp, 1969
154. Hundt, Martin, Fritz Krause, *et al.*, *Antikommunismus. Vom Kölner Kommunistenprozess 1852 bis zu den Berufsverboten heute*, Frankfurt, Verlag Marxistische Blätter, 1972
155. Huster, E.U., *et al.*, *Determinanten der westdeutschen Restauration 1945-1949*, Frankfurt, Suhrkamp, 1972
156. Jacobsen, H.A. and H. Dollinger, eds., *Der Kampf um die Hochschulreform*, Munich, Dtv, 1969
157. Jaeggi, Urs, *Macht und Herrschaft in der Bundesrepublik*, Frankfurt, Fischer, 1970
158. Kaden, Albrecht, *Einheit oder Freiheit. Die Wiedergründung der SPD 1945/46*, Hanover, Dietz, 1964

159. Kaiser, Josef, *Reden und Gedanken. Der Soziale Staat* (brochure), Berlin, Union-Verlag, 1945
160. Kaltefleiter, Werner, *Wirtschaft und Politik in Deutschland. Konjunktur als Bestimmungsfaktor des Parteiensystems*, Cologne and Opladen, Westdeutscher Verlag, 1966
161. Kitzinger, Uwe, *German Electoral Politics. A Study of the 1957 Campaign*, Oxford, Clarendon Press, 1960
162. Kluth, Hans, *Die KPD in der Bundesrepublik. Ihre politische Tätigkeit und Organisation 1945-1956*, Cologne and Opladen, Westdeutscher Verlag, 1959
163. Koepcke, Cordula, *Sozialismus in Deutschland*, Munich, Olzog, 1970
164. Kogon, Eugen, Abendroth, *et al.*, *Der totale Notstandsstaat*, Reinbek, ro-ro-ro, 1965
165. Kogon, Eugen, *Die unvollendete Erneuerung. Deutschland im Kraftfeld 1945-63*, Frankfurt, Europäische Verlagsanstalt, 1964
166. Kopsch, Hartmut, *The Evolution of German Social Democracy*, unpublished M.A. thesis, University of British Columbia, 1966
167. KPD (PV), ed., *Die ideologisch-politische Festigung unserer Partei auf der Grundlage des Marxismus-Leninismus*, *Materialien der 14. PV-Tagung* Frankfurt, KPD, n.d.
168. KPD, *The Karlsruhe Trial for Banning the Communist Party of Germany. White Paper*, trans. C.P. Dutt, London, Lawrence & Wishart, 1956
169. KPD, *KPD 1945-1965. Abriss, Dokumente, Zeittafel*, E. Berlin, 1966
170. KPD, *Die KPD lebt und kämpft. Dokumente der KPD 1956-1962*, E. Berlin, Dietz, 1963
171. KPD (ZK), *Die Lage in der Bundesrepublik und der Kampf um Frieden und Demokratie. Entwurf eines Beschlusses zur Parteikonferenz der KPD* (brochure), n.p. (E. Berlin), n.d. (1959?)
172. Kralewski, Wolfgang and Karlheinz Neunreither, *Oppositionelles Verhalten im ersten deutschen Bundestag 1949-53*, Cologne and Opladen, Westdeutscher Verlag, 1963
173. Krasomil, Dean H., *The German Social Democratic Party after 1945. A Contribution to the Study of the SPD in the Period 1945-1952*, unpublished doctoral thesis, University of Frankfurt, 1953
174. Krueger, Horst, *Was ist heute links? Thesen und Theorien zu einer politischen Position*, Munich, List, 1963
175. Kuczynski, Jürgen, *Darstellung der Lage der Arbeiter in Westdeutschland seit 1945*, 2 vols., E. Berlin, Akademie-Verlag, 1963
176. ———, *So war es wirklich. Ein Rückblick auf 20 Jahre Bundesrepublik*, E. Berlin, Staatssekretariat für westdeutsche Fragen, 1969
177. ———, *Studien zur Geschichte des deutschen Imperialismus*, E. Berlin, Dietz, 1952
178. Kühnl, Reinhard, *Deutschland zwischen Demokratie und Faschismus*, Munich, Carl Hanser Verlag, 1969
179. ———, *Das Dritte Reich in der Presse der Bundesrepublik. Kritik eines Geschichtbildes*, Frankfurt, Europäische Verlagsanstalt, 1966
180. ———, *Formen bürgerlicher Herrschaft I. Liberalismus-Faschismus*, Reinbek, ro-ro-ro, 1971
181. ———, ed., *Formen bürgerlicher Herrschaft II. Der bürgerliche Staat der Gegenwart.* Reinbek, ro-ro-ro, 1972
182. ———, *Die von F.J. Strauss repräsentierten politischen Kräfte und ihr Verhältnis zum Faschismus. Ein Gutachten*, Cologne, Pahl-Rugenstein, 1971
183. ———, *Die nationalsozialistische Linke 1925-1930*, Meisenheim, Anton Hain, 1966
184. ———, *Die NPD*, W. Berlin, Voltaire Verlag, 1967
185. Kumpf, Richard, *Tendenzen der Formierung einer klassenmässigen Opposition in der Sozialdemokratie unter den Bedingungen der Grossen Koalition*, unpublished doctoral thesis, Humboldt University, E. Berlin, 1970
186. Lamm, Fritz, *Briefwechsel mit der SPD* (brochure), Stuttgart, Author, 1963
187. Lamm, Fritz, Ursula Schmiederer, *et al.*, *Die Grosse Koalition und die nächsten Aufgaben der Linken*, Frankfurt, Verlag Neue Kritik, 1967

304 The German Left Since 1945

188. Lange, Max Gustav, ed., *Parteien in der Bundesrepublik*, Stuttgart and Düsseldorf, Ring-Verlag, 1955
189. Lehmann, Lutz, *Legal und Opportun. Politische Justiz in der Bundesrepublik*, W. Berlin, Voltaire Verlag, 1966
190. Leonhard, Wolfgang, *Die Revolution entlässt ihre Kinder*, Frankfurt & W. Berlin, Ullstein Taschenbücher, (1955), 20th ed., 1965
191. Lesius (pseudonym of Wilhelm Lüke), *Der Weg von unten! Zur Gründung christlicher Arbeiter- und Angestellten-Gewerkschaften in Deutschland*, Essen-West, mimeograph, 1954
192. Litten, Jens, *Eine verpasste Revolution? Nachruf auf den SDS*, Hamburg, Hoffmann und Campe, 1969
193. Lochner, Louis Paul, *Tycoons and Tyrant. German Industry from Hitler to Adenauer*, Chicago, Regnery, 1954
194. Löwke, Udo F., *Für den Fall, dass . . . SPD und Wehrfrage 1949-1955*, Hanover, Verlag für Literatur und Zeitgeschehen, 1969
195. MacIver, Robert, *The Web of Government*, New York, Macmillan, 1960.
196. Mandel, Ernest, *Die deutsche Wirtschaftskrise. Lehren aus der Rezession 1966/67*, Frankfurt, Europäische Verlagsanstalt, 1969
197. Mannschatz, Gerhard and Josef Seider, *Zum Kampf der KPD im Ruhrgebiet für die Einigung der Arbeiterklasse und die Entmachtung der Monopolherren 1945 bis 1947*, E. Berlin, Dietz, 1962
198. Marcus, Hermann, *Die Macht der Mächtigen. Deutschland und seine Wirtschaftsriesen*, Dusseldorf, Droste Verlag, 1970
199. Marcuse, Herbert, *Negations. Essays in Critical Theory*, London, Penguin Press, 1968
200. ———, *Kultur und Gesellschaft 2*, Frankfurt, Suhrkamp, 1965
201. ———, *Ideen zu einer kritischen Theorie der Gesellschaft*, Frankfurt, Suhrkamp, 1969
202. *Marxistische Blätter*, special issue, *Autoritäre Herrschaftsstrukturen. Demokratische Alternativen*, Frankfurt, Sept./Oct. 1968
203. ———, special issue, *Klassen und Klassenkampf heute. Beiträge zu einer internationalen wissenschaftlichen Konferenz zum 150. Geburtstag von Karl Marx*, Frankfurt, August-Bebel-Gesellschaft, 1968
204. Matthias, Erich, *Sozialdemokratie und Nation. Ein Beitrag zur Ideengeschichte der sozialdemokratischen Emigration in der Prager Zeit des Parteivorstandes 1933-38*, Stuttgart, Deutsche Verlagsanstalt, 1952
205. Maus, Heinz, ed., *Gesellschaft, Recht und Politik. Wolfgang Abendroth zum 60. Geburtstag*, Neuwied und Berlin, Luchterhand, 1968
206. Mehnert, Klaus, *Der deutsche Standort*, Stuttgart, Deutsche Verlagsanstalt, 1967
207. Merkl, Peter, *Germany: Yesterday and Tomorrow*, New York, Oxford University Press, 1965
208. Miliband, Ralph, *The State in Capitalist Society. An Analysis of the Western System of Power*, London, Weidenfeld & Nicolson, 1969
209. Mitscherlich, Alexander and Alfred Weber, *Freier Sozialismus*, Heidelberg, Schneider, 1946
210. Molt, Peter, *Die neutralistische Opposition. Bedingungen und Voraussetzungen der neutralistischen Opposition in der BRD, vor allem der Gesamtdeutschen Volkspartei 1949-54*, unpublished doctoral thesis, University of Heidelberg, 1955
211. Munich Working Group "Kommunistische Infiltration und Machtkampftechnik" im Kommittee "Rettet die Freiheit", ed., *Verschwörung gegen die Freiheit. Die kommunistische Untergrundarbeit in der Bundesrepublik (Rotbuch II)*, n.p. (Munich), n.d. (1960)
212. Narr, Wolf-Dieter, *CDU-SPD Programm und Praxis seit 1945*, Stuttgart, Kohlhammer, 1966
213. Nell-Bruening, Oswald von, *Mitbestimmung*, Landshut, Girnth, 1950
214. *Neokapitalismus, Rüstungswirtschaft, Westeuropäische Arbeiterbewegung*, transcript of a meeting of Sozialistischen Bundes and SDS on 6 and 7 November 1965 in Frankfurt, Frankfurt, Verlag Neue Kritik, 1965

215. Nettl, J.P., *The Eastern Zone and Soviet Policy in Germany 1945-1950*, London, Oxford University Press, 1951
216. Oppen, Beate von, ed., *Documents on Germany under Occupation*, London, Oxford University Press, 1955
217. Ortlieb, Heinz-Dietrich, *Das Ende des Wirtschaftswunders. Unsere Wirtschafts- und Gesellschaftsordnung in der Wandlung*, Wiesbaden, Steiner, 1962
218. Paterson, William Edgar, *The German Social Democratic Party and European Integration 1949-1957. A Case Study of Opposition in Foreign Affairs*, unpublished doctoral thesis, University of London, (L.S.E.), 1972
219. Petzke, Christian, *Das Wesen der politischen Opposition. Formen und Funktionen der Opposition im staatlichen Leben*, Inaugural dissertation, University of Munich, Faculty of Law, 1959
220. Picht, Georg, *Die deutsche Bildungskatastrophe. Analyse und Dokumentation*, Olten, Walter, 1964
221. Pieck, Wilhelm, *Probleme der Vereinigung von KPD und SPD*, Berlin, Neuer Weg, 1946
222. Pirker, Theo, *Die blinde Macht. Die Gewerkschaftsbewegung in Westdeutschland*, 2 vols., Munich, Mercator Verlag, 1960
223. ———, *Die SPD nach Hitler. Die Geschichte der Sozialdemokratischen Partei Deutschlands 1945-1964*, Munich, Rütten & Loening, 1965
224. Plessner, Helmut, *Die verspätete Nation*, Stuttgart, Kohlhammer, 1959
225. Pollock, James and John Lane, eds., *Source Materials on the Government and Politics of Germany*, Ann Arbor, Wahrs Publishers, 1964
226. Popitz, H., H.P.Bahrdt, *et al.*, *Das Gesellschaftsbild des Arbeiters. Untersuchungen in der Hüttenindustrie*, Tübingen, Mohr, 1957
227. Prittie, Terence, *Adenauer. A Study in Fortitude*, London, Tom Stacey, 1972
228. Pritzkoleit, Kurt, *Gott erhält die Mächtigen*, Düsseldorf, Rauch, 1963
229. Reimann, Max, Ludwig Landwehr, *et al.*, eds., *KPD-Verbot. Ursachen und Folgen 1956-71*, Frankfurt, Verlag Marxistische Blätter, 1971
230. Richert, Ernst, *Die radikale Linke*, W. Berlin, Colloquium Verlag, 1968
231. Richter, Hans-Werner, *Bestandsaufnahme. Eine deutsche Bilanz 1962*, Munich-Vienna-Basel, Kurt Desch, 1962
232. ———, *Plädoyer für eine neue Regierung oder keine Alternative*, Reinbek, ro-ro-ro, 1965
233. Rovan, Joseph, *Le Catholicisme Politique en Allemagne*, Paris, Editions du Seuil, 1956
234. *Der Ruf. Eine deutsche Nachkriegszeitschrift*, Munich, dtv-dokumente, 1962
235. Rupp, Hans-Karl, *Ausserparlamentarische Opposition in der Ära Adenauer. Der Kampf gegen die Atombewaffnung in den fünfziger Jahren*, Cologne, Pahl-Rugenstein, 1970
236. ———, *Der Kampf gegen Atomwaffen in Mitteleuropa — in der BRD der fünfziger Jahre. Eine Studie zu Problematik und Funktionen ausserparlamentarischer oppositioneller Aktivität*, doctoral thesis, University of Bonn, 1969
237. Ryschkowsky, Nikolaus J., *Die linke Linke*, Munich and Vienna, Olzog, 1968
238. Sandoz, Gerard, *La Gauche Allemande. De Karl Marx à Willy Brandt*, Paris, Julliard, 1970
239. Sänger, Fritz, *Soziale Demokratie. Bemerkungen zum Grundsatzprogramm der SPD*, Hanover, Dietz, 1960 (2nd ed. 1962)
240. Schachtner, Richard, *Die deutschen Nachkriegswahlen*, Munich, Isar-Verlag, 1956
241. Schäfer, Gert, Carl Nedelmann, eds., *Der CDU-Staat. Studien zur Verfassungswirklichkeit der Bundesrepublik*, Munich, Szczesny, 1967
242. Schauer, Helmut, ed., *Notstand der Demokratie. Referate, Diskussionsbeiträge und Materialien vom Kongress am 30. Oktober 1966 in Frankfurt*, Frankfurt, Europäische Verlagsanstalt, 1967
243. Schmid, Carlo, *Der Weg des deutschen Volkes nach 1945*, W. Berlin, Haude & Spenersche (SFB Buchreihe NR.5) n.d. (ca. 1966)
244. Schmidt, Eberhard, *Die Bemühungen der Gewerkschaften um eine Neuordnung der Wirtschaftsverfassung in den westlichen Besatzungszonen und in der Bundes-*

republik Deutschland, doctoral thesis, University of Marburg, Institute for Political Science, 1969
245. ———, *Ordnungsfaktor oder Gegenmacht. Die politische Rolle der Gewerkschaften*, Frankfurt, Suhrkamp, 1971
246. ———, *Die verhinderte Neuordnung 1945-1952. Zur Auseinandersetzung um die Demokratisierung der Wirtschaft in den westlichen Besatzungszonen und in der Bundesrepublik Deutschland*, Frankfurt, Europäische Verlagsanstalt, 1970
247. Schmidt, Ute and Tilman Fischer, *Der erzwungene Kapitalismus. Klassenkampfe in den Westzonen 1945-1948*, W. Berlin, Wagenbach, 1972
248. Schöllgen, Werner, *Ohne mich, ohne uns. Recht und Grenzen des Pazifismus*, Graz-Salzburg-Vienna, Pustet, 1951
249. Scholz, Günther, *Ausserer und innerer Wandel der deutschen Gewerkschaftsbewegung in ihrer Entwicklung seit der Entstehungszeit bis zur Neugrundung nach dem Zweiten Weltkrieg*, unpublished doctoral thesis, University of Marburg, Faculty of Law, 1955
250. Schulz, Klaus-Peter, *Auftakt zum Kalter Krieg. Der Freiheitskampf der SPD in Berlin 1945/46*, W. Berlin, Colloquium-Verlag, 1965
251. ———, *Opposition als politisches Schicksal*, Cologne, Verlag für Politik und Wirtschaft, 1958
252. ———, *Sorge um die deutsche Linke. Eine kritische Analyse der SPD-Politik seit 1945*, Cologne, Verlag für Politik und Wirtschaft, 1954
253. Schumacher, Kurt, *Nach dem Zusammenbruch. Gedanken über Demokratie und Sozialismus*, Hamburg, Christen, 1948
254. ———, *Turmwächter der Demokratie. Ein Lebensbild von Kurt Schumacher*, 2 vols., ed. by Arno Scholz and Walther Oschilewski, Berlin-Grunewald, Arani Verlags GmbH, 1953-1954
255. ———, Erich Ollenhauer, Willy Brandt, *Der Auftrag des demokratischen Sozialismus*, Bonn-Bad Godesberg, Verlag Neue Gesellschaft, 1972
256. Schuster, Dieter, *Die Deutsche Gewerkschaftsbewegung DGB*, Düsseldorf, DGB, 1971 (3rd ed.)
257. Schwarz, Hans-Peter, *Vom Reich zur Bundesrepublik. Deutschland im Widerstreit der aussenpolitischen Konzeptionen in den Jahren der Besatzungsherrschaft 1945-1949*, W. Berlin and Neuwied, Luchterhand, 1966
258. Schwering, Leo, *Frühgeschichte der Christlich-Demokratischen Union*, Recklingshausen, pub. not cited, 1963
259. See, Hans, *Volkspartei in Klassenstaat oder das Dilemma der innerparteilichen Demokratie*, Reinbek, ro-ro-ro
260. Seeliger, Rolf, *Die ausserparlamentarischen Opposition*, Munich, Verlag R. Seeliger, 1968
261. ———, ed., *Quo Vadis SPD?*, Munich, Verlag R. Seeliger, 1971
262. ———, *SPD—Grosser Kompromis ohne Ende?*, Munich, Verlag R. Seeliger, 1971
263. Seifert, Jürgen, *Zur Kritik der Notstandsgesetzgebung*, Frankfurt, Union-Druckerei, 1964
264. Sering, Paul (=Richard Löwenthal) *Jenseits des Kapitalismus. Ein Beitrag zur sozialistischen Neuorientierung*, Nuremberg, Nest-Verlag, 1948 (2nd ed.)
265. Smith, Gordon R., *Party System and Party Structure in West Germany*, unpublished external doctoral thesis, University of London (L.S.E.), 1963
266. SOPADE, ed., *Querschnitt durch Politik und Wirtschaft*, Bonn, Sopade, 1954
267. Sozialistisches Büro, ed., *Für eine neue sozialistische Linke. Analysen, Strategien, Modelle*, Frankfurt, Fischer, 1973
268. SPD (PV), ed., *Acht Jahre sozialdemokratischer Kampf um Einheit, Frieden, und Freiheit. Ein dokumentarischer Nachweis der gesamtdeutschen Haltung der Sozialdemokratie und ihrer Initiativen*, Bonn, mimeograph, 1954
269. ———, *Die alternative unserer Zeit, Auseinandersetzung der Sozialdemokratie mit dem Kommunismus*, Bonn, brochure, 1959
270. ———, *Deutschlandplan der SPD. Kommentare, Argumente, Begründungen*, Bonn, brochure, 1959
271. ———, *Bestandsaufnahme 1966. Eine Dokumentation*, Bonn, 1966
271a ———, *Einheitsgewerkschaft oder christliche Gewerkschaften*, Hanover, 1949

272. ———, *Hintergründe der Atomdebatte im Bundestag*, Bonn, brochure, 1957
273. ———, *Hochverratsprozess gegen getarnte Kommunisten. Eine sozialdemo-kratische Darstellung über den Karlsruher Prozess gegen die 'Sozialistische Aktion'*, Bonn, 1956
274. ———*Jahrbuch der SPD*: 1946, 1954/55, 1956/57, 1958/59, 1959/60, 1961/62, 1963/64, 1965/66, 1967/68, Bonn
275. ———, *Katholik und Godesberger Programm. Zur Situation nach Mater und Magistra*, Bonn, 1962
276. ———, *Material zur Wirtschaftspolitik*, Bonn, 1957
277. ———, *Die Mittelschichten in der modernen Gesellschaft*, Bonn, brochure, 1957
278. ———, *Offensive Auseinandersetzung SED-SPD*, Bad Godesberg, ca. 1966
279. ———, *Professor Abendroth und das Godesberger Programm*, Bonn, mimeo-graph, n.d. (1960)
280. ———, *Protokoll der Verhandlungen des Parteitages der SPD*: 9.-11.5.1946 in Hanover; 29.6.-2.7.1947 in Nuremberg; 11.-14.9.1948 in Düsseldorf; 21.-25.5.1950 in Hamburg; 24.-28.9.1952 in Dortmund; 20.-24.7.1954 in Berlin; 16.-19-6.1956 in Munich; 18.-23.5.1958 in Stuttgart; 13.-15.11.1959 in Bad Godesberg; 21.-25.11.1960 in Hanover; 26.-30.5.1962 in Cologne; 1.-5.6.1966 in Dortmund; 17.-21.3.1968 in Nuremberg
281. Speier, Hans, *German Re-armament and Atomic War. The Views of the German Military and Political Leaders*, Evanston, Ill., Rand Corp. Research Studies, 1957
282. Spiro, Herbert J., *The Politics of German Co-determination*, Cambridge, Mass., Harvard University Press, 1958
283. Statistisches Bundesamt, *Statistisches Jahrbuch für die BRD*, Wiesbaden, 1952 through 1974 (annual)
284. Sund, Olaf, Hans-Georg Conert and Horst Geyer, *Die Parteien der Bundes-republik als Volksparteien*, n.p., Arbeit und Leben Arbeitsgemeinschaft DGB-VHS, 1965
285. Sultan, Herbert and Wolfgang Abendroth, *Bürokratischer Verwaltungsstaat und soziale Demokratie*, Hanover & Frankfurt, Norddeutsche Verlagsanstalt, 1955
286. U.S. Office of the Military Government in Germany (OMGUS), *Opinion Survey Reports*, 1946-1951
287. ———, *Trends in German Public Opinion 1946 Thru 1949*, Bad Godesberg, 1950
288. Ulbricht, Walter, Otto Grotewohl, Friedrich Ebert, *et al.*, *Sprechen zu Dir, sozialdemokratischer Genosse*, n.p., n.d. (ca. 1956)
289. ———, *Zur Geschichte der deutschen Arbeiterbewegung. Aus Reden und Aufsätzen*, vols. II, III, E. Berlin, Dietz, 1955
290. Vilmar, Fritz, *Rüstung und Abrüstung im Spätkapitalismus*, Frankfurt, Europäische Verlagsanstalt, 1965
291. ———, *Strategien der Demokratisierung. Vol. II: Modelle und Kämpfe der Praxis*, Darmstadt and Neuwied, Luchterhand, 1973
292. Wallich, Henry, *Mainsprings of the German Revival*, New Haven, Yale University Press, 1955 (2nd ed. 1960)
293. Wildenmann, Rudolf, *Macht und Konsens als Problem der Innen- und Aussen-politik*, Frankfurt, Athenäum-Verlag, 1963
294. Windsor, Philip, *German Re-unification*, London, Elek Books, 1969
295. Zapf, W., *Wandlungen der deutschen Elite*, Munich, Piper, 1965 (2nd ed. 1966)
296. Zink, Harold, *The United States in Germany 1944-55*, Princeton, Toronto, London, New York, Princeton University Press, 1957
297. Zutz, Heinz-Dieter, *Die DFU und die politische Opposition in der Bundes-republizu Beginn der 60er Jahre*, unpublished Staatsprufung thesis, Pedagogical University Westfalen-Lippe (Bielefeld), n.d. (ca. 1971)

D. RELEVANT PERIODICALS

1. *Agit 883* (W. Berlin) 1968-1971(?)
2. *Die Andere Zeitung* (Hamburg) 1956-1969
3. *Arbeitshefte* (Hanover) 1962-1967

4. *Das Argument* (W. Berlin) 1961-
5. *Atomzeitalter* (Frankfurt) 1961-1968
6. *Berliner Extra-Dienst* (W. Berlin) 1968-
7. *Berliner Stimme* (W. Berlin) 1951-
8. *Berliner Zeitschrift für Politologie* (W. Berlin) 1968-1970
9. *Blätter für deutsche und internationale Politik* (Cologne) 1958-
10. *bulletin* (Frankfurt) 1948-1970
11. *Deutsche Volkszeitung* (Düsseldorf) 1953-
12. *Diskussion* (W. Berlin), 1960-
13. *Elan-Express* (Dortmund) 1971-
14. *Express International* (Frankfurt) 1963-1972
15. *Frankfurter Hefte* (Frankfurt) 1945-
16. *Freie Tribüne* (Düsseldorf) 1950-1951
17. *Freies Volk* (Düsseldorf) 1946-1958
18. *frontal* (W. Berlin) 1960-
19. *Funken* (Stuttgart) 1950-1959
20. *Geist und Tat* (Hamburg) 1948-
21. *Gesellschaft, Staat, Erziehung* (Frankfurt-Berlin-Bonn) 1956
22. *gestern und heute* (Munich) 1964-1969
23. *Gewerkschaftliche Monatshefte* (Cologne) 1950-
24. *Das Gewissen* (Munich) 1961-1966
25. *Informationen der Aktionsgemeinschaft gegen die atomare Aufrüstung der Bundesrepublik* (Düsseldorf) 1960-1961
26. *Informationen der Ausserparlamentarischen Opposition* (Dortmund) 1968-1971
27. *Informationen der Sozialistischen Opposition* (Dortmund) 1967-1969
28. *Informationen des Sozialistischen Zentrums* (Frankfurt) 1967-1968
29. *Informationsdienst des Sozialistischen Bundes* (Frankfurt) 1964-1966
30. *Internationale Politik* (Belgrade) 1955-1968
31. *Junge Kirche* 1945-
32. *konkret* (Hamburg) 1959-
33. *Kürbiskern* (Munich) 1965-
34. *Links* (Offenbach) 1969-
35. *links. Monatsschrift für demokratischen Sozialismus* (Frankfurt) 1952-1963
36. *Marxistische Blätter* (Frankfurt) 1963-1970
37. *Der Monat* (W. Berlin) 1949-
38. *Die Neue Gesellschaft* (Bielefeld) 1954-
39. *Neue Kritik* (Frankfurt) 1960-1969
40. *Neue Politik* (Hamburg) 1956-?
41. *Neue Zeit* (E. Berlin) 1945-1949
42. *New Left Review* (London) 1960-
43. *Periodikum für wissenschaftlichen Sozialismus* (Munich) 1963-1968
44. *Pläne* (Dortmund) 1959-1966?
45. *Die Politische Meinung* (Cologne) 1956-
46. *Politische Studien* (Munich) 1954-
47. *Politische Vierteljahresschrift* (Cologne & Opladen) 1960-
48. *Der Politolog* (W. Berlin) 1959-1967
49. *pro und contra* (W. Berlin) 1948-1953
50. *Die Quelle* (Düsseldorf) 1950-
51. *Rote Presse Korrespondenz* (W. Berlin) 1967-1971
52. *Der Ruf* (Munich) 1946-1949
53. *SDS-Korrespondenz* (Frankfurt) 1960-1968
54. *Der Sozialdemokrat* (Frankfurt) 1953-1968
55. *Der Sozialist* (Stuttgart) 1959-?
56. *Sozialistische Hefte* (Hamburg) 1963-1969
57. *Sozialistische Korrespondenz* (Hamburg) 1959-1969
58. *Sozialistische Politik* (Cologne) 1954-1966
59. *Sozialistische Politik* (W. Berlin) 1969-
60. *Der Staat* (W. Berlin) 1962-
61. *Standpunkt* (W. Berlin) 1947-1959

62. *Studien von Zeitfragen. Materialen zum nonkonformistischen Sozialismus* (Frankfurt) 1962-
63. *Die Tat* (Frankfurt) 1950-
64. *Thomas-Münzer-Briefe* (Stuttgart) 1949-1950
65. *Vierteljahresschrift fur Zeitgeschichte* (Stuttgart) 1953-
66. *Volksstimme* (Cologne) 1945-1956
67. *Von unten auf* (W. Berlin) 1947-1953?
68. *Werkhefte* (Munich) 1946-
69. *Wissen und Tat* (Hilden) 1945-1956, continued illegally
70. *Wirtschaft und Statistik* (Stuttgart) 1949-
71. *WISO: Korrespondenz für Wirtschafts- und sozialwissenschaften* (Cologne) 1956-1958
72. *WWI: Mitteilungen des Wirtschaftswissenschaftliches Institut der Gewerkschaften* (Cologne) 1948-
73. *Zeitschrift für Politik*, new series, 1954-

Index